ORDNANC

STREET ATLAS
East Essex

Contents

IV *Key to maps*

VI *Administrative boundaries*

1 *Street maps*

206 *Index explanation and abbreviations*

207 *Index of towns, villages and rural localities*

208 *Index of street names*

PHILIP'S

First edition published 1994 by

Ordnance Survey	and	Philip's
Romsey Road		an imprint of Reed Consumer Books Limited
Maybush		Michelin House, 81 Fulham Road, London, SW3 6RB
Southampton SO9 4DH		and Auckland, Melbourne, Singapore and Toronto

ISBN 0-540-05850-5 (Philip's, pocket edition)
ISBN 0-319-00402-3 (Ordnance Survey, pocket edition)

To the best of the Publishers' knowledge, the information in this atlas was correct at the time
of going to press. No responsibility can be accepted for any errors or their consequences.

The representation in this atlas of a road, track or path is no evidence of the existence of a
right of way.

Printed in England by Clays Ltd, St Ives plc

Key to map symbols

⇄	British Rail station
⊖	London transport station
Ⓡ	Private railway station
➤●	Bus or coach station
Ⓗ	Heliport
◆	Police station (may not be open 24 hours)
✚	Hospital with casualty facilities (may not be open 24 hours)
◻	Post office
✢	Place of worship
◼	Important building
P	Parking
120	Adjoining page indicator
══	Motorway or dual carriageway
A27(T)	Main or through road (with Department of Transport number)
─┤ ├─	Gate or obstruction to traffic (restrictions may not apply at all times or to all vehicles)
─ ─ ─ ─	Footpath
── ── ──	Bridleway
── ── ──	Path
═══	Track

The representation in this atlas of a road, track or path is no evidence of the existence of a right of way

Amb Sta	Ambulance station	LC	Level crossing
Coll	College	Liby	Library
FB	Footbridge	Mus	Museum
F Sta	Fire station	Sch	School
Hospl	Hospital	TH	Town hall

0	¼	½	¾	1mile
0	250m	500m	250m	1 Kilometre

The scale of the maps is approximately 2½ inches to 1 mile (1:24137)

Key to map pages

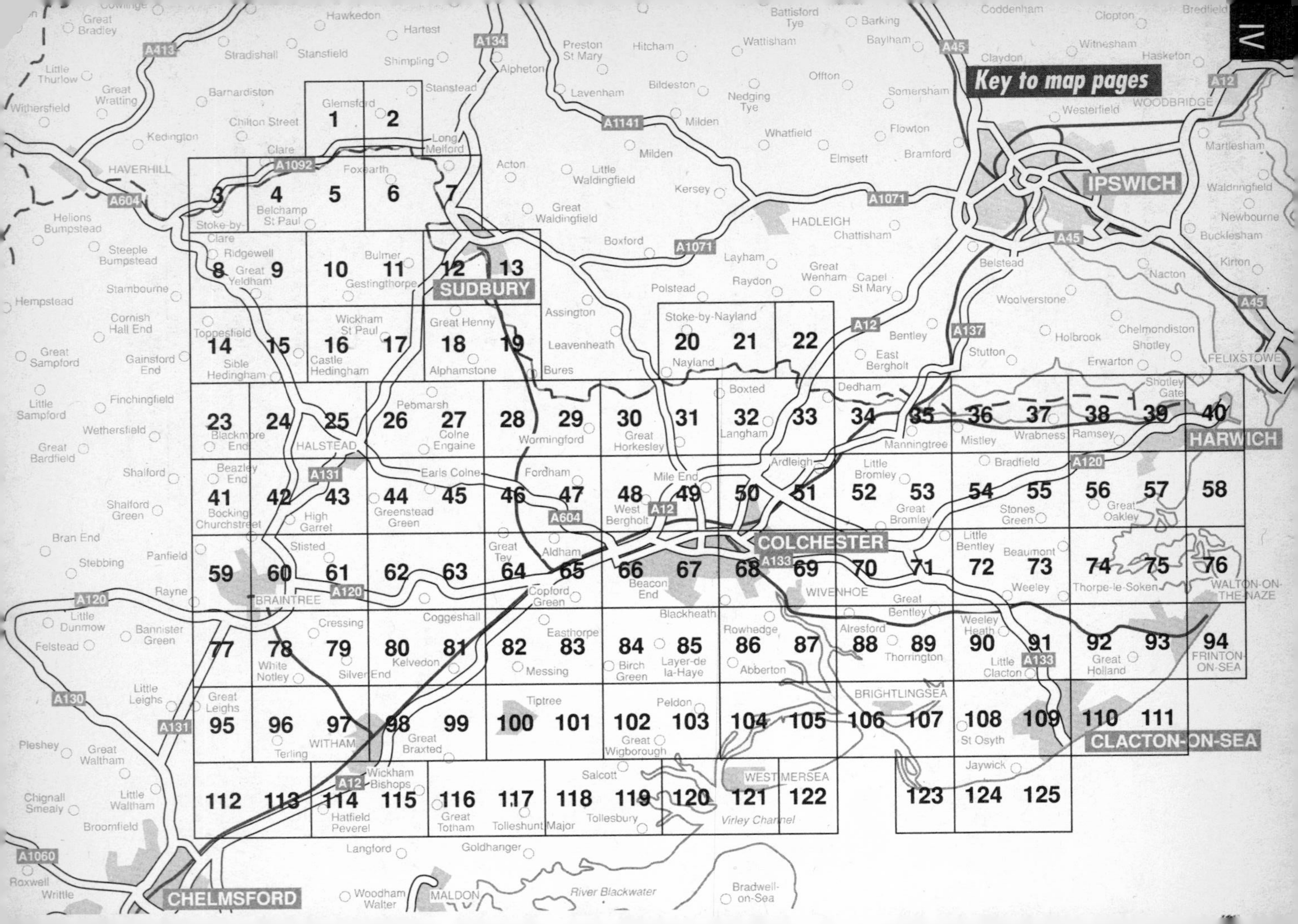

IPSWICH

HARWICH

WOODBRIDGE

FELIXSTOWE

WALTON-ON-THE-NAZE

FRINTON ON SEA

CLACTON-ON-SEA

COLCHESTER

SUDBURY

HADLEIGH

HALSTEAD

BRAINTREE

WITHAM

CHELMSFORD

MALDON

WEST MERSEA

BRIGHTLINGSEA

WIVENHOE

V

NORTH SEA

WEST MERSEA
Virley Channel

Little Waltham
Broomfield
Chignall Smealy
Roxwell
Writtle
Loves Green
Ingatestone
Galleywood
Stock
BILLERICAY
Langdon
Horndon on the Hill
Little Burstead
Laindon
Basildon
Fobbing
Corringham
Stanford le Hope
Mucking
Chadwell St Mary
TILBURY
GRAVESEND

CHELMSFORD
Hatfield Peverel
Langford
Woodham Walter
MALDON
Danbury
Bicknacre
Cold Norton
Woodham Ferrers
South Woodham Ferrers
East Hanningfield
West Hanningfield
South Hanningfield
Runwell
Hullbridge
Hockley
Rayleigh
SOUTH BENFLEET
CANVEY ISLAND
Thames Haven

Great Totham
Tolleshunt Major
Goldhanger
Mundon
Latchingdon
North Fambridge
South Fambridge
Althorne
Mayland
Southminster

Tollesbury
Salcott
River Blackwater
Ramsey Island
Tillingham
Asheldham

Birdbrook on Sea
Bradwell on Sea

BURNHAM-ON-CROUCH
Ostend
Creeksea
Canewdon
River Crouch
Paglesham Churchend
Churchend
FOULNESS ISLAND
Courtsend

Ashingdon
Rochford
Great Wakering
Barling
SHOEBURYNESS
SOUTHEND-ON-SEA

Yantlet Dredged Channel

Grain
Allhallows
Cooling
Cliffe
Cliffe Woods
Hoo St Werburgh
High Halstow
Kingsnorth
ROCHESTER
GILLINGHAM

SHEERNESS
ISLE OF SHEPPEY
Minster
Eastchurch
Leysdown on Sea
Warden

WHITSTABLE
HERNE BAY
Herne
Chestfield
Broomfield
Marshside

126 127 128 129 130 131 132 133 134 135 136 137 138
139 140 141 142 143 144 145 146 147 148 149 150 151
152 153 154 155 156 157 158 159 160 161 162
163 164 165 166 167 168 169 170 171 172 173
174 175 176 177 78 179 180 181 182 183 184
185 186 187 188 189 190 191 192 193 194
195 196 197 198 199 200 201 202
203 204

0 1 2 3 4 5 6 7 8 km
0 1 2 3 4 5 miles

A12 A130 A414 A1060 A414 A132 A127 A130 A13 A129 A1014 A13 A128 A226 A2 A289 A228 A278 A249 A251 A299 A291

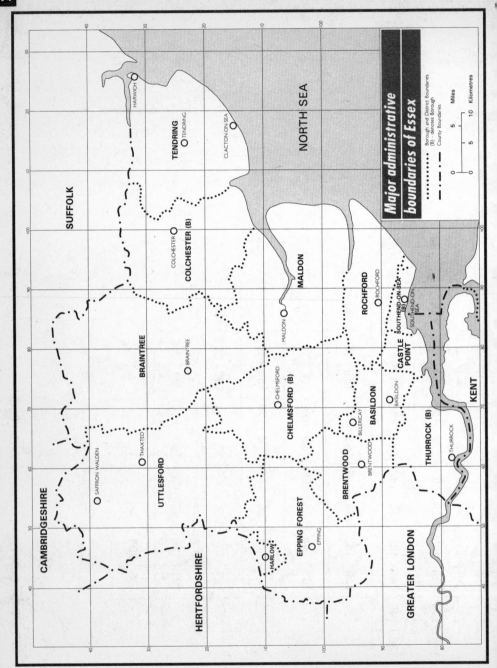

Major administrative boundaries of Essex

A **B** **C**

Moor's Farm

Sparrow's Wood

Truckett's Hall

Lower Barn

4

Wales End Farm

Wales End

49

Wales Farm

Easty Wood

PLUM ST

New Street Farm

NEW ST

3

Robb's Farm

48

Ducks Hall

Colt's Hall

CAVENDISH LA

2

Ark Farm

Blacklands Hall

47

PEACOCKS RD

NETHER RD

Cavendish

WATER LA

Kiln Farm

Vineyard

PH

Sch

Cemy

HIGH ST

LOWER ST

MELFORD RD

A1092

THE COLOURINGS

CLAYS CL

GREENS

1

Alder Carr

Scott's Farm

POOLE ST

GREEN CL

STOUR ST

A1092

B1064

PENTLOW DR

Pentlow Bridge

Pentlow Hall

PENTLOW LA

Moat

Pentlow

River Stour

Pentlow Mill

Pentlow Hall Farm

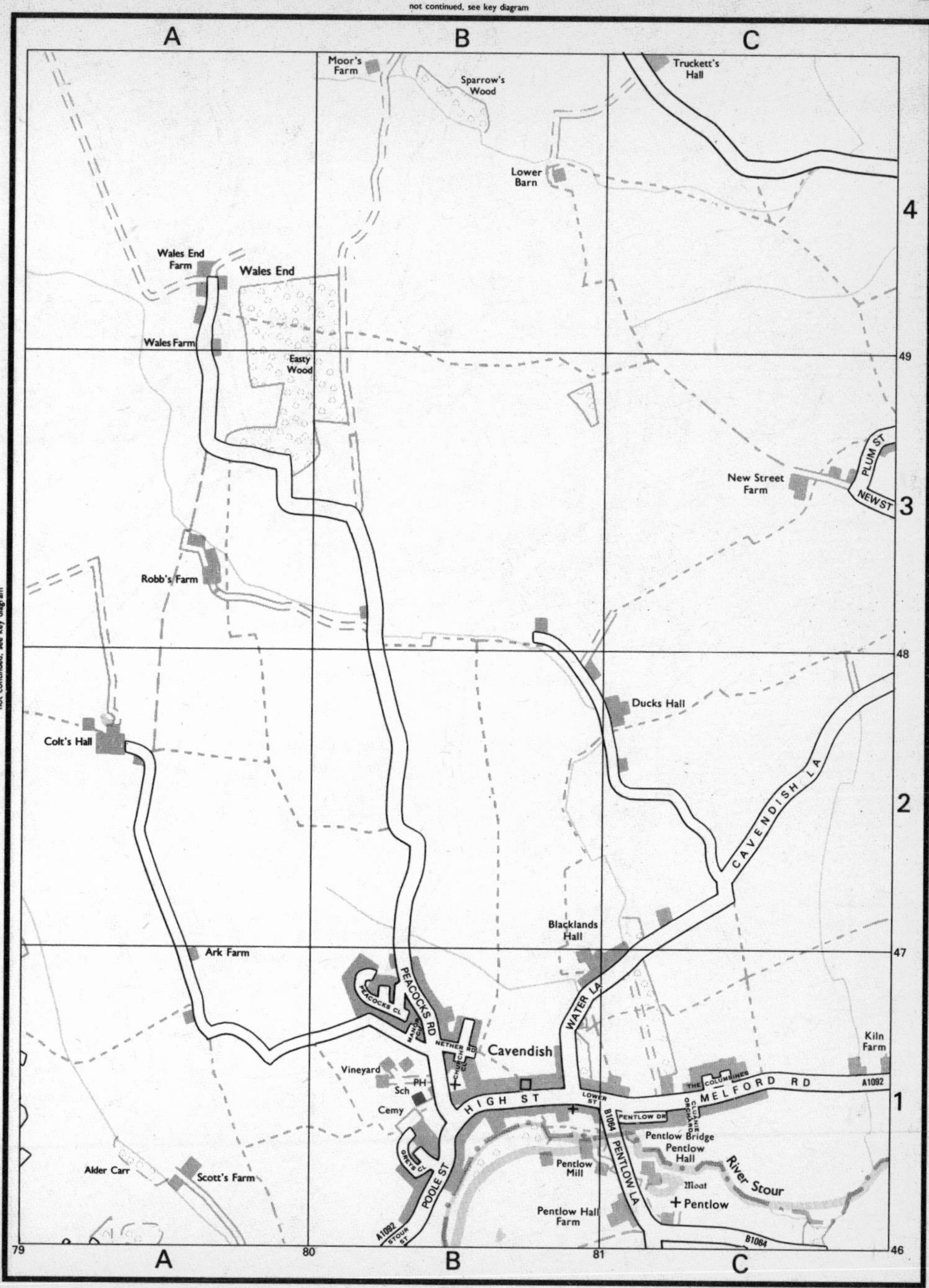

B1064

46

A 80 **B** 81 **C**

79

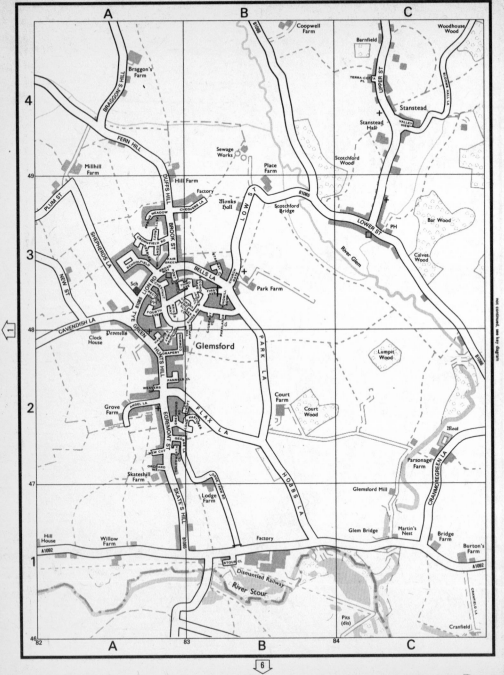

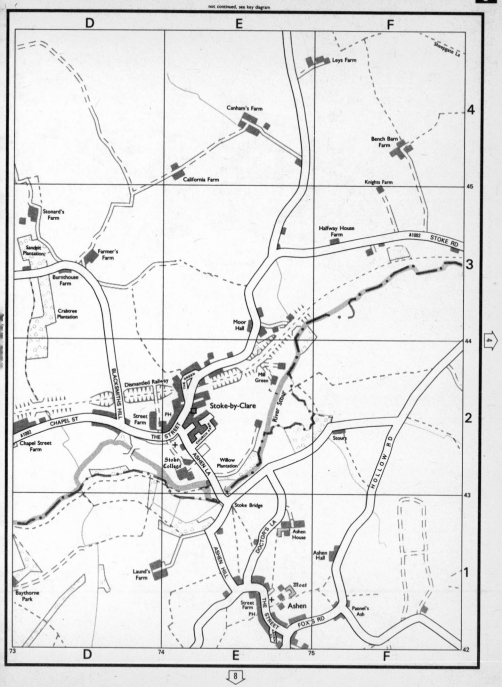

not continued, see key diagram

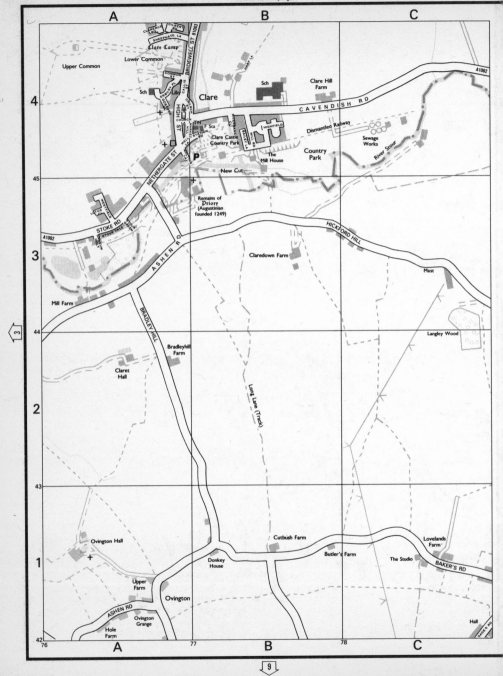

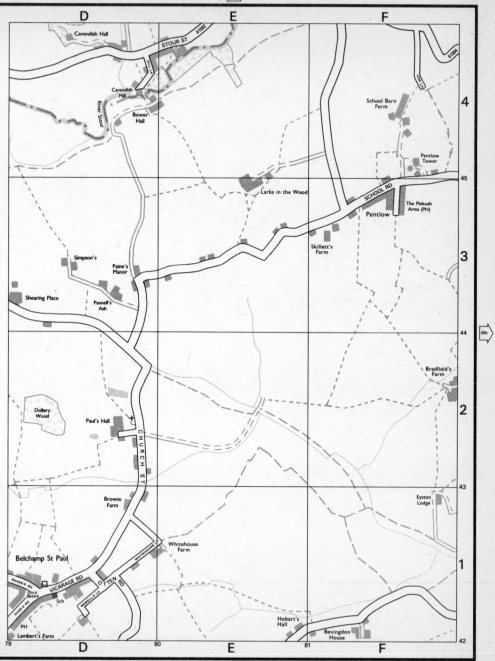

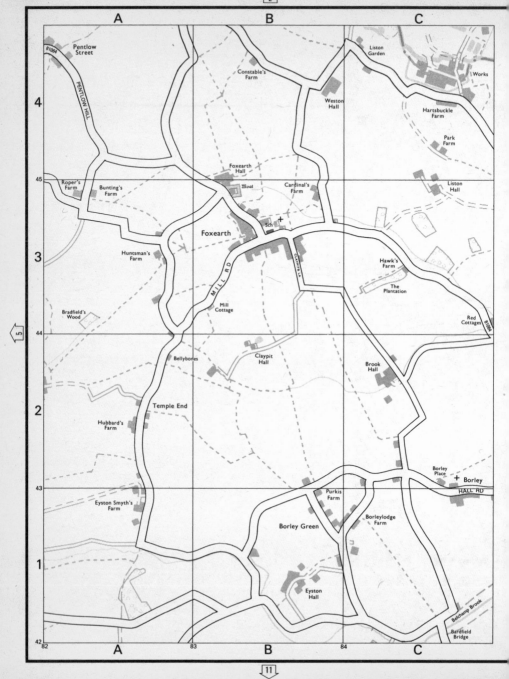

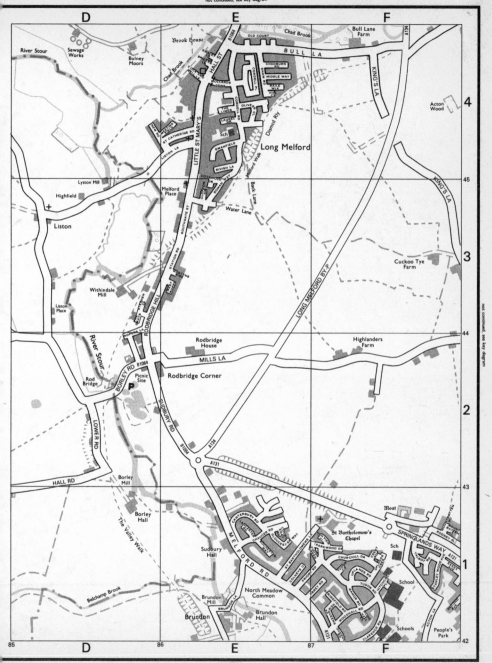

not continued, see key diagram

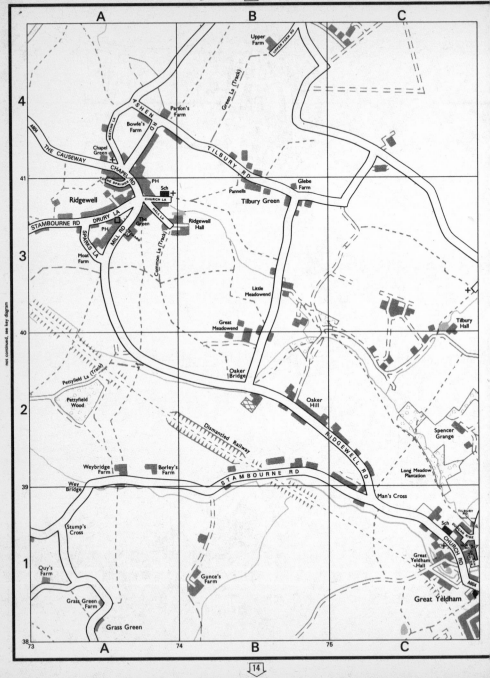

not continued, see key diagram

A   **B**   **C**

Upper Farm

UPPER FARM RD

Green La (Track)

4

ASHEN RD

Parson's Farm

Bowle's Farm

MEETING LA

Chapel Green

A604

THE CAUSEWAY

TILBURY RD

CHAPEL RD

41

COLNE SPRINGS RD

PH

Sch

Glebe Farm

Ridgewell

CHURCH LA

Pannells

Tilbury Green

STAMBOURNE RD

DRURY LA

PH

MILL RD

The Green

HILL LA

Ridgewell Hall

SPARKS LA

Moat Farm

3

Common La (Track)

Little Meadowend

Tilbury Hall

40

Great Meadowend

Oaker Bridge

Pettyfield La (Track)

Pettyfield Wood

Oaker Hill

RIDGEWELL RD

Spencer Grange

2

Dismantled Railway

Long Meadow Plantation

Weybridge Farm

Borley's Farm

STAMBOURNE RD

39

Wey Bridge

Man's Cross

TILBURY RD

Stump's Cross

Sch

DE VERE RISE

CHURCH RD

Great Yeldham Hall

1

Quy's Farm

Gunce's Farm

A604

Grass Green Farm

Great Yeldham

Grass Green

38

73   **A**   74   **B**   75   **C**

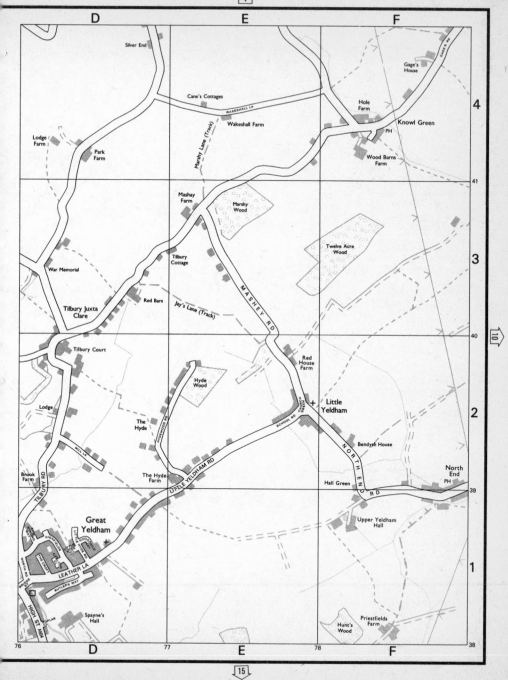

4

D

E

F

Silver End

Cane's Cottages

WAKESHALL LA

Wakeshall Farm

Gage's House

Hole Farm

Knowl Green

PH

4

Lodge Farm

Park Farm

Marshy Lane (Track)

Wood Barns Farm

41

Mashay Farm

Marshy Wood

Twelve Acre Wood

3

War Memorial

Tilbury Cottage

MASHEY RD

Tilbury Juxta Clare

Red Barn

Jay's Lane (Track)

40

Tilbury Court

Red House Farm

Hyde Wood

+ Little Yeldham

2

Lodge

The Hyde

HYDEWOOD RD

SCHOOL RD

CHURCH GREEN

Bendysh House

NORTH END

North End PH

MILL LA

Brook Farm

TILBURY RD

The Hyde Farm

LITTLE YELDHAM RD

Hall Green

RD

39

Great Yeldham

+

Upper Yeldham Hall

HIGHFIELDS

LITTLE YELDHAM RD

NORTH RD

THE CAUSEWAY

LEATHER LA

1

BRIDGE

BUTLERS WAY

HIGH ST A604

POPLAR

Spayne's Hall

Hunt's Wood

Priestfields Farm

76

D

77

E

78

F

38

15

10

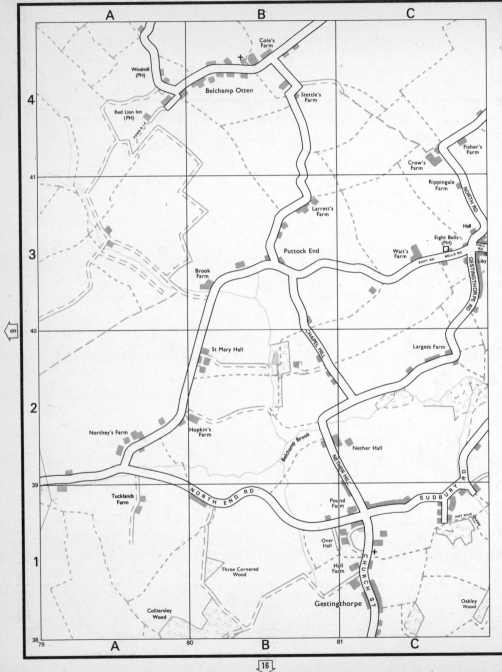

A   B   C

4

Windmill
(PH)

Cole's
Farm

+

Belchamp Otten

Stettle's
Farm

Red Lion Inn
(PH)

POWER LANE

Fisher's
Farm

41

Crow's
Farm

NORTH RD

Rippingale
Farm

Larrett's
Farm

Hall

3

Puttock End

Wait's
Farm

Eight Bells
(PH)

Liby

HALL RD

SOFT RD

BELLS RD

GESTINGTHORPE RD

Brook
Farm

40

St Mary Hall

Largess Farm

CHAPEL HILL

2

Northey's Farm

Hopkin's
Farm

Belchamp Brook

Nether Hall

NETHER HILL

SUDBURY RD

39

Tucklands
Farm

NORTH END RD

Pound
Farm

POT KILN LANE

Over
Hall

+

CHURCH ST

1

Three Cornered
Wood

Hall
Farm

Colliersley
Wood

Gestingthorpe

Oakley
Wood

38
79   80   81

A   B   C

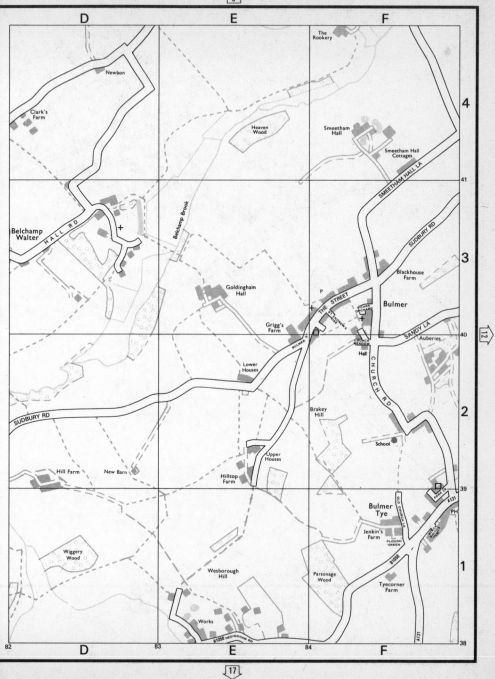

D   E   F

The Rookery

Newbon

Clark's
Farm

4

Heaven
Wood

Smeetham
Hall

Smeetham Hall
Cottages

41

SMEETHAM HALL LA

Belchamp
Walter

Belchamp Brook

SUDBURY RD

3

Blackhouse
Farm

HALL RD

Goldingham
Hall

P

THE STREET

Bulmer

ST ANDREW'S CHURCH

VICARS
ORCHARD

Grigg's
Farm

SANDY LA

Auberies

40

BULMER ●

CHURCH
MEADOW

Hall

CHURCH RD

12

Lower
Houses

Brakey
Hill

SUDBURY RD

2

School

Upper
Houses

Hill Farm   New Barn

Hilltop
Farm

39

PARK LA

Bulmer
Tye

OLD CHURCH LA

A131

PH

Jenkin's
Farm

PLOUGH
GREEN

Wiggery
Wood

B1058

1

Wesborough
Hill

Parsonage
Wood

Tyecorner
Farm

Works

B1058 HEDINGHAM RD

A131

38

D   E   F

82   83   84

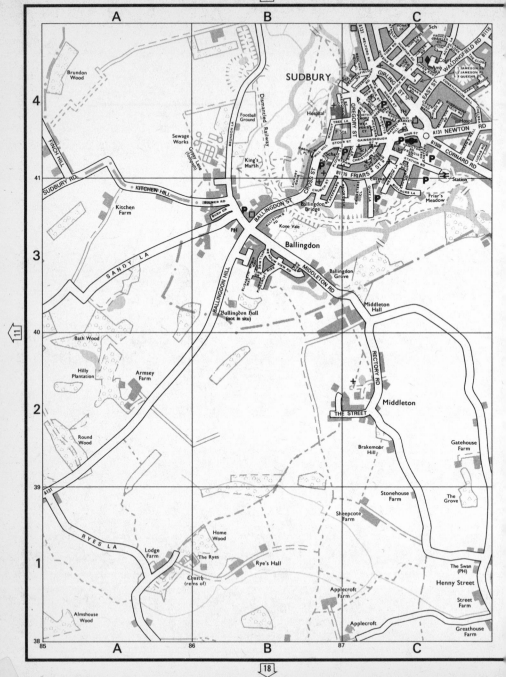

A   B   C

4

Brundon
Wood

SUDBURY

Football
Ground

Hospital

Sewage
Works

King's
Marsh

Dismantled Railway

Tree La

F Sta

GREGORY ST

STOUR ST

GAINSBOROUGH

GIRLING ST

EAST ST

KING ST

NEWTON A131

CORNARD RD

Friar's
Meadow

Station

41

FINCH HILL

SUDBURY RD

KITCHEN HILL

BULMER RD

BUSH GR

PH

Kitchen
Farm

Grey's Lane
(footpath)

BRUNDON LA

BALLINGDON ST

Ballingdon
Bridge

Kone Vale

CROSS ST

FRIARS ST

BULLOCKS LA

QUAY LA

B1115

3

SANDY LA

BALLINGDON HILL

ELIZABETH WAY
RECTORY VIEW RD

MIDDLETON RD

Ballingdon
Grove

Middleton
Hall

Ballingdon

Ballingdon Hall
(not in situ)

40

Bath Wood

Hilly
Plantation

Armsey
Farm

RECTORY RD

Middleton

2

Round
Wood

THE STREET

Brakemoor
Hill

Gatehouse
Farm

Stonehouse
Farm

The
Grove

39

A131

RYES LA

Home
Wood

Lodge
Farm

The Ryes

Rye's Hall

Sheepcote
Farm

1

Church
(rems of)

Applecroft
Farm

The Swan
(PH)

Henny Street

Street
Farm

Almshouse
Wood

Applecroft

Greathouse
Farm

38
85   86   87

A   B   C

11

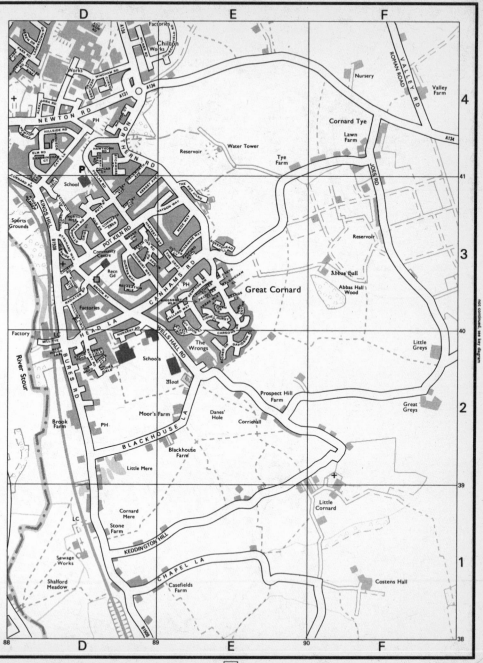

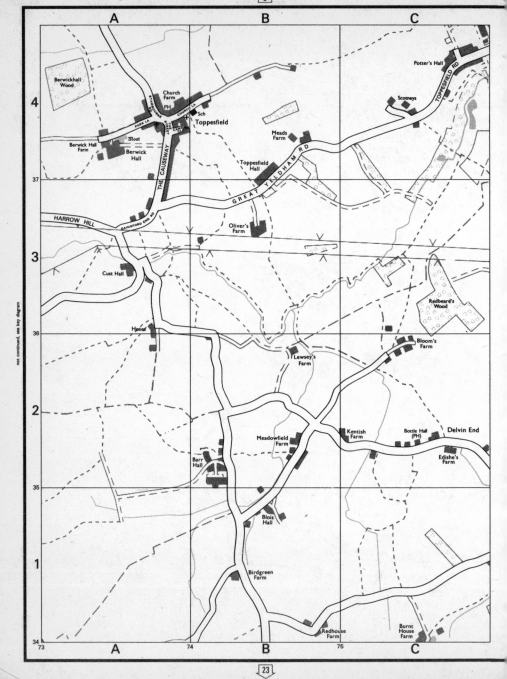

A   B   C

Berwickhall Wood

Church Farm
PH
Park La
Sch
Toppesfield
Moat
Berwick Hall Farm
Berwick Hall
THE CAUSEWAY
Potter's Hall
Scotneys
TOPPESFIELD RD
Meads Farm
Toppesfield Hall
GREAT YELDHAM RD
HARROW HILL
GAINSFORD END RD
Oliver's Farm
Cust Hall
Redbeard's Wood
Hosel
Bloom's Farm
Lewsey's Farm
Meadowfield Farm
Kentish Farm
Bottle Hall (PH)
Delvin End
Barr Hall
Edishe's Farm
Blois Hall
Birdgreen Farm
Redhouse Farm
Burnt House Farm

not continued, see key diagram

A   74   B   75   C

73

34

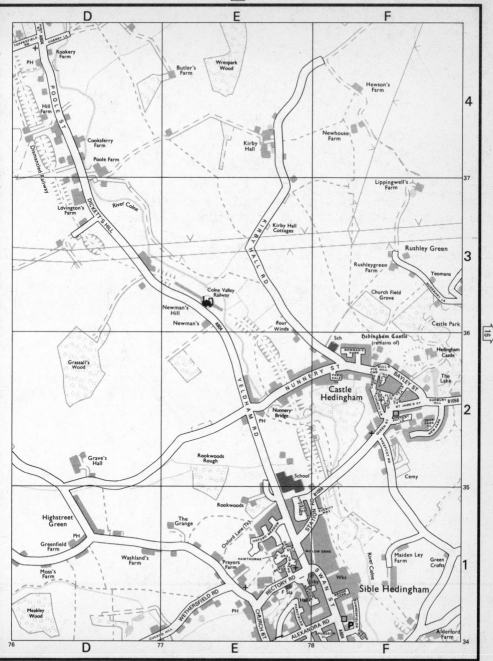

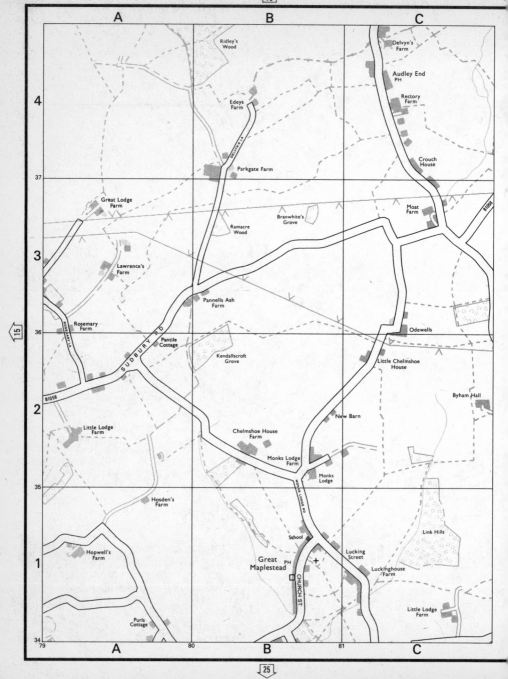

15

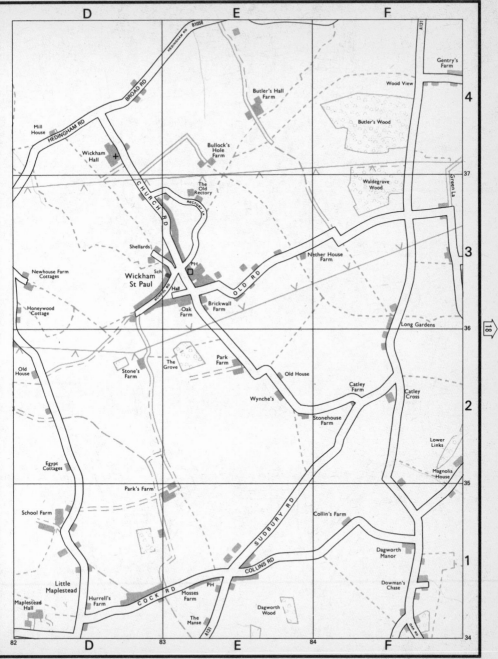

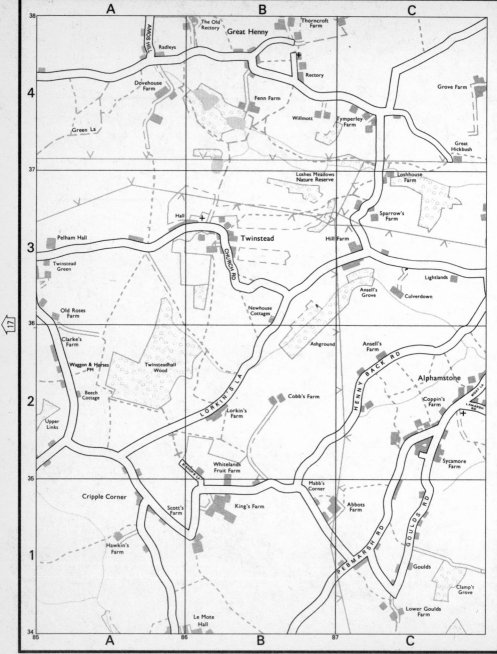

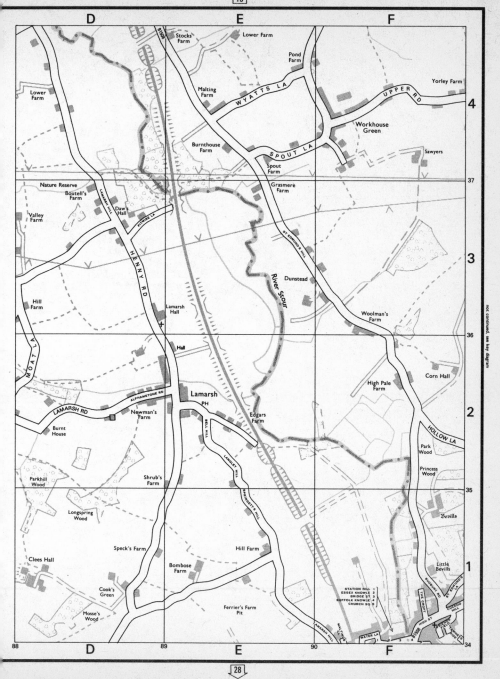

D
E
F

Stocks Farm

Lower Farm

Pond Farm

Yorley Farm

Lower Farm

Malting Farm

WYATTS LA

UPPER RD

4

Workhouse Green

Burnthouse Farm

SPOUT LA

Sawyers

Spout Farm

37

Nature Reserve

Grasmere Farm

Boutell's Farm

Valley Farm

Daws Hall

ST EDMUND'S HILL

3

HENNY RD

LAMARSH HILL

FITWIRE LA

River Scour

Dunstead

Hill Farm

Lamarsh Hall

Woolman's Farm

36

MOAT LA

Hall

High Pale Farm

Corn Hall

Lamarsh

Newman's Farm

ALPHAMSTONE RD

PH

Edgars Farm

HOLLOW LA

2

LAMARSH RD

Burnt House

BELL HILL

Park Wood

Princess Wood

Parkhill Wood

Shrub's Farm

LANGLEY HILL

35

Longspring Wood

Bevills

Speck's Farm

BRANKETT'S HILL

Hill Farm

Little Bevills

Clees Hall

Bombose Farm

1

Cook's Green

Ferrier's Farm Pit

STATION HILL 1
ESSEX KNOWLE 2
BRIDGE ST 3
SUFFOLK KNOWLE 4
CHURCH SQ 8

SUDBURY RD

THE CROFT

ST EDMUND'S LA

Mosse's Wood

LAMARSH HILL

MALTING ST

B1508

HIGH ST

WATER LA

GARDEN HILL

MILL RD

RIVER LA

88
D
89
E
90
F
34

not continued, see key diagram

not continued, see key diagram

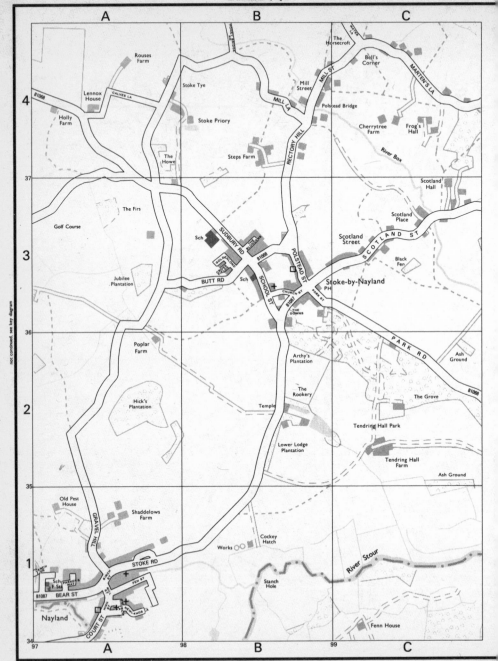

not continued, see key diagram

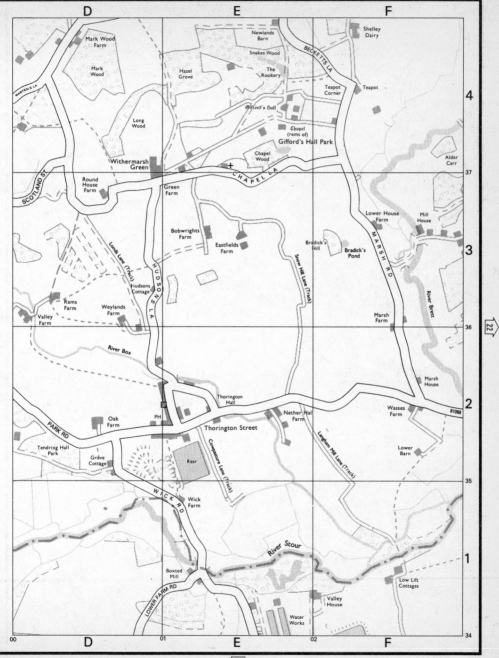

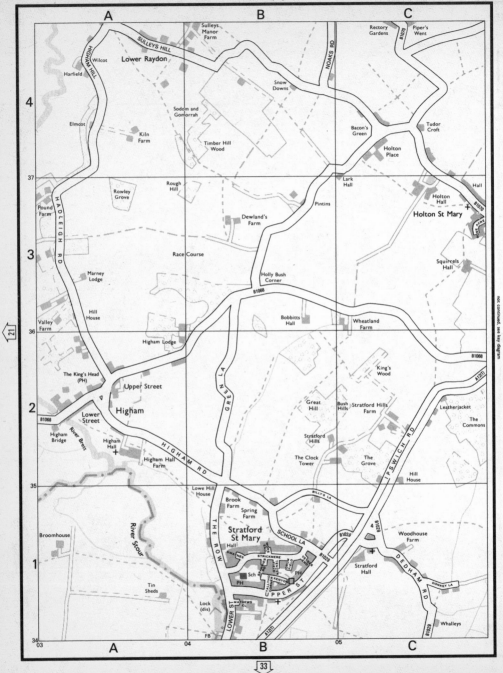

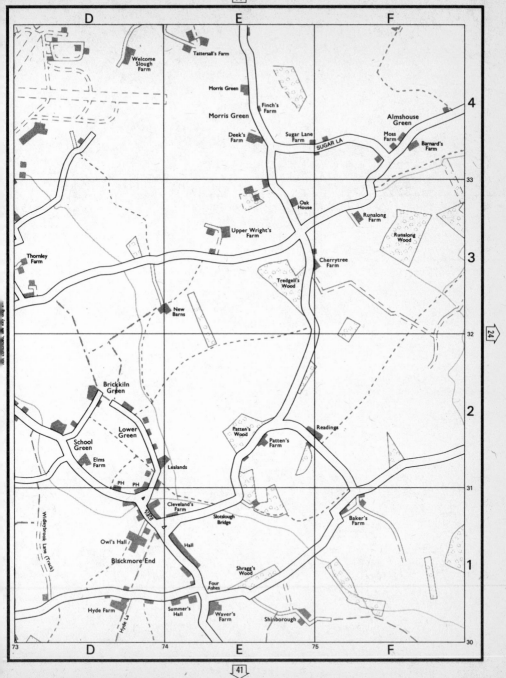

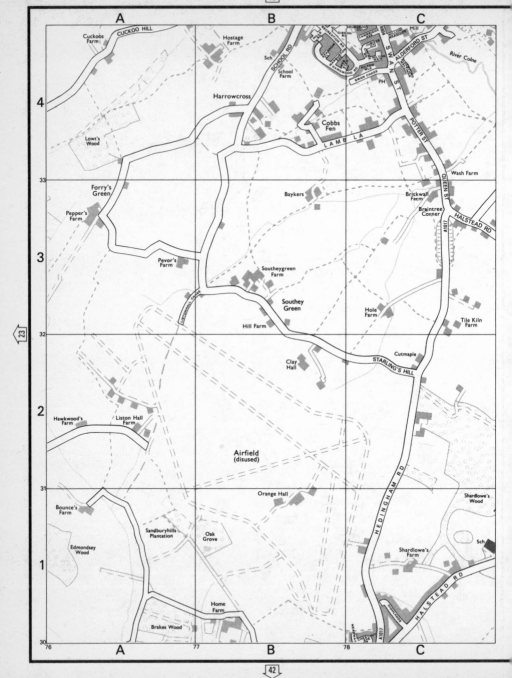

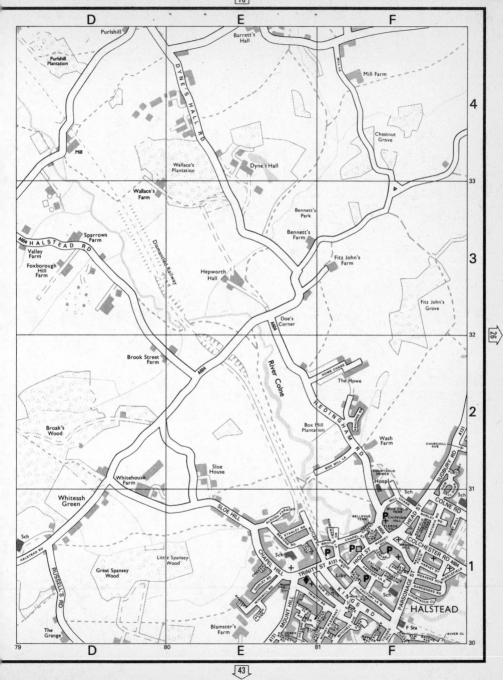

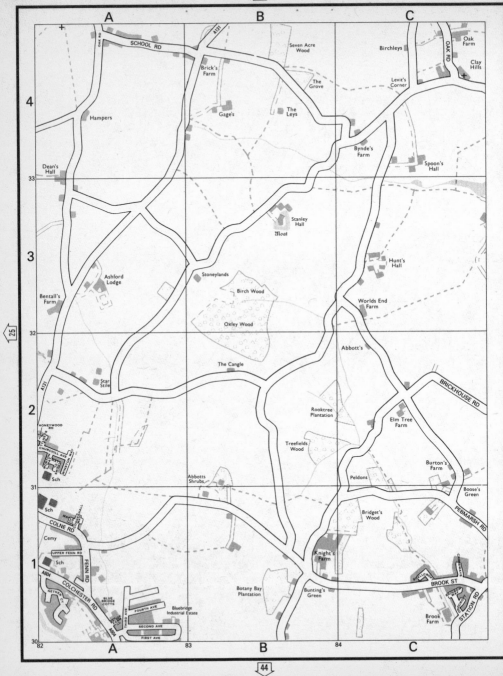

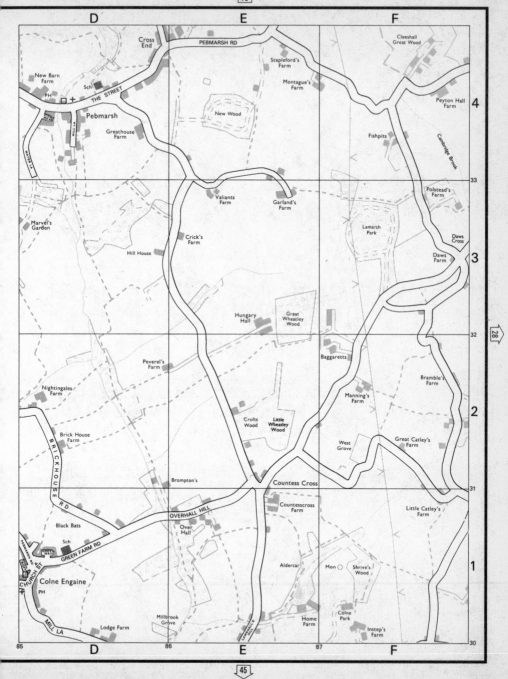

19
27

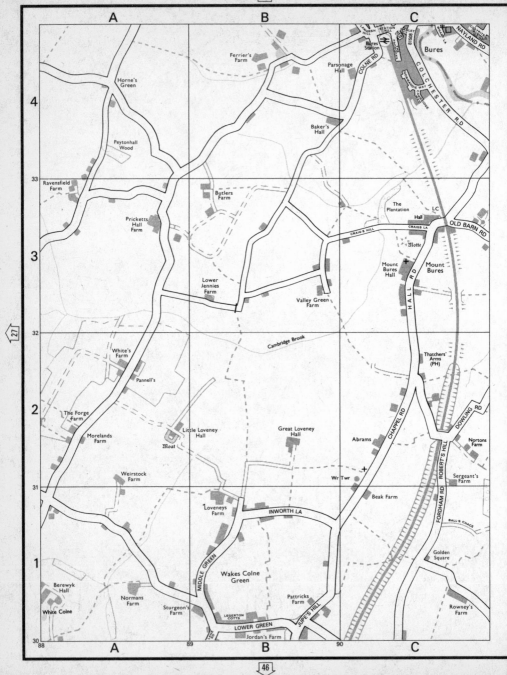

A B C

4

33

3

32

2

31

1

30
88 89 90

A B C

46

Ferrier's Farm

Horne's Green

Peytonhall Wood

Ravensfield Farm

Pricketts Hall Farm

Lower Jennies Farm

White's Farm

Pannell's

The Forge Farm

Morelands Farm

Weirstock Farm

Berewyk Hall

White Colne

Normans Farm

Sturgeon's Farm

Little Loveney Hall

Moat

Loveneys Farm

MIDDLE GREEN

Wakes Colne Green

LEGERTON COTTS

LOWER GREEN

Jordan's Farm

Butlers Farm

Baker's Hall

Valley Green Farm

Cambridge Brook

Great Loveney Hall

INWORTH LA

Pattricks Farm

JUPE'S HILL

Parsonage Hall

COLNE RD

Bures Station

MARSH HILL

STATION HILL

B1508

NAYLAND RD

Bures

COLCHESTER RD

The Plantation

Hall

LC

CRAIG'S HILL

CRAIGS LA

OLD BARN RD

Motte

Mount Bures Hall

Mount Bures

HALL RD

Thatchers' Arms (PH)

Abrams

CHAPPEL RD

Wr Twr

Beak Farm

ROBERT'S HILL

FORDHAM RD

DOWLING RD

Nortons Farm

Sergeant's Farm

BALL'S CHACE

Golden Square

Rowney's Farm

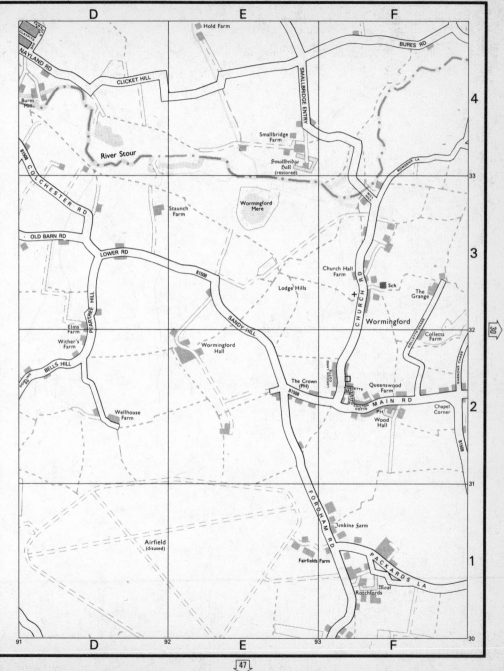

D E F

BURES RD

Hold Farm

NAYLAND RD

CLICKET HILL

SMALLBRIDGE ENTRY

BURES RD

4

Bures
Mill

B1508

Smallbridge
Farm

33

River Stour

Smallbridge
Hall
(restored)

COLCHESTER RD

Wormingford
Mere

Staunch
Farm

Church Hall
Farm

Sch

The
Grange

3

OLD BARN RD

LOWER RD

B1508

Lodge Hills

CHURCH RD

Wormingford

32

PEARTREE HILL

Elms
Farm

SANDY HILL

Colletts
Farm

Wither's
Farm

Wormingford
Hall

COLLETTS CHASE

BELLS HILL

LONDON LANE

ROBERTS
HALL

Queenswood
Farm

GRANGE ROAD

2

Wellhouse
Farm

The Crown
(PH)

B1508

CHILTON
COTTS

MAIN RD

PH

Chapel
Corner

B1508

Wood
Hall

31

FORDHAM RD

Jenkins Farm

Airfield
(disused)

Fairfields Farm

PACKARDS LA

1

Moat
Rotchfords

91 D 92 E 93 F 30

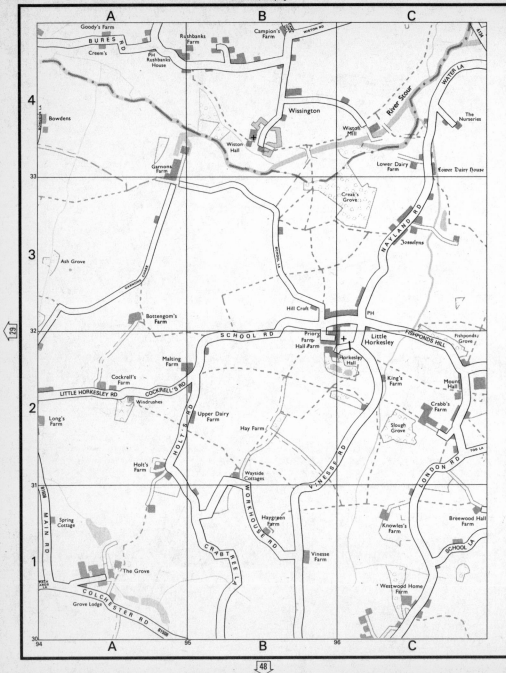

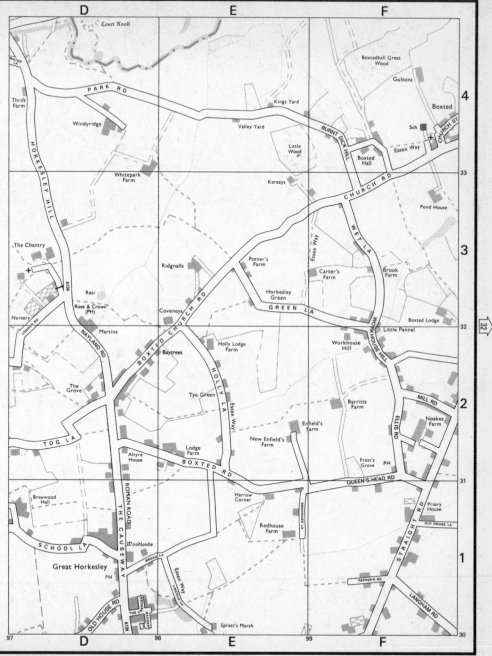

Court Knoll

WATER LA

Thrift Farm

PARK RD

Windyridge

HORKESLEY HILL

Whitepark Farm

The Chantry

A134

Resr

Rose & Crown (PH)

Nursery

LONDON RD

Martins

NAYLAND RD

The Grove

TOG LA

Ridgnalls

Coveneys

BOXTED CHURCH RD

Baytrees

HOLLY LA

ESSEX WAY

Tye Green

Altyre House

Lodge Farm

BOXTED RD

Breewood Hall

ROMAN ROAD

THE CAUSEWAY

SCHOOL LA

Woodlands

Great Horkesley

PH

OLD HOUSE RD

A134

THE GREEN

BROAD LA

LINCOLN'S

Essex Way

Spratt's Marsh

Kings Yard

Valley Yard

Little Wood

Kerseys

Potter's Farm

Horkesley Green

GREEN LA

Holly Lodge Farm

Enfield's Farm

New Enfield's Farm

Harrow Corner

Redhouse Farm

REDHOUSE LA

Boxtedhall Great Wood

Gulsons

Boxted

BURNT DICK HILL

Sch

Essex Way

CHURCH ST

Boxted Hall

CHURCH RD

Pond House

WET LA

Essex Way

Carter's Farm

Brook Farm

Boxted Lodge

Little Pannel

Workhouse Hill

WORKHOUSE HILL

Barritts Farm

MILL RD

Noakes Farm

ELLIS RD

Frost's Grove

PH

QUEEN'S-HEAD RD

STRAIGHT RD

Priory House

OLD HOUSE LA

PEPPER'S RD

LANGHAM RD

4

33

3

32

2

31

1

30

D

E

F

97

98

99

32

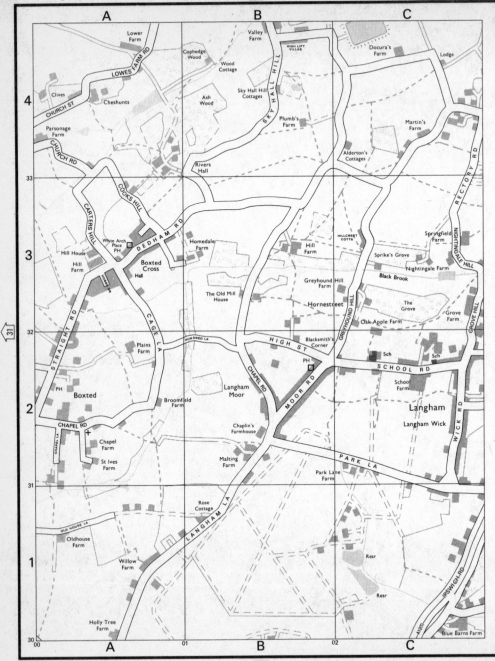

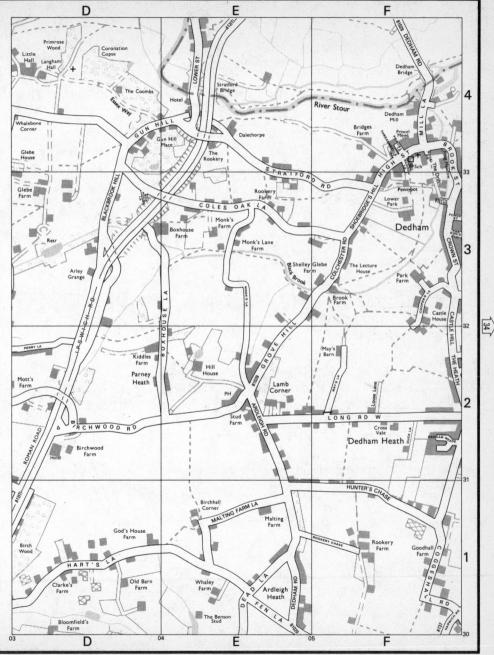

D   E   F

Little Hall

Primrose Wood

Coronation Copse

Langham Hall

The Coombs

Essex Way

Stratford Bridge

Lower St

Hotel

Dedham Bridge

DEDHAM RD

River Stour

Dedham Mill

Whalebone Corner

GUN HILL

Gun Hill Place

Dalethorpe

Bridges Farm

Princh Mews

MILL LA

Glebe House

The Rookery

STRATFORD RD

HIGH ST

BROOK ST

Sch

The Drift

Glebe Farm

COLES OAK LA

Rookery Farm

SHOEBRIDGE'S HILL

Pennypot

Lower Park

Dedham

Monk's Farm

Boxhouse Farm

Monk's Lane Farm

BLACKBROOK HILL

Shelley Glebe Farm

Black Brook

COLCHESTER RD

The Lecture House

Park Farm

CROWN ST

Resr

Arley Grange

MONK'S LA

Brook Farm

Castle House

COOPER'S LA

CASTLE HILL

BOXHOUSE LA

Kiddles Farm

Parney Heath

Hill House

GROVE HILL

May's Barn

MAY'S LA

Louse Lane

THE HEATH

PERRY LA

IPSWICH RD

PH

Lamb Corner

LONG RD W

Mott's Farm

Stud Farm

ARDLEIGH RD

Dedham Heath

Cross Vale

DEDHAM MADE

ROMAN ROAD

BIRCHWOOD RD

Birchwood Farm

HUNTER'S CHASE

Hotel

Birch Wood

God's House Farm

Birchhall Corner

MALTING FARM LA

Malting Farm

ROOKERY CHASE

Rookery Farm

Goodhall Farm

COGGESHALL RD

HART'S LA

Clarke's Farm

Old Barn Farm

Whaley Farm

DEAD LA

FEN LA

Ardleigh Heath

DEDHAM RD

Bloomfield's Farm

The Benson Stud

D   E   F

03   04   05

4
33
3
32
34
2
31
1
30

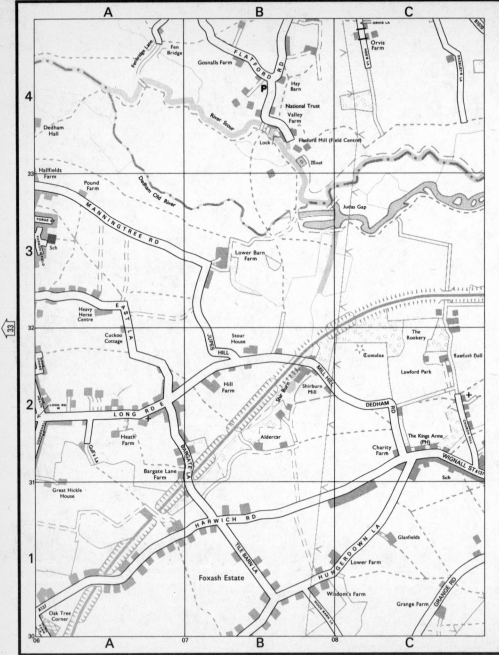

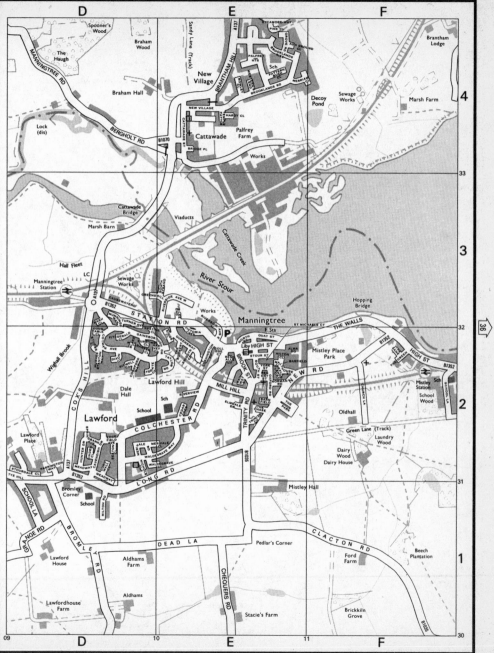

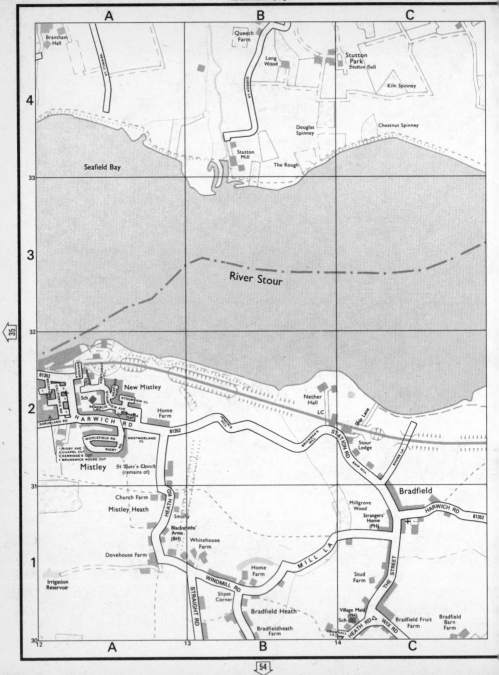

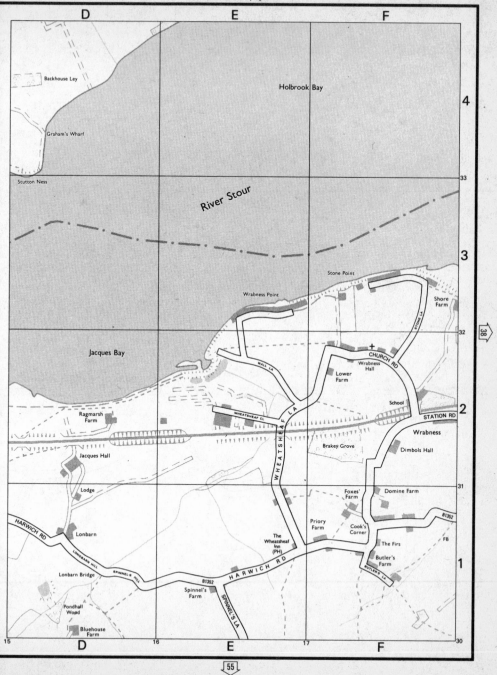

not continued, see key diagram

D   E   F

Backhouse Ley

Holbrook Bay

4

Graham's Wharf

Stutton Ness

33

River Stour

3

Stone Point

Wrabness Point

Shore Farm

Jacques Bay

32

38

CHURCH RD

Wrabness Hall

WALL LA

Lower Farm

School

Ragmarsh Farm

WHEATSHEAF CL

STATION RD

2

Wrabness

WHEATSHEAF LA

Brakey Grove

Dimbols Hall

Jacques Hall

Lodge

Foxes' Farm

Domine Farm

31

HARWICH RD

B1352

Lonbarn

LONBARN HILL

Priory Farm

Cook's Corner

The Firs

FB

The Wheatsheaf Inn (PH)

Butler's Farm

Lonbarn Bridge

SPINNEL'S HILL

B1352

HARWICH RD

BUTLER'S LA

1

Spinnel's Farm

SPINNEL'S LA

Pondhall Wood

Bluehouse Farm

15   D   16   E   17   F   30

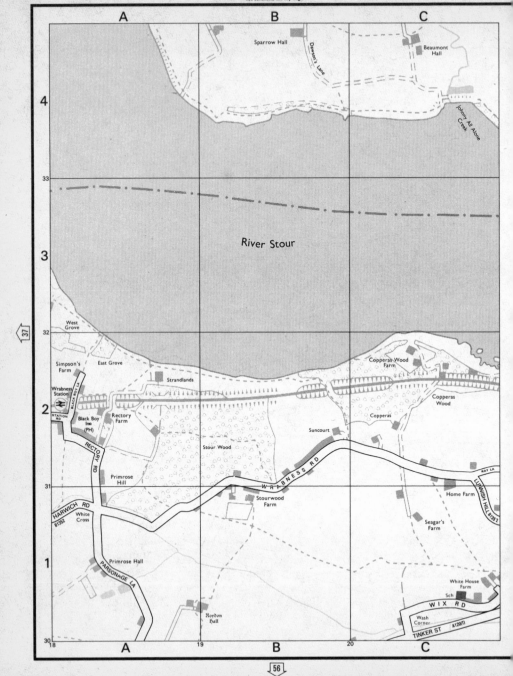

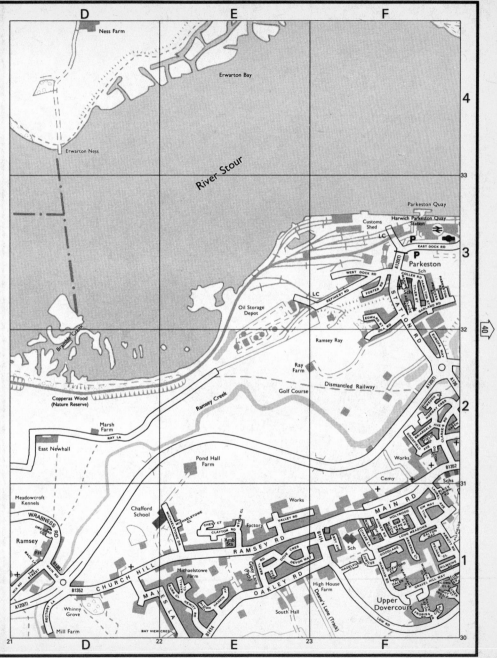

D   E   F

Ness Farm

Erwarton Bay

4

Erwarton Ness

River Stour

33

Parkeston Quay

Customs Shed

Harwich Parkeston Quay Station

LC

P

EAST DOCK RD

P

Parkeston

3

Sch

WEST DOCK RD

COLLIER RD

Oil Storage Depot

LC

REFINERY RD

PORTER RD

GARLAND RD

STATION RD

EDWARD

UNA RD

32

Ramsey Ray

EUROPA WAY

A120(T)

A136

Ray Farm

Golf Course

Dismantled Railway

2

ANNBRIDGE AVE RD

CLARKE RD

Works

GODFREY AVE

B1352

Copperas Wood
(Nature Reserve)

Ramsey Creek

Marsh Farm

Cemy

Schs

RAY LA

East Newhall

Pond Hall Farm

31

Meadowcroft Kennels

Works

MAIN RD

HOLYROOD

DW WAY

WRABNESS RD

Chafford School

MICHAELSTOWE CL

CHEVY CT

CLAYTON RD

STOUR CL

Factory

VALLEY RD

B1414

Sch

LONG MEADOWS

BALTON

ORCHARD CL

Ramsey

PH

Amb Sta

RAMSEY RD

DOVE CRES

DEVON WAY

GOODLAKE

KILMAINE

BACK STREET

MAIN RD

Michaelstowe Farm

OAKLEY RD

HAZELVIN

HASTEE

GRAVEL HILL WAY

ACORN

1

Whinny Grove

CHURCH HILL

MAYES LA

B1352

High House Farm

Deane's Lane (Track)

Upper Dovercourt

A120(T)

Mill Farm

BAY VIEW CRES

South Hall

LOW RD

21   22   23   30

D   E   F

40

not continued, see key diagram

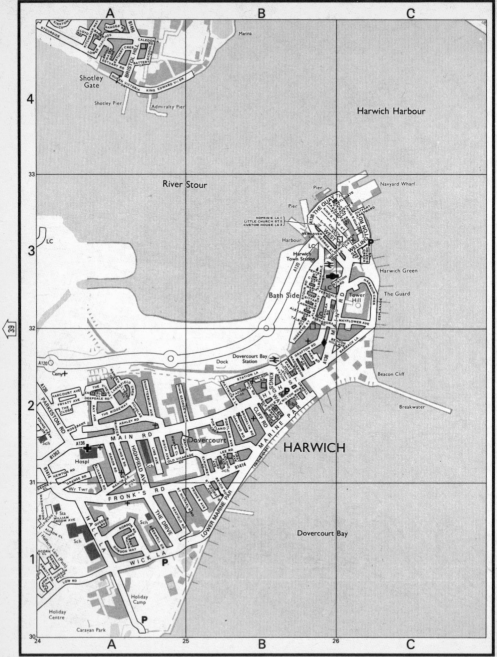

HARWICH

Harwich Harbour

River Stour

Shotley Gate

Shotley Pier

Admiralty Pier

Marina

Navyard Wharf

Pier

Pier

THE QUAY

HOPKIN'S LA 1
LITTLE CHURCH ST 2
CUSTOM HOUSE LA 3

Harbour

Harwich Town Station

Harwich Green

Bath Side

Tower Hill

The Guard

Mayflower Ave

Dovercourt Bay Station

Dock

Beacon Cliff

Breakwater

Dovercourt

Hospl

Cemy

MAIN RD

FRONK'S RD

HALL LA

WICK LA

THE DRIVE

LOWER MARINE PAR

MARINE PAR

Dovercourt Bay

Holiday Camp

Holiday Centre

Caravan Park

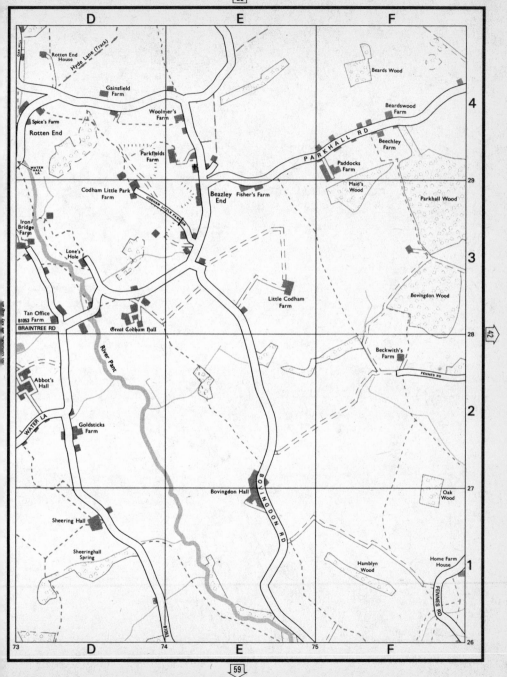

D E F

Oak Hill

Rotten End House

Hyde Lane (Track)

Gainsfield Farm

Woolmer's Farm

Spice's Farm

Rotten End

Parkfields Farm

WATER HALL LA

Codham Little Park Farm

CODHAM LITTLE PARK RD

Iron Bridge Farm

Lone's Hole

Tan Office Farm

B1053

BRAINTREE RD

River Pant

Abbot's Hall

WATER LA

Goldsticks Farm

Sheering Hall

Sheeringhall Spring

B1053

Beazley End

Fisher's Farm

Little Codham Farm

Great Codham Hall

BOVINGDON RD

Bovingdon Hall

Beards Wood

Beardswood Farm

PARKHALL RD

Beechley Farm

Paddocks Farm

Maid's Wood

Parkhall Wood

Bovingdon Wood

Beckwith's Farm

FENNES RD

Oak Wood

Hamblyn Wood

Home Farm House

FENNES RD

4

29

3

28

2

27

1

26

42

73 D 74 E 75 F 26

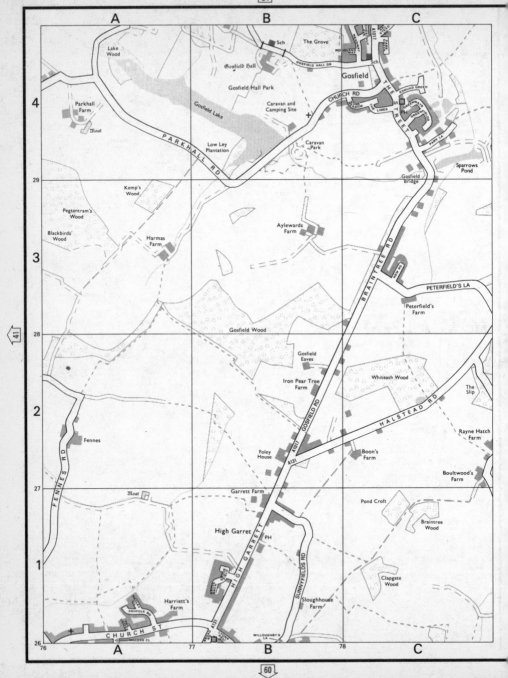

25

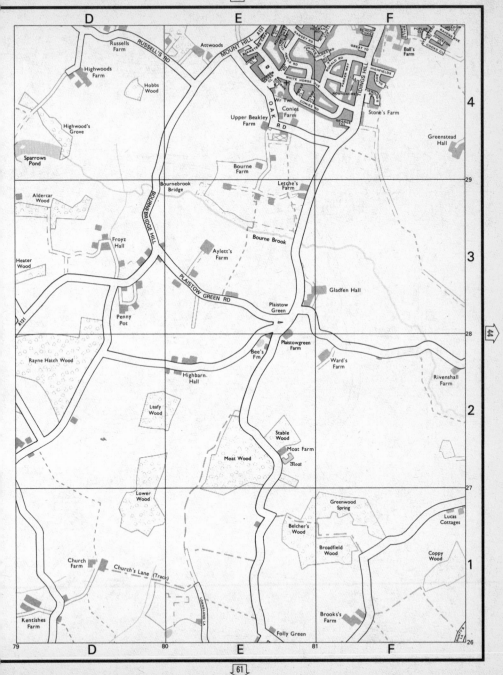

44

26

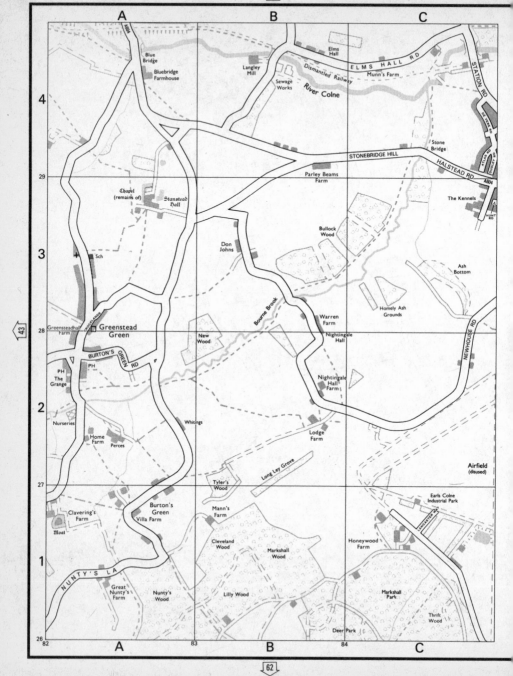

A **B** **C**

4

Blue
Bridge

Bluebridge
Farmhouse

Langley
Mill

Elms
Hall

ELMS HALL RD

Dismantled Railway

Munn's Farm

STATION RD

Sewage
Works

River Colne

Stone
Bridge

STONEBRIDGE HILL

HALSTEAD RD.

A604

29

Parley Beams
Farm

The Kennels

Chapel
(remains of)

Stanstead
Hall

HUNT
RD

Bullock
Wood

Ash
Bottom

3

Sch

Don
Johns

Homely Ash
Grounds

Warren
Farm

Bourne Brook

43

Greensteadhall
Farm

Greenstead
Green

New
Wood

Nightingale
Hall

NEWHOUSE RD

28

BURTON'S GREEN RD

PH

PH
The
Grange

Nightingale
Hall
Farm

2

Nurseries

Whitings

Lodge
Farm

Home
Farm

Perces

Airfield
(disused)

Long Ley Grove

27

Tyler's
Wood

Earls Colne
Industrial Park

Clavering's
Farm

Burton's
Green
Villa Farm

Mann's
Farm

Honeywood
Farm

LANCASTER PK

Moat

Cleveland
Wood

Markshall
Wood

1

NUNTY'S LA.

Great
Nunty's
Farm

Nunty's
Wood

Lilly Wood

Markshall
Park

Thrift
Wood

Deer Park

26
82

A 83 **B** 84 **C**

62

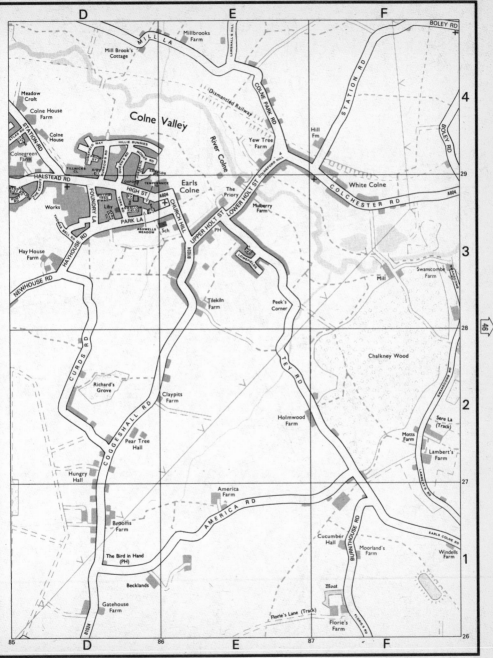

D E F

BOLEY RD

MILL LA

Millbrooks Farm

Mill Brook's Cottage

Meadow Croft

Colne House Farm

Colne Valley

Colne House

STATION RD

Colnegreen Farm

NORTHGATE WAY

HILLIE BUNNIES

MOAT RD

EMERALDS

TILLWICKS CL.

TEMPERANCE

Halstead RD

FOUNDRY LA

HIGH ST

OXFORD

Earls Colne

The Priory

Works

Liby

PARK LA

ASHWELLS MEADOW

CHURCH HILL

Sch

UPPER HOLT ST

LOWER HOLT ST

Mulberry Farm

LOWERHOUSE

B1024

PH

Hay House Farm

HAYHOUSE RD

NEWHOUSE RD

Tilekiln Farm

Peek's Corner

Dismantled Railway

COLNE PARK RD

LAWSHALL'S HILL

River Colne

Yew Tree Farm

EGGMFORD HILL

Hill Fm

STATION RD

BOLEY RD

4

29

White Colne

COLCHESTER RD

A604

Mill

Swanscombe Farm

3

TEY RD

28

Chalkney Wood

CURDS RD

Richard's Grove

COGGESHALL RD

Claypits Farm

Holmwood Farm

Pear Tree Hall

SWANSCOMBE RD

Motts Farm

Sere La (Track)

Lambert's Farm

LAMBERTS RD

2

27

Hungry Hall

America Farm

AMERICA RD

Brooms Farm

The Bird in Hand (PH)

Cucumber Hall

BURNTHOUSE RD

Moorland's Farm

EARLS COLNE RD

Windells Farm

1

Becklands

Gatehouse Farm

B1024

Florie's Lane (Track)

FLORIE'S RD

Moat

Florie's Farm

26

85 86 87

D E F

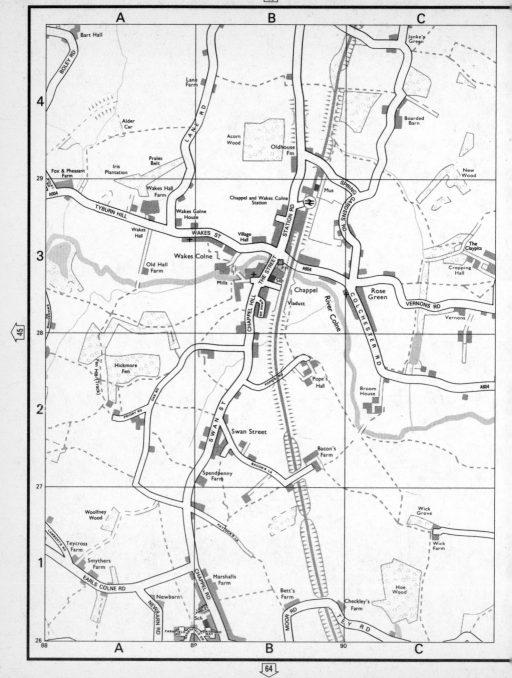

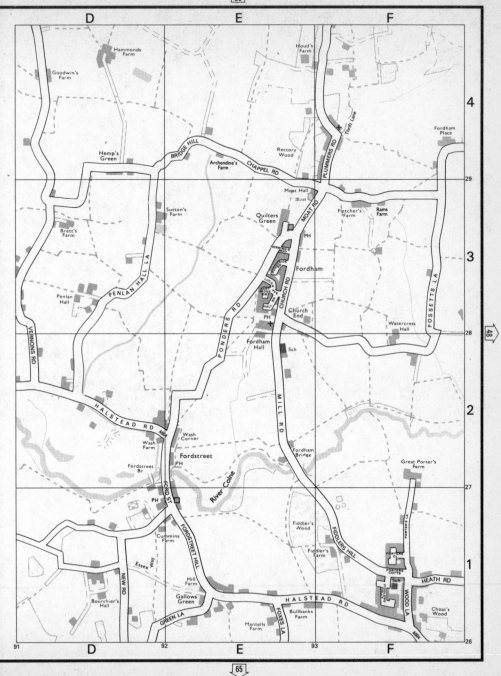

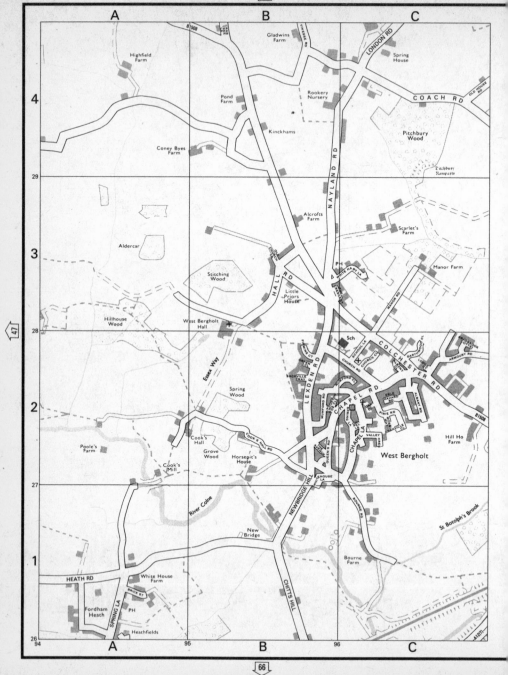

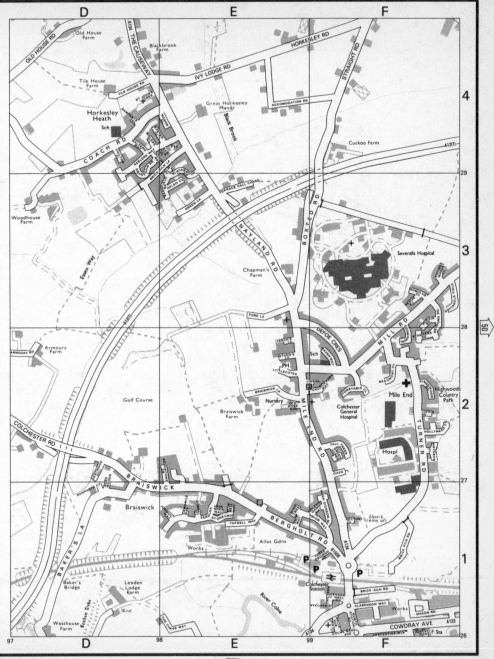

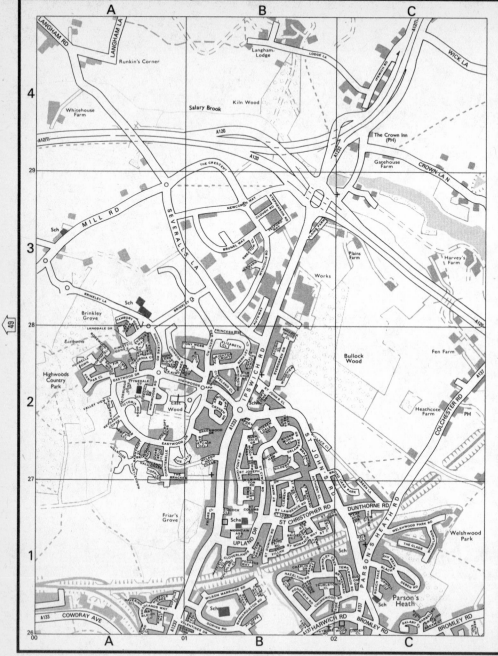

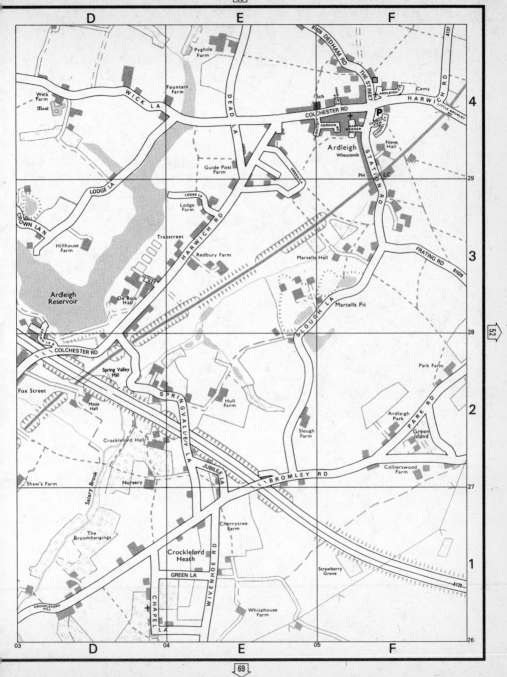

D   E   F

4

29

3

28

2

27

1

26

Wick Farm

Moat

Pyghtle Farm

Fountain Farm

WICK LA

DEDHAM RD

B1029

DEAD LA

GREEN LA

THE STREET

Sch

ARDLEIGH

Cemy

HARWICH RD

A137

LITTLE BROMLEY

COLCHESTER RD

GERNON

MANSE WARNER

CONGREG CHAPEL

P

New Hall

Ardleigh

Wheatlands

Guide Post Farm

LODGE LA

STATION RD

PH

LC

CROWN LA N

LODGE LA

Lodge Farm

HARWICH RD

Hillhouse Farm

Trapstreet

Redbury Farm

Martells Hall

FRATING RD

B1029

Ardleigh Reservoir

De Bois Hall

Martells Pit

SLOUGH LA

COLCHESTER RD

28

Park Farm

Spring Valley Mill

Fox Street

SPRING VALLEY LA

Moze Hall

Hull Farm

Slough Farm

Ardleigh Park

PARK RD

Green Island

Crockleford Hall

JUBILEE LA

Collierswood Farm

Salary Brook

Shaw's Farm

Nursery

BROMLEY RD

The Broomhangings

Cherrytree Farm

Crockleford Heath

WIVENHOE RD

GREEN LA

CHAPEL LA

Strawberry Grove

A120

CROCKLEFORD HILL

Whitehouse Farm

03   04   05

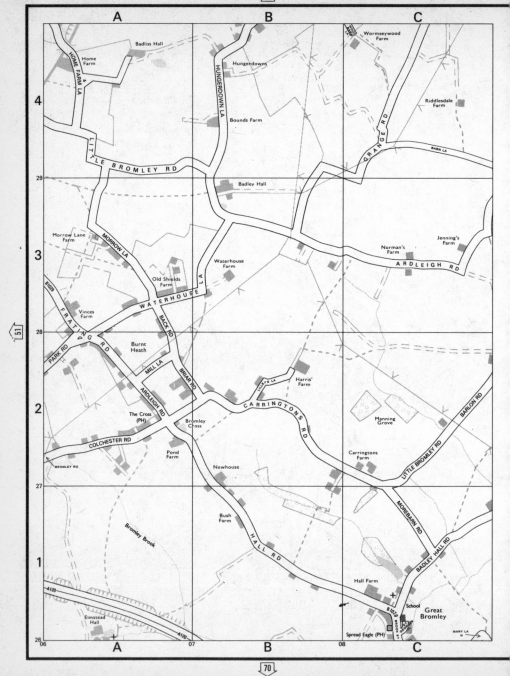

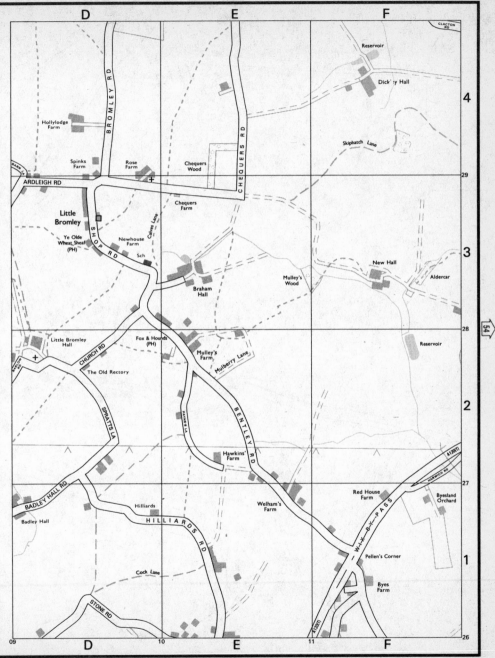

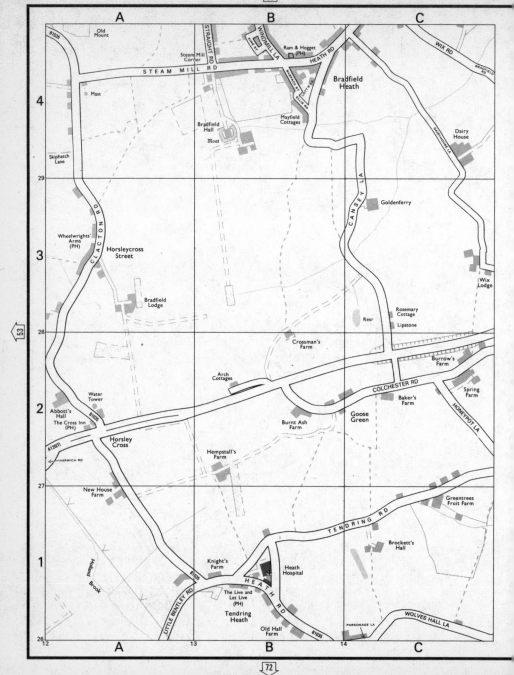

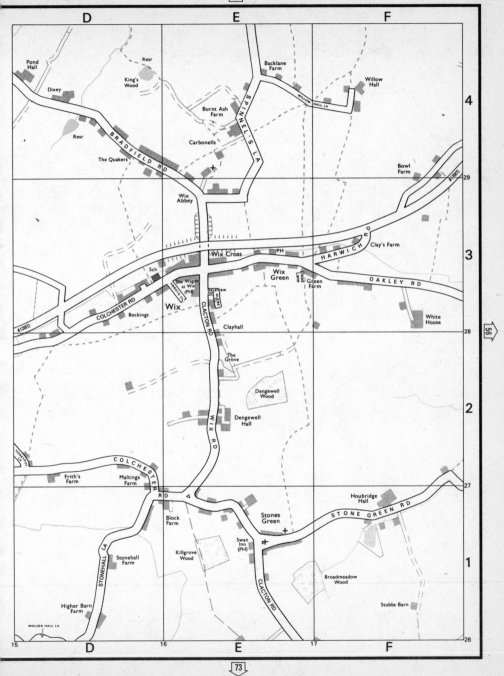

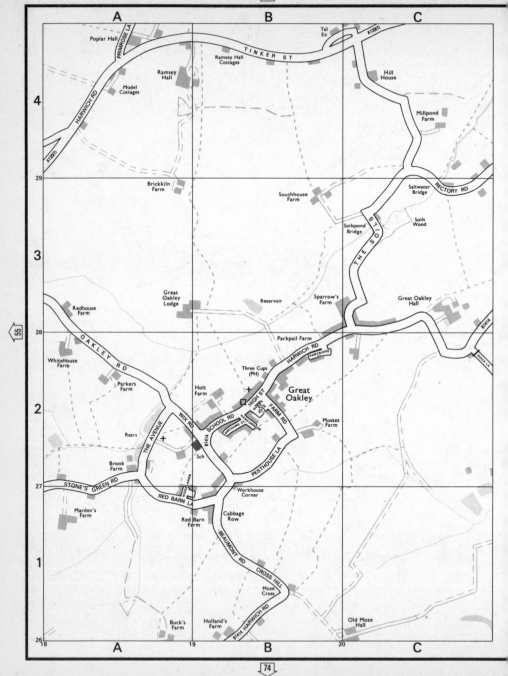

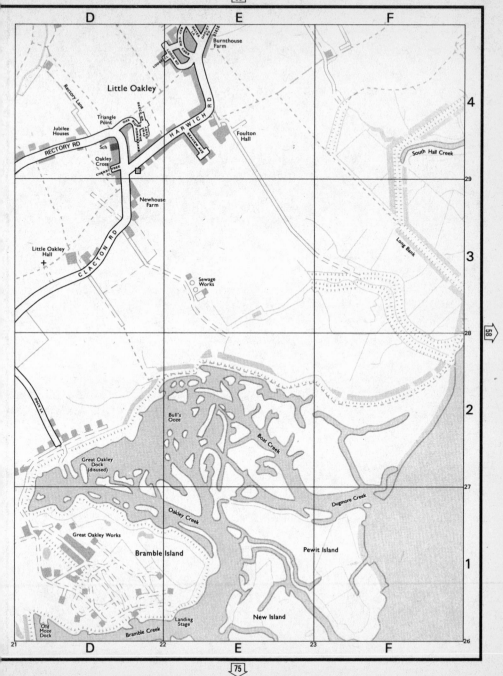

D E F

4

Burnthouse
Farm

Little Oakley

Triangle
Point

Jubilee
Houses

RECTORY RD

Sch

Oakley
Cross

Rectory Lane

HARWICH RD

Foulton
Hall

South Hall Creek

29

Newhouse
Farm

CLACTON RD

Little Oakley
Hall

Long Bank

3

Sewage
Works

28

Bull's
Ooze

Boat Creek

2

Great Oakley
Dock
(disused)

27

Oakley Creek

Dugmore Creek

Great Oakley Works

Bramble Island

Pewit Island

1

Old
Moze
Dock

Landing
Stage

New Island

Bramble Creek

21 D 22 E 23 F 26

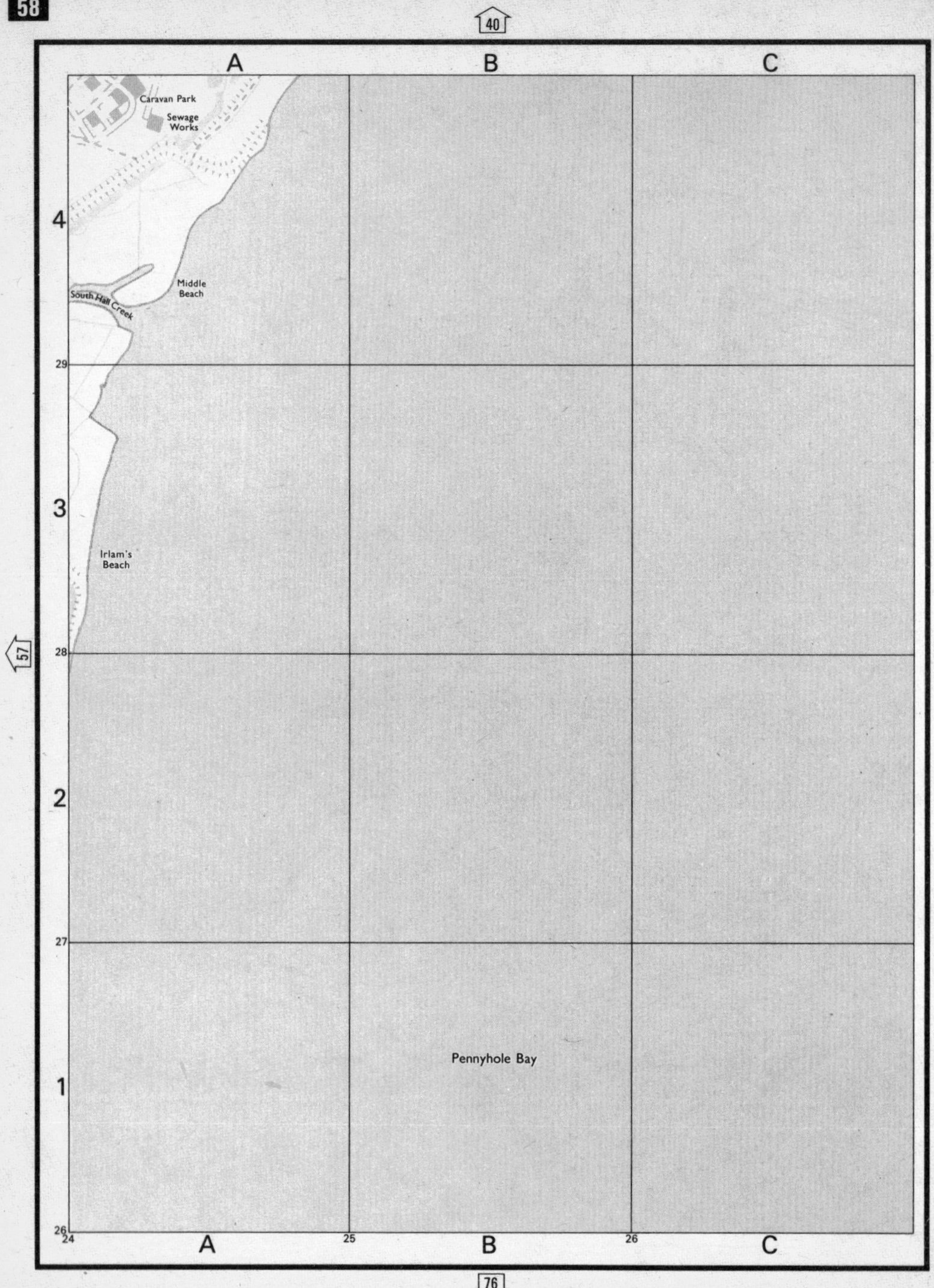
40
A
B
C
Caravan Park
Sewage Works
4
Middle Beach
South Hall Creek
29
3
Irlam's Beach
57
28
2
27
Pennyhole Bay
1
26
24
25
26
A
B
C
76

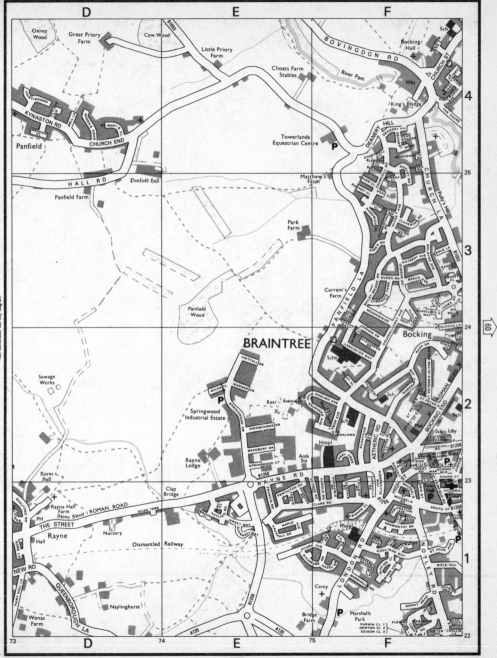

D   E   F

Oxney Wood

Great Priory Farm

Cow Wood

Little Priory Farm

Choats Farm Stables

River Pant

BOVINGDON RD

Bocking Hall

Sch

CHURCH ST

Wks

King's Bridge

4

THE TLEDOWN

KYNASTON RD

MARY C

QUEENS GDNS

Panfield

CHURCH END

Towerlands Equestrian Centre

P

DEANERY HILL

DEANERY HILL

CHURCH LA

25

HALL RD

Panfield Hall

Matthew's Farm

Panfield Farm

Park Farm

B1256

3

Currant's Farm

MAYSENT AVE

BEECH

PANFIELD LA

Bocking

24

MEADOWSIDE

BRAINTREE

LANCASTER WAY

Schs

Bocking

CRITTALL DR

WARNER DR

WICKES CL

P

Resr

ENGLISH AVE

BUNGALOWS

Sch

ST PETERS RD

ROMAN ROAD

BOCKING END

Sch

Liby

2

Springwood Industrial Estate

SWINBOURNE DR

BRADBURY DR

SPRINGWOOD CT

Rayne Lodge

B1256

Hospl

Amb Sta

AETHERIC RD

COGGESHALL

Sewage Works

RAYNE RD

HIGH

Victoria

23

Rayne Hall

Clap Bridge

Rayne Hall Farm

Stane Street ROMAN ROAD

GILDA TERR

FRANCIS RD

PENTLOW DR

CLARE RD

B1256

SOUTH ST

PH

THE STREET

Rayne

Hall

Nursery

JERSEY WAY

MAPLE

ACORN AVE

LONDON RD

HOSP

NOTLEY RD

1

Dismantled Railway

SWEET WAY

NEW RD

ST JOHN

RIFLE CL

QUEENSBOROUGH LA

Naylinghurst

Cemy

Bridge Farm

Marshalls Park

DARWIN CL 1
NEWTON CL 2
EDISON CL 3

CHALLIS

Wenas Farm

B1256

A120

A120

22

73   D   74   E   75   F

60

not continued, see key diagram

42

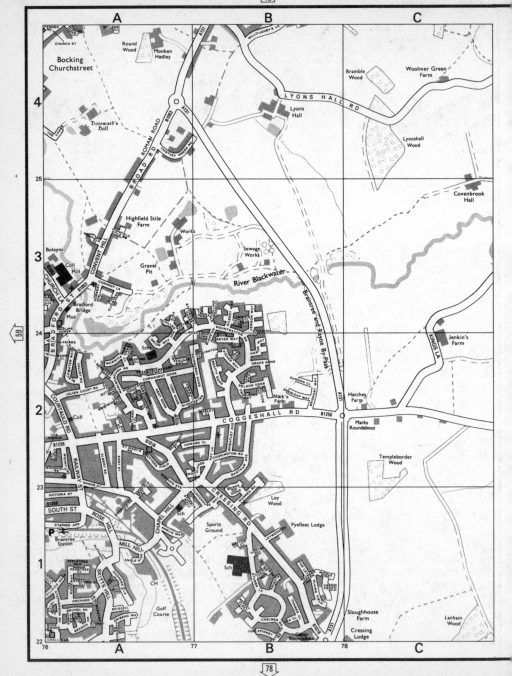

59

78

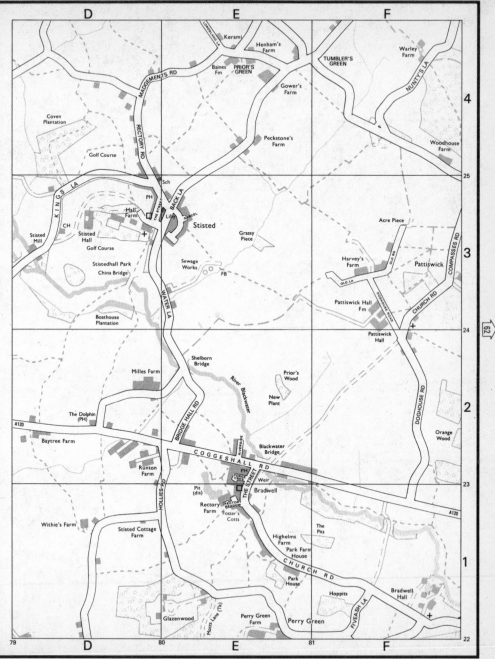

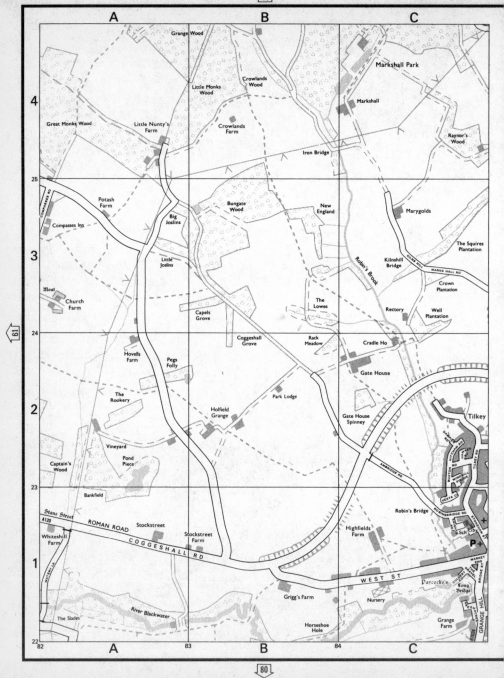

A B C

4

Grange Wood

Markshall Park

Little Monks
Wood

Crowlands
Wood

Markshall

Great Monks Wood

Little Nunty's
Farm

Crowlands
Farm

Iron Bridge

Raynor's
Wood

25

Potash
Farm

Big
Joslins

Bungate
Wood

New
England

Marygolds

The Squires
Plantation

Compasses Inn

3

Little
Joslins

Robin's Brook

Kilnshill
Bridge

KILNS HILL

MARKS HALL RD

Crown
Plantation

Moat

Church
Farm

Capels
Grove

The
Lowes

Rectory

Well
Plantation

24

Hovells
Farm

Pegs
Folly

Coggeshall
Grove

Rack
Meadow

Cradle Ho

Gate House

The
Rookery

Park Lodge

Gate House
Spinney

Tilkey

2

Holfield
Grange

Vineyard

Captain's
Wood

Pond
Piece

AMBRIDGE RD

VESTA

23

Bankfield

Robin's Bridge

Stane Street

ROMAN ROAD

Stockstreet

Highfields
Farm

Sch

P

A120

Whiteshill
Farm

COGGESHALL RD

Stockstreet
Farm

MARKET
END

1

WEST ST

Paycocke's

Long
Bridge

Grigg's Farm

Nursery

GRANGE HILL

River Blackwater

The Slades

Horseshoe
Hole

Grange
Farm

22

82

A

83

B

84

C

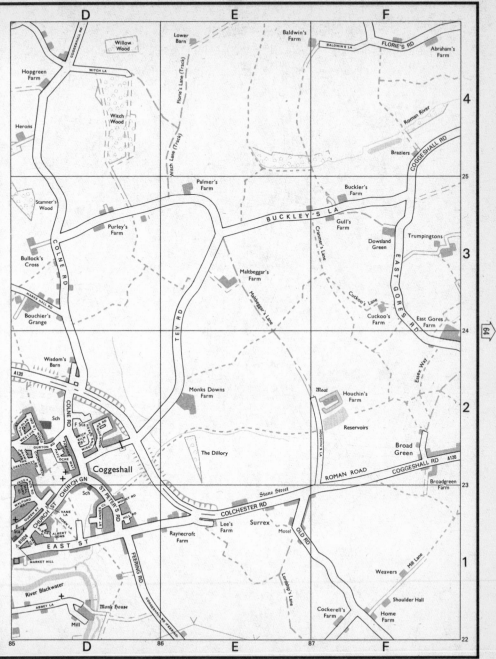

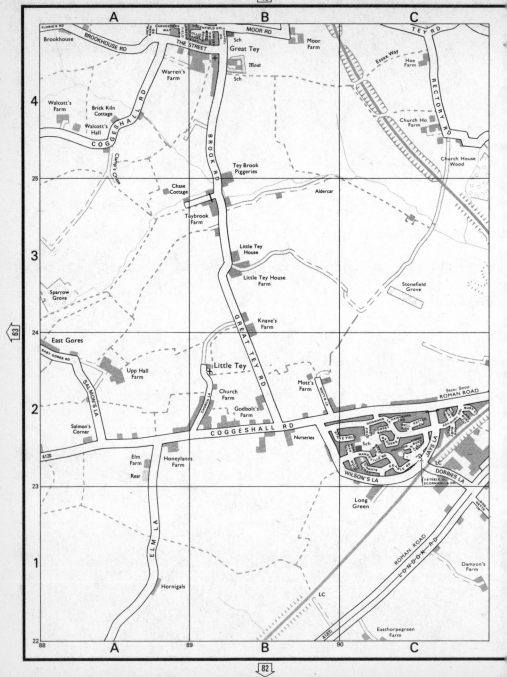

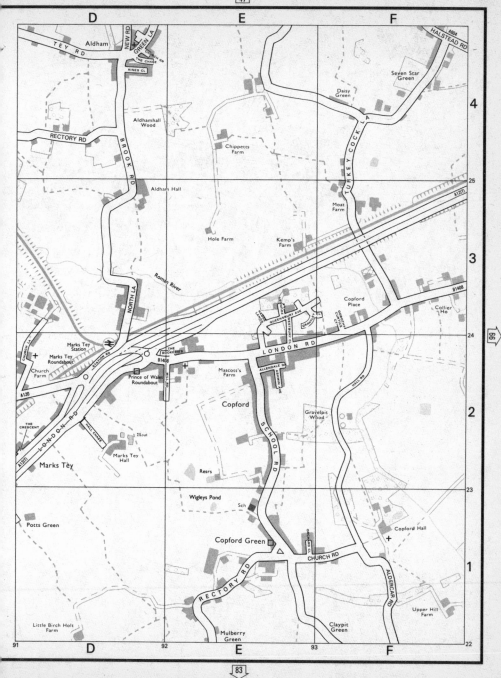

D   E   F

TEY RD

Aldham

NEW RD

GREEN LA

CHURCH OR
THE CHASE

HINES CL

HALSTEAD RD

A604

Seven Star
Green

Daisy
Green

4

RECTORY RD

Aldhamhall
Wood

Chippetts
Farm

TURKEY COCK LA

25

BROOK RD

Aldham Hall

Hole Farm

Kemp's
Farm

Moat
Farm

A12(T)

B1408

3

Roman River

NORTH LA

Copford
Place

Collier
Ho

HENDON CL
QUEENSBURY AVE
WEST BURY CL
GRANCLEY CTCE
DOMOTHY CTCE
LARGE

Marks Tey
Station

THE
BROOKFIELD

B1408

LONDON RD

24

CHURCH LA

Marks Tey
Roundabout

STATION RD

Mascott's
Farm

ALLENDALE DR
ASHWIN AVE

HALL RD

Gravelpit
Wood

Church
Farm

Prince of Wales
Roundabout

BELL HILL RD

Copford

SCHOOL RD

A120

THE
CRESCENT

L-O-N-D-O-N---R-D

HALL CHASE

Moat

2

A120

Marks Tey
Hall

Resrs

Marks Tey

Wigleys Pond

Sch

23

Potts Green

Copford Green

RECTORY RD

ORCHARD RD

CHURCH RD

Copford Hall

ALDERCAR RD

1

Little Birch Holt
Farm

Mulberry
Green

Claypit
Green

Upper Hill
Farm

91   D   92   E   93   F 22

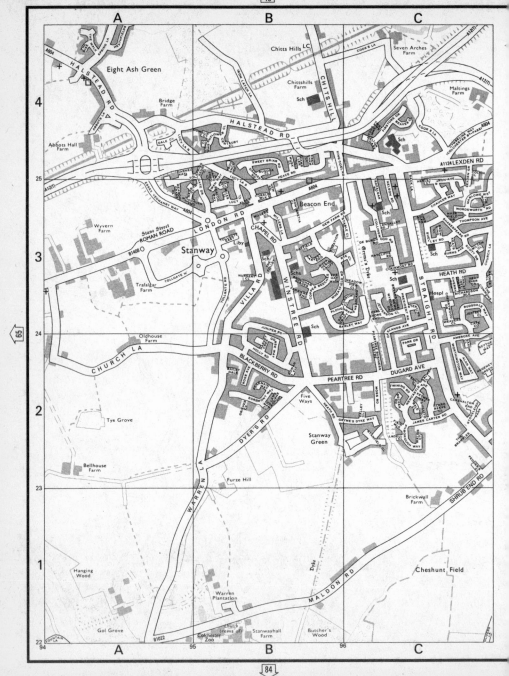

ELECTRICAL CONTRACTORS

19-31

16 VULCANO ROAD

CSL LIMITED

Tel: (04023) 71767
Fax: (04023) 77016

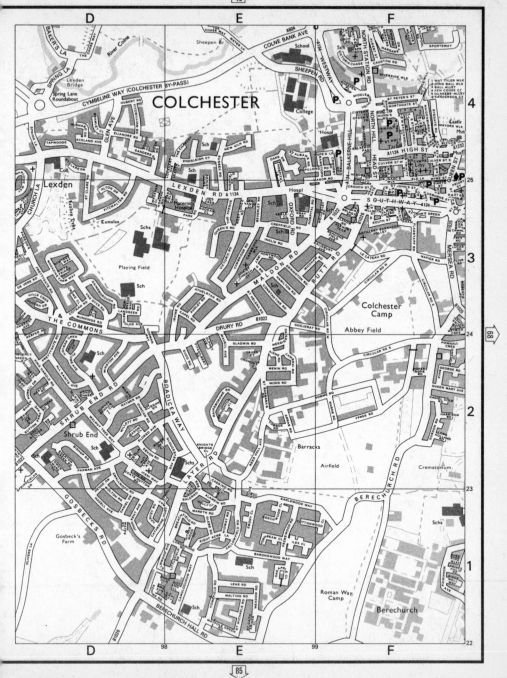

COLCHESTER

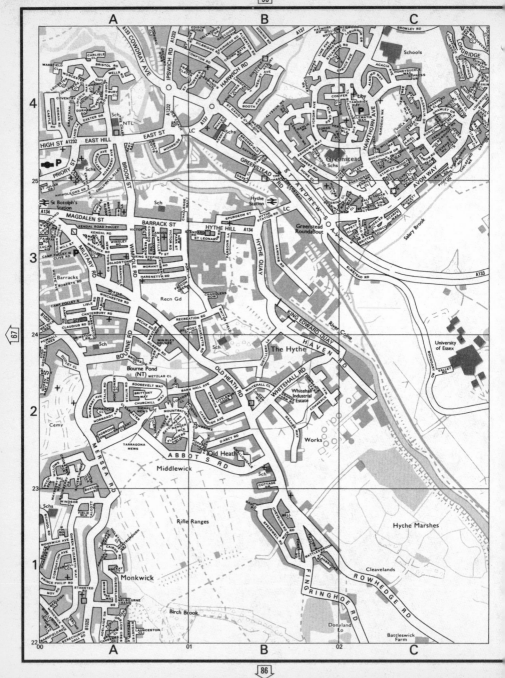

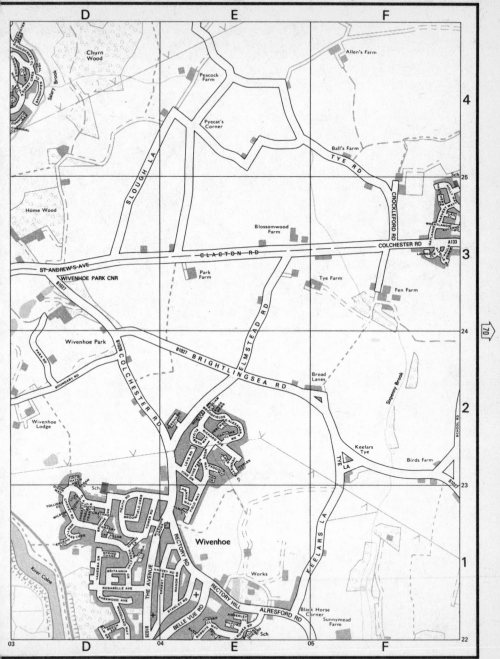

70

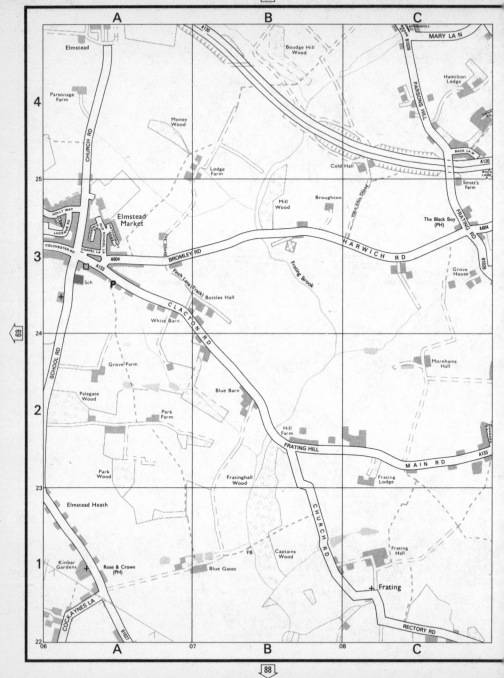

53

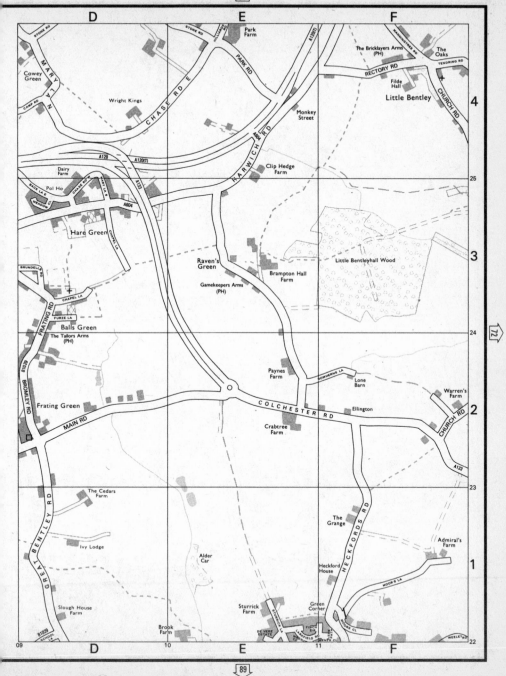

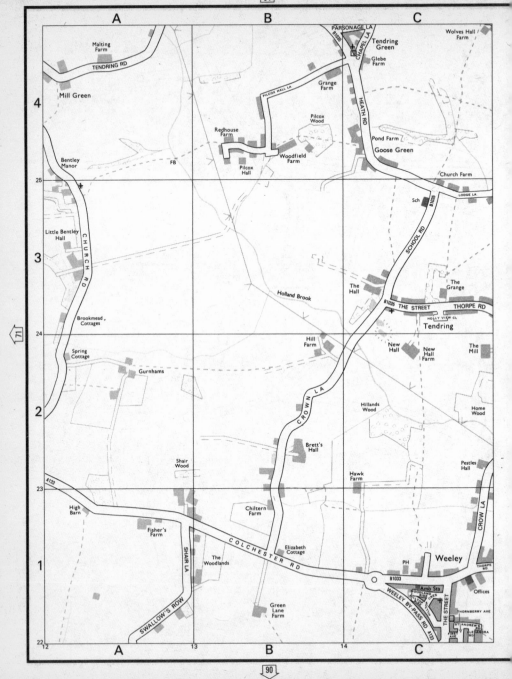

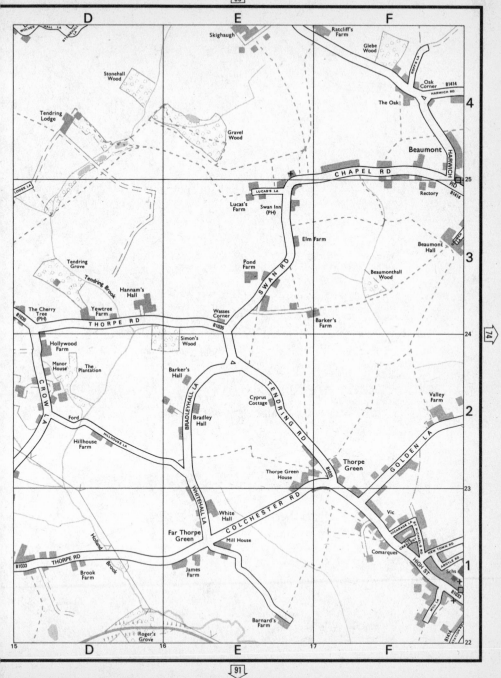

56

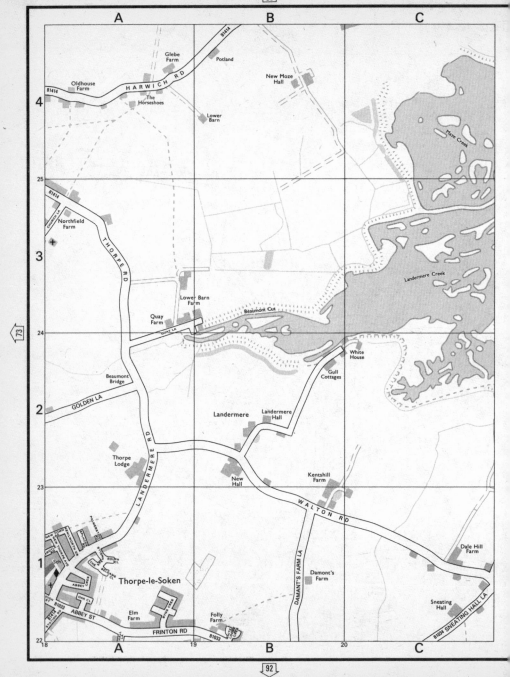

B1414

Glebe
Farm

Potland

New Moze
Hall

Oldhouse
Farm

HARWICH RD

B1414

The
Horseshoes

4

Lower
Barn

Maze Creek

25

B1414

Northfield
Farm

THORPE RD

3

Landermere Creek

Lower Barn
Farm

Quay
Farm

Beaumont Cut

QUAY LA

24

White
House

Beaumont
Bridge

Gull
Cottages

GOLDEN LA

2

Landermere

Landermere
Hall

LANDERMERE RD

Thorpe
Lodge

23

New
Hall

Kentshill
Farm

WALTON RD

New Town

KNIGHTS DR

FERN CRES
ROLPH
ROLPH
CL
REDGATE
CL

Sch

Thorpe-le-Soken

ABBEY

OAK CL

DAMANT'S FARM LA

Damont's
Farm

Dale Hill
Farm

1

HIGH
ST
B1033

STATION RD

B1414

ABBEY ST

Elm
Farm

Folly
Farm

Sneating
Hall

B103A SNEATING HALL LA

FRINTON RD

B1033

22
18

73

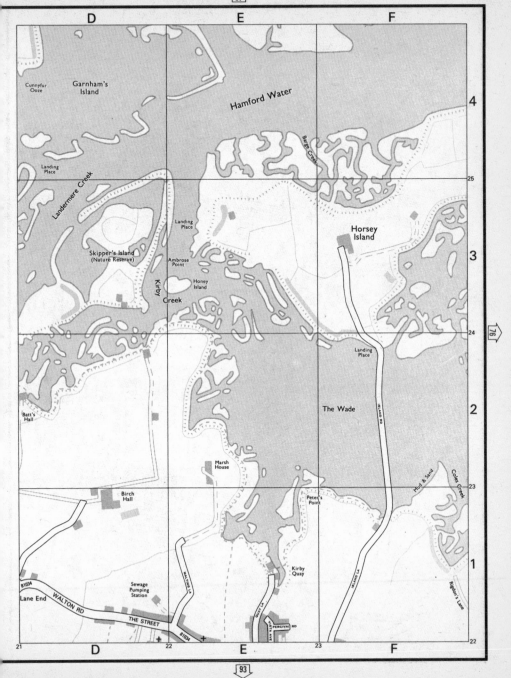

D E F

Cunnyfur
Ooze

Garnham's
Island

Hamford Water

4

Landing
Place

25

Landermere Creek

Landing
Place

Horsey
Island

Skipper's Island
(Nature Reserve)

Ambrose
Point

Kirby Creek

Honey
Island

3

76

24

Landing
Place

Batt's
Hall

The Wade

2

ISLAND RD

Mud & Sand

Coles Creek

Marsh
House

23

Birch
Hall

Peter's
Point

Kirby
Quay

MALTING LA

QUAY LA

ISLAND LA

Rigbon's Lane

1

B1034

WALTON RD

Lane End

Sewage
Pumping
Station

THE STREET

B1034

E

PERCIVAL RD

HUBYS AVE

23

22

21 D 22 E F 22

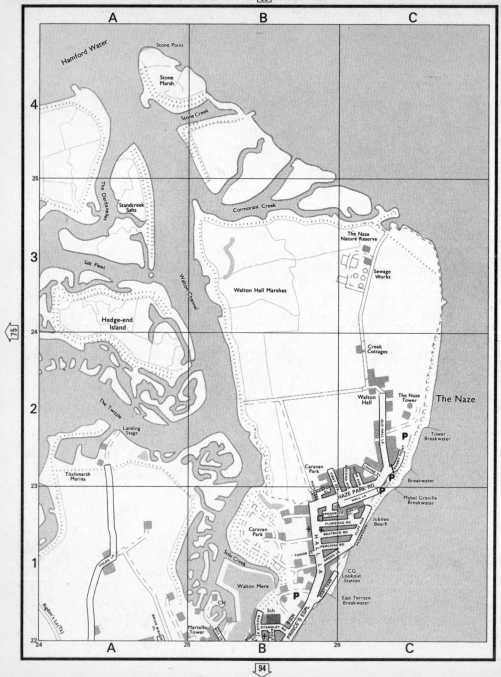

59

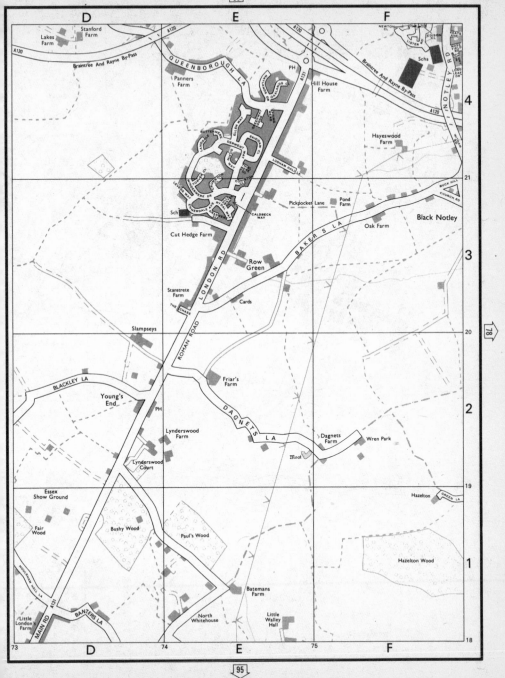

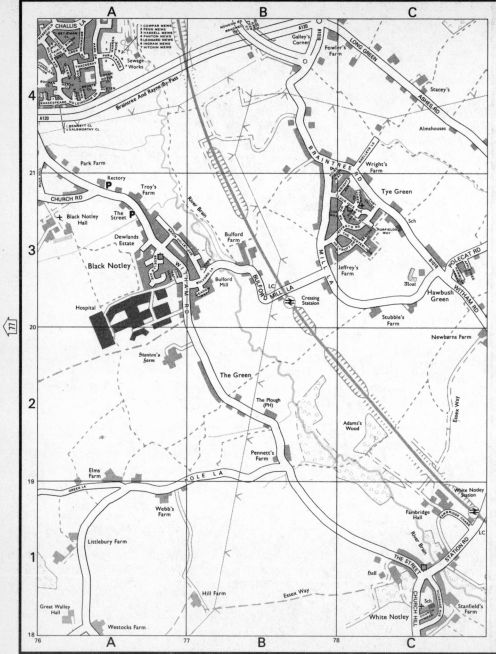

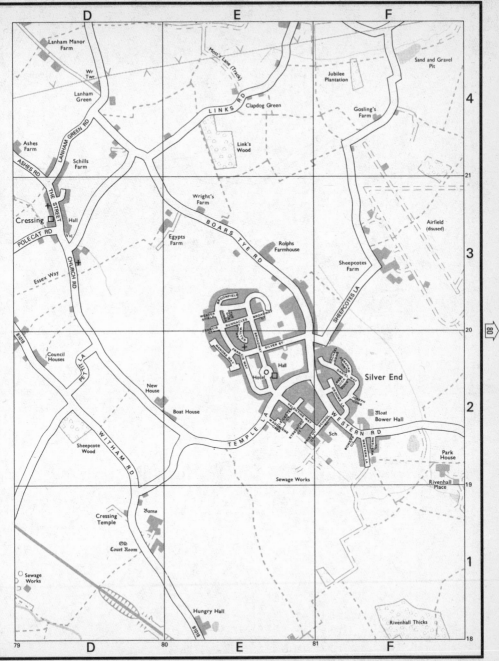

D
E
F

Lanham Manor Farm

Wr Twr

Lanham Green

Ashes Farm

Schills Farm

LANHAM GREEN RD

ASHES RD

THE STREET

Cressing

Hall

Vic

POLECAT RD

Essex Way

CHURCH RD

Council Houses

New House

Boat House

PETTY LA

WITHAM RD

Sheepcote Wood

Cressing Temple

Old Court Room

Sewage Works

Barns

Hungry Hall

B1018

B1018

Mott's Lane (Track)

LINKS RD

Clapdog Green

Link's Wood

Wright's Farm

BOARS TYE RD

Egypts Farm

Rolphs Farmhouse

Jubilee Plantation

Gosling's Farm

Sand and Gravel Pit

Airfield (disused)

Sheepcotes Farm

SHEEPCOTES LA

BROOMFIELD

WEAVER SPINK

FRANCIS

RUNNACLES

BROADWAY ST

BROADWAY

SILVER ST

PRINCE CLOSE

MANORS WAY

FRANCIS WAY

Hotel

Hall

TEMPLE LA

WESTERN RD

Silver End

DANIEL WAY

JOSEPH RD

VALENTINE WAY

MAGDALENE

SCHOOL

Sch

Moat Bower Hall

Park House

Rivenhall Place

Rivenhall Thicks

Sewage Works

80

4

21

3

20

2

19

1

18

79
D
80
E
81
F

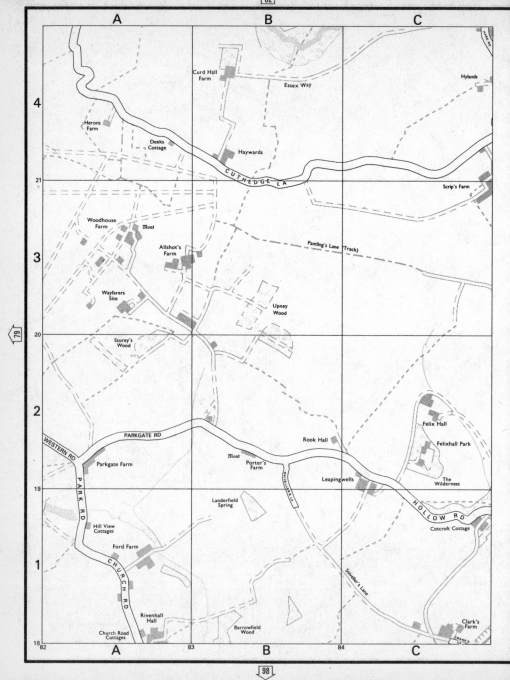

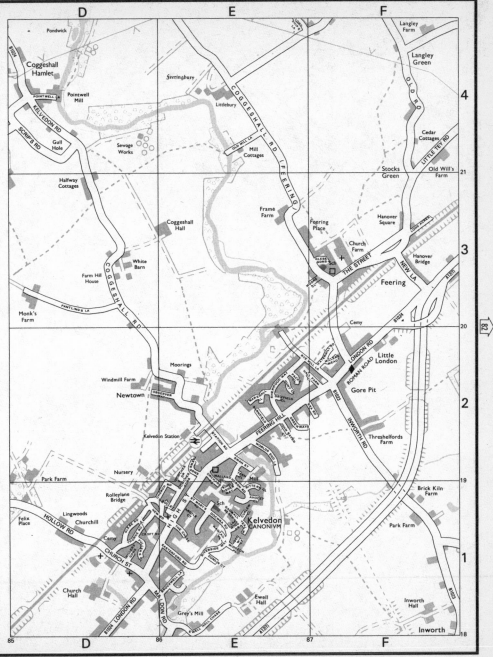

D E F

Pondwick

Coggeshall Hamlet

POINTWELL LA
Pointwell Mill

Seeringbury

Langley Farm

Langley Green

OLD RD

KELVEDON RD

SCRIP'S RD

Gull Hole

Littlebury

OLD MILL LA

Mill Cottages

Sewage Works

Cedar Cottages

LITTLE TEY RD

Stocks Green

Old Will's Farm

21

Halfway Cottages

Frame Farm

Feering Place

Hanover Square

COGGESHALL RD (FEERING)

White Barn

Coggeshall Hall

Church Farm

Hanover Bridge

A12/T1

3

Farm Hill House

GLEBE GDNS
Sch
THE STREET

MOORE CL

NEW LA

Feering

PANTLING'S LA

Monk's Farm

COGGESHALL RD

Cemy

B1024

20

82

Moorings

LONDON RD

Little London

Windmill Farm

OBSERVER

Newtown

RYE MILL LA
STRETTERS RD
HALL FARM
MARSHALL
DRYFIELD
WALLIS MEAD
ROMAN ROAD

Gore Pit

INWORTH RD

2

Kelvedon Station

STATION RD

FEERING HILL

GOLD'S NOOK
GREENWAYS

Threshelfords Farm

Nursery

Mill

19

Park Farm

SWAN ST

Brick Kiln Farm

Rolleylane Bridge

Sch

AVOCET CL

Felix Place
Lingwoods

HIGH ST

Kelvedon
CANONIVM

Park Farm

B1023

HOLLOW RD
Churchill

Cemy

MALDON RD

1

Church St

CHURCH ST

Church Hall

LONDON RD
B1024

Grey's Mill

Ewell Hall

Inworth Hall

A12/T1

Inworth

18

85 86 87

D E F

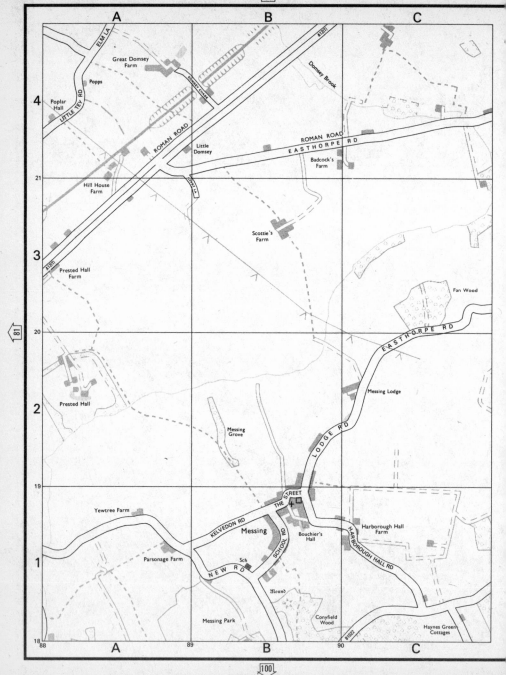

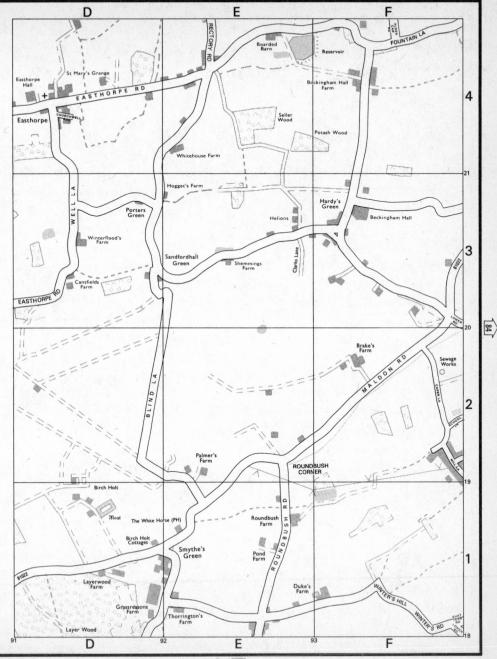

D   E   F

FOUNTAIN LA

ALDER CAR

Boarded Barn

Reservoir

St Mary's Grange

Easthorpe Hall

Bockingham Hall Farm

EASTHORPE RD

4

Easthorpe

CHURCHWELL

Seller Wood

Potash Wood

RECTORY RD

Whitehouse Farm

21

Hogget's Farm

Hardy's Green

WELL LA

Porters Green

Helions

Beckingham Hall

Winterflood's Farm

Clarks Lane

3

Sandfordhall Green

Shemmings Farm

B1022

EASTHORPE RD

Cantfields Farm

LOWER RD

20

84

BLIND LA

Brake's Farm

MALDON RD

Sewage Works

CARR LA

2

SCHOOL

Palmer's Farm

ROUNDBUSH CORNER

WELLS

19

Birch Holt

Moat

The White Horse (PH)

Roundbush Farm

ROUNDBUSH RD

Birch Holt Cottages

Smythe's Green

Pond Farm

1

B1022

Layerwood Farm

Duke's Farm

WINTER'S HILL

Grassreasons Farm

WINTER'S RD

Thorrington's Farm

Layer Wood

SHAT TENHALL ROVER

18

91   D   92   E   93   F

66

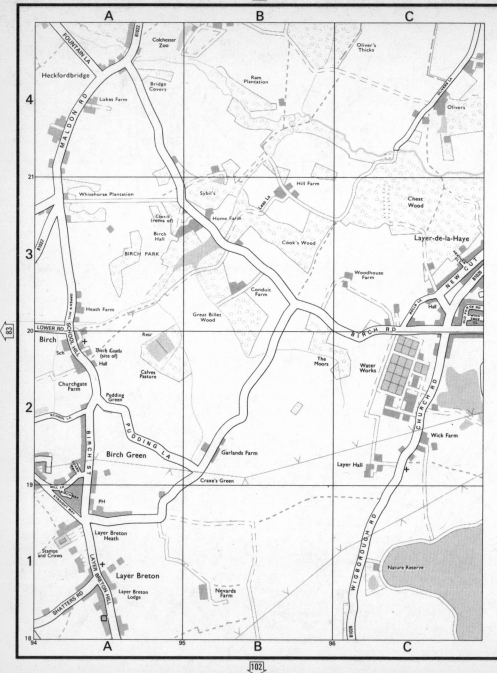

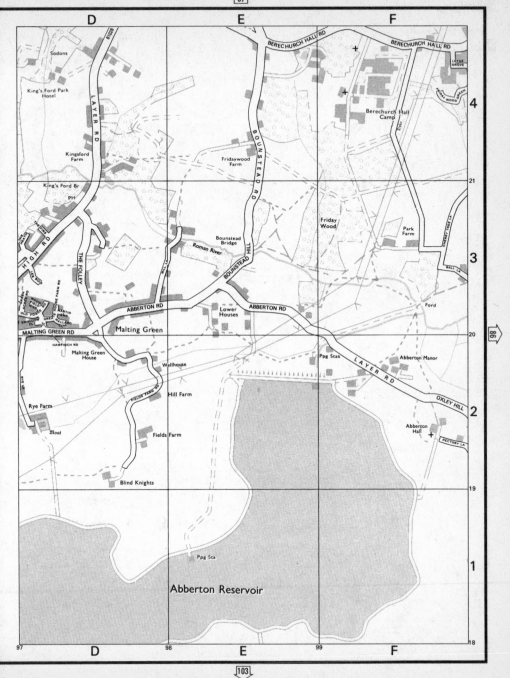

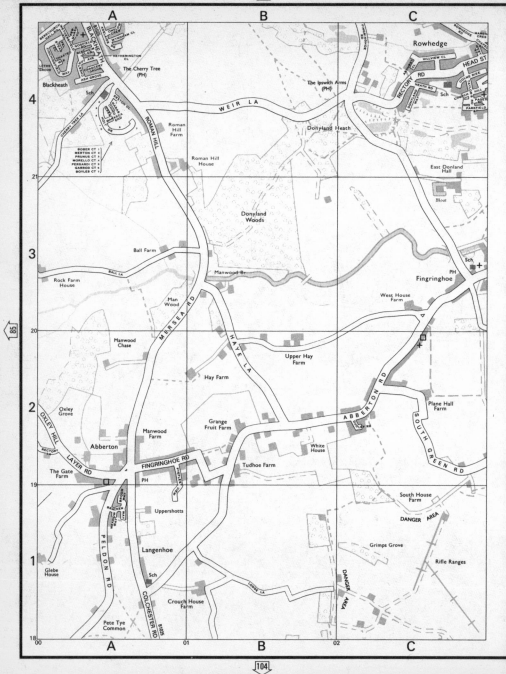

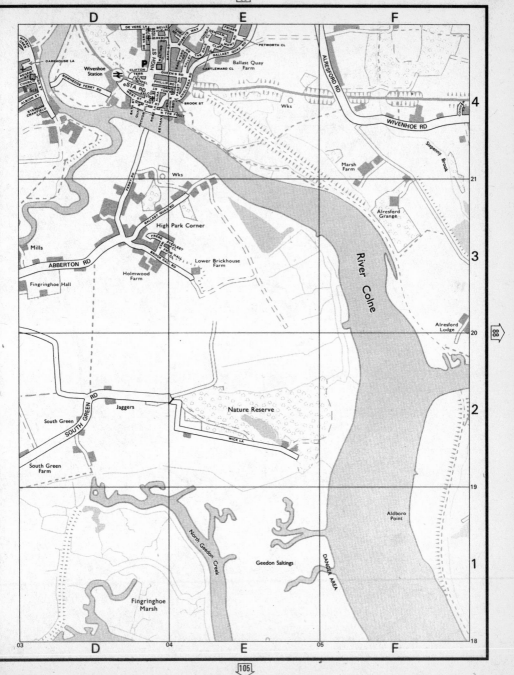

69

88

D   E   F

DE VERE LA
BELLE
B1028
HIGH ST
Wivenhoe Station
CLIFTON TERR
STA RD
ROWHEDGE FERRY RD
DAREHOUSE LA
REGENT ST
Sch
ALBION ST
SHEEPFIELD CRANFIELD CL
PHILLIP RD
BROOK ST
WEST ST
EAST ST
THE FOLLY
BETHANY ST
FALCON
QUEEN'S RD
COWDRAY
FRIARS
PETWORTH CL
DENDY
CLARKHOUSE
CASTLEWARD CL
BALLAST QUAY RD
Ballast Quay Farm
Wks

ALRESFORD RD
WIVENHOE RD
Sixpenny Brook
Marsh Farm
Alresford Grange

21

Wks

FERRY RD
BALLAST QUAY RD
High Park Corner
FREE HALL
THE MILL
BROOK HALL RD
Mills
ABBERTON RD
Holmwood Farm
Fingringhoe Hall
Lower Brickhouse Farm

River Colne

Alresford Lodge

20

3

SOUTH GREEN RD
Jaggers
South Green
South Green Farm
Nature Reserve
WICK LA

2

19

Aldboro Point

North Geedon Creek
Geedon Saltings
DANGER AREA
Fingringhoe Marsh

1

18

03   04   05

D   E   F

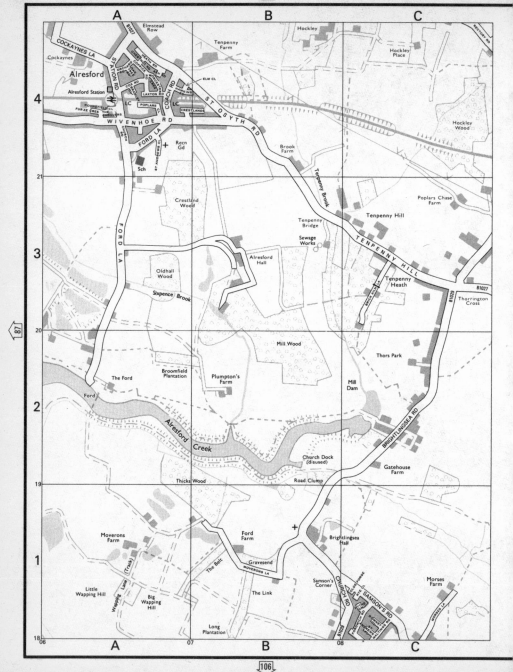

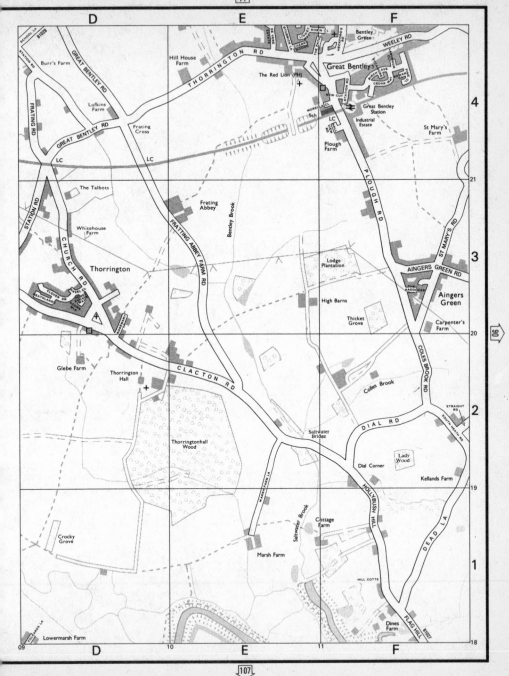

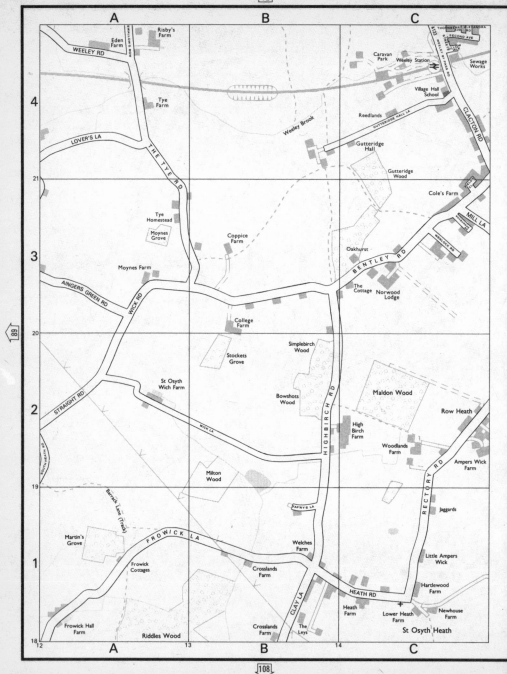

A   B   C

4

21

3

20

2

19

1

18
12   13   14

A   B   C

89

WEELEY RD
Risby's Farm
Eden Farm
SWALLOW'S ROW
Tye Farm
LOVER'S LA
THE TYE RD
Tye Homestead
Moynes Grove
Moynes Farm
AINGERS GREEN RD
WICK RD
Coppice Farm
College Farm
STRAIGHT RD
SOUTH HEATH RD
St Osyth Wich Farm
WICK LA
Stockets Grove
Milton Wood
Barrack Lane (Track)
Martin's Grove
Frowick Cottages
FROWICK LA
Frowick Hall Farm
Riddles Wood
Crosslands Farm
Welches Farm
Crosslands Farm
The Leys
CLAY LA
FAPNY'S LA
Weeley Brook
Simplebirch Wood
Bowshots Wood
HIGHBIRCH RD
High Birch Farm
Maldon Wood
Row Heath
Woodlands Farm
RECTORY RD
Ampers Wick Farm
Jaggards
Little Ampers Wick
Hartlewood Farm
Newhouse Farm
Heath Farm
Lower Heath Farm
HEATH RD
St Osyth Heath
Caravan Park
Weeley Station
Sewage Works
THORNBURY
ALEXANDRA AVE RD
SECOND AVE
WEELEY BY PASS RD
MILTON RD
A133
Village Hall
School
CLACTON RD
Reedlands
Gutteridge Hall
GUTTERIDGE HALL LA
Gutteridge Wood
Cole's Farm
MILL LA
Oakhurst
BENTLEY RD
WENLOCK RD
The Cottage
Norwood Lodge

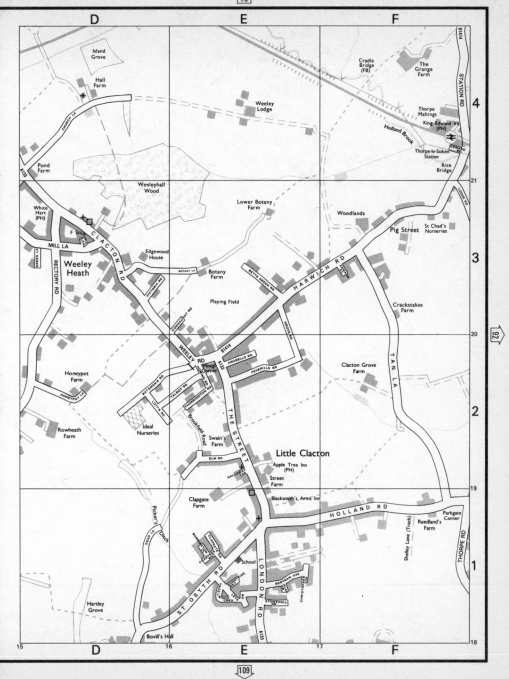

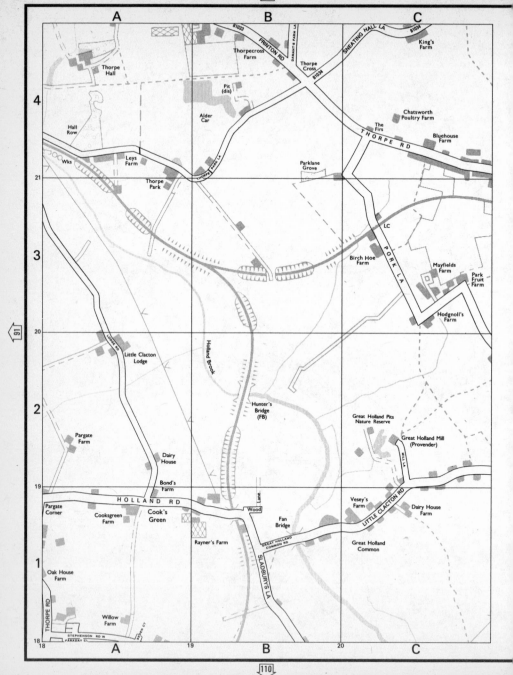

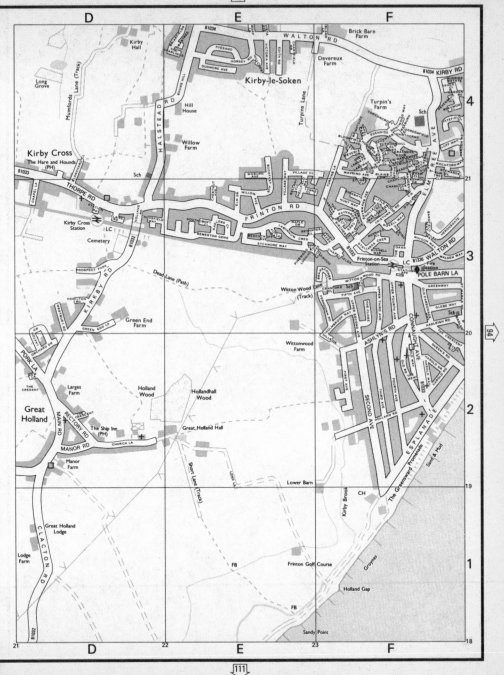

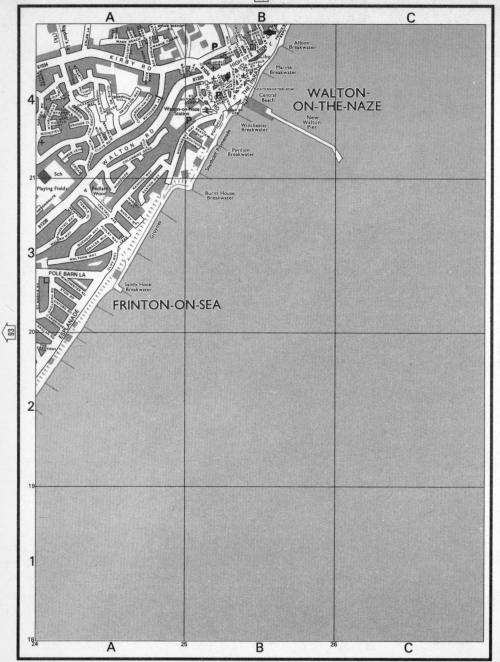

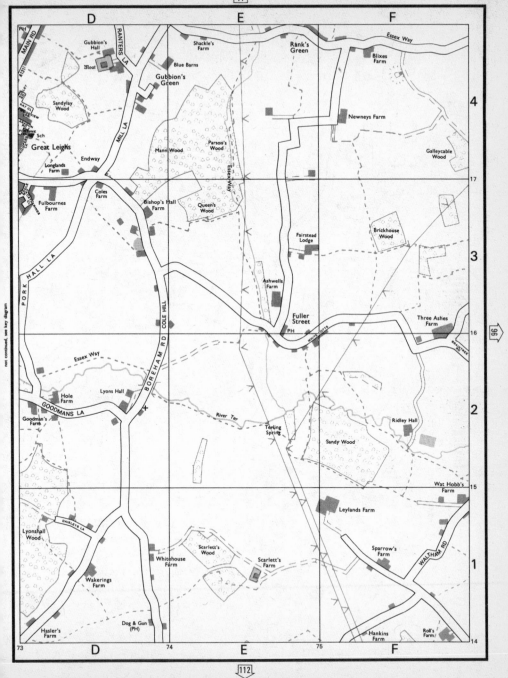

D   E   F

PH

MAIN RD

Gubbion's Hall

RANTERS LA

Shackle's Farm

Rank's Green

Essex Way

Blixes Farm

Moat

Blue Barns

Gubbion's Green

4

Sandylay Wood

MILL LA

Newneys Farm

Galleycable Wood

Sch

Great Leighs

Mann Wood

Parson's Wood

Endway

Longlands Farm

17

Fulbournes Farm

Coles Farm

Bishop's Hall Farm

Queen's Wood

ESSEX WAY

Fairstead Lodge

Brickhouse Wood

3

PORK HALL LA

COLE HILL

BOREHAM RD

Ashwells Farm

Fuller Street

PH

Three Ashes Farm

16

96

not construed, see key diagram

BRAINTREE

WHITE OTTER

Essex Way

Hole Farm

Lyons Hall

GOODMANS LA

River Ter

Terling Spring

Ridley Hall

2

Goodman's Farm

Sandy Wood

Wat Hobb's Farm

15

Leylands Farm

DAIRLEYS LA

Lyonshall Wood

Scarlett's Wood

Sparrow's Farm

WALTHAM RD

1

Whitehouse Farm

Scarlett's Farm

Wakerings Farm

Dog & Gun (PH)

Hankins Farm

Roll's Farm

Hasler's Farm

14

73   D   74   E   75   F

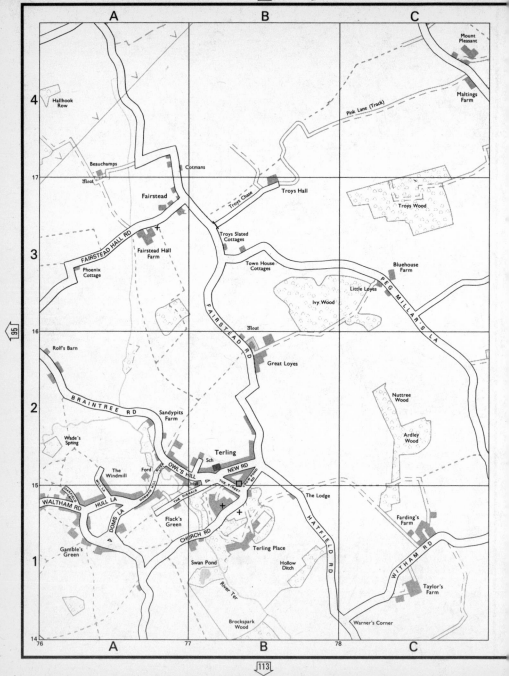

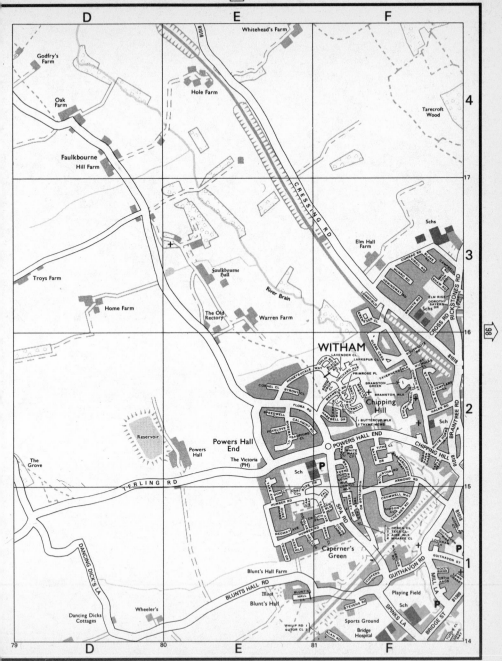

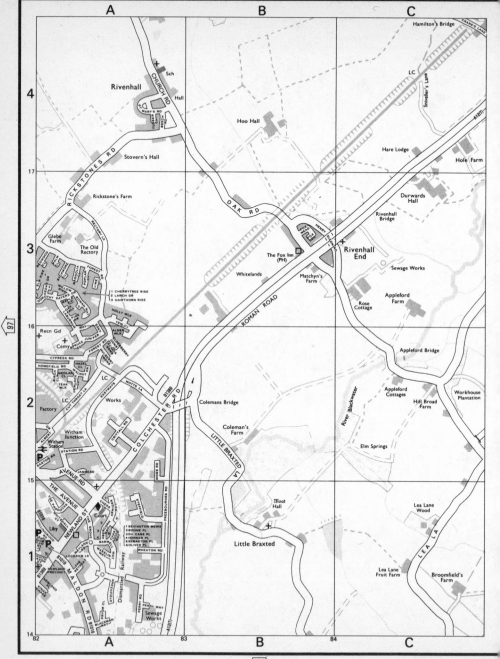

A B C

97

4

Rivenhall

CHURCH RD

Sch

Hall

MARY'S RD
BEECH

Hamilton's Bridge

CRANE'S LANE

LC

Sniveller's Lane

A12(T)

Hoo Hall

Hare Lodge

Hole Farm

17

RICKSTONES RD

Stovern's Hall

OAK RD

Durwards Hall

Rivenhall Bridge

Rickstone's Farm

RECTORY LA

The Fox Inn (PH)

FOX MEAD RD

HENRY RD

Rivenhall End

Sewage Works

3

Glebe Farm

The Old Rectory

Whitelands

Matchyn's Farm

Appleford Farm

Rose Cottage

1 CHERRYTREE RISE
2 LARCH GR
3 HAWTHORN RISE

WILLOW GR
SAYERS DR

DOROTHY
FOREST RD

HOLLY WLK
TEW

ROMAN ROAD

16

Recn Gd

Cemy

JUNIPER

ALDER WLK

SPRUCE

Appleford Bridge

CYPRESS RD

HAZEL

HOMEFIELD RD
MEDLAND

KNUT

Appleford Cottages

Hill Broad Farm

Workhouse Plantation

TEAK WLK
EASTWAYS

LC

MOTTS LA

LC

Works

River Blackwater

2

Factory

CUT THROAT LA

COLCHESTER RD

B1389

Colemans Bridge

LITTLE BRAXTED LA

Elm Springs

Witham Junction

Witham Station

CRITTALL RD

STATION RD

Coleman's Farm

ALBERT RD
EASTON RD

P

15

AVENUE RD

JANHEAD

ROSS RD

FREEBOURNES RD

THE AVENUE

NEWLAND ST

Court

Moat Hall

Lea Lane Wood

Lea La

Liby

P P

LOCKRAM LA

1 BEVINGTON MEWS
2 BOONE PL
3 OLI CANE PL
4 HORNER PL
5 KYNASTON PL
6 OLIVER PL

BARWELL

WHEATON RD

Little Braxted

1

MALDON RD

NEWLAND PRECINCT

B1018

Dismantled Railway

PERRY WAY

Lea Lane Fruit Farm

Broomfield's Farm

B1389

FERRY RD

Sewage Works

BLACKMAN

A12(T)

14

82 83 84

A B C

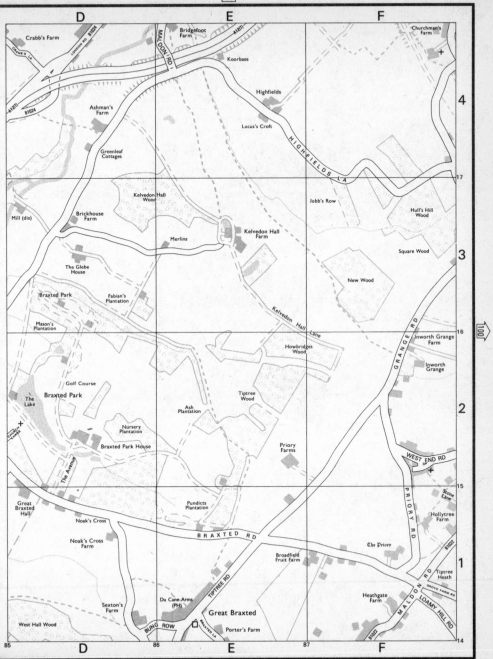

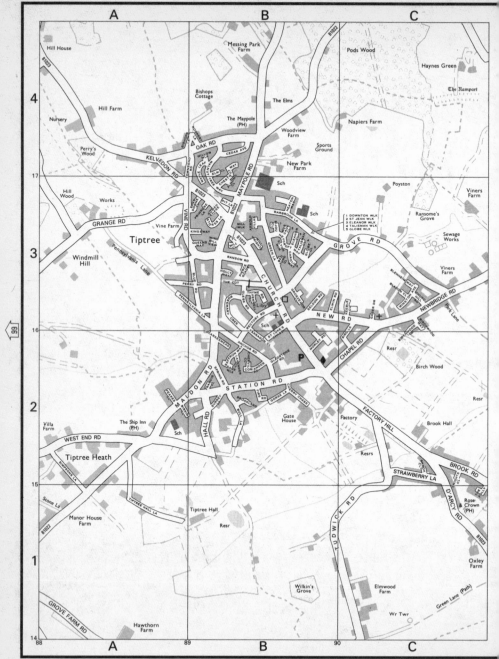

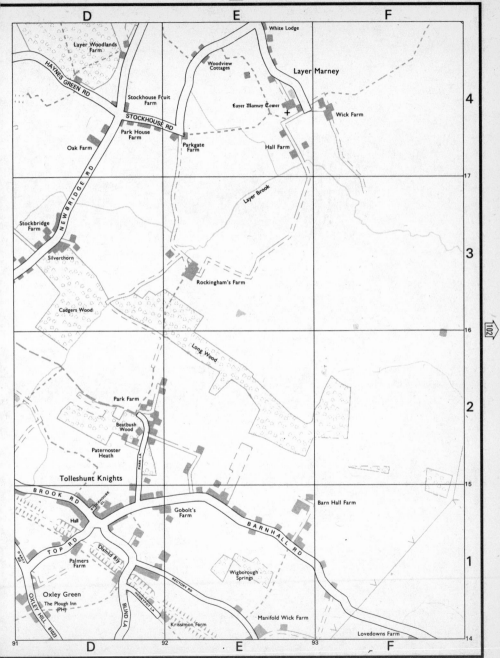

D   E   F

White Lodge

Layer Woodlands
Farm

HAYNES GREEN RD

Woodview
Cottages

Layer Marney

Stockhouse Fruit
Farm

Layer Marney Tower

Wick Farm

STOCKHOUSE RD

Park House
Farm

Parkgate
Farm

Hall Farm

Oak Farm

NEW BRIDGE RD

Layer Brook

Stockbridge
Farm

Silverthorn

Rockingham's Farm

Cadgers Wood

Long Wood

Park Farm

Beatbush
Wood

Paternoster
Heath

PARK LA

Tolleshunt Knights

BROOK RD

Barn Hall Farm

Hall

Gobolt's
Farm

BARNHALL RD

TOP RD

Palmers
Farm

District Rd

Wigborough
Springs

Oxley Green

The Plough Inn
(PH)

OXLEY HILL B1023

BLIND LA

RECTORY RD

Krissimon Farm

Manifold Wick Farm

Lovedowns Farm

91   D   92   E   93   F

4

17

3

16

2

15

1

14

102

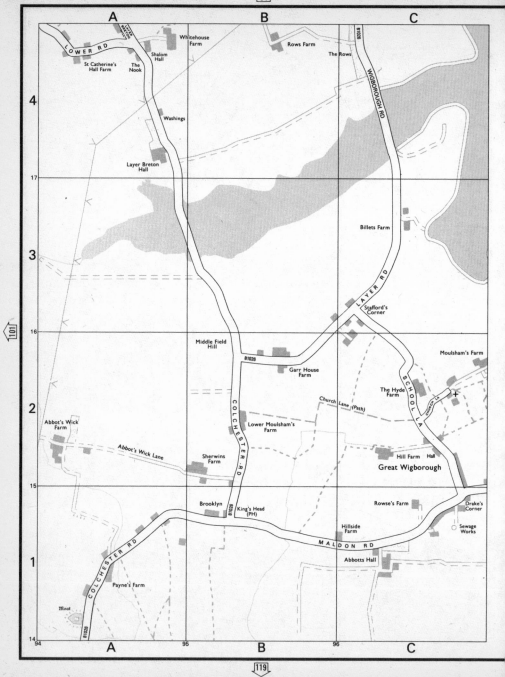

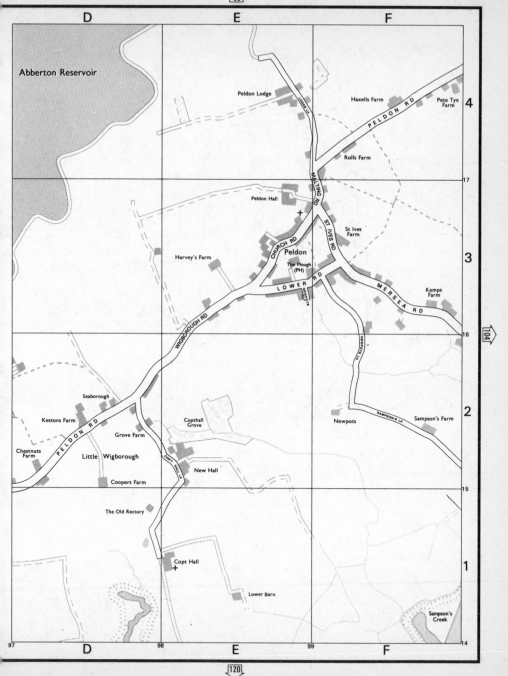

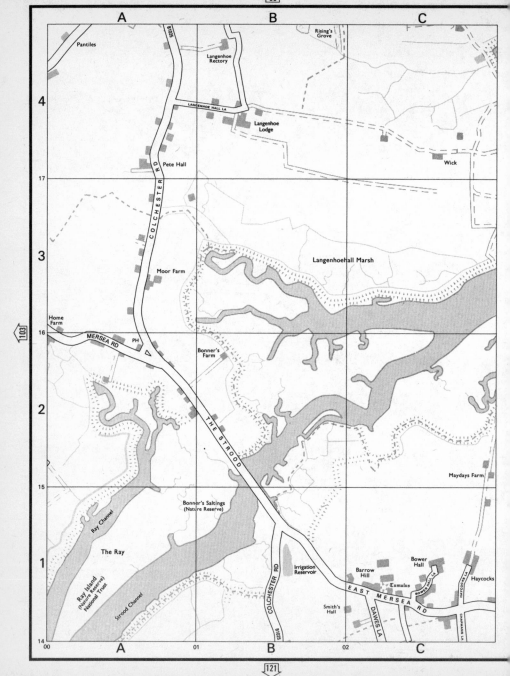

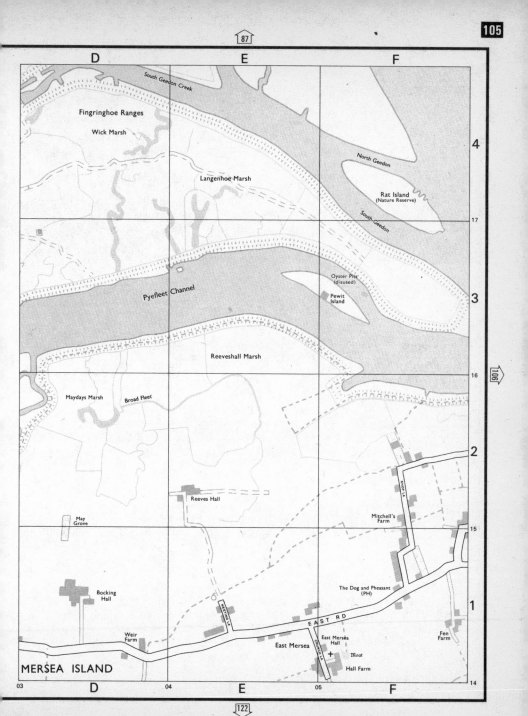

D E F

South Geedon Creek

Fingringhoe Ranges

Wick Marsh

4

North Geedon

Langenhoe Marsh

Rat Island
(Nature Reserve)

South Geedon

17

Oyster Pits
(disused)

Pyefleet Channel

Pewit
Island

3

Reeveshall Marsh

16

106

Maydays Marsh   Broad Fleet

2

Reeves Hall

Mitchell's
Farm

May
Grove

15

SHOP LA

Bocking
Hall

The Dog and Pheasant
(PH)

1

EAST RD

Fen
Farm

Weir
Farm

East Mersea

East Mersea
Hall

MERSEA ISLAND

✝   Moat

Hall Farm

03   D   04   E   05   F   14

88

105

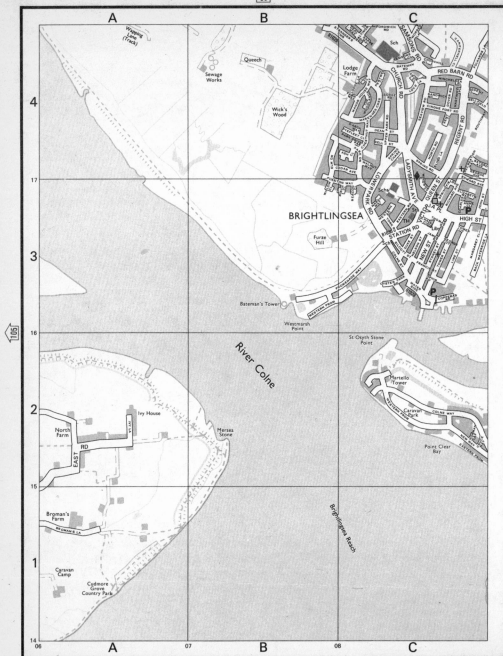

BRIGHTLINGSEA

River Colne

Brightlingsea Reach

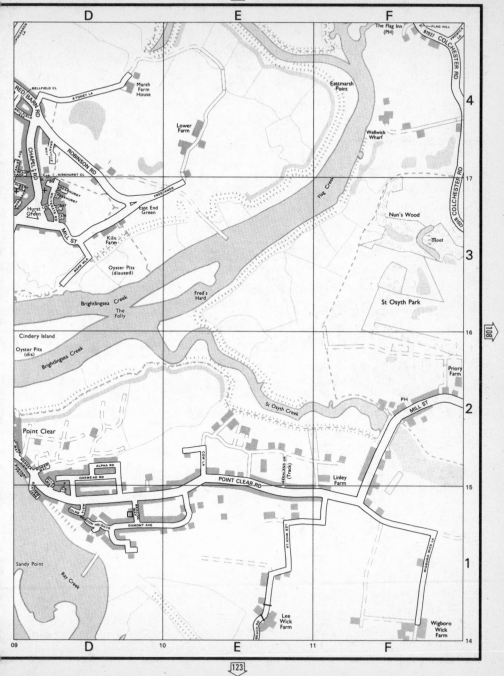

D   E   F

The Flag Inn (PH)

FLAG HILL

B1027 COLCHESTER RD

Eastmarsh Point

4

BELLFIELD CL

STONEY LA

Marsh Farm House

RED BARN RD

Wellwick Wharf

Lower Farm

ROBINSON RD

CHAPEL RD

GRANVILLE WAY

KIRKHURST CL

17

B1027 COLCHESTER RD

FREE LANDS

Flag Creek

GREENHURST

WYTCHWOOD RD

East End Green

Nun's Wood

Hurst Green

MILL ST

Kiln Farm

Moat

3

ROPE WALK

Oyster Pits (disused)

Fred's Hard

St Osyth Park

Brightlingsea Creek

The Folly

Cindery Island

16

108

Oyster Pits (dis)

Brightlingsea Creek

Priory Farm

St Osyth Creek

PH

MILL ST

2

Point Clear

ALPHA RD

COW LA

OAKMEAD RD

GREENLAND DR (Track)

POINT CLEAR RD

Linley Farm

15

COLNE HEIGHTS

DUMONT AVE

LEE WICK LA

MIDDLE WICK LA

Sandy Point

Ray Creek

1

Lee Wick Farm

BEACH RD

Wigboro Wick Farm

14

09   D   10   E   11   F

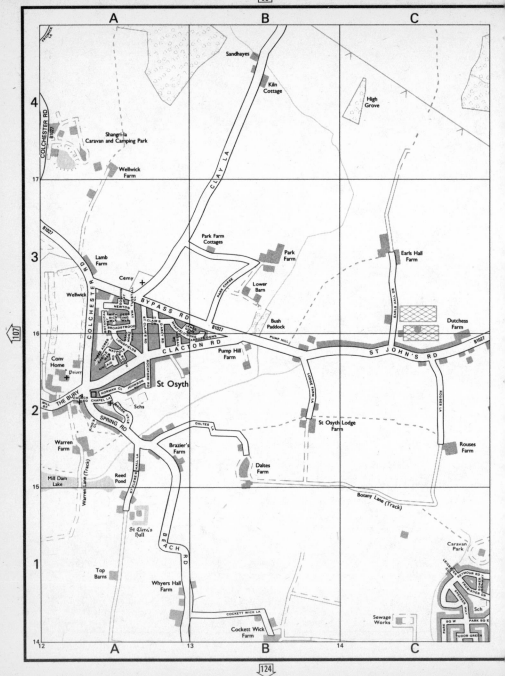

A   B   C

4

17

3

16

2

15

1

14

Sandhayes

Kiln Cottage

High Grove

CLAY LA

COLCHESTER RD

B1027

Shangri-la Caravan and Camping Park

Wellwick Farm

B1027

Lamb Farm

Park Farm Cottages

Park Farm

Earls Hall Farm

Cemy

Wellwick

BYPASS RD

COLCHESTER RD

NEWTON

DEER
BICKLING
ACRE

BROADSTROOD

St CLAIR'S

WIMB ACRES

LONGFIELDS

MAYPOLE

KING LA
ARB

DARCY RD

ARBOUR DONS

HEATH FIELD DOWN

CLARK RD

ROCHFORD RD

Lower Barn

Bush Paddock

B1027

Dutchess Farm

EARLS HALL DR

St JOHN'S RD

B1027

CLACTON RD

Pump Hill Farm

PUMP HILL

Conv Home

Priory

THE BURY

CHURCH

CHAPEL LA

HORNAH CL

JOHNSON RD

TUDOR CL

Schs

St Osyth

LODGE FARM LA

ROUSES LA

SPRING RD

MILL RD

Warren Farm

WARREN LANE (Track)

St CLERE'S HALL LA

Reed Pond

Brazier's Farm

DALTES LA

St Osyth Lodge Farm

Rouses Farm

Mill Dam Lake

Daltes Farm

Botany Lane (Track)

BEACH RD

St Clere's Hall

Caravan Park

LEICESTER CL

SEYMOUR RD

FROBISHER WAY

LANCASTER RD

Top Barns

Whyers Hall Farm

Sewage Works

Sch

PARK SQ W

SPENSER WAY

PARK SQ E

TUDOR GREEN

COCKETT WICK LA

Cockett Wick Farm

12   13   14

A   B   C

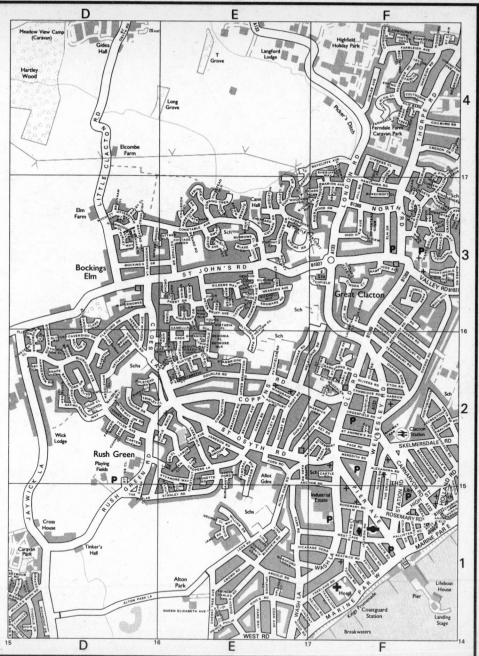

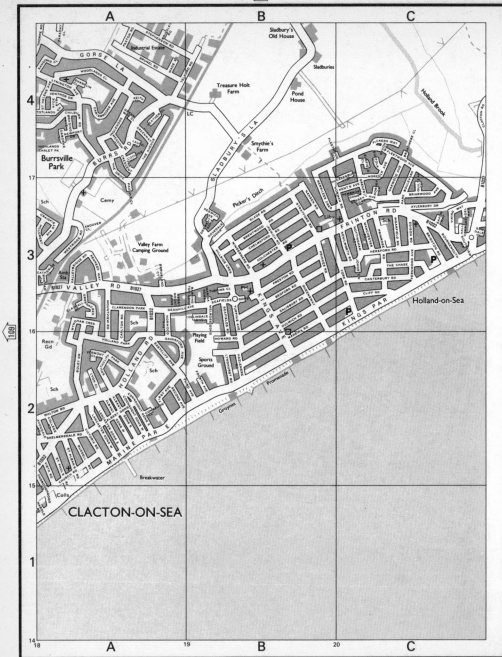

CLACTON-ON-SEA

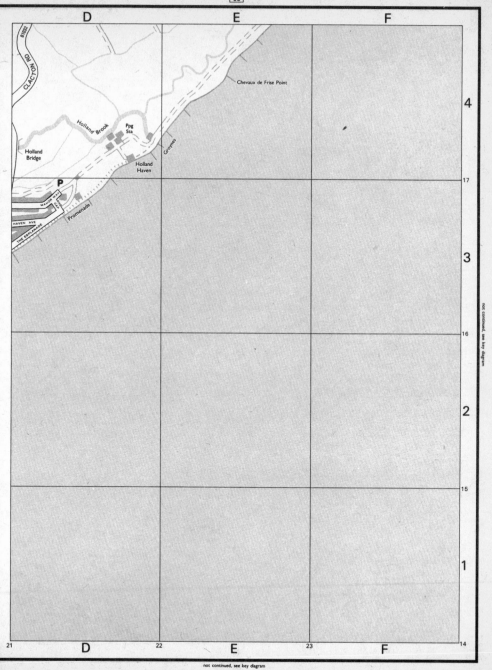

D   E   F

CLACTON RD
BRIDGE

Chevaux de Frise Point

Holland Brook

Ppg
Sta

Holland
Bridge

Holland
Haven

Groynes

P

MANOR WAY

Promenade

HAVEN AVE

THE ESPLANADE

4

17

3

16

2

15

1

14

21   D   22   E   23   F

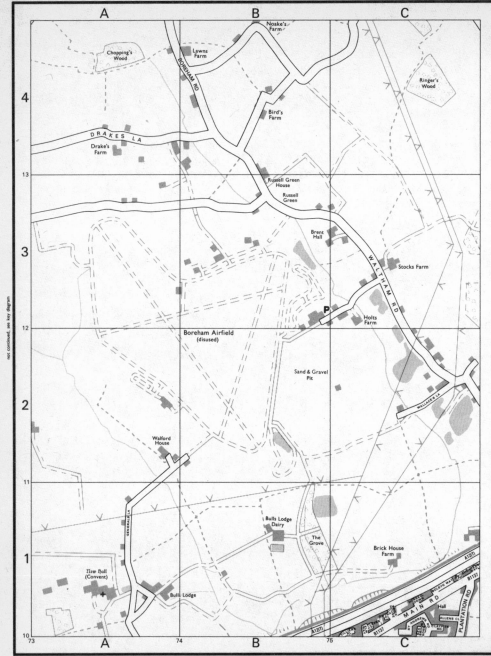

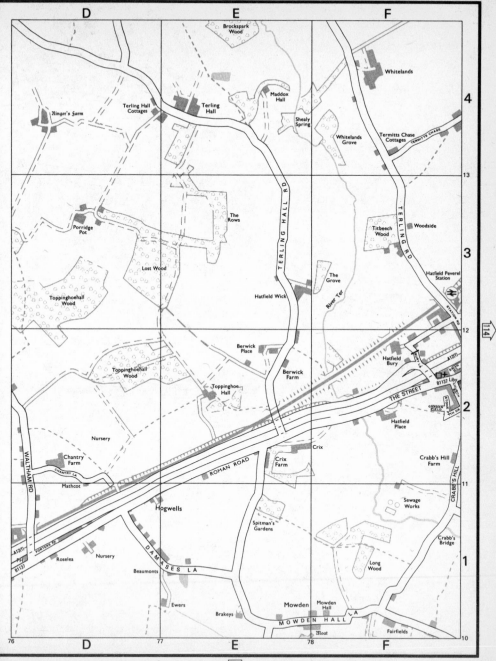

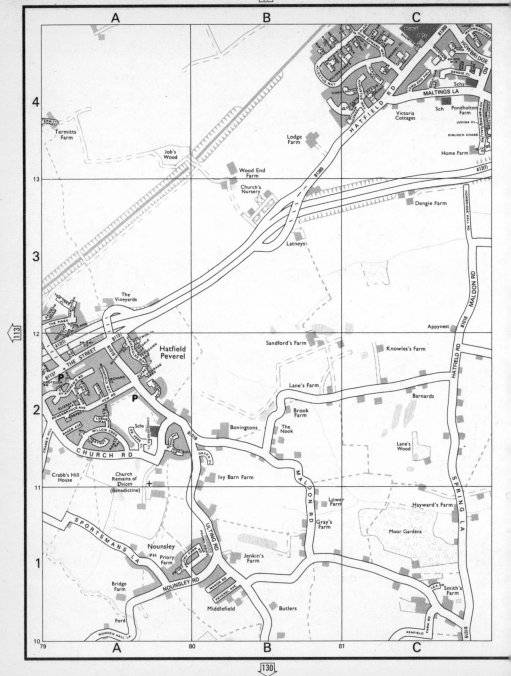

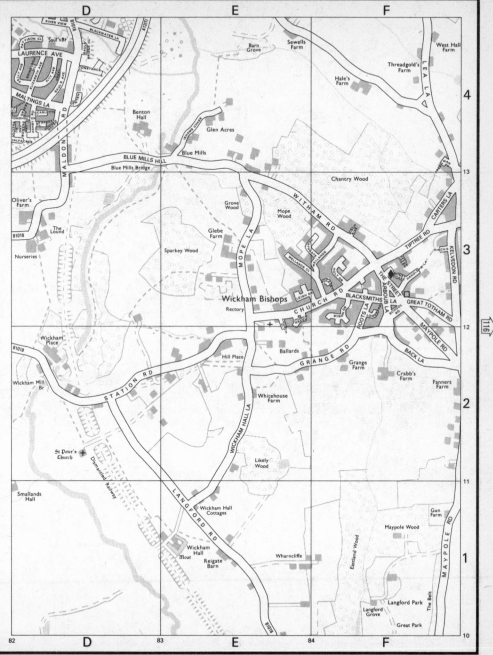

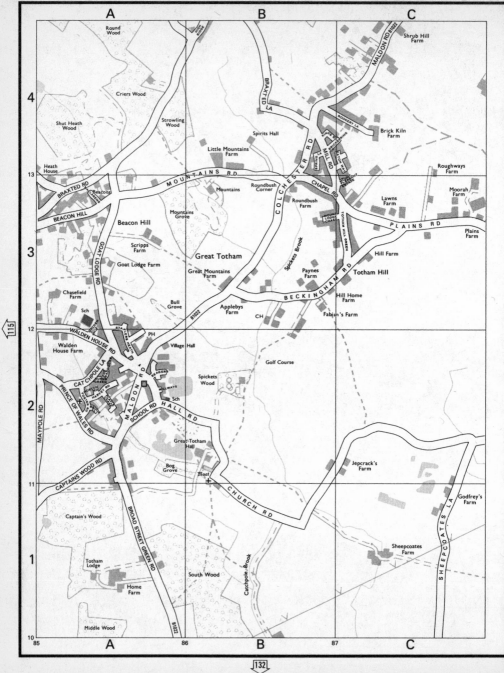

115

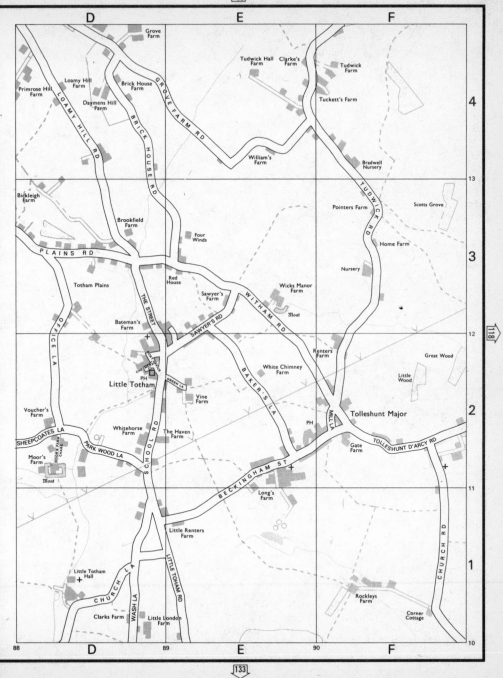

118

D E F

Grove Farm

Tudwick Hall Farm

Clarke's Farm

Tudwick Farm

Loamy Hill Farm

Brick House Farm

Tuckett's Farm

Primrose Hill Farm

Daymens Hill Farm

LOAMY HILL RD

GROVE FARM RD

BRICK HOUSE RD

William's Farm

Bradwell Nursery

4

13

Bickleigh Farm

TUDWICK RD

Pointers Farm

Scotts Grove

Brookfield Farm

Four Winds

Home Farm

PLAINS RD

3

Totham Plains

Red House

Sawyer's Farm

Wicks Manor Farm

Nursery

THE STREET

SAWYER'S RD

WITHAM RD

Moat

Bateman's Farm

Renters Farm

Great Wood

12

OFFICE LA

CHURCH HOUSE

PH

Little Totham

GREEN LA

White Chimney Farm

Little Wood

Vine Farm

BAKER'S LA

Voucher's Farm

MILL LA

PH

Tolleshunt Major

2

Whitehorse Farm

The Haven Farm

Gate Farm

TOLLESHUNT D'ARCY RD

SHEEPCOATES LA

PARK WOOD LA

SCHOOL RD

KINGS BROOK CHASE

Moor's Farm

BECKINGHAM ST

Moat

Long's Farm

11

Little Renters Farm

CHURCH RD

1

LITTLE TOHAM RD

Little Totham Hall

CHURCH LA

WASH LA

Rockleys Farm

Clarks Farm

Little London Farm

Corner Cottage

88 89 90 10

D E F

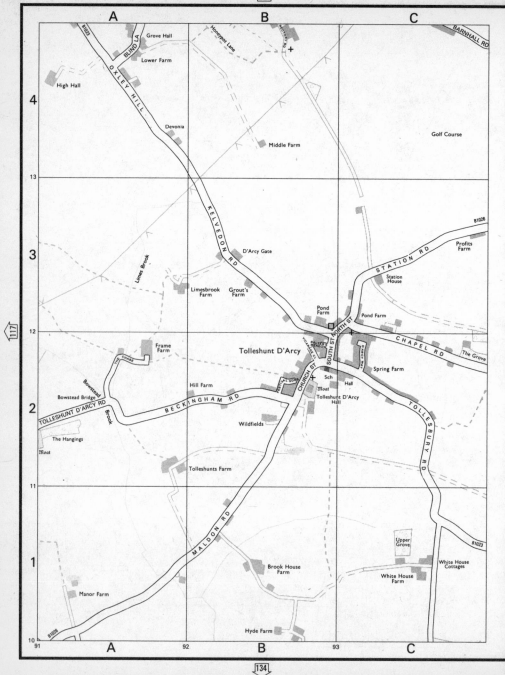

Tolleshunt D'Arcy

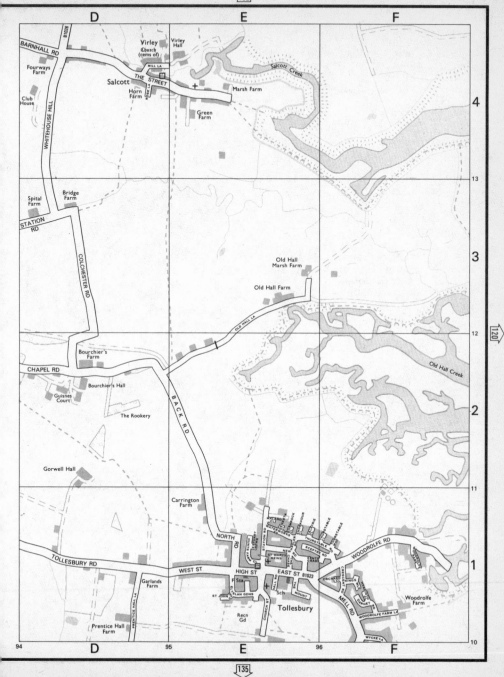

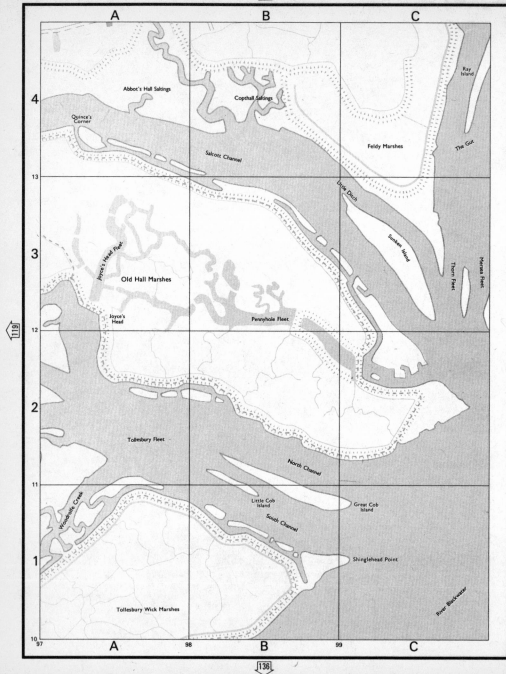

A   B   C

Ray Island

Abbot's Hall Saltings

Copthall Saltings

4

Quince's Corner

Feldy Marshes

The Gut

Salcott Channel

13

Little Ditch

Sunken Island

Joyce's Head Fleet

3

Old Hall Marshes

Thorn Fleet

Mersea Fleet

Joyce's Head

Pennyhole Fleet

12

2

Tollesbury Fleet

North Channel

11

Woodrolfe Creek

Little Cob Island

Great Cob Island

South Channel

1

Shinglehead Point

River Blackwater

Tollesbury Wick Marshes

10

97   A   98   B   99   C

ELECTRICAL CONTRACTORS

01245
221042

- HILLBRIDGE ROAD
- CLEMENTS GREEN LANE
- LONGFIELD ROAD
- ALGARS WAY
- DOWNLEAZE

CSL LIMITED

Tel: (04023) 71767
Fax: (04023) 77016

KEITH BELL

23 DOWNLANE

SWP

01245 321042

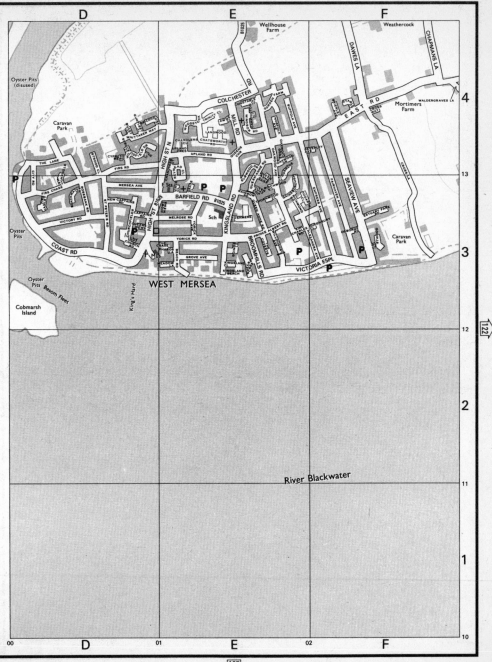

Oyster Pits
(disused)

Caravan
Park

Wellhouse
Farm

Weathercock

Mortimers
Farm

WALDERGRAVES LA

COLCHESTER RD

THE LANE

FIRS CHASE

MERSEA AVE

NEW CAPTAINS

VICTORY RD

Oyster
Pits

COAST RD

Oyster
Pits Besom Fleet

King's Hard

Cobmarsh
Island

WEST MERSEA

UPLAND RD

BARFIELD RD

MELROSE RD

YORICK RD

GROVE AVE

Sch

KINGSLAND RD

BROOMHILLS RD

Kingsland
Beach

VICTORIA ESPL

SEAVIEW AVE

Caravan
Park

DAWES LA

CHAPMANS LA

EAST RD

CROSS LA

River Blackwater

4

13

3

12

11

2

1

10

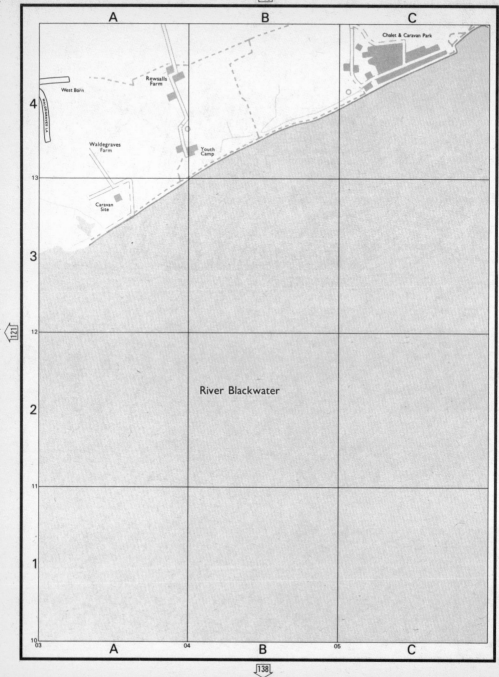

A B C

4

West Barn

Rewsalls
Farm

Waldegraves
Farm

Youth
Camp

Caravan
Site

Chalet & Caravan Park

121

River Blackwater

13

3

12

2

11

1

10
03 A 04 B 05 C

107

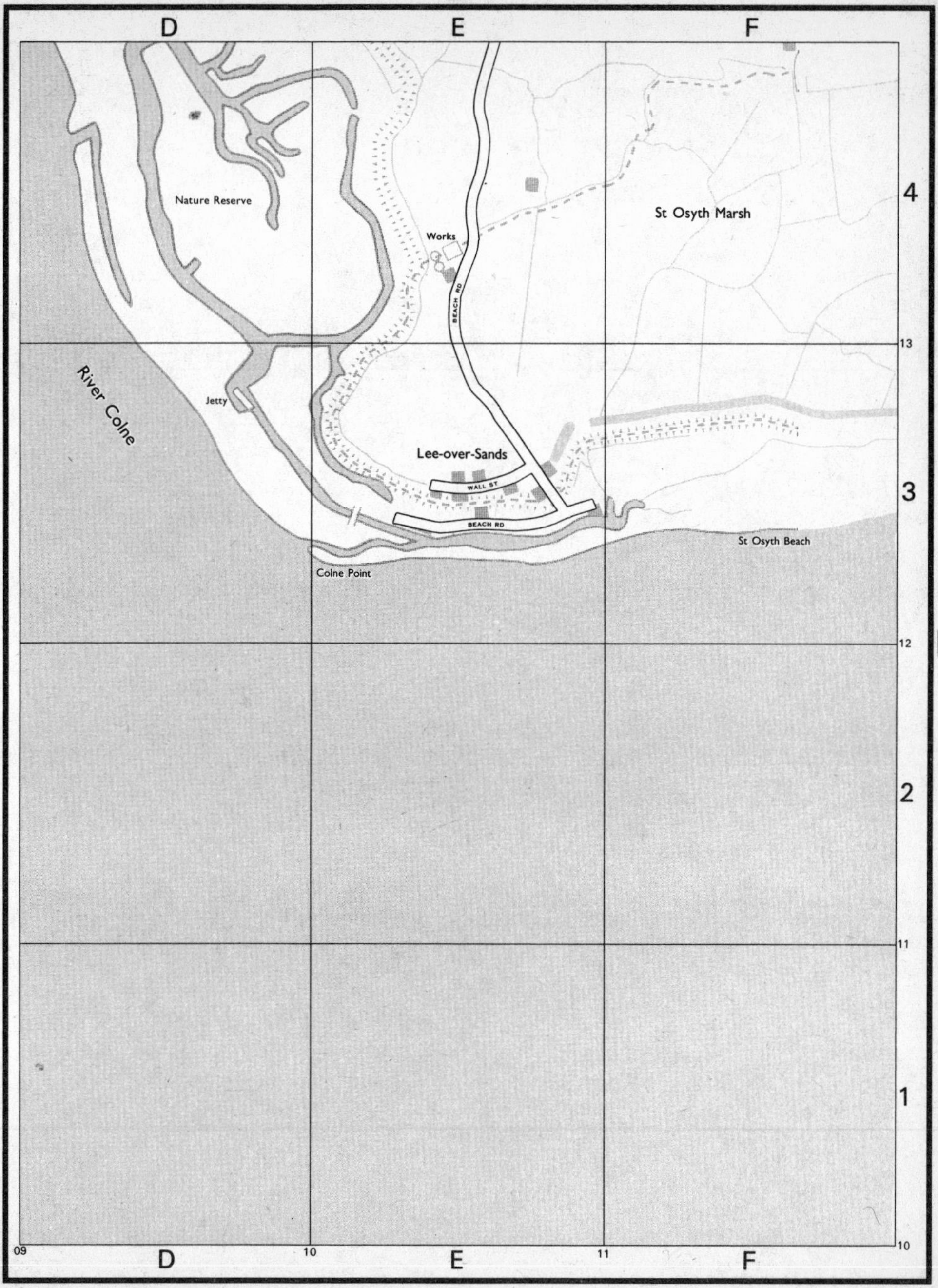

| D | E | F |

124

Nature Reserve

St Osyth Marsh

4

Works

BEACH RD

13

River Colne

Jetty

Lee-over-Sands

3

WALL ST

BEACH RD

St Osyth Beach

Colne Point

12

2

11

1

| D | E | F |

09   10   11   10

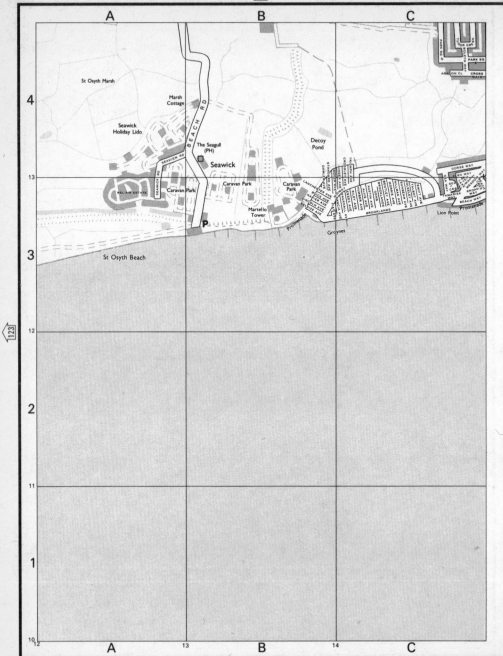

A   B   C

4

St Osyth Marsh

Marsh
Cottage

Seawick
Holiday Lido

The Seagull
(PH)

Seawick

Decoy
Pond

13

BEACH RD

SEAVIEW RD

SEAWICK RD

BEL AIR ESTATE

Caravan Park

Caravan Park

Caravan
Park

Martello
Tower

P

Promenade

LANCHESTER AVE

Groynes

Brooklands

GORSE WAY

Lion Point

Promenade

PARK SQ

TUDOR GDN

PARK SQ

AVALON CL

CROSS
WAYS

TAMARISK WAY

BEACH WAY

3

St Osyth Beach

12

2

11

1

10

12   13   14

A   B   C

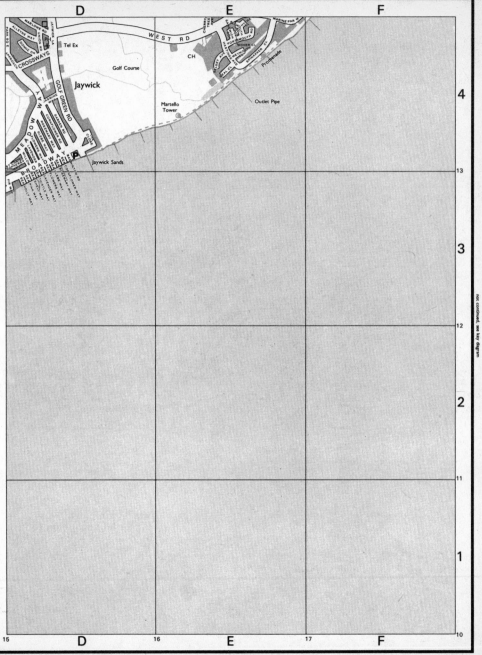

WEST RD

Tel Ex

Golf Course

CH

Jaywick

CROSSWAYS

GOLF GREEN RD

MEADOW WAY

BROADWAY

Martello
Tower

Outlet Pipe

Promenade

Jaywick Sands

4

13

3

12

2

11

1

10

15

16

17

D

E

F

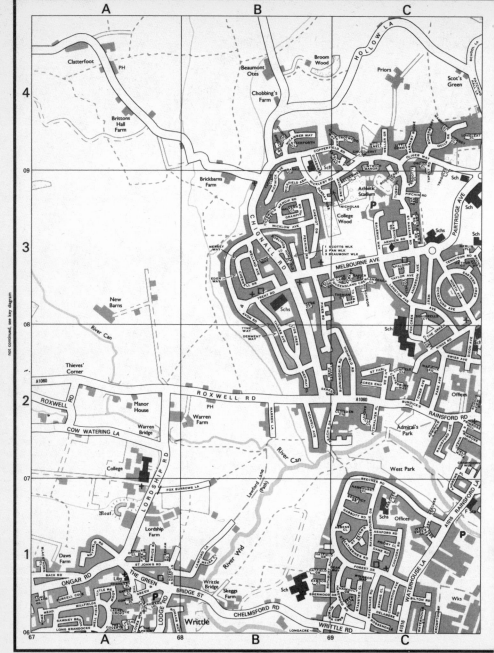

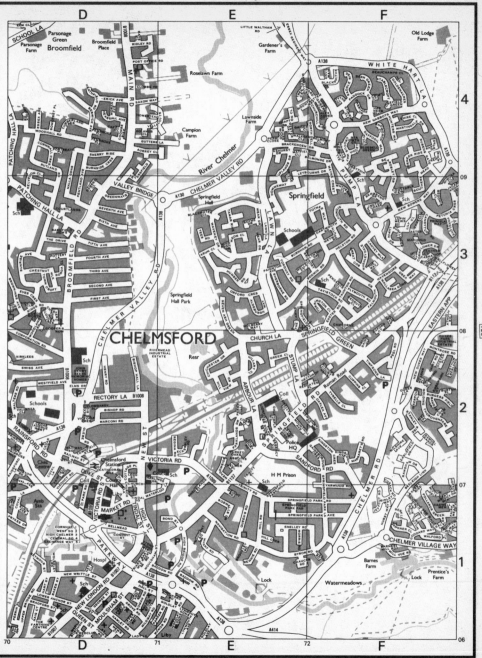

CHELMSFORD

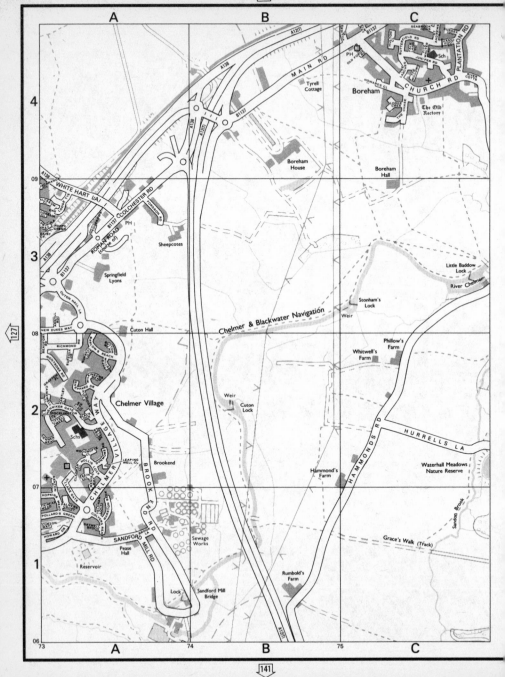

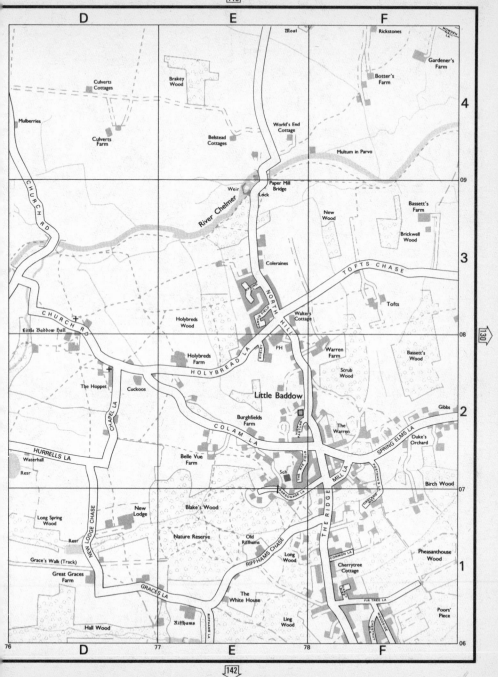

113
130

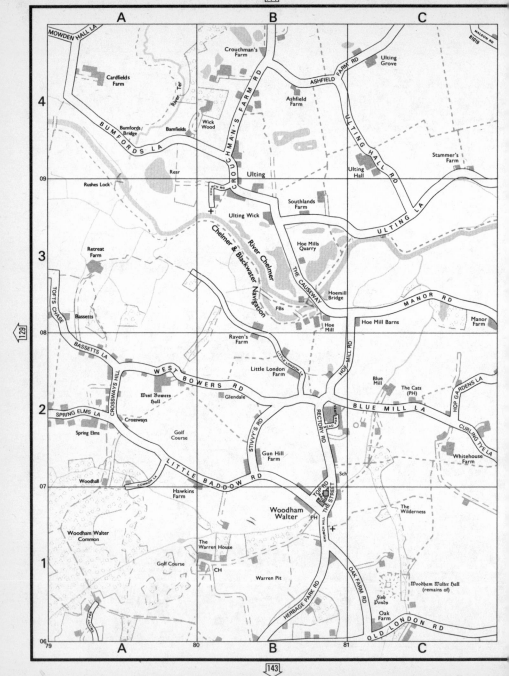

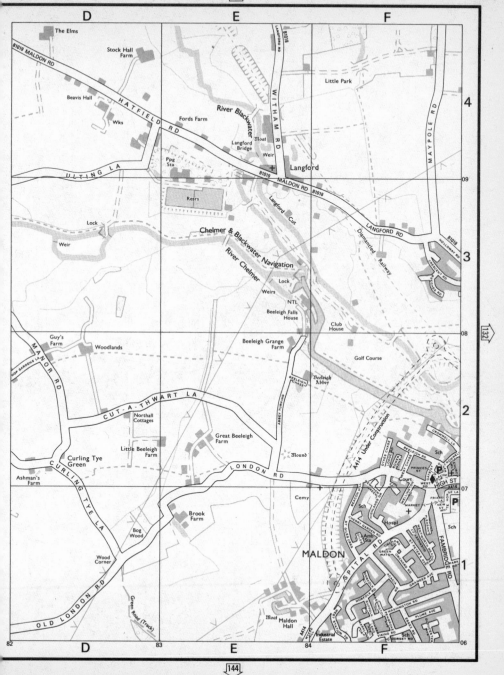

115
144
132

D E F

The Elms

Stock Hall Farm

B1019 MALDON RD

Beavis Hall

HATFIELD RD

Wks

Fords Farm

River Blackwater

WITHAM RD

LANGFORD RD

B1019

Little Park

MAYPOLE RD

4

Moat

Langford Bridge

Weir

Langford

ULTING LA

Ppg Sta

MALDON RD B1019

09

Resrs

Langford Cut

LANGFORD RD

Lock

Chelmer & Blackwater Navigation

Dismantled Railway

B1019 HOLLOWAY RD

Weir

River Chelmer

CRESCENT RD

STONEY CORNER RD

3

Lock

Weirs

NTL

Beeleigh Falls House

Club House

08

Guy's Farm

Woodlands

Beeleigh Grange Farm

Golf Course

MANOR RD

BISHOP GARDENS LA

BEELEIGH CHASE

Beeleigh Abbey

CHURCH ALLEY

CROMWELL LA

2

CUT-A-THWART LA

Northall Cottages

Great Beeleigh Farm

Mound

A14 Under Construction

BEELEIGH RD

Sch

Curling Tye Green

Little Beeleigh Farm

LONDON RD

Court

HIGH ST

PRINCES ST

A14

07

CURLING TYE LA

Ashman's Farm

Cemy

Sch

Hospl

P

Sch

FAMBRIDGE RD

Brook Farm

MALDON

1

Bog Wood

Wood Corner

SPITAL RD

GRANGER AVE

PLUME AVE

OLD LONDON RD

Green Road (Track)

Moat

Maldon Hall

A14

Industrial Estate

VIKING RD

DORSET RD

82 83 84 06

D E F

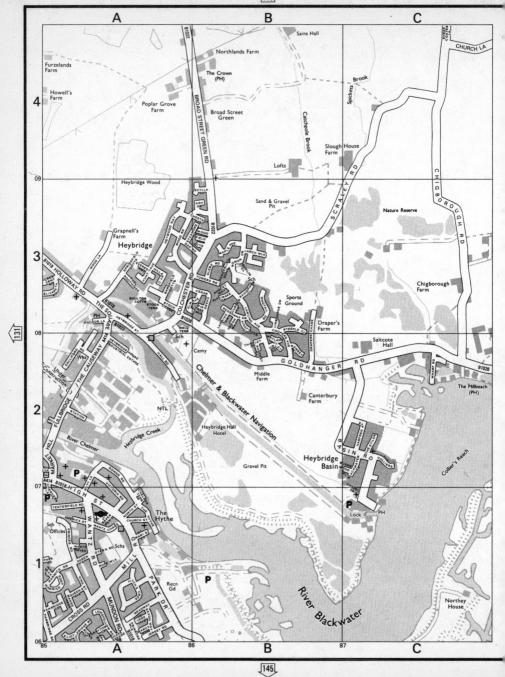

117

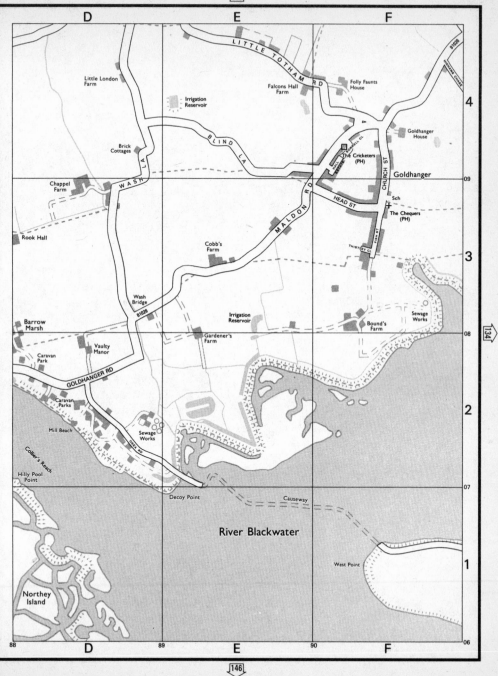

D E F

LITTLE TOTHAM RD

Little London
Farm

Irrigation
Reservoir

Falcons Hall
Farm

Folly Faunts
House

B1026

4

BLIND LA

Goldhanger
House

Brick
Cottages

The Cricketers
(PH)

Goldhanger

WASH LA

Chappel
Farm

09

HEAD ST

CHURCH ST

Sch

MALDON RD

The Chequers
(PH)

Rook Hall

THISTLEY CL

Cobb's
Farm

3

Wash
Bridge

B1026

Irrigation
Reservoir

Sewage
Works

Barrow
Marsh

Gardener's
Farm

Bound's
Farm

08

Caravan
Park

Vaulty
Manor

GOLDHANGER RD

Caravan
Parks

2

Mill Beach

SEA RD

Sewage
Works

Collier's Reach

07

Hilly Pool
Point

Decoy Point

Causeway

River Blackwater

West Point

1

Northey
Island

88 D 89 E 90 F 06

134

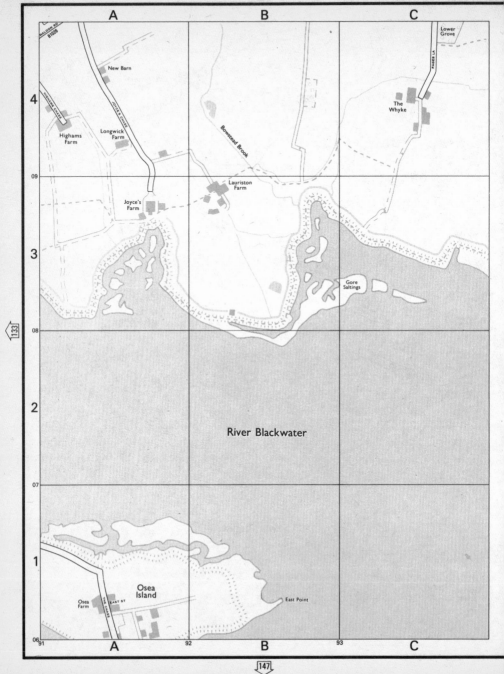

A
B
C

133

147

MALDON RD B1026

JOYCE'S CHASE

New Barn

Highams Farm

Longwick Farm

Joyce's Farm

Lauriston Farm

Bowstead Brook

Gore Saltings

PAGES LA.

Lower Grove

The Whyke

4

09

3

08

2

07

1

06

River Blackwater

Osea Island

Osea Farm

EAST ST

THE CHASE

East Point

91
92
93

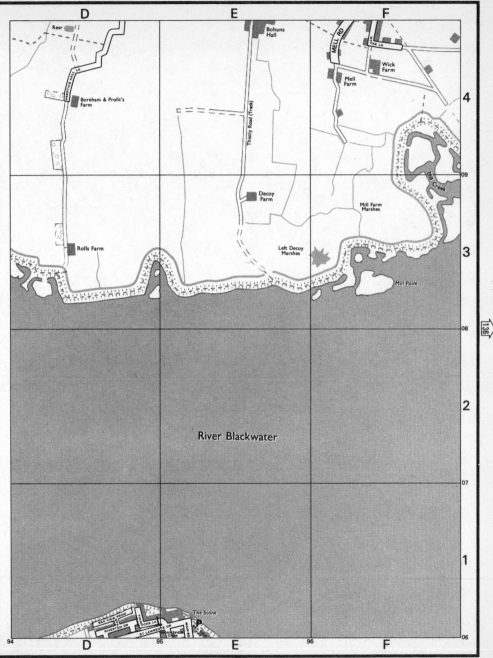

D   E   F

Resr

Bohuns Hall

MELL RD

OXE LA

Wick Farm

Boreham & Profit's Farm

Mell Farm

4

09

Thirsty Road (Track)

Decoy Farm

Mill Farm Marshes

Mill Creek

Rolls Farm

Left Decoy Marshes

Mill Point

3

08

136

River Blackwater

2

07

1

SEA VIEW PROM

RIVERTON DR

OCKS LA

ST LAWRENCE DR

COURTVIEW CRES

The Stone

06

94   D   95   E   96   F

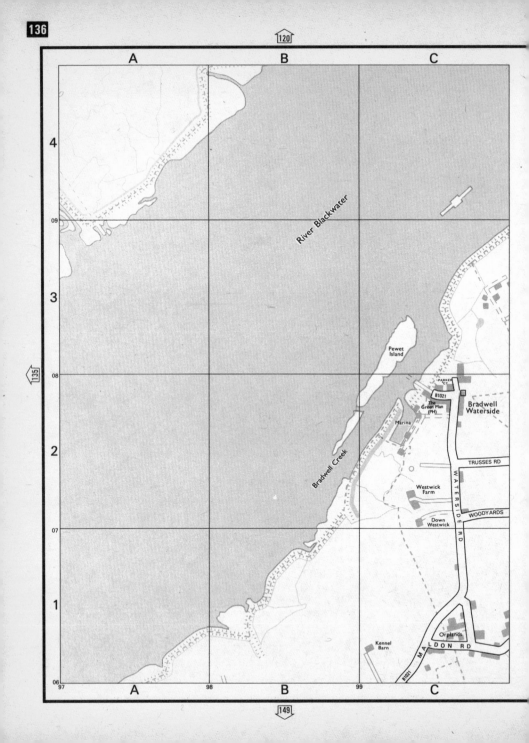

A   B   C

4

09

River Blackwater

3

Pewet
Island

08

PARKER
CT
B1021
The
Green Man
(PH)
Bradwell
Waterside

Marina

2

TRUSSES RD

Bradwell Creek

Westwick
Farm

W
A
T
E
R
S
I
D
E

R
D

WOODYARDS

Down
Westwick

07

1

Orplands

Kennel
Barn

M
A
L
D
O
N   RD

B1021

06
97   98   99

A   B   C

135

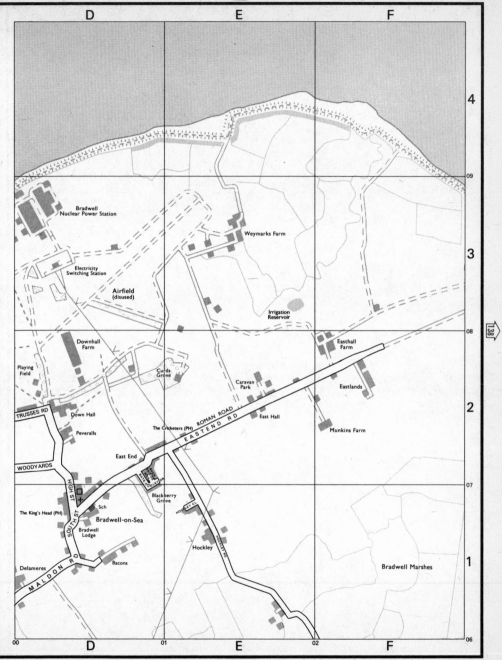

D   E   F

4

Bradwell
Nuclear Power Station

Weymarks Farm

09

3

Electricity
Switching Station

Airfield
(disused)

Irrigation
Reservoir

138

Downhall
Farm

Easthall
Farm

08

Playing
Field

Curds
Grove

Caravan
Park

Eastlands

TRUSSES RD

Down Hall

The Cricketers (PH)

ROMAN ROAD

EASTEND RD

East Hall

Munkins Farm

2

Peveralls

WOODYARDS

East End

HIGH ST

Blackberry Grove

07

The King's Head (PH)

SOUTH RD

Sch

HOCKLEY CL

Bradwell-on-Sea

Bradwell
Lodge

HOCKLEY RD

Hockley

Bradwell Marshes

1

Delameres

MALDON RD

Bacons

00   01   02   06

D   E   F

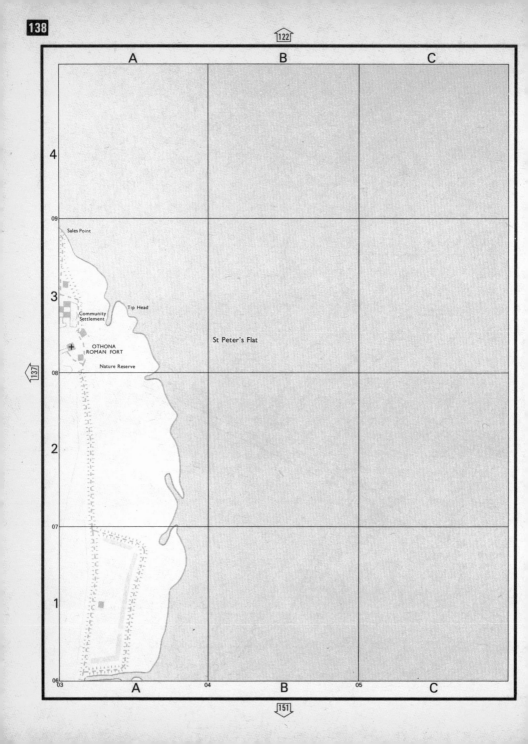

A B C

4

09

Sales Point

3

Tip Head

Community
Settlement

St Peter's Flat

OTHONA
ROMAN FORT

Nature Reserve

08

2

07

1

06

03   04   05

A   B   C

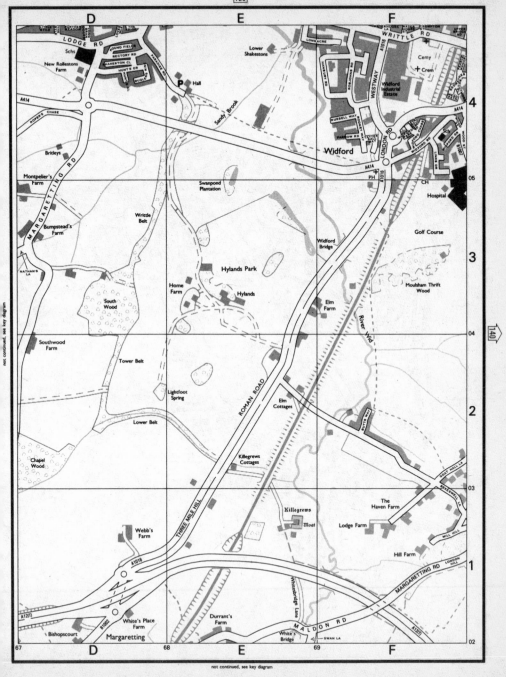

D   E   F

LODGE RD

New Rollestons Farm

Schs

ROUND FIELD

RECTORY RD

MAKESTON CL

HUNT'S DR

FARQUHAR RD

P Hall

Lower Shakestons

LONGACRE

WRITTLE RD

A1016

Cemy

+ Crem

Widford Industrial Estate

WESTWAY

A414

4

Britleys

Montpelier's Farm

Sandy Brook

RUSSELL WAY

FARROW WAY

ROOKERY WAY

Widford

LONDON RD

A1016

PH

A414

CH

05

Bumpstead's Farm

NATHAN'S LA

Swanpond Plantation

Writtle Belt

Hospital

Golf Course

3

South Wood

Home Farm

Hylands Park

Hylands

Widford Bridge

Moulsham Thrift Wood

Southwood Farm

Tower Belt

Elm Farm

River Wid

04

Lightfoot Spring

ROMAN ROAD

Lower Belt

Elm Cottages

BUTTS WAY

2

Chapel Wood

Killegrews Cottages

GOAT HALL LA

BEAKSWELL LA

03

THREE MILE HILL

Killegrews

Moat

The Haven Farm

Lodge Farm

MILL HILL

Webb's Farm

A1016

Hill Farm

MARGARETTING RD

LONDON HILL

1

A12(T)

B1002

White's Place Farm

Bishopscourt

Margaretting

Durrant's Farm

Wheatbridge Lane

White's Bridge

MALDON RD

SWAN LA

A130

F

02

67   D   68   E   69   F

not continued, see key diagram

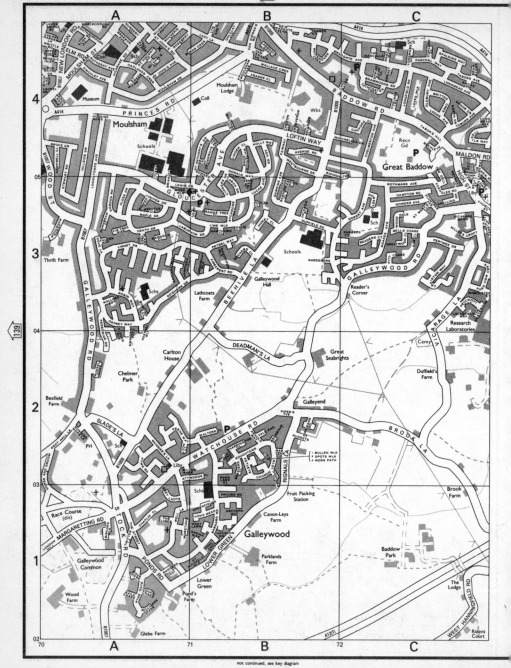

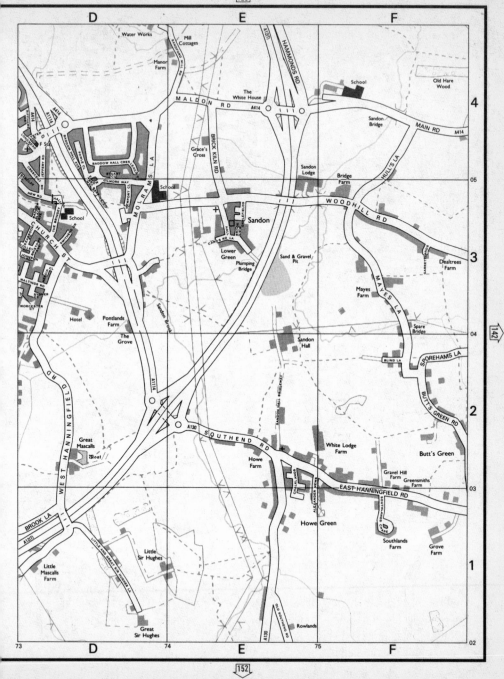

129

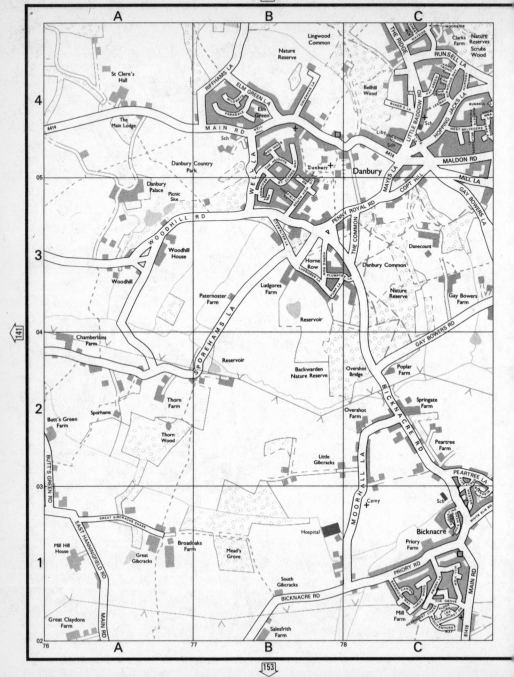

141

153

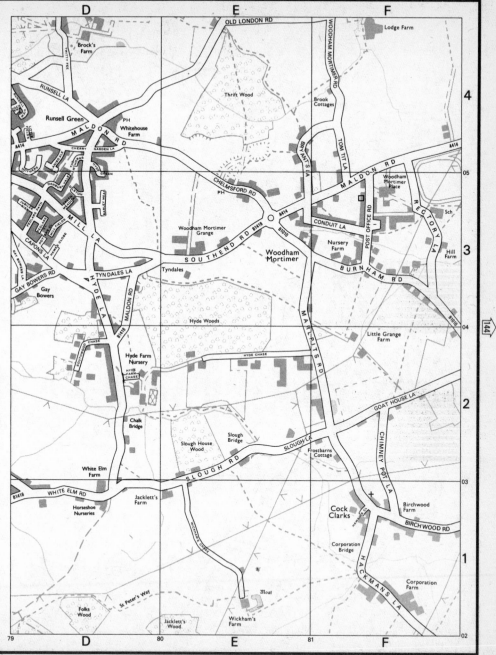

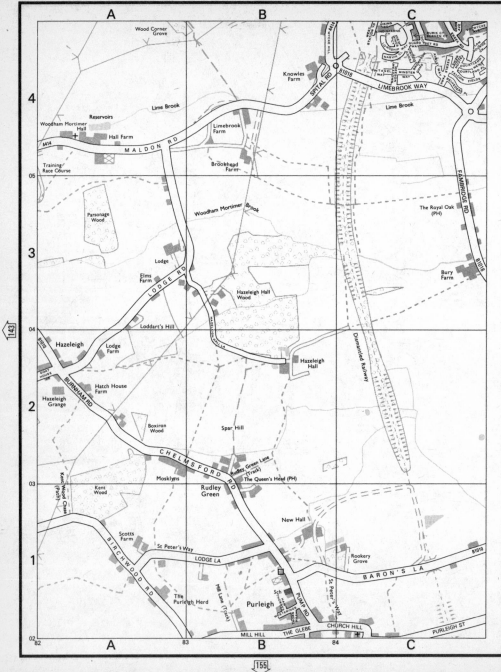

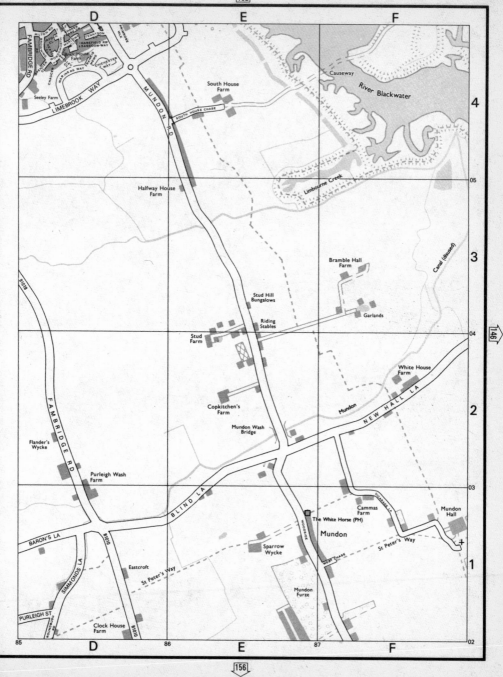

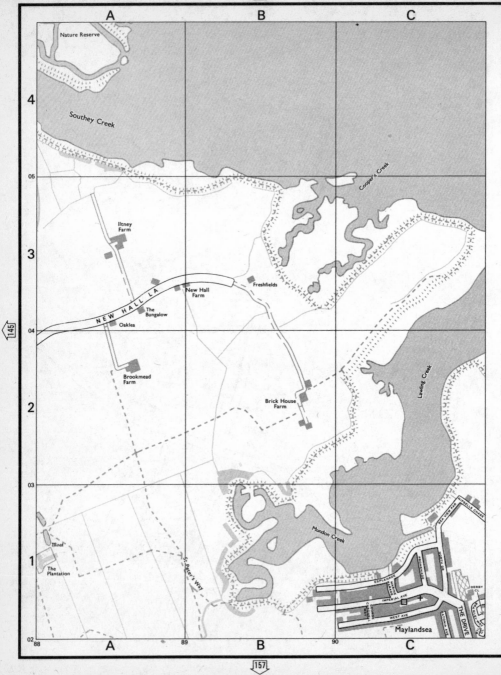

A   B   C

4

Nature Reserve

Southey Creek

Cooper's Creek

05

Iltney
Farm

3

Freshfields

NEW HALL LA
New Hall
Farm

The
Bungalow
Oaklea

04

Brookmead
Farm

Lawling Creek

2

Brick House
Farm

03

Mundon Creek

Moat

1

The
Plantation

St. Peter's Way

Maylandsea

02
88   89   90

A   B   C

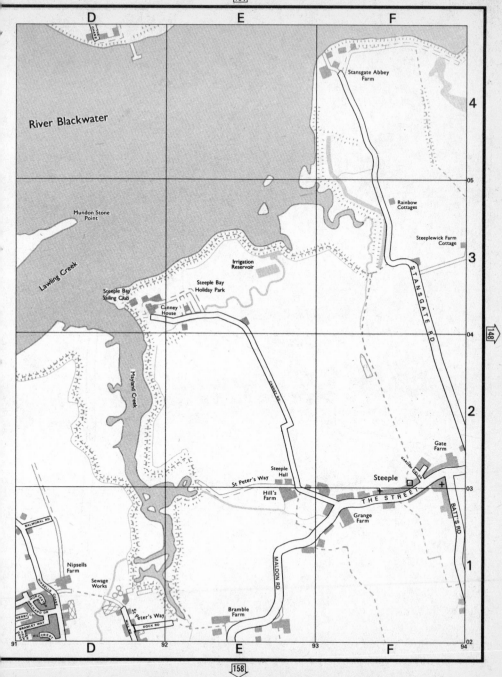

D   E   F

River Blackwater

Stansgate Abbey Farm

4

05

Mundon Stone Point

Rainbow Cottages

Lawling Creek

Steeplewick Farm Cottage

Irrigation Reservoir

3

Steeple Bay Holiday Park

Steeple Bay Sailing Club

Canney House

STANSGATE RD

04

Mayland Creek

2

Gate Farm

Steeple Hall

Steeple

St Peter's Way

Hill's Farm

THE STREET

03

Grange Farm

BATT'S RD

Balmoral Rd

1

Nipsells Farm

Sewage Works

MALDON RD

St Peter's Way

DOCK RD

Bramble Farm

02

91   D   92   E   93   F   94

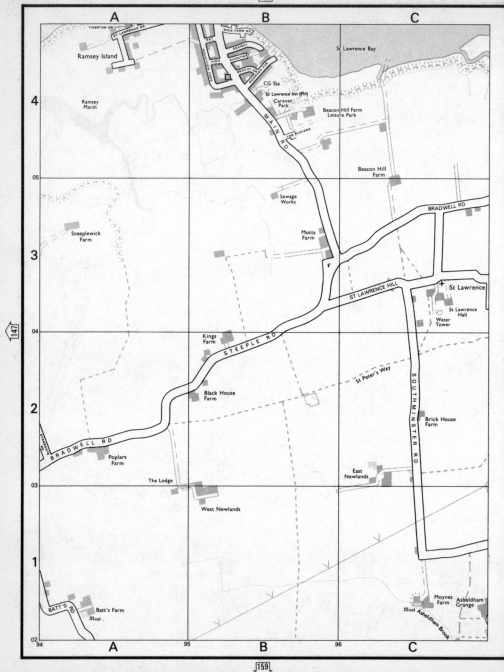

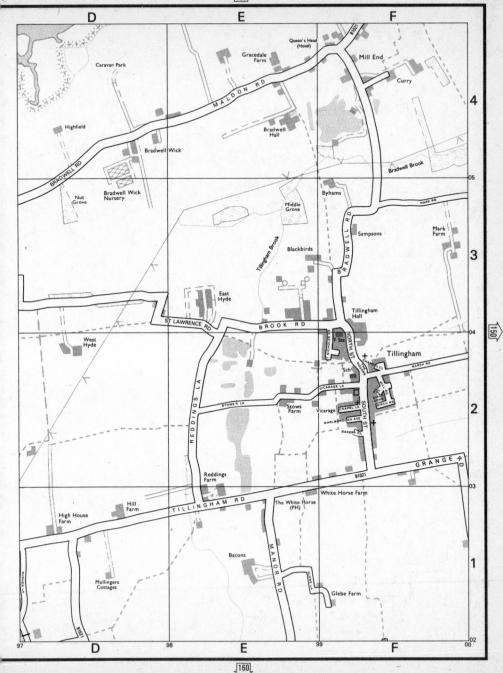

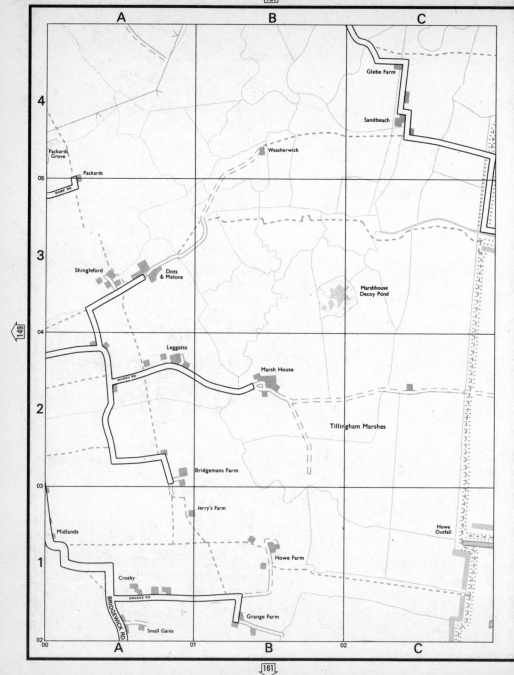

A   B   C

4

Glebe Farm

Sandbeach

Packards
Grove

Weatherwick

05 Packards

MARK RD

3

Shingleford

Dots
& Melons

Marshhouse
Decoy Pond

04

Leggatts

MARSH RD

Marsh House

2

Tillingham Marshes

03

Bridgemans Farm

Jerry's Farm

Midlands

Howe
Outfall

1

Howe Farm

Crosby

BRIDGEWICK RD

GRANGE RD

Grange Farm

02 Small Gains

00   01   02

A   B   C

138

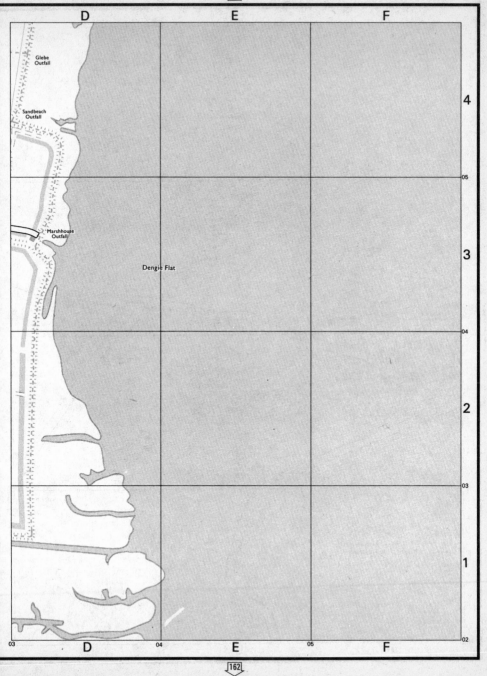

162

141

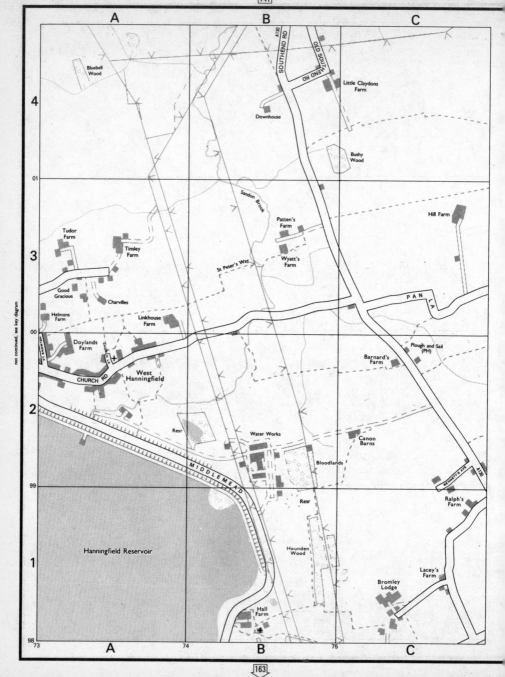

A   B   C

4

01

3

00

2

99

1

98

73   74   75

A   B   C

Bluebell Wood

Little Claydons Farm

SOUTHEND RD

A130

OLD SOUTHEND RD

Downhouse

Bushy Wood

Sandon Brook

Patten's Farm

Hill Farm

Tudor Farm

Tinsley Farm

Wyatt's Farm

St Peter's Way

Good Gracious

Charvilles

P A N

Helmons Farm

Linkhouse Farm

ST THOMAS

Doylands Farm

Plough and Sail (PH)

Barnard's Farm

CHURCH RD

West Hanningfield

Resr

Water Works

Canon Barns

MIDDLEMEAD

Bloodlands

Resr

Ralph's Farm

BENNETT'S AVE

A130

Hanningfield Reservoir

Hounden Wood

Lacey's Farm

Bromley Lodge

Hall Farm

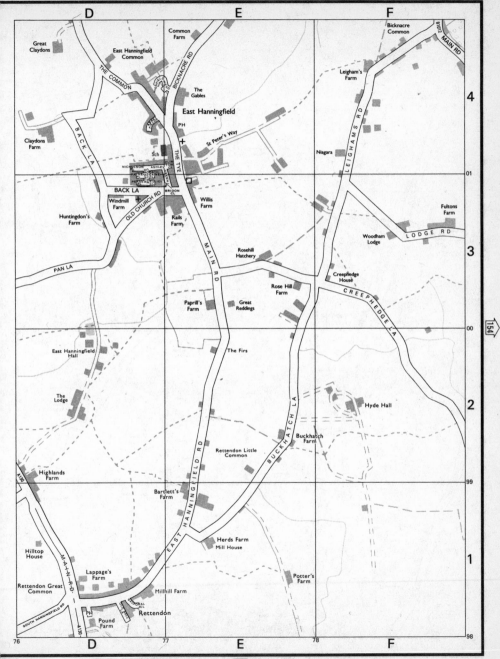

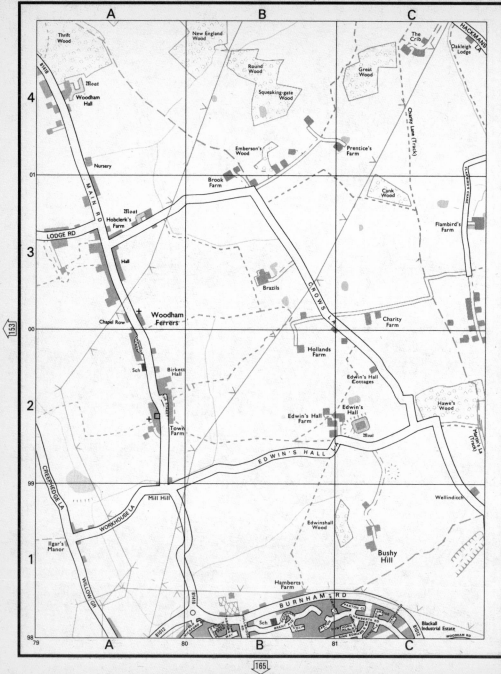

A   B   C

Thrift Wood

New England Wood

Round Wood

Squeaking-gate Wood

Great Wood

The Crib

Oakleigh Lodge

HACKMANS LA

Moat

Woodham Hall

4

Emberson's Wood

Prentice's Farm

Charity Lane (Track)

FLAMBIRD'S CHASE

Nursery

01

Brook Farm

Cank Wood

Flambird's Farm

Moat

Hobclerk's Farm

LODGE RD

MAIN RD

3

Hall

Brazils

CROWS LA

Charity Farm

Chapel Row

Woodham Ferrers

00

Hollands Farm

Sch

Birkett Hall

Edwin's Hall Cottages

Hawe's Wood

2

Edwin's Hall Farm

Edwin's Hall

Town Farm

Moat

Mayes's La (Track)

EDWIN'S HALL LA

99

CREEPHEDGE LA

Mill Hill

Wellinditch

WORKHOUSE LA

Edwinshall Wood

Ilgar's Manor

Bushy Hill

1

WILLOW GR

Hamberts Farm

B1418

BURNHAM RD

Sch

Blackall Industrial Estate

B1012

98

79   A   80   B   81   C   WOODHAM RD

153

144
156
166

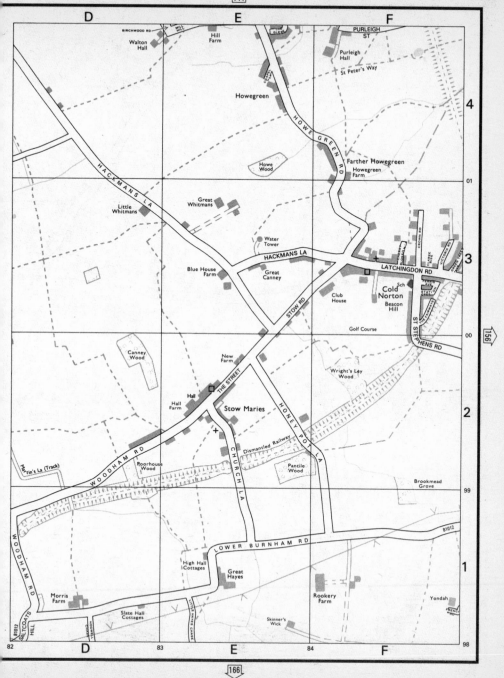

D   E   F

BIRCHWOOD RD

Walton Hall

Hill Farm

PURLEIGH ST

Purleigh Hall

St Peter's Way

Howegreen

4

HOWE GREEN RD

Howe Wood

Farther Howegreen

Howegreen Farm

01

HACKMANS LA

Little Whitmans

Great Whitmans

Water Tower

HACKMANS LA

LATCHINGDON RD

3

Blue House Farm

Great Canney

Club House

Cold Norton

Sch

Beacon Hill

STOW RD

Golf Course

ST STEPHENS RD

00

Canney Wood

New Farm

Wright's Ley Wood

THE STREET

Hall Farm

Hall

Stow Maries

HONEY POT LA

2

WOODHAM RD

Morris Farm

Poorhouse Wood

Dismantled Railway

Pantile Wood

CHURCH LA

Brookmead Grove

99

Ma'tin's La (Track)

B1012

LOWER BURNHAM RD

High Hall Cottages

Great Hayes

1

WOODHAM RD

Morris Farm

Slate Hall Cottages

Rookery Farm

Yondah

SALTCOATS HILL

Skinner's Wick

82   D   83   E   84   F   98

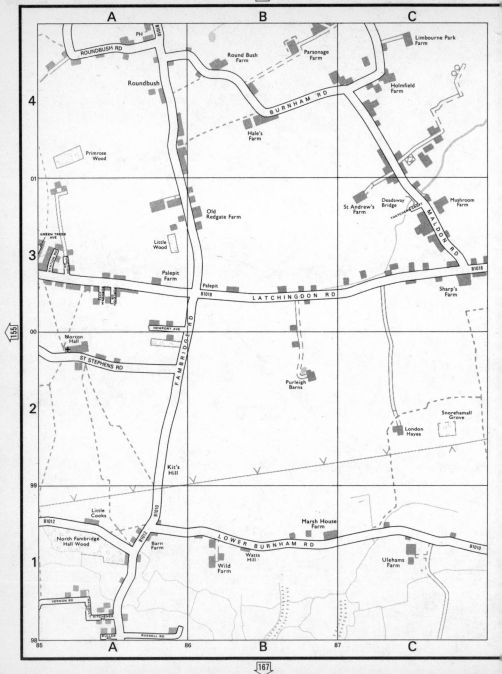

A
B
C

ROUNDBUSH RD
PH
B1010
Roundbush
Round Bush Farm
Parsonage Farm
Limbourne Park Farm
BURNHAM RD
Holmfield Farm
4
Hale's Farm
Primrose Wood
01
Old Redgate Farm
St Andrew's Farm
Deadaway Bridge
Mushroom Farm
GREEN TREES AVE
Little Wood
THATCHERS CROFT
MALDON RD
3
STATION RD
Palepit Farm
Palepit
B1018
Sharp's Farm
B1018
LATCHINGDON RD
NEWPORT AVE
00
Norton Hall
FAMBRIDGE RD
ST STEPHENS RD
Purleigh Barns
2
Snorehamall Grove
London Hayes
Kit's Hill
99
Little Cooks
B1012
Marsh House Farm
North Fambridge Hall Wood
B1010
B1012
Barn Farm
LOWER BURNHAM RD
B1012
B1010
1
Wild Farm
Watts Hill
Ulehams Farm
VERNON RD
KITCHENER
BULLER
RUSSELL RD
98
85
86
87

A
B
C

146

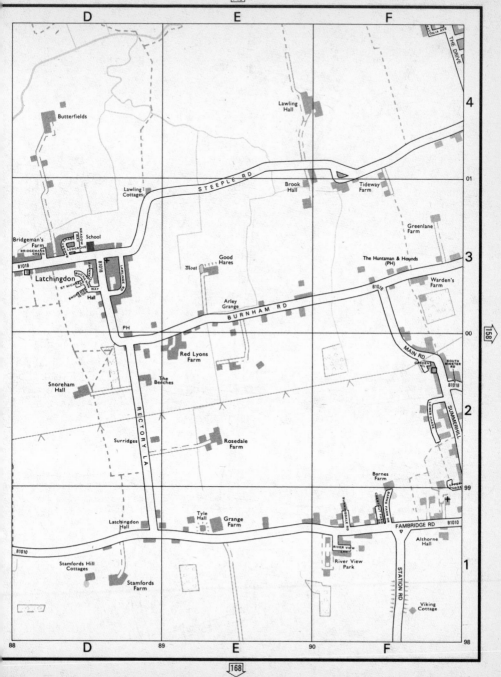

168
158

D   E   F

Butterfields

Lawling
Hall

STEEPLE RD

Lawling
Cottages

Brook
Hall

Tideway
Farm

Greenlane
Farm

Bridgeman's
Farm

BRIDGEMANS
GREEN

School

MEADOW
RISE

LUDGROVE

The Huntsman & Hounds
(PH)

Warden's
Farm

B1018

Latchingdon

ST MICHAELS

BUCKINGHAM WAY

SNOREHAM

LAWLING RD

Hall

PH

Moat

Good
Hares

Arley
Grange

BURNHAM RD

B1018

MAIN RD

SOUTH
MINSTER
RD

GARDEN
CL

B1018

SUMMERHILL

Snoreham
Hall

The
Beeches

Red Lyons
Farm

LOWER CHASE

RECTORY LA

Surridges

Rosedale
Farm

Barnes
Farm

UPPER
CHASE

Latchingdon
Hall

Tyle
Hall

Grange
Farm

FAMBRIDGE RD

B1010

Althorne
Hall

B1010

Stamfords Hill
Cottages

SUMMERDALE RD

CHANTRY LA

BARNS FARM DR

River View
Park

RIVER VIEW
FARM

STATION RD

Stamfords
Farm

Viking
Cottage

THE DRIVE

Lawling
Hall

4

01

3

00

2

99

1

98

88   89   90

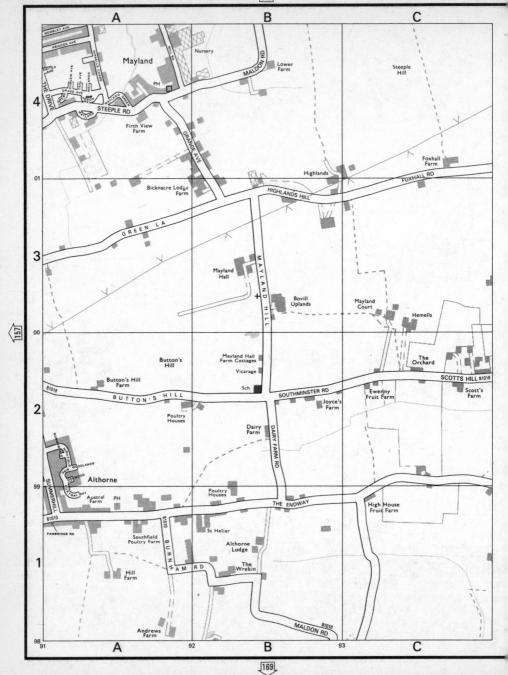

A   B   C

4

01

3

00

2

99

1

98
91   92   93

A   B   C

WEMBLEY AVE
PRINCES AVE
TINWELLS CLOSE
Nursery
MALDON RD
Lower Farm
Steeple Hill

Mayland
THE DRIVE
FINNELLS AVE
ASH WAY AVE
GOBBS WAY
DRAKE AVE
MAYLAND GREEN
PH
STEEPLE RD
Firth View Farm
GRANGE AVE
Highlands
Foxhall Farm
FOXHALL RD

Bicknacre Lodge Farm
HIGHLANDS HILL

GREEN LA

Mayland Hall
MAYLAND HILL
Bovill Uplands
Mayland Court
Hemells

+

The Orchard

Button's Hill
Mayland Hall Farm Cottages
Vicarage
Sch
SCOTTS HILL B1018

Button's Hill Farm
B1018
BUTTON'S HILL
SOUTHMINSTER RD
Ewenny Fruit Farm
Scott's Farm

Poultry Houses
Joyce's Farm

Dairy Farm
DAIRY FARM RD

SUMMERHILL
HIGH FIELD
WOODLANDS
WOOD
LAURAL WAY
Althorne
Poultry Houses
THE ENDWAY
High House Fruit Farm

Austral Farm
PH
B1010
FAMBRIDGE RD
Southfield Poultry Farm
BURNHAM RD
St Helier
Althorne Lodge
The Wrekin

Hill Farm
Andrews Farm
MALDON RD
B1010

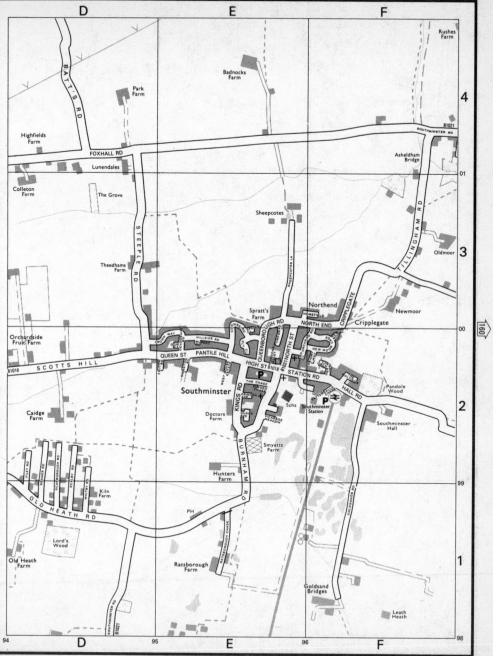

D   E   F

4

Rushes
Farm

Badnocks
Farm

Park
Farm

B1021

SOUTHMINSTER RD

Highfields
Farm

FOXHALL RD

Asheldham
Bridge

Lunendales

01

Colleton
Farm

The Grove

Sheepcotes

T
I
L
L
I
N
G
H
A
M
R
D

Oldmoor

3

S
T
E
E
P
L
E
R
D

Theedhams
Farm

Spratt's
Farm

Northend

Newmoor

HOMEFIELD

Cripplegate

C
R
I
P
P
L
E
G
A
T
E

NORTH END

00

Orchardside
Fruit Farm

CROSS WAY

HILLSIDE RD
ALBERT

QUEENBOROUGH RD

NORTH ST

NEW MOO

QUEEN ST

PANTILE HILL

Pandole
Wood

B1018

SCOTTS HILL

HIGH ST B1018

B1021

STATION RD

HALL RD

WEST ST

K
I
N
G
S
R
D

THE CHASE

Southminster

Schs

P

Southminster
Station

Southminster
Hall

2

Caidge
Farm

Doctors
Farm

DUKE

GRANGE
MEADOW

PRINCE AVE

Smyatts
Farm

C
O
L
D
S
A
N
D
S
R
D

99

FILEY RD

B
U
R
N
H
A
M
R
D

Hunters
Farm

BEAMER RD

SCARBOROUGH RD

ECLABY DR

WHITBY RD

Kiln
Farm

OLD HEATH RD

PH

R
A
T
S
B
O
R
O
U
G
H
C
H
A
S
E

Lord's
Wood

Old Heath
Farm

Ratsborough
Farm

Goldsand
Bridges

Leath
Heath

1

94   95   96   98

D   E   F

SOUTHMINSTER RD   B1021

149
159
171

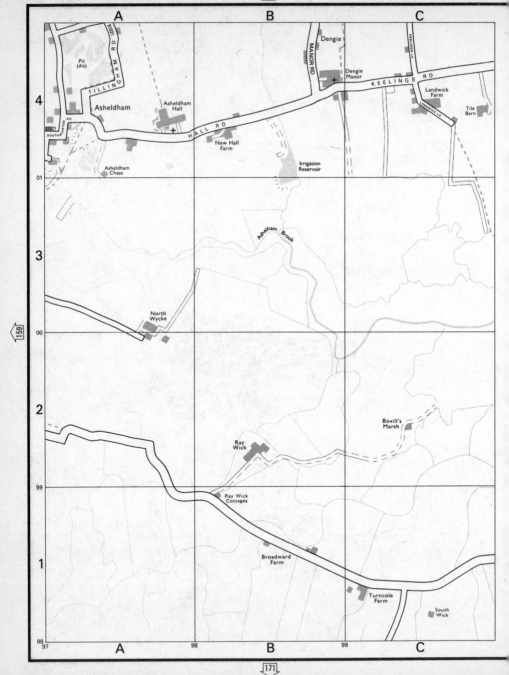

A   **B**   **C**

Pit (dis)

TILLINGHAM RD (1018)

Asheldham

Asheldham Hall

MANOR RD

Dengie

Dengie Manor

KEELINGS LA

KEELINGS RD

Landwick Farm

Tile Barn

4

B1021

SOUTH ... RD

HALL RD

New Hall Farm

LANDWICK LA

Asheldham Chase

Irrigation Reservoir

Asheldham Brook

3

North Wycke

00

2

Ray Wick

Bovill's Marsh

99

Ray Wick Cottages

Broadward Farm

1

Turncole Farm

South Wick

98

97   98   99

A   **B**   **C**

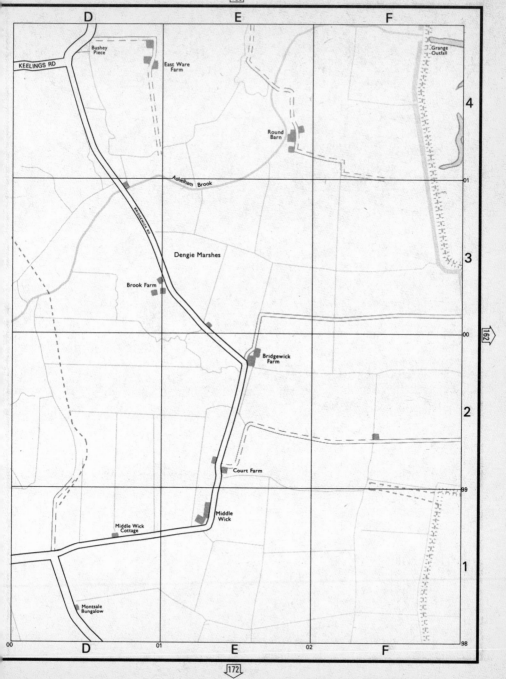

150

D E F

KEELINGS RD

Bushey
Piece

East Ware
Farm

Grange
Outfall

4

Round
Barn

Asheldham Brook

01

Dengie Marshes

3

Brook Farm

00

Bridgewick
Farm

2

Court Farm

99

Middle Wick
Cottage

Middle
Wick

1

Montsale
Bungalow

00

D E F

98

01 02

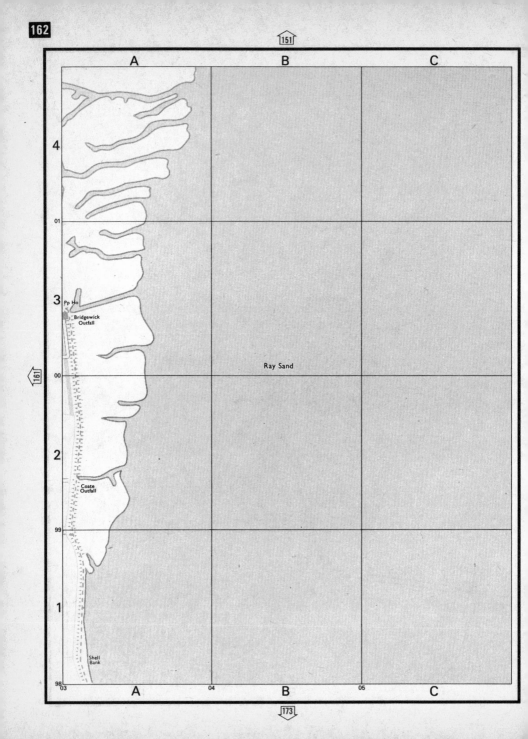

A   B   C

4

01

3   Pp Ho

Bridgewick
Outfall

Ray Sand

00

2

Coate
Outfall

99

1

Shell
Bank

98
03   A   04   B   05   C

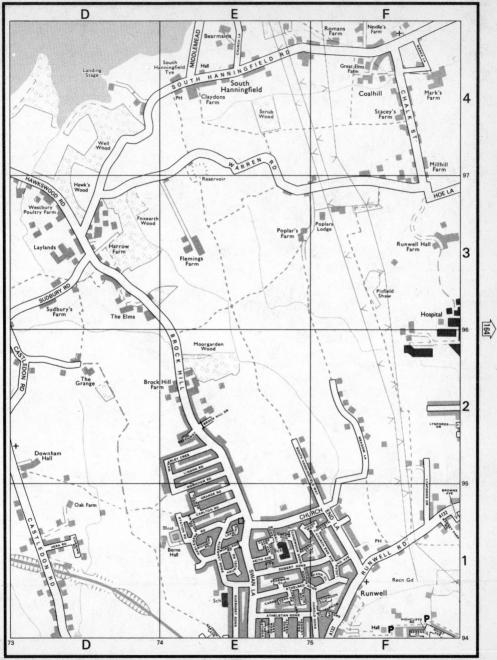

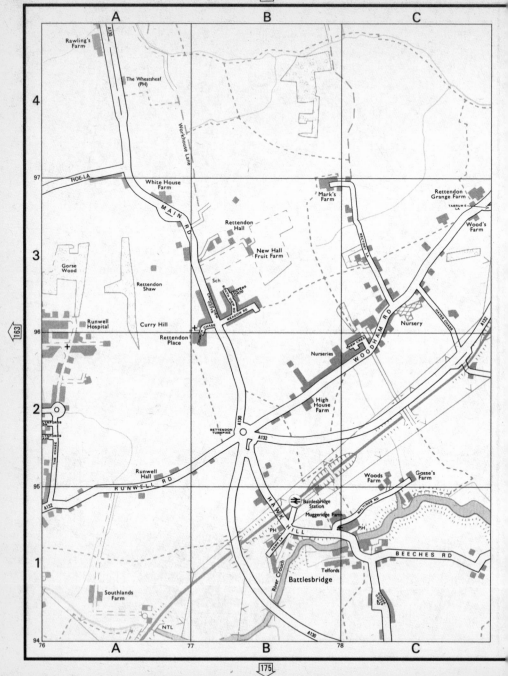

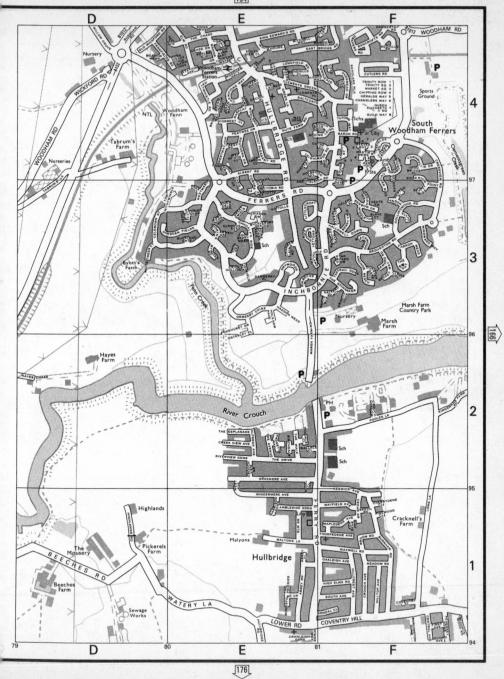

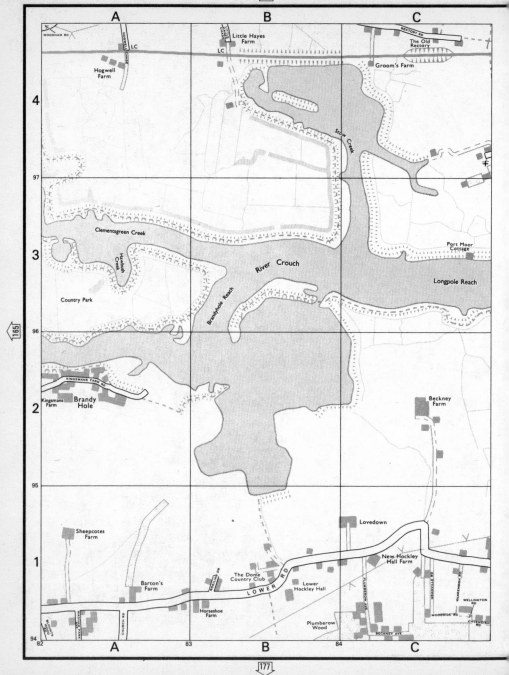

165

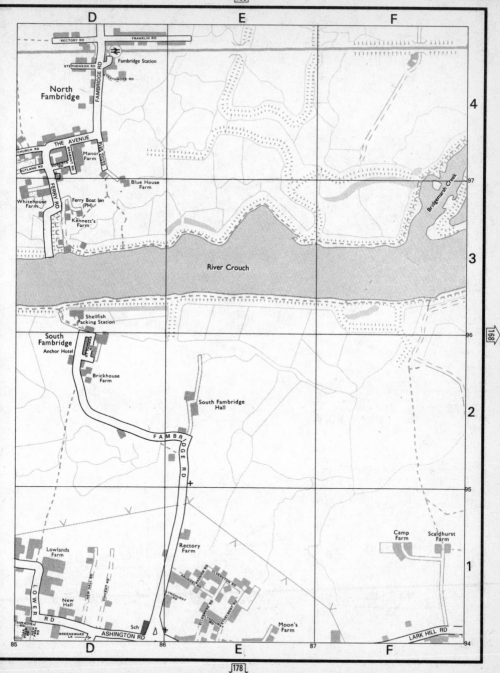

156
178
168

North Fambridge

RECTORY RD

FRANKLIN RD

STEPHENSON RD

STRATHMORE RD

Fambridge Station

FAMBRIDGE RD

THE AVENUE

CHURCH RD

RUTLAND RD

Manor Farm

Blue House Farm

FERRY RD

Whitehouse Farm

Ferry Boat Inn (PH)

Kennett's Farm

River Crouch

Bridgemarsh Creek

Shellfish Packing Station

South Fambridge

Anchor Hotel

Brickhouse Farm

South Fambridge Hall

FAMBRIDGE RD

Lowlands Farm

LOWER RD

NEW HALL RD

VINCENT RD

New Hall

Rectory Farm

Sch

CAVENDISH RD

GREENSWARD LA

ASHINGTON RD

ASHINGFORD RD

ULVERSTON RD

ELLESMERE RD

LYNHURST RD

Moon's Farm

Camp Farm

Scaldhurst Farm

LARK HILL RD

D E F

4 97 3 96 2 95 1 94

85 86 87

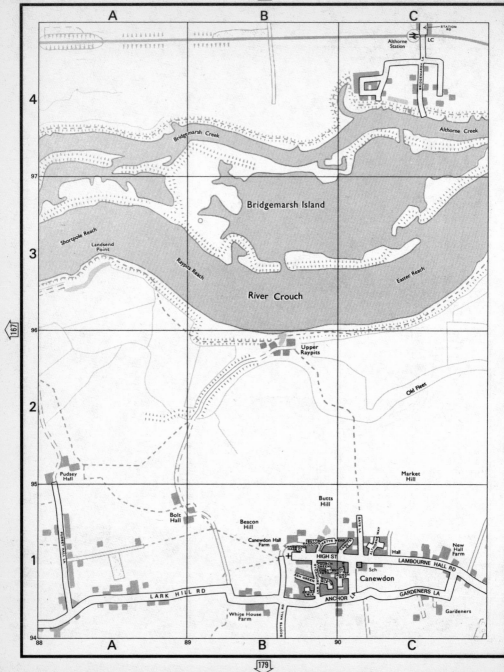

A B C

4
97
3
96
2
95
1
94

88 89 90

STATION RD

Althorne Station

LC

BRIDGEMARSH

Althorne Creek

Bridgemarsh Creek

Bridgemarsh Island

Shortpole Reach

Landsend Point

Raypits Reach

River Crouch

Easter Reach

Upper Raypits

Old Fleet

Pudsey Hall

Market Hill

Butts Hill

Bolt Hall

Beacon Hill

Canewdon Hall Farm

New Hall Farm

PUDSEY LA

HIGH ST

LAMBOURNE HALL RD

Hall

GATE LA

ALTHORNE WAY

CHAPEL LA

CHURCH

Sch

Canewdon

ASH GREEN RD

ANCHOR LA

GARDENERS LA

Gardeners

LARK HILL RD

White House Farm

SCOTTS HALL RD

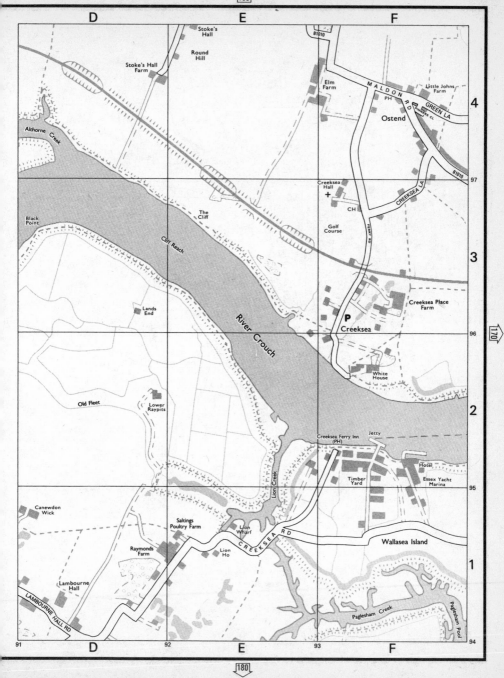

D   E   F

Stoke's Hall

Round Hill

Stoke's Hall Farm

B1010

Elm Farm

MALDON RD

Little Johns Farm

GREEN LA

PH

CHINESE CL

4

Ostend

Althorne Creek

B1010

97

Creeksea Hall

+

CREEKSEA LA

CH

Black Point

The Cliff

Golf Course

Cliff Reach

FERRY RD

3

Creeksea Place Farm

Lands End

River Crouch

P

Creeksea

96

170

White House

Old Fleet

Lower Raypits

2

Creeksea Ferry Inn (PH)

Jetty

Hotel

Lion Creek

Timber Yard

Essex Yacht Marina

95

Canewdon Wick

Saltings Poultry Farm

Lion Wharf

CREEKSEA RD

Wallasea Island

Raymonds Farm

Lion Ho

1

Lambourne Hall

LAMBOURNE HALL RD

Paglesham Creek

Paglesham Pool

91   D   92   E   93   F   94

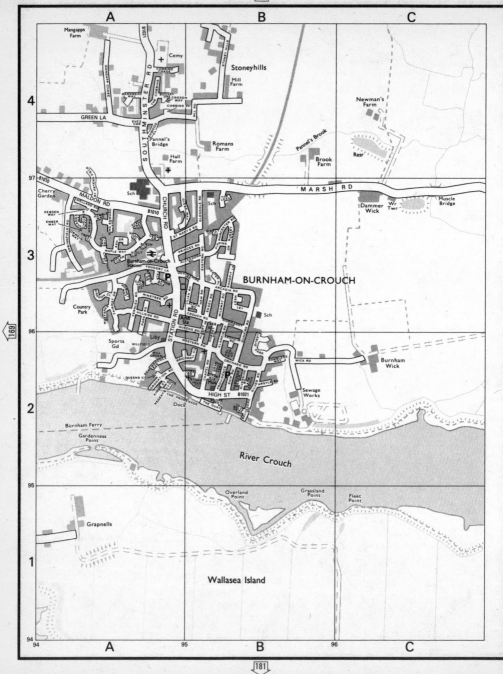

BURNHAM-ON-CROUCH

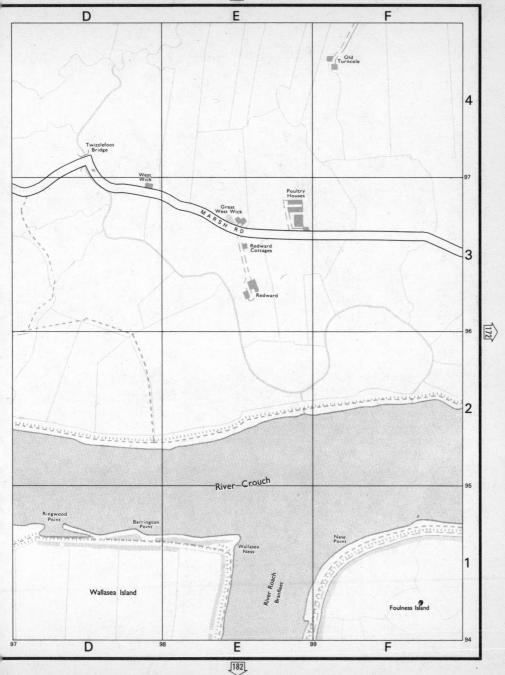

D E F

4

97

Old
Turncole

Twizzlefoot
Bridge

West
Wick

MARSH RD

Great
West Wick

Poultry
Houses

3

Redward
Cottages

Redward

96

172

2

River—Crouch

95

Ringwood
Point

Barrington
Point

Nase
Point

Wallasea
Ness

1

Wallasea Island

River Roach
Bramfleet

Foulness Island

94

97 D 98 E 99 F

171

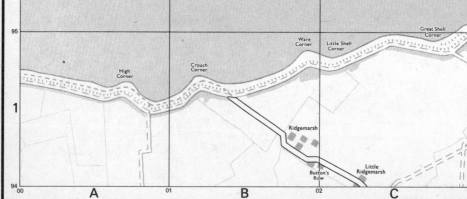

A   B   C

4

Old
Montsale

New
Montsale

Deal Hall

97

East Wick
Cottages

Coney
Hall

East
Wick

3

MARSH RD

Holliwell
Farm

Holliwell
Point

96

2

River Crouch

95

Great Shell
Corner

Ware
Corner

Little Shell
Corner

High
Corner

Crouch
Corner

1

Ridgemarsh

Little
Ridgemarsh

Button's
Row

94

00   A   01   B   02   C

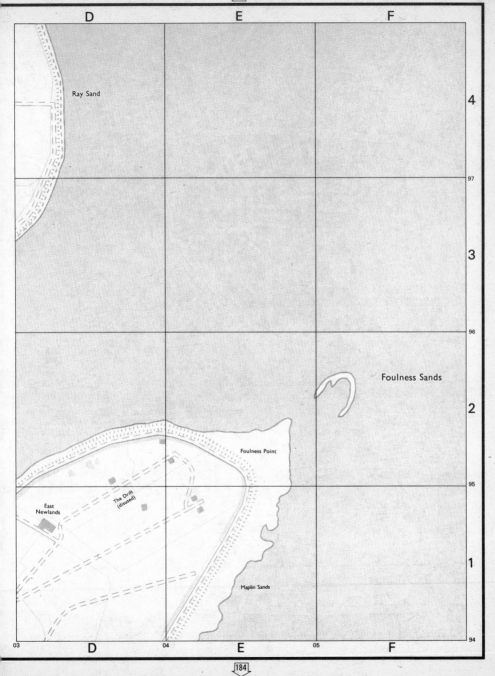

D   E   F

Ray Sand

4

97

3

96

Foulness Sands

2

Foulness Point

95

The Drift
(disused)

East
Newlands

1

Maplin Sands

94

03   D   04   E   05   F

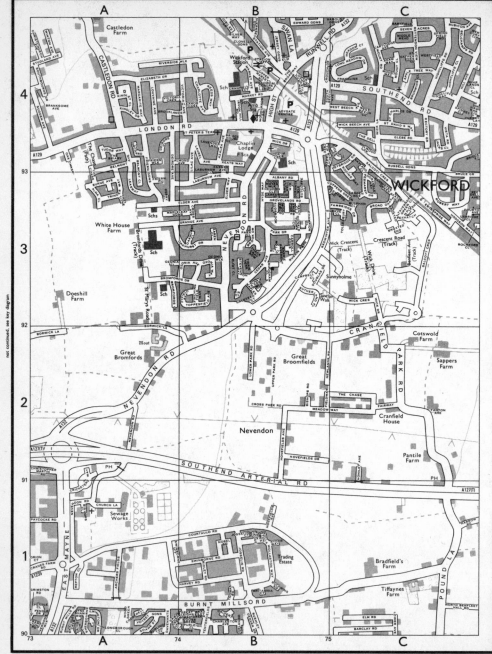

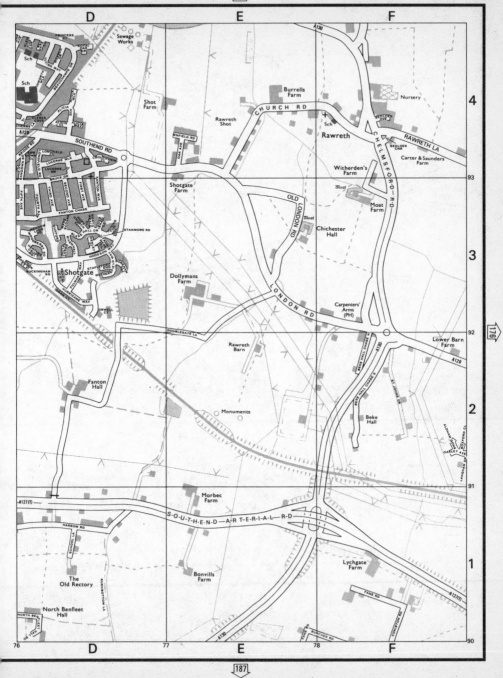

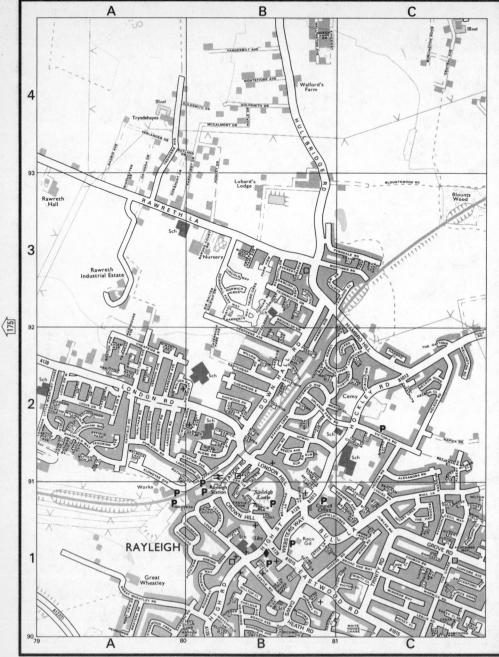

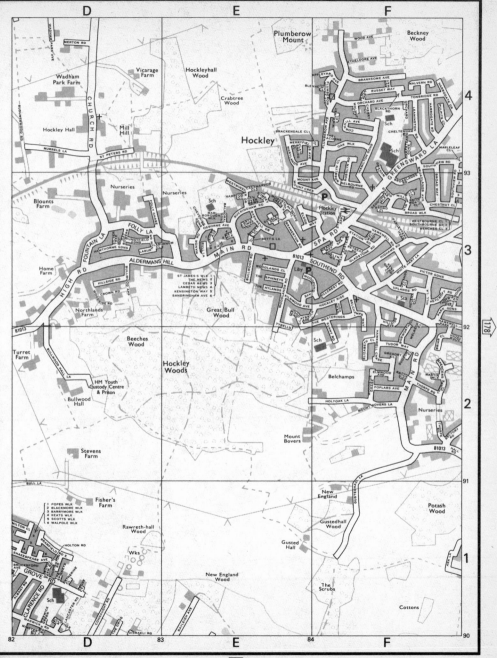

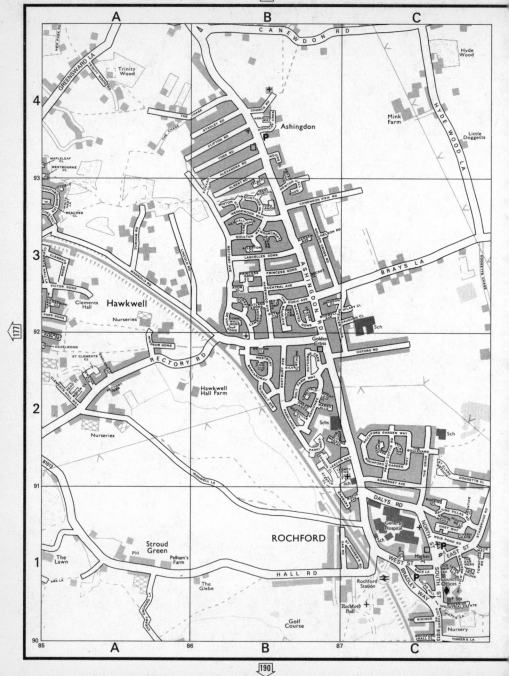

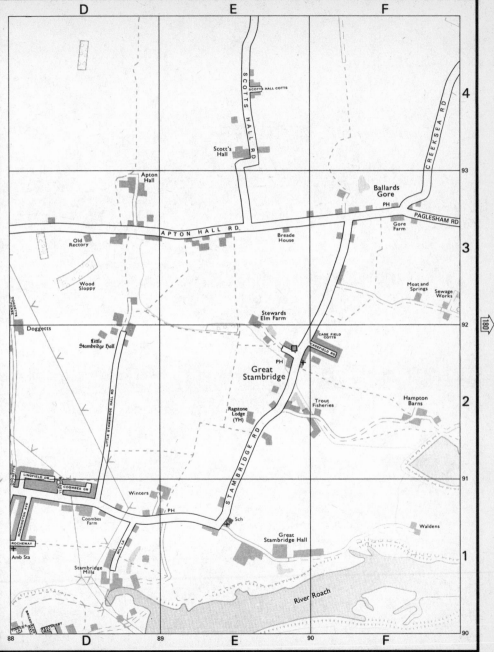

D   E   F

180

4

93

3

92

2

91

1

90

88   D   89   E   90   F

SCOTTS HALL RD

SCOTTS HALL COTTS

Scott's Hall

Apton Hall

Ballards Gore

PH

PAGLESHAM RD

Gore Farm

CREEKSEA RD

APTON HALL RD

Old Rectory

Breade House

Wood Sloppy

DOGGETTS

Moat and Springs

Sewage Works

Doggetts

Little Stambridge Hall

Stewards Elm Farm

CAGE FIELD COTTS

CAGEFIELD RD

PH

Great Stambridge

LITTLE STAMBRIDGE HALL RD

Hampton Barns

Ragstone Lodge (YH)

Trout Fisheries

STAMBRIDGE RD

LINGFIELD DR

COOMBES GR

Winters

PH

Coombes Farm

Sch

Great Stambridge Hall

Waldens

MILL LA

DODGETTS

DORRINGTON AVE

ROCHEWAY

Amb Sta

Stambridge Mills

River Roach

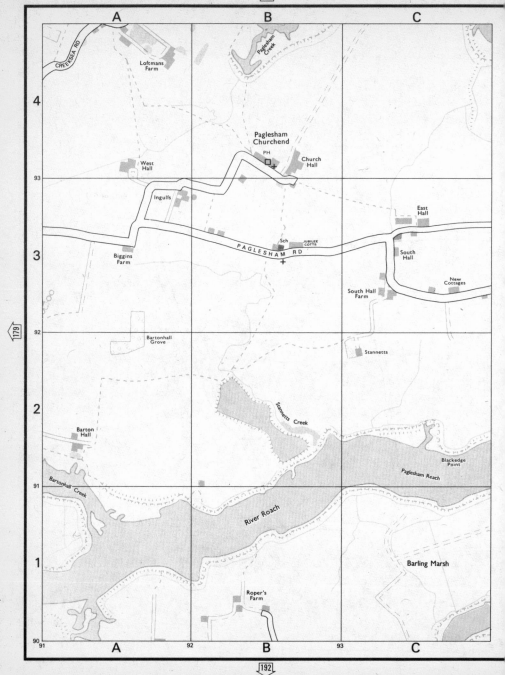

179

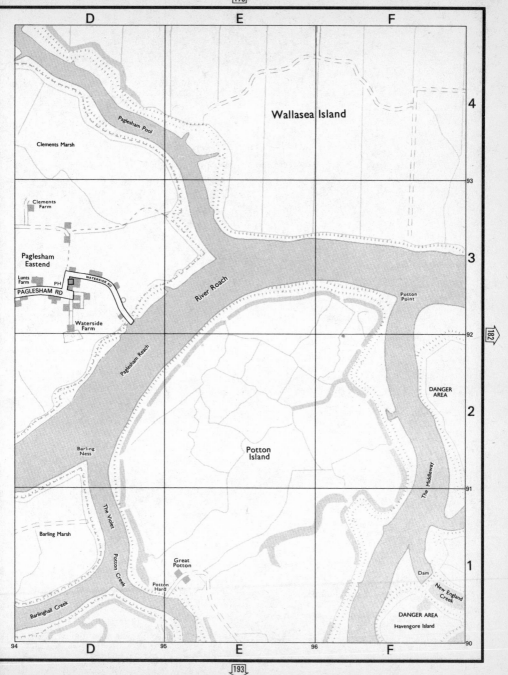

D E F

4

Wallasea Island

Paglesham Pool

Clements Marsh

93

Clements
Farm

3

Paglesham
Eastend

River Roach

Potton
Point

Lunts
Farm   PH
PAGLESHAM RD   WATERSIDE RD

182

92

Waterside
Farm

Paglesham Reach

DANGER
AREA

2

Barling
Ness

Potton
Island

91

The Violet

The Middleway

Barling Marsh

Potton Creek

1

Great
Potton

Dam

New England
Creek

Potton
Hard

Barlinghall Creek

DANGER AREA

Havengore Island

90

94   D   95   E   96   F

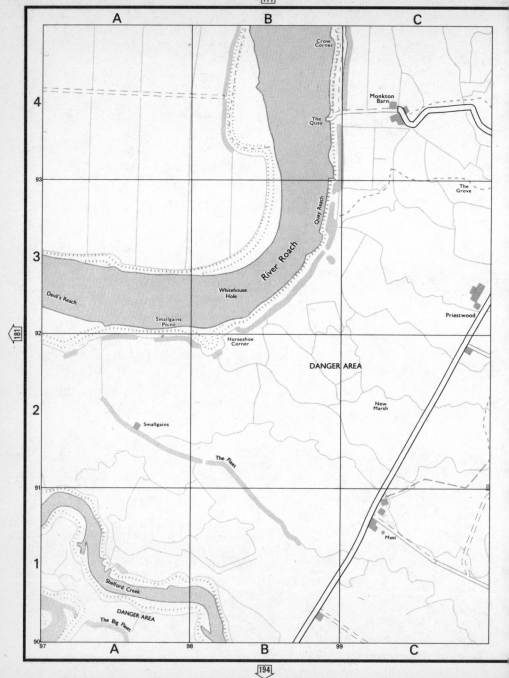

A B C

4

93

3

181

92

2

91

1

90
97 A 98 B 99 C

Crow
Corner

Monkton
Barn

The
Quay

The
Grove

Quay Reach

River Roach

Devil's Reach

Whitehouse
Hole

Smallgains
Point

Priestwood

Horseshoe
Corner

DANGER AREA

New
Marsh

Smallgains

The Fleet

Mast

Shelford Creek

DANGER AREA

The Big Fleet

172

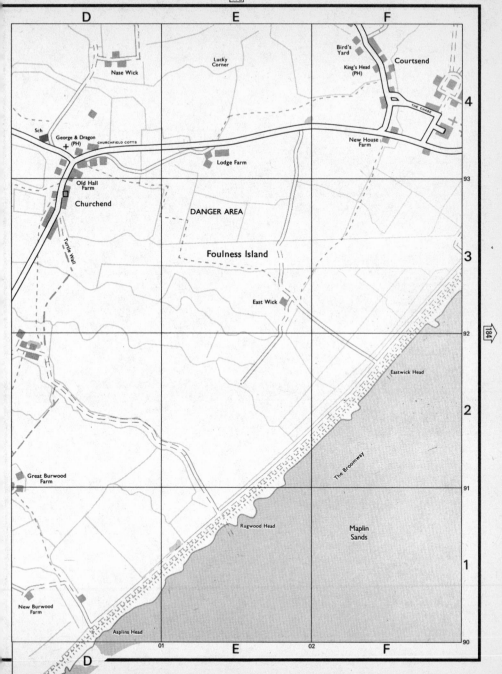

D

E

F

Nase Wick

Lucky
Corner

Bird's
Yard

King's Head
(PH)

Courtsend

THE CHASE

4

Sch

George & Dragon
(PH)

CHURCHFIELD COTTS

Lodge Farm

New House
Farm

93

Old Hall
Farm

Churchend

DANGER AREA

Foulness Island

Turtle Wall

East Wick

3

92

Eastwick Head

2

The Broomway

Great Burwood
Farm

91

Maplin
Sands

Rugwood Head

New Burwood
Farm

1

Asplins Head

01

E

02

F

90

D

00

184

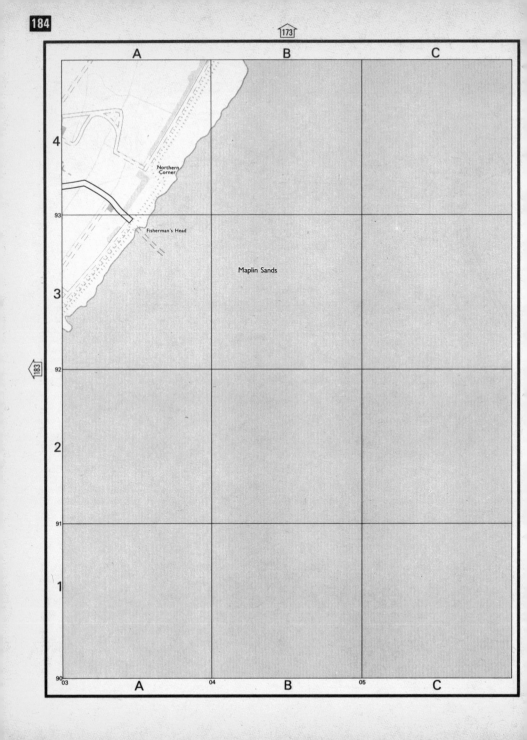

Northern
Corner

Fisherman's Head

Maplin Sands

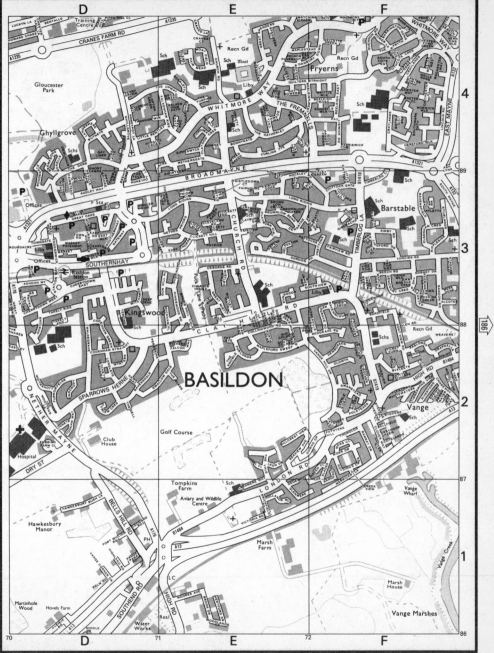

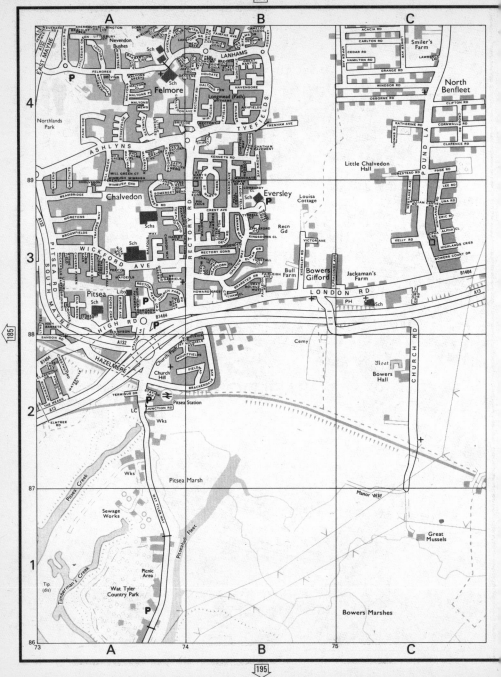

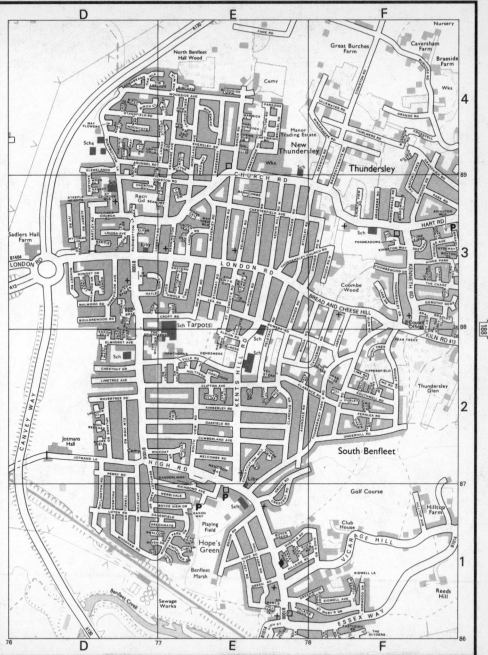

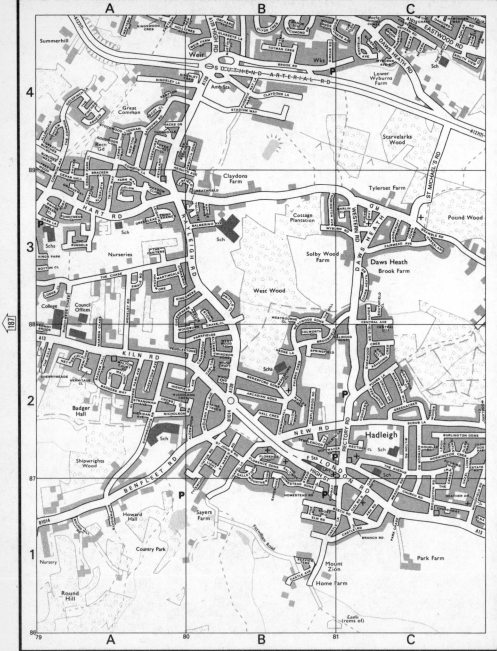

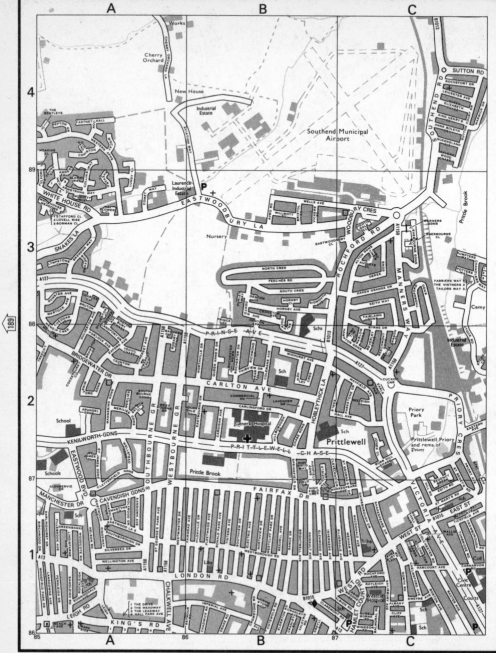

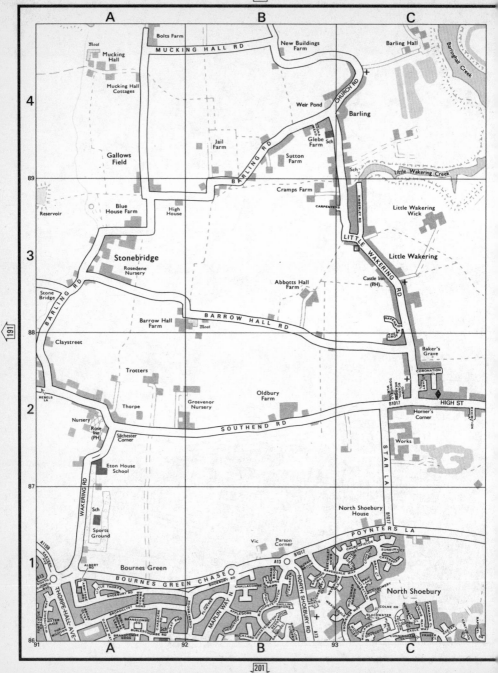

191

A **B** **C**

4

Bolts Farm

Moat

Mucking Hall

MUCKING HALL RD

New Buildings Farm

Barling Hall

Barlinghall Creek

Mucking Hall Cottages

Weir Pond

CHURCH RD

Barling

Gallows Field

Jail Farm

BARLING RD

Glebe Farm Sch

Sutton Farm

Sch

Little Wakering Creek

89

Cramps Farm

Reservoir

Blue House Farm

High House

CARPENTERS

Little Wakering Wick

KIMBERLEY RD

LITTLE WAKERING

Little Wakering

3

Stonebridge

Rosedene Nursery

Abbotts Hall Farm

Castle Inn (PH)

BARLING RD

Stone Bridge

BARROW HALL RD

Barrow Hall Farm

Moat

HAVENGORE

88

Claystreet

CROP

Baker's Grave

Trotters

CORONATION

Thorpe

REBELS LA

Grosvenor Nursery

Oldbury Farm

HIGH ST

Horner's Corner

2

Nursery

Rose Inn (PH)

Silchester Corner

SOUTHEND RD

B1017

Works

STAR LA

Eton House School

WAKERING RD

87

North Shoebury House

B1017

Sch

Sports Ground

POYNTERS LA

A1159

Vic

Parson Corner

A13

1

Albert

Bournes Green

BOURNES GREEN CHASE

SHOEBURY RD

MARLIN WAY

NORTH SHOEBURY RD

A13

North Shoebury

THORPE HALL AVE

86

91 **A** 92 **B** 93 **C**

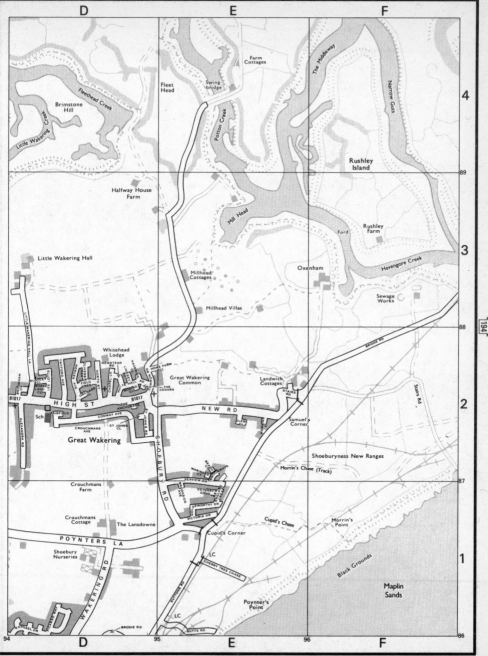

D   E   F

Fleethead Creek

Brimstone
Hill

Little Wakering Creek

Farm
Cottages

Swing-
bridge

Fleet
Head

Potton Creek

The Middleway

Narrow Guts

4

89

Rushley
Island

Halfway House
Farm

Mill Head

Ford

Rushley
Farm

3

Little Wakering Hall

Millhead
Cottages

Oxenham

Havengore Creek

Sewage
Works

Millhead Villas

88

Whitehead
Lodge

NEWSTEAD RD

HOPE FARM RD

THE CEDARS

Great Wakering
Common

Landwick
Cottages

BRIDGE RD

STAIRS RD

Stairs Rd

2

HIGH ST

B1017

B1017

THE ANCHORAGE

NEW RD

Samuel's
Corner

Sch
FAIRFIELD

CONWAY AVE

ST JOHNS
CL

CROUCHMANS
AVE

ST JOHN'S RD

SHOEBURY RD

Great Wakering

ALEXANDRA RD

Shoeburyness New Ranges

Morrin's Chase (Track)

87

Crouchmans
Farm

MARINE CL
SEAVIEW DR
ESTUARY GDNS
OSWORTHY DR
VICTORIA DR

Cupid's Chase

Morrin's
Point

Crouchmans
Cottage

The Lansdowne

Cupid's Corner

POYNTERS LA

WAKERING RD

LC

Shoebury
Nurseries

CHERRY TREE CHASE

Black Grounds

1

Maplin
Sands

POTTONS RD

LC

Poynter's
Point

BRODIE RD

LC

BUTTS RD

86

94   D   95   E   96   F

182

193

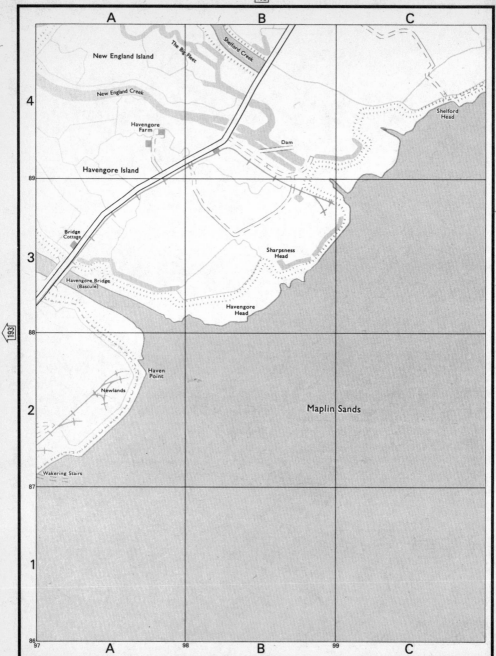

New England Island

The Blk. Fleet

Shelford Creek

New England Creek

Shelford Head

Havengore Farm

Dam

Havengore Island

Bridge Cottage

Sharpsness Head

Havengore Bridge (Bascule)

Havengore Head

Haven Point

Newlands

Maplin Sands

Wakering Stairs

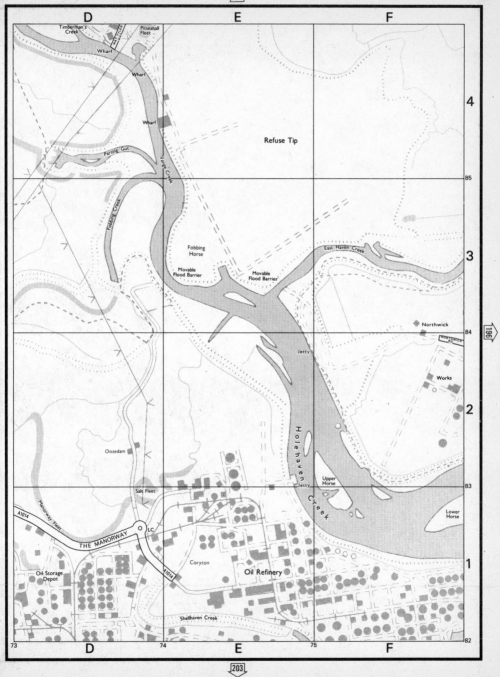

D E F

4

85

3

84 196

2

83

1

82

D E F

Timberman's Creek
Pitseahall Fleet
Wharf
Wharf
Wharf
Parting Gut
Fobbing Creek
Vange Creek
Refuse Tip
Fobbing Horse
Movable Flood Barrier
Movable Flood Barrier
East Haven Creek
Northwick
Jetty
Works
Oozedam
Upper Horse
Salt Fleet
Jetty
Holehaven Creek
Lower Horse
A1014
Manorway Fleet
THE MANORWAY
LC
A1014
Coryton
Oil Refinery
Oil Storage Depot
Shellhaven Creek

73 74 75

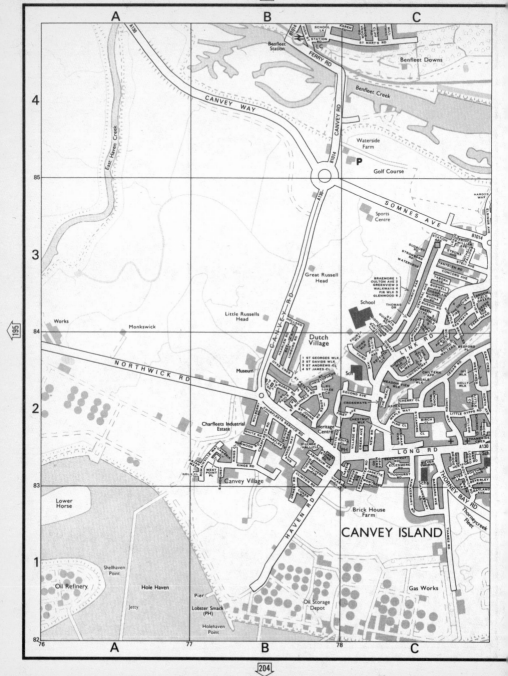

CANVEY ISLAND

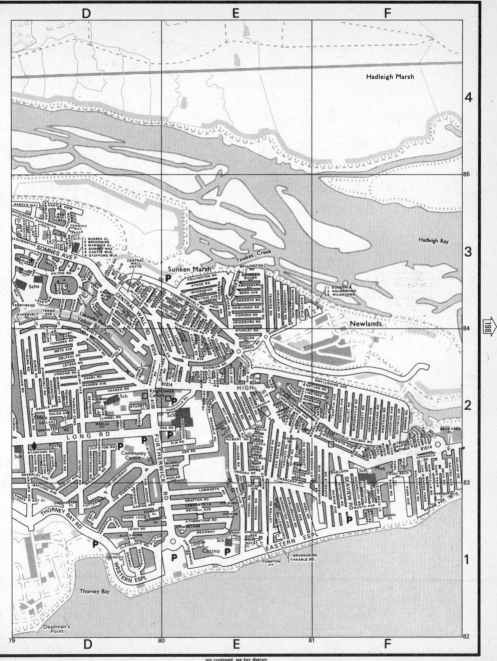

189

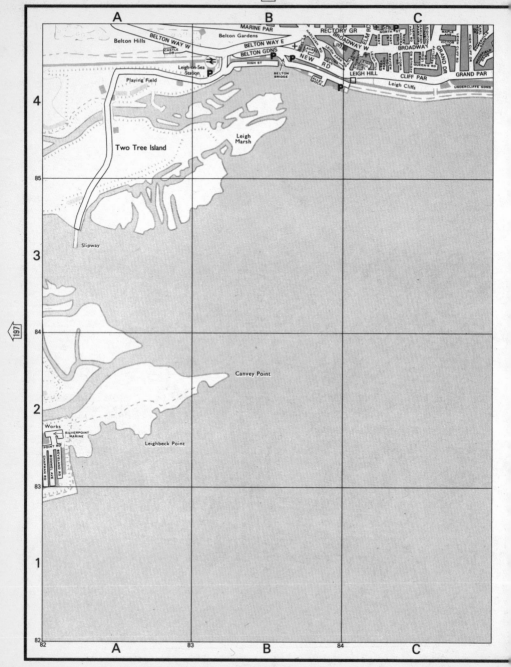

197

A   B   C

MARINE PAR
RECTORY GR
Belton Gardens
BELTON WAY W
Belton Hills
BROADWAY
BELTON WAY E
BELTON GDNS
BROADWAY W
CASTLE DR
NEW RD
Leigh-on-Sea Station
HIGH ST
BELTON BRIDGE
LEIGH HILL
CLIFF PAR
GRAND PAR
BROADWAY
Playing Field
Leigh Cliffs
UNDERCLIFFE GDNS

4

Leigh Marsh

Two Tree Island

85

Slipway

3

84

Canvey Point

2

Works
SILVERPOINT MARINE
POINT RD
Leighbeck Point

83

1

82
82   83   84

A   B   C

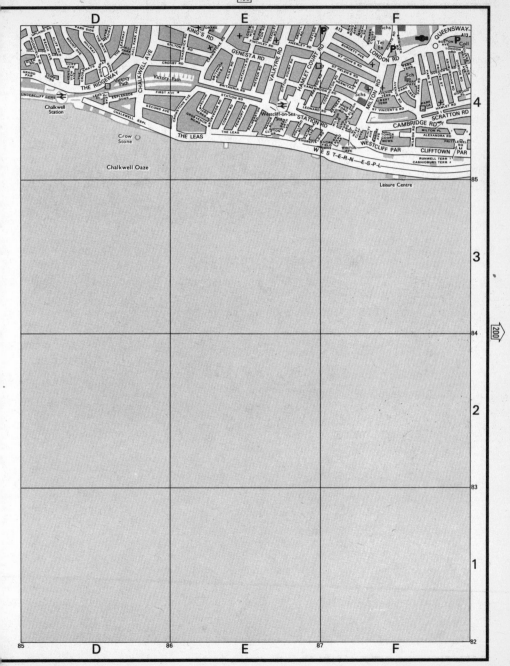

THE RIDGEWAY

KING'S RD

GENESTA RD

CHALKWELL AVE

VALKYRIE RD

HAMLET COURT RD

QUEENSWAY

LONDON RD

Victory Path

First Ave

Station Rd

Westcliff-on-Sea

STATION RD

CAMBRIDGE RD

SCRATTON RD

CLIFFTOWN

WESTCLIFF PAR

Chalkwell Station

Esplanade Gdns

Second Ave

Chalkwell Espl

THE LEAS

THE LEAS

WESTERN ESPL

Crow Stone

Chalkwell Oaze

Leisure Centre

D · E · F

85 86 87

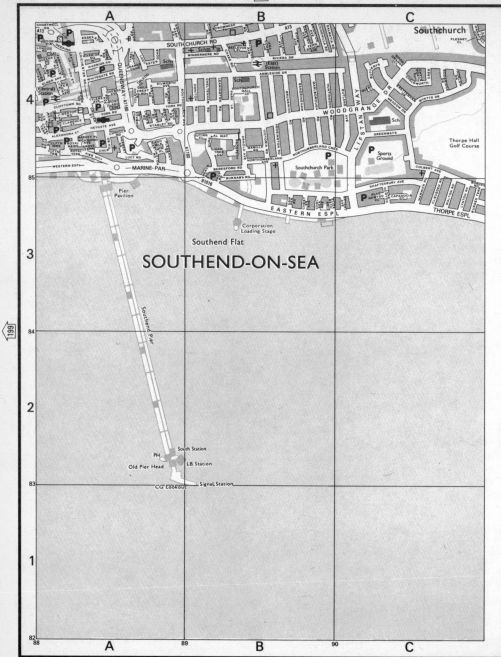

199

SOUTHEND-ON-SEA

Southend Flat

Southchurch

Thorpe Hall
Golf Course

Southchurch Park

Sports
Ground

Pier
Pavilion

Southend Pier

Corporation
Loading Stage

South Station
PH
Old Pier Head
LB Station
CG Lookout
Signal Station

MARINE PAR

WESTERN ESPL

EASTERN ESPL

THORPE ESPL

Central
Station

SOUTHCHURCH RD

(East)
Station

WOODGRANGE DR

LIFSTAN WAY

QUEENSWAY-A1160

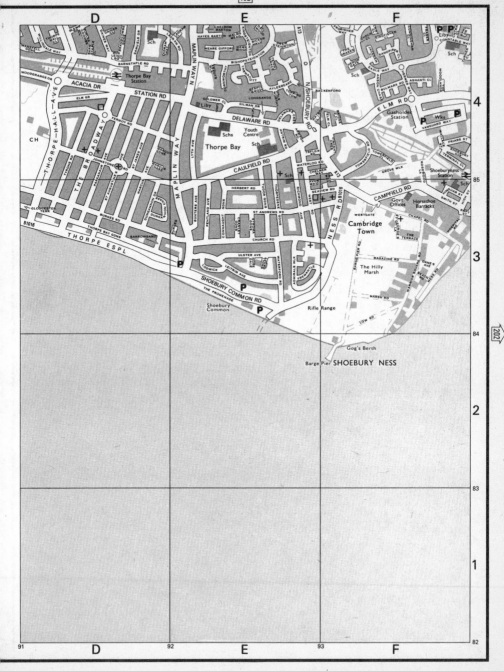

SHOEBURY NESS

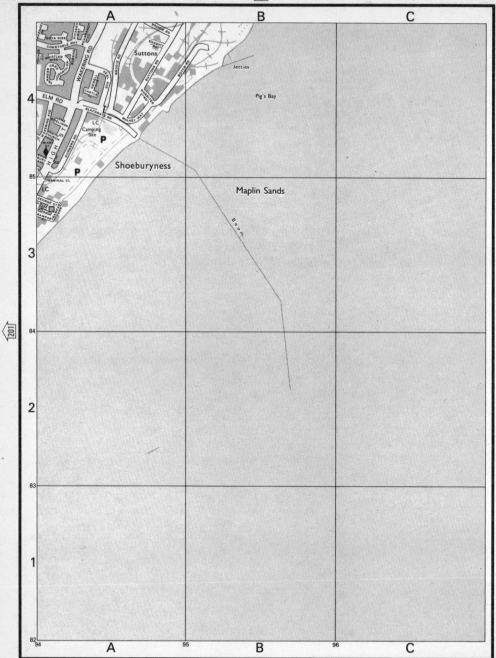

A B C

4

Suttons

Jetties

Pig's Bay

ELM RD

LC
Camping
Site

P

P

Shoeburyness

85

Maplin Sands

LC

3

B o o m

201

84

2

83

1

82

94 95 96

A B C

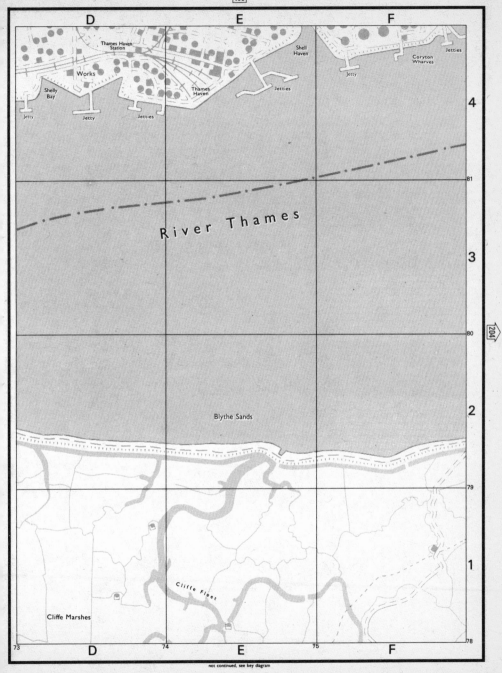

204

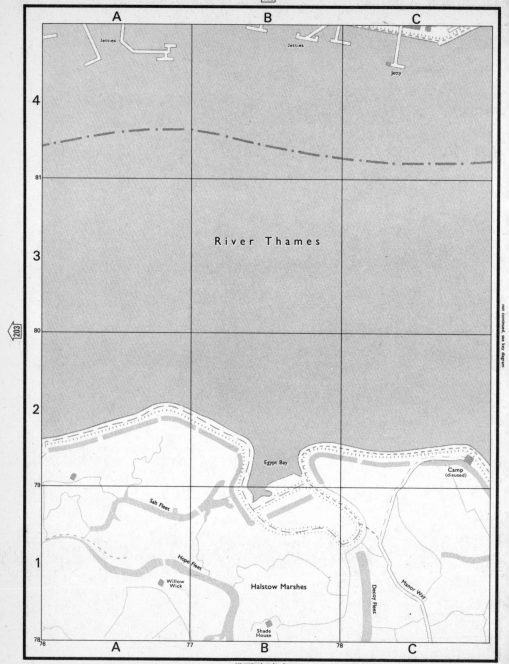

A   B   C

Jetties

Jetties

Jetty

Jetty

4

81

River Thames

3

not continued, see key diagram

80

2

Egypt Bay

Camp
(disused)

79

Salt Fleet

Hope Fleet

1

Willow
Wick

Halstow Marshes

Decoy Fleet

Manor Way

Shade
House

78

76   77   78

A   B   C

USER'S NOTES

EXPLANATION OF THE STREET INDEX REFERENCE SYSTEM

Street names are listed alphabetically and show the locality, the page number and a reference to the square in which the name falls on the map page.

Example: Cedar Way.   Gt Ben...89 F4

Cedar Way   This is the full street name, which may have been abbreviated on the map.

Gt Ben   This is the abbreviation for the town, village or locality in which the street falls.

89   This is the page number of the map on which the street name appears.

F4   The letter and figure indicate the square on the map in which the centre of the street falls. The square can be found at the junction of the vertical column carrying the appropriate letter and the horizontal row carrying the appropriate figure.

ABBREVIATIONS USED IN THE INDEX
Road Names

Approach	App	Lane	La
Avenue	Ave	North	N
Boulevard	Bvd	Orchard	Orch
Broadway	Bwy	Parade	Par
By-Pass	By-Ps	Passage	Pas
Causeway	Cswy	Place	Pl
Common	Comm	Pleasant	Plea
Corner	Cnr	Precinct	Prec
Cottages	Cotts	Promenade	Prom
Court	Ct	Road	Rd
Crescent	Cres	South	S
Drive	Dr	Square	Sq
Drove	Dro	Street, Saint	St
East	E	Terrace	Terr
Gardens	Gdns	Walk	Wlk
Grove	Gr	West	W
Heights	Hts	Yard	Yd

Towns, Villages and Rural Localities

Name	Abbr	No	Grid
Aldham	Ald	65	D4
Alphamstone	Alph	18	C2
Alresford	Alres	88	A4
Althorne	Alth	158	A2
Ardleigh	Ard	51	F4
Asheldham	Ashe	160	A4
Ashen	Ashe	3	E1
Ashington	Ashi	178	B4
Barling	Barl	192	C4
Basildon	Basil	185	E2
Beaumont	Beau	73	F4
Belchamp Otten	Bel O	10	B4
Belchamp St Paul	Bel S P	5	D1
Belchamp Walter	Bel W	11	D3
Birch	Birch	84	A2
Black Notley	Bl Not	78	A3
Boreham	Bore	128	C4
Boxted	Box	31	F4
Bradfield	Brad	36	C1
Bradwell	Bradw	61	E1
Bradwell-on-Sea	Brad O S	137	D1
Braintree	Brain	59	E2
Brightlingsea	Brigh	106	B3
Broomfield	Broom	127	D4
Bulmer	Bul	11	F3
Bures	Bures	28	C4
Burnham-On-Crouch	Burn	170	B3
Canewdon	Cane	168	C1
Canvey Island	Canv	196	C1
Castle Hedingham	Ca Hed	15	F2
Cattawade	Catt	35	E4
Cavendish	Cav	1	B1
Chelmsford	Chelm	127	D2
Churchend	Church	183	D3
Clacton-on-Sea	Clact	110	A1
Clare	Cla	4	B4
Coggeshall	Cogg	63	D2
Colchester	Colch	67	E4
Cold Norton	Col N	155	F3
Colne Engaine	Col En	27	D1
Copford	Copf	65	E2
Corringham	Corr	185	D1
Danbury	Dan	142	C4
Dedham	Ded	33	F3
Dengie	Deng	160	B4
Earls Colne	Ea Col	45	E3
East Hanningfield	E Han	153	E4
East Mersea	E Mers	105	E1
Eight Ash Green	E A Gr	66	A4
Elmstead Market	Elmst M	70	A3
Fairstead	Fair	96	A3
Faulkbourne	Faulk	97	D4
Feering	Fee	81	F3
Fingringhoe	Fing	86	C3
Fordham	Ford	47	E3
Foxearth	Fox	6	B3
Frating	Frat	70	C1
Frinton-on-Sea	Frin	96	A3
Gestingthorpe	Gest	10	B1
Glemsford	Glems	2	B2
Goldhanger	Gold	133	F4
Gosfield	Gos	42	C4
Great Baddow	Gt Bad	140	C4
Great Bentley	Gt Ben	89	F4
Great Braxted	Gt Brx	99	E1
Great Bromley	Gt Bro	52	C1
Great Henny	Gt H	18	B4
Great Horkesley	Gt Hor	31	D1
Great Leighs	Gt Le	95	D4
Great Maplestead	Gt Map	16	B1
Great Oakley	Gt Oak	56	B2
Great Stambridge	Gt Stam	179	E2
Great Tey	Gt T	64	B4
Great Totham	Gt Tot	116	B3
Great Wakering	Gt Wak	193	D2
Great Wigborough	Gt Wig	102	C2
Great Yeldham	Gt Y	9	D1
Hadleigh	Hadl	188	C2
Halstead	Hals	25	E1
Harwich	Harw	40	B2
Hatfield Peverel	Hat Per	114	A2
Hawkwell	Hawk	178	A3
Hazeleigh	Haze	144	A2
Higham	High	22	A2
Hockley	Hock	177	E4
Hullbridge	Hull	165	E1
Kelveden	Kelv	81	E1
Lamarsh	Lam	19	E2
Langenhoe	Lang	86	A1
Langford	Langf	131	E4
Langham	Langh	32	C2
Latchingdon	Latch	157	D3
Lawford	Lawf	35	d2
Layer Breton	Lay Br	84	A1
Layer Marney	Lay M	101	E4
Layer-de-la-Haye	Lay H	84	C3
Little Baddow	Lit Bad	129	E2
Little Bentley	Lit Ben	71	F4
Little Braxted	Lit Brx	98	B1
Little Bromley	Lit Bro	53	D3
Little Clacton	Lit Cla	91	E2
Little Horkesley	Lit Hor	30	C2
Little Maplestead	Lit Map	17	D1
Little Oakley	Lit Oak	57	D4
Little Totham	Lit Tot	117	D2
Little Waltham	Lit Wal	112	A4
Little Yeldham	Lit Y	9	F2
Long Melford	L Mel	7	E4
Maldon	Mald	131	F1
Manningtree	Mann	35	E3
Margaretting	Marg	139	D1
Marks Tey	Mks T	65	D2
Mayland	May	158	A4
Messing	Mess	82	B1
Middleton	Midd	12	C2
Mistley	Mist	36	A2
Mount Bures	M Bure	29	C3
Mundon	Mund	145	F1
Nayland	Nay	20	A1
North Fambridge	N Fam	167	D4
Ovington	Ovi	4	A1
Paglesham Churchend	Pag Ch	180	B4
Panfield	Pan	59	D4
Pebmarsh	Peb	27	D4
Peldon	Peld	103	E3
Pentlow	Pent	5	F3
Purleigh	Purl	144	B1
Ramsey	Rams	39	D1
Rayleigh	Rayl	176	A1
Rayne	Ray	59	D1
Rettendon	Rett	153	D1
Ridgewell	Ridge	8	A3
Rivenhall	Rive	98	A4
Rochford	Roch	178	B1
Rowhedge	Rowh	86	C4
Runwell	Runw	163	F1
Sandon	Sand	141	E3
Shotley Gate	Sho G	40	A4
Sible Hedingham	Si Hed	15	F1
Silver End	Silv E	79	F2
South Benfleet	S Ben	188	F2
South Hanningfield	S Han	163	E4
South Woodham Ferrers	S Woo F	165	F4
Southend-On-Sea	South	200	B3
Southminster	Soum	159	E2
Springfield	Sprin	127	F3
St Lawrence	St L	148	C3
St Osyth	St O	108	A2
Stanway	Stanw	66	B3
Steeple	Steep	147	F2
Stisted	Stis	61	E3
Stonebridge	Stobr	192	A3
Stow Maries	Stow M	155	E2
Stratford St Mary	Str S M	22	B1
Sudbury	Sud	12	B4
Tendring	Tend	72	C3
Terling	Terl	96	B2
Thorpe-le-Soken	Th L S	74	A1
Thorrington	Thor	89	D3
Thundersley	Thund	187	F4
Tillingham	Till	149	F2
Tiptree	Tipt	100	A3
Tollesbury	Tolle	119	E1
Tolleshunt D'Arcy	Toll D	118	B2
Tolleshunt Knights	Toll K	101	D2
Tolleshunt Major	Toll M	117	F2
Toppesfield	Topp	14	B4
Twinstead	Twin	18	B3
Tye Green	T Gr	78	C3
Ulting	Ult	130	B4
Virley	Virl	119	D4
Wakes Colne	Wa Col	46	B3
Walton on the Naze	Walt	94	B4
Weeley	Weel	72	C1
West Bergholt	W Berg	48	C2
West Hanningfield	W Han	152	A2
West Mersea	W Mers	121	E3
Wethersfield	Weth	23	D1
White Notley	Wh Not	78	C1
Wickford	Wick	174	C3
Wickham Bishops	Wic Bis	115	E3
Wickham St Paul	Wic S P	17	D3
Witham	With	97	F2
Wivenhoe	Wiv	69	E1
Wix	Wix	55	E3
Woodham Mortimer	Woo Mor	143	E3
Woodham Walter	Woo Wa	130	B1
Wormingford	Worm	29	F3
Wrabness	Wrab	37	F2
Writtle	Writ	126	B1

Aalten Ave. Canv 197 F2
Abbas Wlk. Sud 13 E3
Abberton Rd. Fing 86 C2
Abberton Rd. Lay H 85 D3
Abbess Cl. Chelm 126 C1
Abbey Cl. Hull 165 E1
Abbey Cres. Th L S 74 A1
Abbey Fields. E Han 153 D4
Abbey La. Cogg 63 D1
Abbey Rd. Hull 165 E1
Abbey Rd. Sud 7 F1
Abbey St. Th L S 74 A1
Abbey Turning. Mald 131 E2
Abbeygate St. Colch 67 F3
Abbot's Rd. Colch 68 A2
Abbots Cl. Clact 109 F3
Abbots Cl. Wix 55 E3
Abbots Gdns. St O 108 B2
Abbots La. E A Gr 66 A4
Abbots Wlk. South 201 E4
Abbotsleigh Rd. S Woo F 165 F3
Abbotswood. Thund 188 B3
Abbott Rd. Harw 39 F1
Abbotts Cl. Chelm 127 E2
Abbotts Cl. South 189 F3
Abdy Ave. Harw 39 F1
Abels Rd. Hals 43 E4
Abensburg Rd. Canv 197 E3
Abercorn Way. With 98 A1
Aberdeen Gdns. Hadl 189 D1
Abingdon Ct. Basil 174 A1
Abinger Cl. Clact 109 E3
Abraham Dr. Silv E 79 F2
Abreys. Thund 188 A4
Acacia Ave. Colch 68 C4
Acacia Dr. Mald 131 F1
Acacia Dr. South 201 D4
Acacia Rd. South 98 A2
Acacia Rd. Basil 186 C4
Accomodation Rd. Box 49 E4
Achilles Way. Brain 60 A3
Achnacone Dr. Canv 49 E2
Ackland Ave. Colch 67 D4
Acorn Ave. Brain 59 F3
Acorn Ave. Hals 25 E1
Acorn Cl. Colch 50 B2
Acorn Cl. Harw 40 A1
Acorn Wlk. Thor 89 D3
Acorns The. Hock 177 F4
Acres End. Chelm 126 C2
Acton Cl. Sud 12 C4
Acton Green. Sud 12 C4
Acton La. Sud 7 F1
Adalia Cres. Hadl 189 D2
Adalia Way. Hadl 189 D1
Adam Way. Wick 174 C4
Adams Glade. Hawk 178 B3
Addison Pavement. Basil 186 A3
Addison Rd. Sud 13 D4
Adelaide Dr. Colch 68 A1
Adelaide Gdns. S Ben 187 E1
Adelaide St. Rams 39 F3
Adelsburg Rd. Canv 197 E2
Admirals Wlk. Chelm 126 C2
Admirals Wlk. South 201 E3
Aetheric Rd. Brain 59 F2
Affleck Rd. Colch 68 C4
Agar Rd App. Walt 94 B4
Agate Rd. Clact 109 F1
Agincourt Rd. Clact 109 E2
Agnes Ave. Hadl 189 D2
Ailsa Rd. South 199 E4
Ainger Rd. Harw 39 F1
Aingers Green Rd. Gt Ben 90 A3
Airborne Cl. South 189 F3
Aire Wlk. With 97 F1
Aisne Rd. Colch 67 E2
Ajax Cl. Brain 60 A3
Akenfield Cl. S Woo F 165 F4
Alamein Rd. Burn 170 B2
Alamein Rd. Chelm 126 C3
Alamein Rd. Colch 67 E1
Alan Cl. South 189 F3
Alan Dr. Lit Cla 91 E1
Alan Gr. South 189 F3
Alan Rd. With 97 F1
Alan Way. Colch 66 C2
Alanbrooke Rd. Colch 68 B1
Albany Ave. South 190 C1
Albany Cl. Chelm 126 C3
Albany Cl. W Berg 48 C2
Albany Gdns. E. Clact 110 A2
Albany Gdns W. Clact 110 A2
Albany Rd. Rayl 177 D1
Albany Rd. W Berg 48 C2
Albert Cl. Brain 60 B3
Albermarle Gdns. Brain 60 B3
Albermarle St. Harw 40 B3
Albert Ave. Ashi 178 B3
Albert Cl. Rayl 176 C2
Albert Gdns. Colch 110 A2
Albert Gdns. Cogg 63 D1
Albert Pl. Cogg 63 D1
Albert Rd. Ashi 178 B3
Albert Rd. Brigh 107 D3
Albert Rd. Burn 170 B2
Albert Rd. Rayl 176 C2
Albert Rd. S Woo F 165 E4

Albert Rd. South 192 A1
Albert Rd. South 200 A4
Albert Rd. Thund 187 D3
Albert Rd. With 98 A2
Albert St. Colch 67 F4
Albert St. Harw 40 B3
Albert Terr. South 199 F4
Albertine Cl. Stanw 66 B3
Albion Gr. Colch 68 A3
Albion Rd. S Ben 187 E2
Albion Rd. South 190 C1
Albion St. Rowh 57 D4
Albrighton Croft. Colch 50 B2
Albury. South 191 F1
Alcotes. Basil 185 F3
Aldeburgh Cl. Clact 109 D2
Aldeburgh Gdns. Colch 50 A2
Aldeburgh Way. Sprin 127 E3
Alder Dr. Chelm 140 A3
Alder Wlk. With 98 A2
Alderbury Lea. S Woo F 142 C1
Aldercar Rd. Copf 65 F1
Alderford Maltings. Si Hed 24 C4
Alderford St. Si Hed 24 C4
Alderleys. Thund 188 A3
Aldermans Hill. Hock 177 D3
Alderney Gdns. Runw 163 E1
Alderton Rd. Colch 68 B4
Alderwood Way. S Ben 188 B2
Aldham Gdns. Rayl 175 F2
Aldon Cl. Harw 39 E1
Aldridge Cl. Sprin 128 A2
Aldrin Way. South 190 A3
Alefounder Cl. Colch 68 C3
Alexander Ct. Sprin 127 F4
Alexander Mews. Sand 141 E1
Alexander Rd. Brain 59 F2
Alexandra Ave. W Mers 121 E4
Alexandra Dr. Wiv 69 E2
Alexandra Rd. Ashi 178 B4
Alexandra Rd. Burn 170 B3
Alexandra Rd. Clact 109 F2
Alexandra Rd. Colch 67 F3
Alexandra Rd. Gt Wak 193 D2
Alexandra Rd. Harw 40 B3
Alexandra Rd. Rayl 176 C2
Alexandra Rd. S Ben 187 E1
Alexandra Rd. Si Hed 15 E1
Alexandra Rd. South 198 C4
Alexandra Rd. South 199 F4
Alexandra Rd. Sud 13 D4
Alexandra Rd. Wee! 72 C1
Alexandra St. Harw 40 B3
Alexandra St. South 200 A4
Alexandra Terr. Colch 67 F3
Alexandria Dr. Rayl 176 A2
Alfells Rd. Elmst M 69 F3
Alfred Gdns. Runw 163 E1
Alfred Terr. Walt 94 B4
Alfreda Ave. Hull 165 E2
Alfreg Rd. With 114 B4
Algars Way. S Woo F 165 E4
Alicia Ave. Wick 175 D4
Alicia Cl. Wick 175 D4
Alicia Way. Wick 175 D4
Alicia Wlk. Wick 175 D4
Alison Cl. Harw 40 A1
All Saints Ave. Colch 67 D2
All Saints Cl. Sprin 127 F2
Allandale. Thund 188 A4
Allectus Way. With 114 B4
Allen Way. St O 107 D2
Allendale Dr. Copf 65 E2
Allens Cl. Bore 112 C1
Allerton Cl. Hawk 178 B3
Alley Dock. South 198 B4
Alleyn Pl. South 190 B1
Alleyne Way. Clact 125 D4
Allfields. Harw 39 F1
Allfields. Harw 40 A1
Alma Cl. Hadl 189 E1
Alma Cl. Wick 174 A3
Alma Dr. Chelm 127 D1
Alma Rd. Hadl 189 D1
Alma Sq. Mann 35 E2
Alma St. Wiv 87 D4
Almere. S Ben 187 E2
Almond Ave. Wick 174 B4
Almond Cl. Clact 109 E2
Almond Cl. Tipt 100 C3
Almond Cl. Wiv 69 E1
Almond Way. Colch 68 C4
Almond Wlk. Canv 196 C2
Alpha Cl. Basil 186 C3
Alpha Rd. Basil 186 C3
Alpha Rd. Burn 170 B3
Alpha Rd. With 97 D2
Alphamstone Rd. Lam 19 D2
Aiport Ave. Colch 67 E2
Alresford Rd. Elmst M 87 F4
Alston Cl. Colch 67 D3
Althorne Cl. Basil 174 A1
Altforne Way. Cane 168 C1
Althorpe Cl. Hock 177 E3
Alton Dr. Colch 67 D3
Alton Gdns. South 190 C3
Alton Park La. Clact 109 D1
Alton Park Rd. Clact 109 E1

Alton Rd. Clact 109 F1
Aluf Cl. With 114 C4
Alvis Ave. Clact 124 C3
Alyssum Cl. Bore 128 A3
Alyssum Wlk. Colch 68 B4
Amarells Rd. Lit Cla 91 E2
Amberley Cl. Elmst M 69 E1
Ambleside Dr. South 200 B4
Ambleside Gdns. Hull 165 E1
Ambleside Wlk. Canv 196 C2
Ambridge Rd. Cogg 62 C2
Ambrose Ave. Colch 66 C2
Ameland Rd. Canv 197 D3
America Rd. Ea Col 45 E1
America St. Mald 132 A1
Amid Rd. Canv 197 E3
Amos Hill. Gt H 18 A4
Amoss Rd. Gt Bad 140 C4
Ampers End. Basil 185 E3
Anchor End. Mist 36 A4
Anchor Hill. Wiv 87 D4
Anchor La. Cane 168 B1
Anchor La. Mald 132 A3
Anchor La. Mist 36 A2
Anchor Rd. Clact 109 F2
Anchor Rd. Tipt 100 B2
Anchor Reach. S Woo F 165 F3
Anchor St. Chelm 127 D1
Anchorage The. Gt Wak 193 D2
Anders Fall. South 190 A3
Anderson Ave. Chelm 126 C3
Andover Cl. Clact 109 D3
Andrew Cl. Brain 59 F3
Andrews Pl. Chelm 126 C2
Andyk Rd. Canv 197 F2
Anerley Rd. South 199 E4
Angel Cl. Basil 185 E2
Angel La. Glems 2 A2
Angle Side. Brain 60 A1
Anglefield. Clact 109 F1
Anglesea Rd. Wiv 87 E4
Anglia Cl. Colch 67 D2
Anglia Way. Brain 60 A1
Anne Boleyn Dr. Roch 190 C4
Anne Cl. Brigh 106 C3
Anson Ciease. South 201 F4
Anson Cl. S Woo F 165 F3
Anson Way. Brain 60 B2
Anstey Cl. South 189 E4
Anthony Cl. Colch 50 B1
Antonio Wlk. Colch 68 C4
Antrim Rd. South 201 E4
Anvil Way. Sprin 127 F4
Anzio Cres. Colch 67 E2
Apple Tree Way. Wick 174 C4
Appledore. South 192 B1
Appleford Ct. Basil 186 B3
Appletow. South 189 F3
Appleton Rd. S Ben 187 D1
Appletree Cl. South 191 F2
Appletree Ct. Tipt 78 C3
Appletree Wlk. Brain 60 A1
Appleyard Ave. Hock 177 F4
Approach Rd. Canv 197 F2
Approach The. Clact 125 D4
Approach The. Rayl 176 B2
Apton Hall Rd. Gt Stam 179 E3
Apton Hall Rd. Roch 179 E3
Aragon Cl. Clact 124 C4
Aragon Cl. South 190 C2
Arakan Cl. Colch 67 D1
Arboub La. Wic Bis 115 F3
Arbour La. Sprin 127 E2
Arbour Way. Colch 50 B2
Arbutus Cl. Chelm 140 A3
Arcade Rd. Clact 110 A3
Arcadia Rd. Burn 170 B3
Arcadia Rd. Canv 197 E2
Arcadian Gdns. Hadl 188 B2
Archer Ave. South 191 F2
Archer Cl. South 191 F2
Archers Fields. Basil 174 A1
Archibald Cl. Chelm 109 D3
Ardens Cl. South 50 B2
Arderne Cl. Harw 39 F1
Ardleigh Ct. Ard 51 F4
Ardleigh Rd. Ded 33 E2
Ardleigh Rd. Gt Bro 52 A2
Ardleigh Rd. Lit Bro 52 A2
Ardleyway. Rayl 176 B2
Argyle Ct. Kelv 81 E1
Argyll Rd. Burn 170 B2
Argyll Rd. Th L S 73 F1
Argyll Rd. Bore 128 A3
Argyll Rd. South 199 E4
Argyll Rd. South 190 C1
Arjan Way. Canv 196 B2
Ark La. Roch 178 A1
Arlington Rd. South 191 F1
Armadale. Canv 196 C3
Armagh Rd. South 201 E4
Armidale Wlk. Colch 68 A4
Armiger Way. With 98 A1
Armitage Rd. South 192 A1
Armond Rd. With 97 F2
Armoury Rd. W Berg 48 C2
Armstrong Cl. Dan 142 C4
Armstrong Rd. Thund 187 E4
Armstrong Way. Gt Y 9 D1

Arnheim Rd. Burn 170 B2
Arnhem Gr. Brain 59 F2
Arnhem Rd. Chelm 126 C3
Arnold Ave. South 200 B4
Arnold Dr. Colch 68 C3
Arnold Rd. Clact 109 E3
Arnold Villas. Tipt 100 B3
Arnold Way. Chelm 140 B2
Arnolds Way. Ashi 178 B4
Arnstones Cl. Colch 68 B4
Arras Rd. Colch 67 E2
Arrow Rd. Colch 68 C4
Arthur Cl. Chelm 126 C3
Arthur St. Colch 67 F3
Arthy Cl. Hat Pev 114 A2
Artillery Barracks Folley. Colch 67 F3
Artillery St. Colch 68 A3
Arun Cl. Sprin 128 A2
Arundel Dr. South 190 A2
Arundel Rd. Ashi 167 E1
Arundel Rd. Runw 163 E1
Arundel Rd. Thund 187 D4
Arwen Gr. S Woo F 165 E3
Asbury Cl. Colch 68 B4
Ascot Cl. Thund 188 A4
Ash Bungalows. Brain 59 F2
Ash Cl. Brigh 106 C4
Ash Cl. Clact 109 E2
Ash Fall. With 97 F3
Ash Gr. Burn 170 A3
Ash Gr. Chelm 140 B4
Ash Gr. Mald 132 C3
Ash Gr. Sud 13 E3
Ash Gr. Wiv 69 E2
Ash Green. Cane 168 B1
Ash Ground Cl. Catt 35 E4
Ash Grove. Colch 86 A4
Ash Rd. Alres 88 A4
Ash Rd. Canv 197 E3
Ash Rd. Hadl 188 C1
Ash Tree Cres. Chelm 126 C1
Ash Tree Cres. Chelm 126 C1
Ash Tree Wlk. Basil 185 F3
Ash Way. Hock 177 F4
Ash Wlk. South 200 A4
Ashanti Cl. South 201 F4
Ashburnham Rd. South 199 F4
Ashbury Dri. Mks T 64 C2
Ashby Rd. With 115 D4
Ashcombe Cl. South 189 D3
Ashcombe Way. Rayl 176 C1
Ashcombe. Hawk 178 B2
Ashdene Cl. Hull 165 F1
Ashdon Way. Basil 185 D3
Ashdown Cres. Hadl 188 C2
Ashdown Way. Colch 68 B4
Ashe Cl. Ashe 3 E1
Ashen Hill. Ashe 3 E1
Ashen La. Cla 3 E2
Ashen Rd. Bel S P 4 A3
Ashen Rd. Ovi 4 A1
Ashen Rd. Wick 93 F4
Ashes Rd. T Gr 78 C4
Ashfield Farm Rd. Ult 130 B4
Ashfields. Basil 186 B4
Ashford Rd. Chelm 126 C1
Ashingdale Cl. Canv 197 E1
Ashingdon Rd. Ashi 178 B3
Ashingdon Rd. Roch 178 B3
Ashleigh Cl. Canv 197 D3
Ashleigh Dr. South 198 C4
Ashley Gdns. Colch 67 E4
Ashley Green. E Han 153 D4
Ashley Rd. Harw 40 A2
Ashlong Gr. Hals 25 F2
Ashlyn's Rd. Frin 93 F2
Ashlyns. Basil 186 A4
Ashmans Row. S Woo F 165 E3
Ashmere Rise. Sud 13 D4
Ashmole Dr. Walt 93 F3
Ashpole Rd. Brain 42 A1
Ashurst Ave. South 191 F1
Ashurst Dr. Rowh 86 C4
Ashurst Dr. Sprin 127 E4
Ashwells Meadow. Ea Col 45 D3
Ashwin Ave. Copf 65 E2
Ashwood Cl. Burn 170 A4
Ashworths. Canv 197 E4
Ashworths. Hawk 178 B3
Aspen Cl. Canv 196 C2
Aspen Way. Colch 68 B4
Aspen Way. Lit Oak 57 D4
Asquith Ave. Thund 188 B3
Asquith Gdns. Thund 188 B4
Assandune Cl. Ashi 178 B4
Astell Ct. Frin 93 F2
Aster Cl. Clact 109 E2
Aster Ct. Sprin 127 F3
Astley Rd. Clact 109 F3
Athelstan Gdns. Runw 163 E1
Athelstan Rd. Colch 67 E3
Atherstone Cl. Canv 197 E1
Atherstone Rd. Canv 197 E1
Athol Cl. Canv 197 E3
Atholl Rd. Sprin 127 F3
Athos Rd. Canv 197 E3

Baker's La. Dan

Atlas Ct. Ea Col 45 D4
Atlas Rd. Ea Col 44 C4
Attlee Gdns. Colch 68 A3
Attwoods Cl. Chelm 140 B2
Aubrey Cl. Chelm 127 D4
Aubrey Dr. Chelm 126 C3
Audley Rd. Colch 67 E3
Audley Way. Basil 185 F4
Audley Way. Frin 94 A3
Audleys Cl. South 190 C3
Audries Estate. Walt 94 A4
Augusta Way. S Woo F 142 C1
Augustus Way. With 114 C4
Austen Cl. Brain 78 A4
Austin Ave. Clact 124 C3
Autoway. Colch 50 B3
Autumn Cl. Clact 109 E3
Avebury Rd. South 190 C1
Aveley Way. Mald 144 C4
Aveline Rd. Ard 51 F4
Avenue Rd. Corr 185 D1
Avenue Rd. Gt Bad 140 B4
Avenue Rd. S Ben 187 F2
Avenue Rd. South 198 C4
Avenue Rd. With 98 A2
Avenue Terr. South 199 F4
Avenue The. Brain 59 F2
Avenue The. Canv 197 D1
Avenue The. Clact 110 A4
Avenue The. Gt Oak 56 A2
Avenue The. Hadl 188 C2
Avenue The. Hull 165 F1
Avenue The. N Fam 167 D4
Avenue The. W Berg 48 B2
Avenue The. With 98 A1
Aviation Way. Roch 190 B4
Avignon Cl. Colch 68 A2
Avila Chase. Chelm 140 A1
Avington Wlk. Thund 187 F3
Avocet Cl. Kelv 81 E1
Avon Cl. Mald 132 B3
Avon Cl. Hawk 178 B3
Avon Rd. Chelm 126 B3
Avon Way. Colch 68 C3
Avon Way. South 201 E4
Avon Wlk. With 97 F2
Avondale Cl. Rayl 176 C1
Avondale Dr. South 189 F2
Avondale Rd. Basil 186 A2
Avondale Rd. Clact 110 A2
Avondale Rd. South 189 F2
Avondale Rd. South 187 E2
Avro Rd. South 190 B3
Aylesbeare. South 201 E4
Aylesbury Dr. Clact 110 C3
Aylett Cl. Canv 197 E2
Ayletts. Basil 185 F3
Ayloffe Rd. Colch 50 B1
Azalea Ave. Wick 174 B4
Azalea Way. Clact 109 E2

Baardwyk Ave. Canv 197 F2
Back La E. Gt Bro 71 D3
Back La W. Gt Bro 70 C4
Back La. Brigh 106 C4
Back La. E Han 153 D4
Back La. Gt Tot 115 F2
Back La. Rams 39 E3
Back La. Roch 178 C1
Back La. Soum 159 E3
Back Rd. Ard 52 A3
Back Rd. Tolle 119 E2
Back Rd. With 97 E2
Back Waterside La. Brigh 106 C3
Bacon's La. Ho Col 46 B2
Baddow Hall Ave. Gt Bad 141 D4
Baddow Place Ave. Gt Bad 141 D3
Baddow Rd. Chelm 127 E1
Baddow Rd. Chelm 140 C4
Baddow Rd. Gt Bad 140 C4
Baden Powell Dr. Colch 67 D2
Badger Hall Ave. S Ben 188 A2
Badgers Cl. Chelm 140 A1
Badgers Cl. South 190 A2
Badgers Gr. Gt Hor 31 D1
Badgers Green. Mks T 64 C2
Badgers Way. S Ben 188 A2
Badley Hall Rd. Gt Bro 71 E4
Badminton Rd. Clact 125 D4
Bailey Bridge Rd. Brain 59 F3
Bailey Dale. Stanw 66 B2
Bailey La. Cla 4 B4
Bailey Rd. Hadl 189 D1
Bailey The. Rayl 176 B1
Bakers Cl. South 189 D3
Baker Ave. Hat Pev 114 A2
Baker Mews. Mald 132 A1
Baker Rd. Sho G 40 A4
Baker St. Chelm 127 D1
Baker's La. Bl Not 77 E3
Baker's La. Cla 49 D1
Baker's La. Dan 142 C4

209

Baker's La. Toll M — Boleyn Cl. Rayl

Baker's La. Toll M 117 E2
Baker's Rd. Bel S P 4 C1
Bakers Cl. S Woo F 165 E4
Bakery Cl. Till 149 F2
Baldwin's La. Gt T 63 D4
Bale Cl. Colch 66 C2
Balfe Ct. Colch 68 C3
Balfour Way. Basil 186 A3
Balkerne Cl. Colch 67 F4
Balkerne Hill. Colch 67 F4
Balkerne Pass. Colch 67 F4
Ball Alley. Colch 67 F4
Ball La. Rowh 86 A3
Ball's Chace. M Bure 28 C1
Ball's Chase. Hals 25 F1
Ballast Quay Rd. Elmst M 69 E1
Ballast Quay Rd. Elmst M 87 E4
Ballast Quay Rd. Fing 87 D3
Ballingdon Hill. Sud 12 B3
Ballingdon St. Sud 12 B3
Balmerino Ave. Thund 188 B3
Balmoral Ave. Clact 109 E2
Balmoral Gdns. Hock 177 E3
Balmoral Rd. South 190 C1
Balmoral Rd. Steep 147 D1
Baltic Ave. South 200 A4
Balton Way. Harw 39 F1
Bancrofts Rd. S Woo F 165 F4
Bandhills Cl. S Woo F 165 E4
Banister Cl. Clact 109 E3
Bank Pass. Colch 67 F4
Bank St. Brain 59 F2
Bankart La. Sprin 127 F2
Bankside Cl. S Woo F 154 C1
Bannister Green. Wick 174 C3
Banters La. Gt Le 77 D1
Banyardway. Hawk 178 B2
Barbara Ave. Canv 196 C1
Barbara Cl. Hawk 178 C1
Barbel Rd. Colch 50 C1
Barbrook La. Tipt 100 B3
Barbrook Way. S Woo F 142 C1
Barclay Cl. Gt Bad 141 D3
Barclay Rd. Basil 174 C1
Bardenville Rd. Canv 197 F2
Bardfield Rd. Colch 68 A1
Bardfield Way. Rayl 176 A2
Bardfield Way. Walt 93 F3
Bardfield. Basil 185 F3
Barfield Rd. W Mers 121 E3
Barfield. Mann 35 E2
Bargate La. Ded 34 A2
Barge Pier Rd. South 201 F3
Barker Cl. Lawf 35 D2
Barkis Cl. Chelm 126 B4
Barkstead Rd. Colch 50 B1
Barley Mead. Dan 143 D3
Barley Way. Colch 66 C3
Barling Rd. Barl 192 B4
Barling Rd. Stobr 192 A3
Barlon Rd. Lit Bro 52 C2
Barlow's Reach. Sprin 128 A2
Barn Green. Sprin 127 F4
Barn Hall Ave. Colch 68 B2
Barn La. Lawf 52 C4
Barnaby Rudge. Chelm 126 C4
Barnard Cl. Basil 185 F1
Barnard Rd. Chelm 140 B1
Barnard Rd. Hadl 189 E1
Barnardiston Rd. Colch 50 B1
Barnardiston Way. With 97 F2
Barnards Ave. Canv 197 E2
Barncombe Cl. Thund 187 E3
Barncroft Cl. Colch 50 A2
Barnes Mill Rd. Sprin 127 F1
Barnet Park Rd. Runw 163 F1
Barneveld Ave. Canv 197 F2
Barnfield Cotts. Mald 132 A3
Barnfield Mews. Chelm 127 D3
Barnfield Rd. Gt Hor 49 E3
Barnfield. Fee 81 E2
Barnfield. Mann 35 E2
Barnfield. Wick 174 C4
Barnhall Rd. Toll K 101 E1
Barnmead Way. Burn 170 A4
Barns Farm Dr. Alth 157 F1
Barnstaple Cl. South 201 D4
Barnstaple Rd. South 201 D4
Barnwell Dr. Hock 177 E3
Baron Rd. S Woo F 165 F4
Baron's La. Purl 144 C1
Baronia Croft. Colch 50 B2
Barons Court Rd. Rayl 176 B3
Baronswood Way. Colch 67 E1
Barpack St. Brad 54 B4
Barr Cl. Wiv 69 E1
Barrack La. Harw 40 C2
Barrack Sq. Chelm 127 D1
Barrack St. Colch 68 A3
Barrie Pavement. Wick 174 B3
Barrington Cl. Basil 185 F4
Barrington Cl. Gt Bad 141 D3
Barrington Cl. Lit Cla 91 E1
Barrington Gdns. Basil 185 F4
Barrington Gdns. Clact 110 B3
Barrington Rd. Colch 68 A3
Barringtons Cl. Rayl 176 B2
Barrow Hall Rd. Barl 192 B3
Barrow Hall Rd. Stobr 192 B3
Barrowsand. South 201 D3
Barrymore Wlk. Rayl 177 D1
Bartlett Cl. May 146 C1
Bartletts. Rayl 189 D4
Bartley Cl. Thund 187 D3
Bartley Rd. Thund 187 D3
Bartlow End. Basil 186 A4
Bartlow Side. Basil 186 A4
Barton Cl. S Woo F 154 B1
Bartram Ave. Brain 60 B2
Barwell Way. With 98 A1
Basin Rd. Mald 132 C2
Bassenthwaite Rd. Thund 187 F4
Bassetts La. Lit Bad 130 A2
Bat View. St L 148 B4
Batavia Rd. Canv 196 B2
Bate-Dudley Dr. Brad O S 137 D2
Bateman Rd. Brigh 106 C4
Bateman's Rd. Clact 91 D2
Bath St. Wiv 87 D4
Bathurst Cl. Colch 68 A1
Batt Hall. Bul 12 A3
Batt's Rd. Steep 148 A1
Battery La. Sho G 40 A4
Battisford Dr. Clact 109 D2
Battlesbrook Rd. Colch 68 B1
Bawn Cl. Brain 60 A2
Bawtree Way. Colch 67 D3
Baxter Ave. South 190 C1
Bay Cl. Canv 197 D1
Bay Rd. Harw 40 B2
Bay View Cres. Lit Oak 57 E4
Bayard Ave. Brigh 106 C4
Bayley St. Ca Hed 15 F2
Baynards Cres. Walt 93 F3
Beach Ave. South 199 D4
Beach Cres. Clact 124 C3
Beach Ct. Gt Wak 193 E2
Beach House Gdns. Canv 197 F1
Beach Rd. Canv 197 E2
Beach Rd. Clact 109 F1
Beach Rd. Harw 40 B1
Beach Rd. South 200 B4
Beach Rd. South 201 F3
Beach Rd. St O 108 A1
Beach Rd. St O 123 E4
Beach Rd. W Mers 121 E3
Beach Way. Clact 124 C3
Beach's Dr. Chelm 126 B2
Beachcroft Ave. Walt 93 E3
Beaches Cl. Hock 178 A3
Beachway. Canv 197 D1
Beachy Dr. St L 148 B4
Beacon Cl. Brigh 106 C3
Beacon Hill Ave. Harw 40 C2
Beacon Hill. Gt Tot 116 A3
Beacon Hill. Mald 131 F1
Beacon Hts. St O 107 D1
Beacon Way. St O 107 D1
Beacon Way. Stanw 66 B3
Beaconsfield Ave. Colch 67 F3
Beaconsfield Cl. Sud 12 C4
Beaconsfield Rd. Clact 109 F2
Beaconsfield Rd. Sud 12 C4
Beadle Way. Gt Le 95 D3
Beadon Dr. Brain 60 A1
Beambridge. Basil 186 A3
Bear St. Nay 20 A1
Beardsley Dr. Sprin 127 F4
Bearsted Dr. Basil 186 B3
Beatrice Ave. Canv 197 D2
Beatrice Rd. Clact 109 F1
Beatrice Rd. Walt 76 C1
Beatty Gdns. Brain 60 B2
Beatty La. Basil 185 F3
Beatty Rise. S Woo F 165 F3
Beauchamps Cl. Sprin 127 F4
Beauchamps Dr. Wick 175 D4
Beaufort Gdns. Brain 60 A2
Beaufort Rd. Sprin 128 A2
Beaufort St. South 191 E1
Beaumont Ave. Brigh 107 D4
Beaumont Ave. Clact 109 E2
Beaumont Cl. Colch 49 F2
Beaumont Cl. Walt 93 F4
Beaumont Park. Dan 142 B3
Beaumont Pl. Brain 60 A2
Beaumont Rd. Gt Oak 56 B1
Beaumont Wlk. Chelm 126 B3
Beaver Cl. Colch 66 C4
Beazley End. Wick 174 C3
Beche Rd. Colch 68 A3
Beck Farm Cl. Canv 197 F2
Beck Rd. Canv 197 F2
Becker Rd. Colch 66 C2
Beckers Green Rd. Brain 60 B1
Becket Cl. Ashi 178 B3
Becket Way. S Woo F 165 F3
Becketts La. High 21 F4
Beckford Rd. Mist 36 A2
Beckingham Rd. Gt Tot 116 B3
Beckingham Rd. Toll D 118 B2
Beckingham St. Toll M 117 E2
Beckney Ave. Hock 166 C1
Becontree Cl. Clact 109 F4
Bedells Ave. Bl Not 78 A3
Bedford Cl. Brain 60 A2
Bedford Cl. Rayl 176 B1
Bedford Cl. Tipt 100 B3
Bedford Pl. Canv 196 C2
Bedford Rd. Clact 110 B3
Bedford Rd. Colch 49 F3
Bedloes Ave. Rayl 175 F4
Bedloes Cnr. Rayl 175 F4
Beech Ave. Brain 59 F3
Beech Ave. Rayl 176 B2
Beech Ave. Wiv 69 D1
Beech Cl. Burn 170 A3
Beech Ct. Basil 185 F3
Beech Gr. Lit Oak 57 D4
Beech Gr. Si Hed 15 E1
Beech Green. Lit Brx 115 F3
Beech Hill. Colch 67 D3
Beech Rd. Basil 185 F3
Beech Rd. Hadl 188 C1
Beech Rd. Hull 165 F1
Beech Rd. Sud 13 D3
Beech Rd. With 98 A4
Beech Rise. Hat Pev 114 A2
Beechcroft Rd. Canv 196 C2
Beeches Cl. Chelm 126 C1
Beeches Cl. Chelm 126 C1
Beeches Rd. Chelm 126 C1
Beeches Rd. Mald 131 F3
Beeches Rd. Rayl 164 C1
Beechmont Gdns. South 190 C2
Beechwood Cl. Colch 67 E1
Beecroft Cres. Canv 197 D3
Beedell Ave. South 190 B1
Beedell Ave. Wick 174 C3
Beehive La. Basil 185 D3
Beehive La. Chelm 140 B3
Beehive La. Gt Bad 140 B3
Beeleigh Chase. Mald 131 E2
Beeleigh Cl. Colch 68 A1
Beeleigh Cl. South 190 C2
Beeleigh Cross. Basil 185 F4
Beeleigh East. Basil 185 F4
Beeleigh Link. Sprin 127 F2
Beeleigh Rd. Mald 131 F2
Beeleigh West. Basil 185 E4
Begonia Cl. Sprin 127 F3
Begonia Pl. Clact 109 E2
Beke Hall Chase N. Rayl 175 F2
Beke Hall Chase S. Rayl 175 F2
Bekeswell La. Chelm 139 F1
Bel-Air Estate. St O 124 A3
Belchamps Rd. Wick 174 C4
Belchamps Way. Hawk 177 F3
Beldams Cl. Th L S 74 A1
Beldowes. Basil 185 E3
Belfairs Cl. Hadl 189 E1
Belfairs Dr. South 189 E1
Belfairs Park Cl. Hadl 189 E3
Belfairs Park Dr. Hadl 189 D3
Belgrave Cl. Gt Bad 140 B4
Belgrave Cl. Rayl 189 D4
Belgrave Rd. Rayl 189 D4
Bell Cl. Colch 68 B1
Bell Hill. Dan 142 B4
Bell Hill. Lam 19 E2
Bell La. Pan 59 D4
Bell St. Gt Bad 140 C3
Bellamy Cl. Walt 93 E3
Belle Vue Rd. Colch 49 F1
Belle Vue Rd. Sud 12 C4
Belle Vue Rd. Wiv 69 E1
Belle Vue. Chelm 127 D1
Bellevue Ave. South 200 B4
Bellevue Pl. South 200 B4
Bellevue Rd. South 191 E1
Bellevue Terr. Hals 25 F1
Bellfield Ave. Brigh 107 D4
Bellfield Cl. Brigh 107 D4
Bellfield. Basil 185 F2
Bellhouse Cres. South 189 E3
Bellhouse La. South 189 E3
Bellhouse Rd. South 189 E3
Bellingham La. Rayl 176 B1
Bellmead. Chelm 127 D1
Bells Chase. Gt Bad 140 C3
Bells Hill Rd. Basil 185 D1
Bells Hill. M Bure 29 D2
Bells La. Glems 2 B3
Bells Rd. Bel W 10 C3
Belmonde Dr. Sprin 127 F4
Belmont Ave. Wick 174 A4
Belmont Cl. Sprin 127 F4
Belmont Cl. Wick 174 A4
Belmont Cres. Colch 50 B2
Belmont Pl. Colch 68 B3
Belsize Ave. Clact 124 B3
Belton Bridge. Hadl 198 B4
Belton Gdns. Hadl 198 B4
Belton Way E. Hadl 198 B4
Belton Way W. Hadl 198 A4
Belvawney Cl. Chelm 126 C3
Belvedere Ave. Hock 177 E3
Belvedere Cl. Dan 142 C4
Belvedere Pl. Mald 144 C4
Belvedere Rd. Burn 170 B2
Belvedere Rd. Dan 142 C4
Belvedere The. Burn 170 B2
Bembridge Cl. Clact 109 F4
Bemerton Gdns. Walt 93 E3
Benbow Dr. S Woo F 165 F3
Bendalls Ct. Lawf 35 E2
Benderloch. Canv 196 C3
Benedict Dr. Chelm 126 C1
Benfield Way. Brain 60 A1
Benfleet Park Rd. S Ben 187 D1
Benfleet Rd. S Ben 188 A2
Bennett Cl. Brain 78 A4
Bennett Cl. Walt 94 A4
Bennett Ct. Colch 68 C3
Bennett Way. Hat Pev 114 A2
Bennett's Ave. E Han 152 C2
Bentalls Cl. South 191 D2
Bentley Ave. Clact 124 C3
Bentley Rd. Lit Bro 53 E2
Bentley Rd. St O 90 B3
Bentley Rd. Weel 90 B3
Bentley Rd. With 97 F2
Bentleys The. South 190 A4
Benton Cl. T Gr 78 C3
Benvenue Ave. South 189 F3
Berdens. Basil 185 E3
Berechurch Hall Rd. Colch 85 F4
Berechurch Rd. Colch 67 F1
Berens Cl. Runw 163 F1
Beresford Cl. Hadl 188 B2
Beresford Gdns. Hadl 188 B2
Beresford Rd. South 200 B4
Berg Ave. Canv 197 E3
Bergen Ct. Mald 144 C4
Bergholt Rd. Colch 49 E1
Bergholt Rd. Str S M 35 D4
Beridge Rd. Hals 25 E1
Berkeley Ave. Canv 197 D2
Berkeley Gdns. Hadl 189 D1
Berkeley Rd. Clact 109 F3
Berkley Cl. Colch 50 B2
Berkshire Cl. South 189 E3
Bernard Cl. Walt 93 F3
Berners Wlk. Basil 185 E4
Bernside. Brain 59 F1
Berrimans Cl. Colch 68 B3
Berry Cl. Wick 174 A3
Berry Vale. S Woo F 165 F3
Bertram Ave. Lit Cla 91 E1
Berwick Ave. Chelm 127 D4
Beryl Rd. Harw 39 E1
Bethany St. Wiv 87 D4
Betjeman Cl. Brain 78 A4
Betjeman Cl. Rayl 176 C2
Betjemens Mews. South 191 D1
Bett's La. Hock 177 E3
Betts Green Rd. Lit Cla 91 E3
Beveland Rd. South 198 A2
Beverley Ave. Canv 197 D2
Beverley Ave. W Mers 121 F4
Beverley Dr. Walt 93 F4
Beverley Gdns. South 190 C2
Beverley Rd. Colch 67 E3
Bevington Mews. With 98 A1
Bickenhall. South 201 E4
Bickerton Point. S Woo F 165 F3
Bicknacre Rd. Dan 142 C2
Bicknacre Rd. E Han 153 E4
Bicknacre Rd. S Woo F 142 C2
Biddenden Ct. Basil 186 B3
Bideford Cl. South 190 A3
Bight The. S Woo F 165 F3
Bignalls Croft. Colch 50 B2
Bijou Cl. Tipt 100 B3
Billy's La. Str S M 22 B1
Bilsdale Cl. Colch 50 B2
Bilton Rd. Chelm 126 C1
Bilton Rd. Hadl 188 C2
Binley Rd. Sprin 127 F1
Birch Ave. Gt Ben 89 F4
Birch Ave. Harw 40 A2
Birch Cl. Brain 59 E1
Birch Cl. Brigh 106 C3
Birch Cl. Cane 168 C1
Birch Cl. Canv 196 C2
Birch Cl. Clact 109 E2
Birch Cl. Rayl 176 B2
Birch Cl. Thund 187 D4
Birch Cl. With 98 A2
Birch Gdns. Till 149 F2
Birch Green. Wick 174 B4
Birch Rd. Lay H 84 C3
Birch Rd. Till 149 F2
Birch Rise. Lit Brx 115 F3
Birch St. Birch 84 A2
Birch St. Nay 20 A1
Bircham Rd. South 191 D1
Birchdale. Hull 165 E2
Birche Cl. South 189 F2
Birches The. Thund 187 E4
Birches The. Walt 93 F3
Birches Wlk. Chelm 140 A1
Birchway. Birch 84 A1
Birchwood Cl. Tipt 100 C3
Birchwood Cl. W Mers 121 E3
Birchwood Dr. South 190 A1
Birchwood Rd. Ded 33 D2
Birchwood Rd. Purl 144 A1
Birchwood Way. Tipt 100 C3
Birchwood. Thund 187 D4
Bird La. Mess 100 C2
Birkdale Rise. Hat Pev 114 A2
Birkin Cl. Tipt 100 A2
Birs Cl. Runw 163 E1
Biscay. South 190 A4
Bishop Hall La. Chelm 127 D2
Bishop Rd. Chelm 127 D2
Bishop Rd. Colch 67 D2
Bishop's Ct. Canv 197 E2
Bishop's La. Twin 18 B2
Bishops Ave. Brain 60 A2
Bishops Cl. Basil 174 A1
Bishops La. Tipt 100 B4
Bishops Rd. Wick 174 B2
Bishopscourt Gdns. Sprin 127 F2
Bishopsteignton. South 192 B1
Bisley Cl. Clact 109 D3
Bittern Cl. Kelv 81 E1
Black Boy La. Wrab 38 A2
Blackberry Rd. Stanw 66 B2
Blackbrook Hill. Langh 33 D3
Blackbrook Rd. Gt Hor 49 E4
Blackfriars. Sud 12 B3
Blackgate Rd. South 202 A4
Blackheath. Colch 86 A4
Blackhouse La. Sud 13 E2
Blackley La. Gt Le 77 D2
Blacklock. Sprin 128 A2
Blackman Way. With 98 A1
Blackmore Ave. Canv 197 D1
Blackmore Wlk. Rayl 177 D1
Blacksmith Cl. Sprin 127 F4
Blacksmiths Hill. Cla 3 D2
Blacksmiths La. Bul 11 F1
Blacksmiths La. Wic Bis 115 F3
Blackthorn Cl. Writ 126 A1
Blackthorn Rd. Harw 39 F1
Blackthorn Rd. Hock 177 F4
Blackthorn Rd. With 97 F2
Blackthorne Ave. Colch 68 C4
Blackthorne Rd. Canv 197 E2
Blackwater Ave. Colch 50 C1
Blackwater Cl. Mald 132 C2
Blackwater Cl. South 192 C1
Blackwater Cl. Sprin 127 E3
Blackwater Dr. W Mer 121 D3
Blackwater La. With 115 D4
Blackwater Way. Brain 60 A2
Blackwood Chine. S Woo F 165 F3
Bladon Cl. Brain 59 F4
Bladon Cl. Tipt 100 C3
Blaine Dr. Walt 93 F4
Blake Cl. Lawf 35 D2
Blake Ct. S Woo F 165 F3
Blake Dr. Brain 60 B2
Blake Dr. Clact 109 E3
Blake Hall Dr. Wick 175 D3
Blake Rd. With 97 F3
Blamsters Cres. Hals 43 E4
Blanchard Cl. Walt 93 D4
Blatches Chase. South 189 F4
Blenheim Chase. South 189 F2
Blenheim Cl. S Woo F 142 C1
Blenheim Cres. South 189 F1
Blenheim Dr. Colch 86 A4
Blenheim Gdns. Steep 147 D1
Blenheim Mews. South 189 F2
Blenheim Park Cl. South 189 F2
Blenheim Rd. Clact 109 E1
Blenheim Way. Tipt 100 C3
Blenheim Cl. Brain 59 F4
Blind La. Birch 83 D2
Blind La. Brigh 106 C4
Blind La. Gold 133 E4
Blind La. Purl 145 E1
Blind La. Sand 141 F2
Blind La. Toll K 101 D1
Bloomfield Ave. Walt 93 F4
Blooms Hall La. Glems 2 C4
Blott Rise. With 114 C4
Blountswood Rd. Hull 177 D4
Blower Cl. Rayl 176 C2
Blue Bridge Cotts. Hals 26 A1
Blue House Ave. Clact 109 D2
Blue House Fm Chase. N Fam 167 D4
Blue Mill La. Woo Wa 130 C2
Blue Mills Hill. With 115 E4
Blue Rd. Tipt 100 B3
Bluebell Ave. Clact 109 E2
Bluebell Cl. With 97 F2
Bluebell Green. Sprin 127 F4
Bluebell Way. Colch 49 E1
Bluehouse. Basil 185 D3
Blundens The. Nay 20 B3
Blunt's Hall Dr. With 97 E1
Blunts Hall Rd. With 97 E1
Blyford Rd. Clact 109 D2
Blyth's Meadow. Brain 59 F2
Blythe Way. Thund 187 E4
Blyton Cl. Wick 174 B3
Boadicea Way. Colch 67 E2
Boars Tye Rd. Silv E 79 E3
Bobbing Cl. Roch 178 C1
Bobbits Way. Wiv 87 E4
Bober Ct. Rowh 86 A4
Bocking End. Brain 59 F2
Bocking's Gr. Clact 109 D3
Bockingham Green. Basil 186 A4
Bodmin Rd. Sprin 127 F3
Bohemia Chase. South 189 E3
Bois Field Terr. Hals 25 F1
Bois Hall Gdns. Hals 25 F2
Boley Dr. Clact 110 A2
Boley Rd. Wa Col 46 A4
Boleyn Cl. Rayl 189 E4

Boleyn Way. Bore 112 C1
Boleyn Way. Clact 124 C4
Boleyns Ave. Brain 59 F3
Bolls La. Lay H 84 C3
Bolney Dr. Rayl 189 E4
Bommel Ave. South 198 A2
Bonchurch Ave. South 189 E1
Bond St. Chelm 127 E1
Bonham Cl. Clact 110 A3
Bonington Chase. Sprin 127 F3
Bonnygate. Basil 185 E4
Boone Pl. With 98 A1
Booth Ave. Colch 68 B4
Borda Cl. Chelm 127 D3
Boreham Cl. Wick 175 D3
Boreham Rd. Gt Le 95 D2
Borley Rd. L. Mel 7 F3
Borman Cl. South 190 A3
Borrett Ave. Canv 197 D2
Borrowdale Cl. Thund 187 F3
Borrowdale Rd. Thund 187 F3
Boscawen Gdns. Brain 60 B2
Boscombe Rd. South 191 D1
Boston Ave. Rayl 176 A2
Boston Ave. South 190 C1
Boswell Ave. Roch 178 B3
Boswells Dr. Chelm 127 E1
Bosworth Cl. Hawk 177 F2
Bosworth Rd. Rayl 176 A2
Botanical Way. St O 108 A3
Botany La. Weel 91 E3
Bouchers Mead. Sprin 127 F4
Bouldrewood Rd. S Ben 187 D3
Boulevard The. Roch 178 C2
Boulton Cotts. Mald 132 A3
Boundary Rd. Colch 68 C2
Boundary Rd. Rayl 189 D4
Bounderby Gr. Chelm 126 C3
Bounstead Hill. Lay H 85 E3
Bounstead Rd. Colch 85 E4
Bourchier Way. Hals 43 E4
Bourne Cl. Hals 43 E4
Bourne Rd. Colch 68 A2
Bourne Rd. W Berg 48 C1
Bournebridge Hill. Hals 43 D3
Bournemouth Park Rd. South 191 D1
Bournemouth Rd. Clact 110 C3
Bournes Green Chase. South 192 A1
Bouvel Dr. Burn 170 A4
Bouverie Rd. Chelm 41 E1
Bovingdon Rd. Brain 41 F1
Bower Way. South 191 F1
Bowbank Cl. South 192 C1
Bowdens La. Worm 29 F4
Bower Gdns. Mald 131 F2
Bower Hall La. W Mers 104 C1
Bower La. Basil 185 F4
Bowers Cl. Silv E 79 F2
Bowers Court Dr. Basil 186 C3
Bowers Rd. S Ben 187 E3
Bowes Rd. Elmst M 69 E1
Bowman Ave. Rayl 189 D3
Bowman's Park. Ca Hed 15 F2
Box Mill La. Hals 25 F2
Boxford Cl. Rayl 175 F2
Boxhouse La. Ded 33 E3
Boxted Church Rd. Gt Hor 31 E2
Boxted Cl. Colch 49 F3
Boxted Rd. Gt Hor 31 E2
Boyce Green. S Ben 187 E1
Boyce Hill Cl. Hadl 189 D3
Boyce Rd. South 202 A4
Boyce View Dr. S Ben 187 E1
Boyden Cl. South 191 F1
Boydin Cl. With 114 C4
Boyles Ct. Rowh 86 A4
Boyne Dr. Sprin 127 E3
Boyton Cl. Thund 187 F3
Brabant Rd. N Fam 167 D4
Brace Wlk. S Woo F 165 F3
Bracken Dell. Rayl 176 C1
Bracken The. Colch 50 A2
Bracken Way. Lang 86 A1
Bracken Way. Thund 188 A3
Brackendale Ave. Basil 186 B2
Brackendale Cl. Hock 177 F4
Brackenden Dr. Sprin 127 E4
Brackley Cres. Basil 174 A1
Bradbourne Way. Basil 186 B3
Bradbrook Cotts. W Berg 48 C2
Bradbury Dr. Brain 59 E2
Bradfield Rd. Wix 55 D4
Bradford St. Brain 60 A1
Bradford St. Chelm 127 D1
Bradfordbury. Hadl 189 E3
Brading Ave. Clact 110 A4
Bradley Ave. Thund 187 F3
Bradley Cl. Canv 197 D3
Bradley Cl. Thund 187 F3
Bradley Green. Basil 174 B1
Bradley Hill. Ovi 4 A3
Bradley Way. Roch 178 C1
Bradleyhall La. Th L S 73 E2
Bradwell Cl. Brain 78 B4
Bradwell Rd. Brad O S 149 D4
Bradwell Rd. St L 148 C3
Bradwell Rd. Steep 147 E4
Bradwell Rd. Till 149 F3
Braemar Ave. Chelm 140 A4

Braemar Cres. Hadl 189 D1
Braemore Cl. Colch 50 B2
Braemore. Canv 196 C3
Braggon's Hill. Glems 2 A4
Brain Rd. With 97 F2
Brain Valley Ave. Bl Not 78 A3
Braintree Rd. Gos 42 C3
Braintree Rd. T Gr 78 C4
Braintree Rd. Terl 96 A2
Braintree Rd. With 97 F2
Braiswick La. Colch 49 E2
Braiswick. Colch 49 D1
Bramble Cl. Rayl 189 D4
Bramble Cres. Hadl 189 D3
Bramble Rd. Canv 197 E2
Bramble Rd. Hadl 188 C3
Bramble Rd. Rayl 189 D4
Bramble Rd. With 97 F2
Brambles The. Colch 66 C2
Brambles. Walt 94 A4
Bramerton Rd. Hock 177 E3
Bramfield Rd E. Rayl 177 D1
Bramfield Rd W. Rayl 176 C1
Bramley Cl. Alres 88 A4
Bramley Cl. Brain 60 A2
Bramley Cl. Colch 67 D4
Bramley Way. May 146 C1
Bramleys The. Cogg 63 D2
Bramleys The. Hawk 178 B3
Brampton Cl. South 190 A2
Bramston Green. With 97 F2
Bramston Wlk. With 97 F2
Bramstone Ct. Gt Bad 140 C4
Bramwoods Rd. Gt Bad 140 C4
Branch Rd. Hadl 188 C1
Brandenburg Rd. Canv 197 E3
Brandon Rd. Brain 59 E1
Brands Cl. Sud 13 E3
Branksome Ave. Hock 177 F4
Branksome Rd. South 191 E1
Branscombe Cl. Frin 93 F3
Branscombe Gdns. South 201 D4
Branscombe Sq. South 192 A1
Branscombe Wlk. South 192 A1
Branston Rd. Clact 109 E3
Brantham Hill. Catt 35 E4
Braxted Cl. Hawk 178 B2
Braxted La. Gt Tot 116 B4
Braxted Rd. Gt Brx 99 E1
Braxted Rd. Lit Brx 116 A3
Bray Ct. South 192 C1
Braybrooke. Basil 185 E3
Brays La. Roth 178 C3
Braziers Cl. Chelm 140 B2
Breachfield Rd. Colch 67 E1
Bread and Cheese Hill. Thund 187 F3
Bream Ct. Colch 50 C1
Brecon Cl. Basil 186 B4
Bree Ave. Mks T 64 C2
Bree Hill. S Woo F 165 E3
Brempsons. Basil 185 D4
Brendon Pl. Chelm 126 C1
Brendon Way. South 190 A3
Brent Ave. S Woo F 154 B1
Brent Cl. Walt 93 F4
Brent Cl. With 97 F1
Brentwood Rd. Clact 110 B3
Bressingham Gdns. S Woo F 165 E4
Brettenham Dr. South 200 C4
Bretts Bldgs. Colch 68 A3
Brewster Cl. Canv 197 E2
Brian Bishop Cl. Walt 76 B2
Brian Cl. Chelm 140 A3
Briar Cl. Hawk 177 F2
Briar Rd. Gt Bro 52 A2
Briardale Ave. Harw 39 F2
Briarfields. Walt 93 E4
Briarswood. Canv 197 D3
Briarswood. Sprin 127 E4
Briarwood Ave. Clact 110 C3
Briarwood Cl. South 189 E3
Briarwood Dr. South 189 F3
Briarwood End. Colch 50 A2
Briary The. Wick 174 A4
Brices Way. Glems 2 A3
Brick House La. Bore 112 C1
Brick House Rd. Toll M 117 D4
Brick Kiln Cl. Cogg 63 D2
Brick Kiln La. Alres 88 C3
Brick Kiln La. Gt Hor 49 D4
Brick Kiln Rd. Colch 49 F1
Brick Kiln Rd. Sand 141 E4
Brick St. E A Gr 48 A1
Brickfield Rd. Basil 185 E1
Brickfields Rd. S Woo F 165 F4
Brickfields Way. Roch 179 D1
Brickhouse Cl. W Mers 121 E4
Brickhouse Rd. Col En 27 D2
Brickman's Hill. Brad 36 B2
Brickspring La. Gt Tot 116 B4
Brickwall Ct. Burn 170 A2
Bridewell St. Cla 4 A4
Bridge Cl. South 201 F4
Bridge Hall Rd. Bradw 61 E2
Bridge Hill. Ford 47 E4
Bridge House Cl. Wick 174 B4
Bridge Pl. Catt 35 E4
Bridge Rd. Wick 175 D4
Bridge St. Bures 19 F1

Bridge St. Cogg 62 C1
Bridge St. Gt Y 9 D1
Bridge St. Hals 25 F1
Bridge St. With 97 F1
Bridge St. Writ 126 B1
Bridgebrook Cl. Colch 50 B1
Bridgefield Cl. Colch 68 B4
Bridgemans Green. Latch 157 D3
Bridgemarsh La. Alth 168 C4
Bridgend Cl. S Woo F 165 F4
Bridgewater Dr. South 190 A2
Bridgewick Rd. Deng 161 D3
Bridon Cl. E Han 153 D3
Bridport Rd. Sprin 127 E3
Bridport Way. Brain 60 B2
Brierley Ave. W Mers 121 F4
Bright Cl. Clact 109 E3
Brighten Rd. South 199 F4
Brightlingsea Rd. Thor 88 C2
Brightlingsea Rd. Wiv 69 E2
Brighton Ave. South 200 B4
Brighton Rd. Clact 110 C3
Brightside. Walt 93 F4
Brightwell Ave. South 190 B1
Brindles. Canv 196 C3
Brindley Rd. Clact 110 A4
Bringey The. Gt Bad 141 D3
Brinkley Cres. Colch 50 B1
Brinkley La. Colch 50 B3
Brinkworth Cl. Hock 177 F3
Brisbane Way. Colch 68 A1
Briscoe Rd. Basil 186 A4
Brise Cl. Brain 60 A2
Bristol Cl. Rayl 176 B3
Bristol Ct. Silv E 79 F2
Bristol Hill. Sho G 40 A4
Bristol Rd. Colch 68 A4
Bristol Rd. South 190 B3
Bristowe Ave. Gt Bad 141 D3
Britannia Cr. Wiv 69 D1
Britannia Ct. Basil 174 B1
Britannia Gdns. South 199 E4
Britannia Rd. South 199 E4
Brittany Way. Colch 68 A2
Brixham Cl. Rayl 176 B3
Broad Cl. Hock 177 F3
Broad Green. Basil 185 E4
Broad La. Gt Hor 31 D1
Broad Oak Way. Rayl 176 C1
Broad Oaks Park. Colch 50 C1
Broad Rd. Wick 174 C3
Broad Par. Hock 177 F3
Broad Rd. Brain 60 A4
Broad Rd. Wic S P 17 D4
Broad Street Green Rd. Gt Tot 116 A1
Broad Street Green Rd. Mald 132 B4
Broad Way. Hock 177 F3
Broad Wlk. Hock 177 F3
Broadclyst Ave. South 189 E3
Broadclyst Cl. South 192 A1
Broadclyst Gdns. South 192 A1
Broadfields. Wiv 69 E2
Broadlands Ave. Hock 177 F2
Broadlands Rd. Hock 177 F3
Broadlands Way. Colch 50 A1
Broadlands. Thund 187 F3
Broadlawn. Hadl 189 D2
Broadmayne. Basil 185 E3
Broadmead Rd. Colch 50 C1
Broadmere Cl. Clact 110 C4
Broadstrood. St O 108 A3
Broadwater Gdns. Sho G 40 A4
Broadway Cl. Silv E 79 E3
Broadway North. Basil 186 A3
Broadway The. South 201 D4
Broadway The. South 201 D4
Broadway W. South 198 B4
Broadway. Clact 125 D4
Broadway. Glems 2 A3
Broadway. Silv E 79 E2
Broadway. South 198 B4
Brock Cl. With 114 C4
Brock Hill. Dt Runw 163 E2
Brock Hill. Runw 163 E2
Brockenhurst Way. S Woo F 142 C1
Brockham Cl. Clact 109 D3
Brockley Rd. Chelm 127 E1
Brocksford Ave. Rayl 176 C1
Brockwell La. Kelv 81 E1
Brockwell Wlk. Wick 174 B3
Brodie Rd. South 202 A4
Brograve Cl. Chelm 140 B2
Broman's La. E Mers 106 A1
Bromfords Cl. Wick 174 B3
Bromfords Dr. Wick 174 B3
Bromley Rd. Ard 51 E2
Bromley Rd. Colch 50 C1
Bromley Rd. Elmst M 70 A3
Bromley Rd. Frat 71 D2
Bromley Rd. Lawf 35 D1
Brompton Gdns. Mald 144 C4
Bronte Cl. Brain 78 A4
Bronte Mews. South 191 D1
Bronte Rd. With 97 F3
Brook Cl. Brain 59 E1
Brook Cl. Gt Tot 116 A2

Brook Cl. Roch 191 D4
Brook Cl. Tipt 100 C2
Brook Cl. Woo Wa 130 B1
Brook Dr. Basil 185 E1
Brook Dr. Wick 174 B3
Brook End Rd. Sprin 128 A2
Brook Farm Cl. Hals 26 A1
Brook Hall Rd. Fing 87 D3
Brook La. Chelm 140 C2
Brook La. Sprin 128 A1
Brook La. W Han 140 C2
Brook Meadow. Si Hed 15 E1
Brook Pl. Hals 25 F1
Brook Rd. Ald 65 D4
Brook Rd. Gt T 64 B4
Brook Rd. Rayl 188 B4
Brook Rd. S Ben 187 E1
Brook Rd. Till 149 E3
Brook Rd. Toll K 101 D1
Brook St. Col En 26 C4
Brook St. Colch 68 A4
Brook St. Ded 33 F4
Brook St. Glems 2 A3
Brook St. Gt Bro 52 C1
Brook St. Mann 35 E2
Brook St. Wiv 87 D4
Brook Terr. Si Hed 15 F1
Brook Vale. St O 108 A2
Brook View. Sand 141 E3
Brook Wlk. With 114 C4
Brooke Sq. Mald 132 A1
Brookfields Cl. South 189 E3
Brookfields. South 189 E3
Brookhouse Rd. Gt T 64 A4
Brookhurst Cl. Sprin 127 E2
Brookland. Tipt 100 B2
Brooklands Ave. South 189 F3
Brooklands Gdns. Clact 124 C3
Brooklands Gdns. Catt 35 E4
Brooklands Rise. Catt 35 E4
Brooklands Sq. Canv 196 C2
Brooklands Wlk. Chelm 140 A4
Brooklands. Clact 124 C3
Brooklands. Wick 174 A4
Brooklyn Dr. Rayl 176 B3
Brooklyn Rd. Harw 40 A1
Brookside Ave. Gt Wak 193 E1
Brookside. Colch 68 A2
Brookside. Canv 197 D3
Brookside. Hawk 177 F2
Broom Hill. Hals 25 F1
Broom Rd. Hadl 165 F1
Broom St. Sud 13 D3
Broom Way. Lang 86 A1
Broome Gr. Wiv 69 D1
Broomfield Ave. Rayl 176 A2
Broomfield Ave. South 189 F3
Broomfield Cres. Wiv 69 D1
Broomfield Green. Canv 196 C3
Broomfield Rd. Chelm 127 D3
Broomfield. Hadl 188 B2
Broomfield. Silv E 79 E3
Broomfields. Basil 186 A3
Broomhills Rd. W Mers 121 E3
Broomways. Gt Wak 193 E2
Brosdon Dr. Hals 25 F1
Brougham Cl. Gt Wak 193 D2
Brougham Glades. Stanw 66 B3
Broughton Cl. Colch 67 E2
Broughton Rd. Hadl 188 C1
Broughton Rd. S Woo F 165 F3
Browning Ave. South 191 D1
Browning Cl. Colch 66 C3
Browning Rd. Mald 145 D4
Brownings Ave. Chelm 127 E3
Brownlow Bend. Basil 185 E3
Brownlow Cross. Basil 185 E3
Brownlow Green. Basil 185 E3
Browns Ave. Runw 163 F1
Brownsea Way. Colch 67 D2
Broxted Dr. Wick 174 C3
Broxted End. Wick 174 C3
Bruce Gr. Chelm 140 A4
Bruce Gr. Wick 175 D4
Bruff Dr. Walt 94 A4
Bruges Rd. Canv 197 E1
Brundells Rd. Gt Bro 71 D4
Brunel Cl. Basil 186 A3
Brundon La. Sud 12 B4
Brunel Rd. Brain 60 A1
Brunel Rd. Clact 110 A4
Brunel Rd. South 189 E3
Brunel Rd. Thund 187 E4
Brunel Way. Colch 50 B3
Brunswick House Cut. Mist 36 B2
Brunswick Rd. South 200 B4
Brunwins Cl. Wick 174 C4
Brussum Rd. Canv 197 E1
Brust Rd. Canv 197 E1
Bruton Ave. South 190 A3
Bryanston Ave. Colch 66 C3
Bryant Ave. South 200 C3
Bryant's La. Woo Mor 143 E4
Bryce Way. Basil 186 B3
Buchan Cl. Brain 78 A4
Buchanan Way. Latch 157 D3

Buck Hill. Bl Not 77 F3
Buckeridge Way. Brad O S 137 D2
Buckerills. Basil 186 A3
Bucklast Ave. Walt 93 E3
Buckhatch La. Rett 153 E2
Buckingham Dr. Colch 68 C4
Buckingham Rd. Hock 177 E3
Buckingham Sq. Wick 175 D3
Buckland Gate. S Woo F 165 E3
Buckland. South 192 B1
Bucklebury Heath. S Woo F 165 E3
Buckley's La. Gt T 63 E3
Bucklleys Cl. Wic Bis 115 F3
Buckleys. Gt Bad 140 C4
Buckwins Sq. Basil 174 B1
Buckwoods Rd. Brain 60 A1
Buddleia Dr. Wiv 69 D1
Budna Rd. Canv 196 C3
Buffett Way. Colch 68 C3
Buglers Rise. Writ 139 D4
Buick Ave. Clact 124 B3
Bulbecks Wlk. S Woo F 165 E3
Bulford La. Bl Not 78 B3
Bulford Mill La. T Gr 78 B3
Bull Hill Rd. Clact 109 F3
Bull La. Hock 177 E3
Bull La. L Mel 7 F4
Bull La. Mald 132 A2
Bull La. Rayl 176 C1
Bull La. Tipt 100 B2
Bull's Hill. Ca Hed 15 F2
Bullace Cl. Colch 50 B2
Bullfen Wlk. Chelm 140 B2
Buller Rd. N Fam 156 A1
Bullfinch Cl. Colch 68 C4
Bullock Wood Cl. Colch 50 B2
Bullocks La. Sud 12 C3
Bullwood App. Hock 177 E3
Bullwood Hall La. Rayl 177 D2
Bullwood Rd. Hock 177 E3
Bulmer Rd. Sud 12 B2
Bulmer St. Bul 11 E2
Bulow Ave. Canv 197 D2
Bulphan Cl. Wick 174 C3
Bulwark Rd. South 201 F4
Bumfords La. Hat Pev 130 A4
Bumfords La. Lit 130 A4
Bundick's Hill. Chelm 126 C2
Bung Row. Gt Brx 99 E1
Bunters Ave. South 201 E3
Bunting Cl. Chelm 140 A3
Bunyan Rd. Brain 59 E2
Burches Mead. Thund 188 A4
Burches Rd. Thund 187 F4
Burdett Ave. South 199 F4
Burdett Rd. South 200 B4
Burdun Cl. With 114 B4
Bure Dr. With 97 E2
Buren Ave. Canv 197 E1
Bures Rd. Bures 30 A4
Bures Rd. Sud 13 D2
Burfield Cl. South 189 E3
Burfield Rd. South 189 E3
Burgate Cl. Clact 109 D2
Burges Cl. South 201 E3
Burges Rd. South 201 D3
Burges Terr. South 200 C3
Burgess Field. Sprin 127 F2
Burgundy Gdns. Basil 186 A4
Burkitts La. Sud 12 C4
Burleigh Sq. South 201 D4
Burlescombe Leas. South 192 A1
Burlescombe Rd. South 192 A1
Burlington Ct. Basil 174 A1
Burlington Gdns. Hadl 188 C2
Burlington Gdns. Hull 176 C4
Burlington Rd. Colch 67 F4
Burmanny Cl. Clact 109 E2
Burnaby Rd. South 200 B4
Burne Ave. Wick 174 C3
Burnham Ave. Col N 156 A3
Burnham Cl. Walt 94 A4
Burnham Rd. Alth 158 A1
Burnham Rd. Latch 157 D2
Burnham Rd. Mund 156 B4
Burnham Rd. S Woo F 154 B4
Burnham Rd. South 191 D1
Burnham Rd. Woo Mor 143 F3
Burns Ave. Basil 186 A3
Burns Ave. Colch 66 C3
Burns Cl. Mald 132 A1
Burns Cres. Chelm 140 B4
Burns Way. S Woo F 165 E4
Burnside Cres. Chelm 127 D3
Burnside. Canv 197 D3
Burnt Dick Hill. Box 31 F4
Burnt Mills Rd. Basil 174 B1
Burnthouse Rd. Ea Col 45 F1
Burr Cl. Lit Oak 39 E1
Burr Hill Chase. South 191 F2
Burroughs Piece Rd. Sud 12 C4
Burrow's Rd. Ea Col 45 D4
Burrows Cl. Clact 124 C3
Burrows Cl. Lawf 35 D2
Burrows Way. Rayl 176 B1

211
Burrs Rd. Clact
Cherrytree Rd. Sud

Burrs Rd. Clact 110 A4
Burrswood Pl. Mald 132 C2
Burstall Cl. Clact 109 D2
Burton Pl. Sprin 127 F2
Burton's Green Rd. Hals 44 A2
Burwell Ave. Canv 196 C3
Bury Cl. Colch 68 A4
Bury Cl. Mks T 64 C2
Bury La. Hat Pev 113 F2
Bury The. St O 108 A2
Burywoods. Colch 49 D2
Bush Gr. Sud 12 B3
Bushell Way. Walt 93 F3
Bushey Cl. S Woo F 165 F4
Butchers La. Walt 94 A4
Butler Rd. Hals 25 E1
Butler's La. Wrab 37 F1
Butlers Way. Gt Y 9 D1
Butneys. Basil 185 D4
Butt La. Mald 132 A2
Butt Rd. Colch 67 F3
Butt Rd. Nay 20 B3
Butt Rd. Sud 13 D3
Butt's Green Rd. Dan 142 A2
Butt's Green Rd. Sand 141 F2
Butterbur Chase. S Woo F 165 E3
Buttercup Wlk. With 97 F2
Buttercup Wlk. With 97 F2
Butterfield Rd. Bore 128 C4
Buttermere. Bl Not 77 E4
Butterys. South 200 C4
Button's Hill. Alth 158 A2
Butts La. Dan 142 C4
Butts Paddock. Cane 168 B1
Butts Rd. South 193 E1
Butts Way. Chelm 139 F2
Buxey Cl. W Mers 121 D4
Buxton Ave. Hadl 189 D2
Buxton Cl. Hadl 189 D2
Buxton Rd. Cogg 62 C2
Buxton Rd. Colch 68 A2
Buxton Sq. Hadl 189 D2
Buyl Ave. Canv 197 D3
Byfield. South 189 F4
Byfleets. Basil 185 F2
Byford Cl. Rayl 176 C2
Byng Cres. Th L S 74 A1
Byng Gdns. Brain 60 B2
Bypass Rd. St O 108 A3
Byrne Dr. South 190 C2
Byron Ave. Colch 66 C4
Byron Ave. South 191 D1
Byron Cl. Brain 78 A4
Byron Cl. Canv 197 E2
Byron Dr. Wic Bis 115 F3
Byron Rd. Chelm 127 E1
Byrony Cl. With 97 E2
Bywater Rd. S Woo F 165 E3

Cabinet Way. South 189 E3
Cadenhouse Mews. Colch 66 C4
Caernarvon Cl. Hock 177 E3
Cage Field Cotts. Gt Stam 179 F2
Cage La. Box 32 A3
Cagefield Rd. Gt Stam 179 F2
Cairns Rd. Colch 68 A1
Calamint Rd. With 97 E2
Caldbeck Way. Bl Not 77 E3
Caledonia Rd. Sho G 40 A4
California Cl. Colch 50 A2
California Rd. Mist 36 A2
Callis St. Cla 4 A4
Calm Patch. Burn 170 B2
Calvert Dr. Basil 174 B1
Calves La. Nay 20 A4
Cam Way. With 97 E1
Camberton Rd. Brain 59 F3
Camborne Cl. Sprin 127 F3
Cambrai Rd. Colch 67 E2
Cambria Cl. Canv 196 B2
Cambria Cl. Mist 36 A2
Cambridge Gdns. Hawk 178 B3
Cambridge Rd. Canv 196 C2
Cambridge Rd. Clact 109 F2
Cambridge Rd. Colch 67 E3
Cambridge Rd. Frin 94 A3
Cambridge Rd. South 199 F4
Cambridge Way. Bures 28 C4
Cambridge Wlk. Colch 67 E3
Camellia Ave. Clact 109 E2
Camellia Cl. Sprin 127 F3
Camellia Cres. Clact 109 E2
Camelot Gdns. Basil 186 B4
Cameron Cl. Hadl 189 E1
Camoise Cl. Topp 14 A4
Camomile Way. Colch 49 E1
Camp Folley N. Colch 68 A3
Camp Folley S. Colch 68 A3
Camp Rd. Gt Bro 71 D4
Campbell Cl. Chelm 140 A4
Campbell Cl. Wick 174 B3
Campbell Dr. Colch 50 C1
Campbell Rd. With 97 F3
Camper Rd. South 200 B3
Camperdown Rd. Canv 197 E3
Campernell. Brigh 106 C4
Campfield Rd. South 201 F3
Campion Rd. Colch 68 A3
Campion Way. With 97 F2
Campions Hill. Bures 30 B4
Camulodunum Way. Colch 67 E1
Canberra Cl. Chelm 126 C3
Canberra Cl. Colch 68 A1
Candlemakers The. South 191 D3
Candytuft Rd. Sprin 127 F3
Canendon View Rd. Ashi 178 B3
Canewdon Cl. Runw 163 E1
Canewdon Gdns. Runw 163 E1
Canewdon Hall Cl. Cane 168 B1
Canewdon Rd. Ashi 178 B4
Canewdon Rd. South 199 F4
Canford Cl. Gt Bad 140 C4
Canhams Rd. Sud 13 E3
Canney Rd. Steep 147 E2
Canning St. Harw 40 B3
Cannon Leys. Chelm 140 B2
Cannon Rd. Colch 68 A3
Cannon St. Colch 68 A3
Cannons Cl. Colch 67 E2
Canons Cl. S Woo F 142 C1
Canonsleigh Cres. South 189 F1
Cansey La. Brad 54 C3
Canterbury Ave. South 191 F2
Canterbury Cl. Basil 185 F4
Canterbury Rd. Clact 110 C3
Canterbury Rd. Colch 68 A3
Canterbury Rd. Sud 7 E1
Canterbury Way. Chelm 126 C2
Canters The. Thund 188 A3
Canuden Rd. Chelm 126 C1
Canute Cl. Cane 168 C1
Canvey Rd. Basil 186 C3
Canvey Rd. Canv 196 B2
Canvey Rd. Hadl 189 D1
Canvey Way. S Ben 187 D2
Canvey Wlk. Sprin 127 F3
Canwick Gr. Colch 68 B2
Cap Pillar Cl. Wiv 69 D1
Capadocia St. South 200 C3
Cape Cl. Colch 66 C3
Capel Cl. Chelm 127 D4
Capel Park. Walt 93 F4
Capel Rd. Colch 67 E3
Capel Terr. South 200 A4
Caper La. Birch 83 F2
Capons La. Dan 143 D3
Captains Rd. W Mers 121 D3
Captains Wood Rd. Gt Tot 116 A2
Card's Rd. Sand 141 E3
Cardigan Ave. South 190 B2
Cardinal Cl. Colch 69 D4
Carisbrooke Ave. Clact 110 A4
Carisbrooke Dr. S Woo F 165 E3
Carisbrooke Rd. South 190 C1
Carlingford Dr. South 190 B2
Carlisle Cl. Colch 68 A4
Carlton Ave. South 190 B2
Carlton Cl. Gt Y 9 D1
Carlton Dr. South 198 C4
Carlton Dr. Thund 188 B2
Carlton Rd. Basil 186 C4
Carlton Rd. Clact 110 A3
Carlton Rd. Runw 163 E1
Carmania Cl. South 192 C1
Carnarvon Rd. Clact 109 F2
Carnarvon Rd. South 190 C1
Carnation Cl. Sprin 127 F3
Carnival Gdns. South 189 E2
Caro Rd. Canv 197 E2
Carolina Way. Tipt 100 B3
Caroline Cl. Wiv 69 E2
Caroline's Cl. South 190 C3
Carpenters. Barl 192 C3
Carraways. With 115 D4
Carriage Dr. Sprin 127 F4
Carrington Ct. W Mers 121 E4
Carrington Way. Brain 59 F4
Carringtons Rd. Gt Bro 52 B2
Carroll Gdns. Wick 174 B3
Carron Mead. S Woo F 165 F3
Carrs Rd. Clact 109 E2
Carruthers Cl. Runw 163 E1
Carruthers Dr. Runw 163 E1
Carshalton End. Colch 66 C2
Carsons Dr. Sud 13 E3
Cartbridge Cl. Walt 94 A4
Carters Cl. Clact 109 D2
Carters Hill. Box 32 A3
Carters La. Lit Brx 115 F3
Cartlodge Ave. Wick 174 C4
Cartwright Rd. Thund 187 E4
Cartwright Wlk. Sprin 127 F1
Cashiobury Terr. South 199 F4
Cashmere Way. Basil 185 E1
Cassel Ave. Canv 197 E3
Cassino Rd. Chelm 126 C3
Cassino Rd. Colch 67 E2
Castle Ave. Hadl 188 B1
Castle Bailey. Colch 67 F4
Castle Cl. Ca Hed 15 F2
Castle Cl. Rayl 176 B1
Castle Cl. South 202 A4
Castle Dr. Hadl 198 A4
Castle Dr. Rayl 176 B2
Castle Hill. Ded 33 F3
Castle La. Ca Hed 15 F2
Castle La. Hadl 188 C1
Castle Rd. Clact 109 F2
Castle Rd. Colch 68 A4
Castle Rd. Hadl 188 C1
Castle Rd. Rayl 176 B1
Castle Terr. Rayl 176 B1
Castle View Rd. Canv 197 D3
Castle Way. St O 108 A2
Castle Wlk. Canv 197 D3
Castlegate St. Harw 40 B3
Castleton Rd. South 191 F1
Castleward Cl. Elmst M 87 E4
Caswell Mews. Sprin 127 F1
Cat's La. Sud 13 D4
Catchpole La. Gt Tot 116 A2
Catchpool Rd. Colch 67 F4
Caterham Cl. Clact 109 E3
Cathederal Wlk. Chelm 127 D2
Catherine Cl. Clact 110 A3
Catherine Cl. E Han 153 D3
Catherine Hunt Way. Colch 67 E1
Catherine Rd. S Ben 187 F2
Catherines Cl. Gt Le 95 D3
Cattawade End. Basil 185 E4
Cattawade Link. Basil 185 E4
Cattawade St. Catt 35 E4
Caulfield Rd. South 201 E4
Causeway Cl. Glems 2 B3
Causeway Reach. Clact 109 F4
Causeway The. Brain 59 F2
Causeway The. Colch 50 B1
Causeway The. Gt Bad 140 C4
Causeway The. Gt Hor 31 D1
Causeway The. Hals 25 F1
Causeway The. Mald 132 A2
Causeway The. Ridge 8 A4
Causeway The. Topp 14 A4
Causeway The. Ult 130 B3
Causewayend. Lawf 35 D3
Causton Rd. Colch 67 F4
Caustones Cl. Sud 13 E3
Caustonway. Rayl 176 B2
Cavendish Ave. Colch 68 B2
Cavendish Dr. Clact 109 D2
Cavendish Dr. Lawf 35 D2
Cavendish Gdns. Brain 60 B3
Cavendish Gdns. South 190 A1
Cavendish La. Cav 1 C2
Cavendish La. Glems 2 A3
Cavendish Rd. Ashi 166 C1
Cavendish Rd. Cla 4 B4
Cavendish Way. Sud 12 C4
Caversham Ave. South 192 C1
Caversham Park Ave. Rayl 176 B3
Cawkwell Cl. Sprin 128 A2
Cecil Way. Rayl 176 C1
Cedar Ave. Brigh 106 C4
Cedar Ave. Chelm 127 D2
Cedar Ave. Tipt 100 B4
Cedar Ave. Wick 174 B3
Cedar Avenue W. Chelm 127 D2
Cedar Chase. Mald 132 B3
Cedar Cl. Rayl 188 C4
Cedar Cl. South 191 D1
Cedar Cl. Walt 94 A4
Cedar Cres. Lawf 35 E2
Cedar Dr. Hull 165 F1
Cedar Dr. With 98 A3
Cedar Gr. Burn 170 A3
Cedar Hall Gdns. Thund 188 A3
Cedar Mews. Hock 177 E3
Cedar Park Cl. Thund 188 A4
Cedar Rd. Basil 186 C4
Cedar Rd. Canv 196 C2
Cedar Rd. Thund 188 A3
Cedar Way. Gt Ben 89 F4
Cedar Wlk. Cane 168 B1
Cedars Rd. Colch 67 F3
Cedars The. Gt Wak 193 D2
Cedars The. S Woo F 165 E4
Celeborn St. S Woo F 165 D3
Centaury Cl. Stanw 66 B4
Central Ave. Canv 196 C3
Central Ave. Frin 94 A3
Central Ave. Hadl 188 C3
Central Ave. Hawk 178 B3
Central Ave. Hull 176 C4
Central Ave. South 191 E1
Central Ave. Walt 94 A3
Central Cl. Hadl 188 C2
Central Sq. Chelm 127 D1
Central Wall Cotts. Canv 197 D3
Central Wall Rd. Canv 197 D3
Central Wall. Canv 197 D3
Centre The. Hals 25 F1
Centurion Cl. South 201 F4
Ceylon Rd. South 199 E4
Chadacre Rd. South 192 A1
Chadburn Rd. L Mel 7 E4
Chadwick Rd. S Woo F 154 C1
Chadwick Rd. South 199 E4
Chaffinch Cl. South 201 F4
Chaffinch Gdns. Colch 68 C4
Chaingate Ave. South 191 F1
Chalfont Cl. South 189 E2
Chalfont Rd. Colch 50 B2
Chalk End. Basil 186 A3
Chalk St. Rett 163 F4
Chalklands. Sand 141 E2
Chalkwell Ave. South 199 D4
Chalkwell Espl. South 199 D4
Chalkwell Park Dr. South 189 F1
Challacombe. South 192 B1
Challenge Way. Colch 68 A3
Challis La. Brain 59 F1
Challis La. Brain 78 A4
Challock Lees. Basil 186 B3
Chalvedon Ave. Basil 186 A4
Chamberlain Ave. Canv 197 E2
Chamberlain Ave. Walt 94 A4
Chamberlains Rd. S Woo F 165 E3
Champion Cl. Wick 174 B3
Champions Way. S Woo F 165 E4
Champlain Ave. Canv 196 C3
Chancel Cl. Thund 187 E3
Chancel Cl. Till 149 F2
Chancellor Rd. South 200 A4
Chancery Grove. Colch 86 A4
Chancery Pl. Writ 126 A1
Chandlers Cl. Clact 109 D2
Chandlers Cl. W Mers 121 E4
Chandlers Ct. W Mers 121 E4
Chandlers Row. Colch 68 B3
Chandlers Way. S Woo F 165 F4
Chandlers Way. South 191 D3
Chandos Par. Hadl 188 C2
Chaney Rd. Wiv 69 D1
Chanterelle. Colch 50 A2
Chanton Cl. South 189 E4
Chantry La. Bore 113 D2
Chantry The. Colch 67 E4
Chapel Ct. Ard 51 F4
Chapel Cut. Mist 36 A2
Chapel Hill. Bel W 10 B2
Chapel Hill. Brain 60 A1
Chapel Hill. Hals 25 E1
Chapel La. Ard 51 D1
Chapel La. Box 32 A2
Chapel La. Elmst M 70 A3
Chapel La. Gt Bro 71 D3
Chapel La. Gt Wak 193 D2
Chapel La. High 21 E3
Chapel La. Lit Bad 129 D2
Chapel La. Mald 132 C1
Chapel La. Purl 155 E4
Chapel La. S Ben 188 B2
Chapel La. St O 108 A2
Chapel La. Sud 13 E1
Chapel La. Tend 72 C4
Chapel La. Thor 89 D3
Chapel La. Till 149 F2
Chapel La. W Berg 48 C2
Chapel La. Walt 93 D3
Chapel Rd. Beau 73 F4
Chapel Rd. Box 32 A2
Chapel Rd. Brigh 107 D4
Chapel Rd. Burn 170 B2
Chapel Rd. Gt Tot 116 B3
Chapel Rd. Langh 32 B2
Chapel Rd. Ridge 8 A4
Chapel Rd. South 201 F3
Chapel Rd. Stanw 66 B3
Chapel Rd. Tipt 100 C2
Chapel Rd. Toll D 118 C2
Chapel Rd. Tolle 118 C2
Chapel Rd. W Berg 48 C2
Chapel Rd. Wiv 87 D4
Chapel St N. Colch 67 F3
Chapel St S. Colch 67 F3
Chapel St. Cla 3 D2
Chapel St. Hals 25 F1
Chapel St. Wiv 87 D4
Chapelfields. Walt 93 F3
Chaplin Cl. Chelm 140 A1
Chaplin Dr. Colch 50 B1
Chaplins. Walt 93 F4
Chapman Rd. Clact 109 F2
Chapman Rd. South 198 A2
Chapmans Cl. Hadl 189 D1
Chapmans La. W Mers 121 E4
Chapmans Wlk. Hadl 189 D1
Chappel Hill. Wa Col 46 B3
Chappel Rd. Ford 47 E4
Chappel Rd. Gt T 46 B1
Chappel Rd. M Bure 28 C2
Charfleets Cl. Canv 196 B2
Charfleets Rd. Canv 196 B2
Charfleets Service Rd. Canv 196 B2
Charles Cl. South 190 A3
Charles Ct. Wiv 69 E2
Charles Pell Rd. Colch 68 C4
Charles Rd. Brigh 106 C3
Charles St. Colch 68 A3
Charleston Ave. Basil 174 B1
Charlotte Ave. Wick 174 B4
Charlotte Ct. S Woo F 165 E3
Charlotte Dr. Walt 93 F3
Charlotte Way. With 98 A1
Charlton Cl. Basil 186 B4
Charnock Cl. Walt 93 F3
Charnwood Ave. Chelm 126 C1
Charterhouse. Basil 185 E3
Chartfield Dr. Walt 93 E4
Chartwell Cl. Brain 59 F4
Chartwell Sq. South 200 A4
Chase Cl. Thund 187 F3
Chase Ct. Colch 68 C4
Chase Dr. S Woo F 165 E4
Chase End. Rayl 176 C1
Chase Gdns. South 190 B2
Chase La. Harw 39 F1
Chase Rd E. Gt Bro 71 E4
Chase Rd W. Gt Bro 71 D3
Chase Rd. South 200 B4
Chase The. Ald 65 D4
Chase The. Ashi 178 B4
Chase The. Bl Not 77 E3
Chase The. Bore 128 C4
Chase The. Brain 59 F4
Chase The. Church 183 F4
Chase The. Clact 110 C3
Chase The. Colch 68 A4
Chase The. Colch 68 B4
Chase The. Colch 68 C4
Chase The. Ded 34 A2
Chase The. Elmst M 70 A3
Chase The. Gold 134 A1
Chase The. Gt Bad 140 C3
Chase The. Kelv 81 E1
Chase The. Rayl 176 C1
Chase The. Runw 164 A2
Chase The. S Woo F 165 E4
Chase The. Soum 159 E2
Chase The. Thund 188 A3
Chase The. Toll D 118 A2
Chase The. Tolle 119 E1
Chase The. W Mers 121 E3
Chase The. Wick 174 A3
Chase The. Wick 174 C2
Chase Way The. Colch 49 E1
Chaseside. Rayl 188 C4
Chaseway. Basil 185 F2
Chatfield Way. Basil 186 B4
Chatham Pavement. Basil 186 B4
Chatsworth Gdns. Clact 109 E1
Chatsworth Rd. W Mers 121 E4
Chatsworth. Thund 187 F3
Chaucer Cl. Clact 109 D1
Chaucer Cl. Mald 145 D4
Chaucer Cres. Brain 78 A4
Chaucer Rd. Chelm 127 E1
Chaucer Rd. Sud 7 E1
Chaucer Way. Colch 66 C3
Chaucer Wlk. Wick 174 B3
Cheapside E. Rayl 176 B2
Cheapside W. Rayl 176 A2
Cheddar Ave. South 190 A3
Chedington. South 192 B1
Cheldon Barton. South 201 E4
Chelmer Ave. Rayl 176 B1
Chelmer Cl. Lit Tot 117 D2
Chelmer Cl. Walt 93 F4
Chelmer Lea. Gt Bad 140 C4
Chelmer Pl. Chelm 127 E2
Chelmer Rd. Brain 60 B1
Chelmer Rd. Sprin 127 F2
Chelmer Rd. With 97 F1
Chelmer Terr. Mald 132 A1
Chelmer Valley Rd. Chelm 127 E3
Chelmer Village Way. Sprin 128 A2
Chelmer Way. Burn 170 A3
Chelmer Way. South 201 E4
Chelmerton Ave. Gt Bad 140 C4
Chelmesford Rd. Purl 144 B2
Chelmsford Ave. South 190 C1
Chelmsford Rd. Chelm 126 B1
Chelmsford Rd. Clact 110 B3
Chelmsford Rd. Rayl 164 C1
Chelmsford Rd. Rayl 175 F4
Chelmsford Rd. Woo Mor 143 E3
Chelsea Ave. South 200 B3
Chelsea Rd. Sud 12 C4
Chelsworth Ave. Sud 13 D4
Chelsworth Cl. South 200 C4
Chelsworth Cres. South 200 C4
Cheltenham Dr. South 189 F1
Cheltenham dr. Thund 188 A4
Cheltenham Rd. Hock 177 F4
Cheltenham Rd. South 200 B4
Chelwater. Gt Bad 140 B4
Chequers La. Glems 2 B3
Chequers La. Mald 132 A1
Chequers Rd. Lit Bro 53 E4
Chequers The. Alres 88 A4
Cheriton Rd. Brain 60 B1
Cherries The. Canv 197 D1
Cherry Blossom La. Col N 155 F3
Cherry Chase. Tipt 100 B2
Cherry Cl. Canv 196 C2
Cherry Cl. Hock 177 F4
Cherry Garden La. Dan 143 D4
Cherry Garden Rd. Mald 131 F1
Cherry La. Gt Y 15 D4
Cherry La. Wick 175 D4
Cherry Orchard La. Roch 178 A1
Cherry Orchard. Soum 159 F2
Cherry Row. Colch 66 C3
Cherry Tree Ave. Clact 109 E1
Cherry Tree Chase. Gt Wak 193 E1
Cherry Tree Cl. Lit Oak 57 D4
Cherry Tree La. Colch 86 A4
Cherrybrook. South 192 B1
Cherrydene Cl. Hull 165 F1
Cherrydown East. Basil 185 D3
Cherrydown West. Basil 185 D3
Cherrydown. Rayl 176 B2
Cherrygarden La. Chelm 140 A4
Cherrymeade. S Ben 188 A2
Cherrytree Rd. Sud 13 D4

Cherrytree Rise. With

Cherrytree Rise. With 98 A3
Cherrywood Dr. Colch 66 C3
Cherrywoods. Gt Ben 89 E4
Chertsey Cl. South 192 B1
Chervil Cl. Tipt 100 B2
Cherwell Dr. Chelm 126 B3
Cheshunt Dr. Rayl 176 A3
Chess La. With 98 A1
Chester Ave. South 200 B3
Chester Pl. Chelm 127 D3
Chester Way. Basil 185 F4
Chesterfield Ave. Thund 187 E3
Chesterfield Cres. South 189 E3
Chesterford Gdns. Basil 185 F4
Chesterford Green. Basil 185 F4
Chestnut Ave. Clact 109 E2
Chestnut Ave. Colch 86 A4
Chestnut Ave. Gos 42 C4
Chestnut Ave. Hat Pev 114 A2
Chestnut Ave. Mald 132 B3
Chestnut Ave. Wal 93 E3
Chestnut Cl. Burn 170 A3
Chestnut Cl. Hock 177 F3
Chestnut Cl. Basil 186 A2
Chestnut Farm Dr. Alth 157 F1
Chestnut Gr. Brain 59 F1
Chestnut Gr. S Ben 187 D2
Chestnut Gr. South 191 D1
Chestnut Path. Cane 168 B1
Chestnut Rd. Alres 88 A4
Chestnut Rd. Basil 186 A2
Chestnut Rd. Glems 2 A3
Chestnut Way. Brigh 106 C4
Chestnut Way. Tipt 100 B4
Chestnut Wlk. Canv 196 C2
Chestnut Wlk. Chelm 127 D3
Chestnut Wlk. Lit Bad 129 F1
Chestnuts The. Rayl 176 C2
Chestnuts. Basil 186 A4
Cheveling Rd. Colch 68 B1
Chevening Gdns. Hock 177 E3
Chevers Pawen. Basil 186 A3
Cheviot Dr. Chelm 126 B3
Chevy Ct. Harw 39 E1
Cheyne Cl. Sud 12 C3
Chichester Cl. Basil 185 F4
Chichester Cl. Canv 197 D1
Chichester Dr. Sprin 127 E2
Chichester Rd. South 200 A4
Chichester Way. Mald 145 D4
Chigborough Rd. Gt Tot 132 C3
Chignal Rd. Chelm 126 B3
Chilburn Rd. Clact 110 A4
Childwell Alley. Colch 67 F4
Chilham Cl. Basil 186 B3
Chiltern App. Canv 196 C2
Chiltern Cl. Colch 49 F1
Chiltern Cl. Rayl 176 B2
Chilterns The. Canv 196 C2
Chilton Cl. Gt Bad 140 B4
Chilton Cl. Gt Hor 49 D4
Chilton Cotts. Worm 29 F2
Chilton Cl. Sud 13 D4
Chimes The. S Ben 187 F2
Chimney Pot La. Purl 143 F2
Chinchilla Rd. South 200 B4
Chingford Ave. Clact 109 F4
Chinook. Colch 50 B2
Chipping Hill. Hals 25 F1
Chipping Hill. With 97 F2
Chipping Row. S Woo F 165 F4
Chippingdell. With 97 F2
Chipstead Wlk. Clact 109 D3
Chittock Gabl. Basil 185 F3
Chittock Mead. Basil 185 F3
Chitts Hill. E A Gr 48 B1
Chitts Hill. Stanw 66 B4
Cholvedon Sq. Basil 186 A3
Chrismund Way. Gt T 46 B1
Christ Church Ct. Colch 67 E3
Christchurch Ave. Wick 174 A4
Christchurch Rd. South 191 E1
Christina Rd. With 114 C4
Christine Chase. Colch 66 C3
Christmas Field. St Wel 15 E1
Christopher Cl. Sud 12 C4
Christopher Dr. Lit Cla 91 E1
Christopher La. Sud 12 C4
Christy Ave. Chelm 126 C2
Church Chase. Gt Brx 99 D2
Church Chase. Rett 164 B3
Church Cl. Canv 196 C2
Church Cl. Canv 1 B1
Church Cl. W Berg 48 C2
Church Cl. Wic Bis 115 E3
Church Cres. Clact 109 F1
Church End Ave. Runw 163 F1
Church End La. Runw 163 F1
Church End. Pan 59 D4
Church Farm Way. Colch 49 F2
Church Field Rd. Sud 13 E4
Church Fields. Gt Y 8 C1
Church Green. Ald 65 D4
Church Green. Cane 168 B1
Church Green. Cogg 63 D2
Church Green. Lit Y 9 E2
Church Green. Wic Bis 115 E3
Church Hill. Ea Col 45 E3

Church Hill. Lawf 34 C2
Church Hill. Purl 144 C1
Church Hill. Rams 39 D1
Church Hill. Rowh 86 C4
Church Hill. Wh Not 78 C1
Church Hill. Woo Wa 130 B1
Church La. Aid 64 B2
Church La. Basil 174 A1
Church La. Beau 74 A3
Church La. Brain 59 F3
Church La. Ca Hed 15 F2
Church La. Chelm 127 D1
Church La. Cla 4 A4
Church La. Colch 67 F4
Church La. E Mers 105 F1
Church La. Frin 93 D2
Church La. Gt Wig 102 C2
Church La. Harw 40 C3
Church La. Lit Tot 117 D1
Church La. Mist 35 F2
Church La. Mks T 64 B2
Church La. Mks T 65 D2
Church La. Nay 20 A1
Church La. Ridge 8 A3
Church La. S Han 163 E4
Church La. Sprin 127 E2
Church La. Stow M 155 E2
Church La. Topp 14 A4
Church La. W Han 152 A2
Church La. Weel 91 D4
Church La. Wiv 126 A1
Church Mead. Wh Not 78 C1
Church Meadow. Bul 11 F2
Church Par. Canv 196 C3
Church Park Rd. Basil 186 A3
Church Park. Cla 3 E2
Church Rd. Alres 88 A4
Church Rd. Ashi 178 B4
Church Rd. Barl 192 C4
Church Rd. Basil 185 E3
Church Rd. Basil 186 C2
Church Rd. Bl Not 78 A3
Church Rd. Bore 129 D3
Church Rd. Bradw 61 E1
Church Rd. Bradw 61 F3
Church Rd. Brigh 106 C4
Church Rd. Bul 11 F2
Church Rd. Burn 170 A3
Church Rd. Clact 110 A2
Church Rd. Copf 65 F1
Church Rd. Elmst M 70 A2
Church Rd. Ford 47 E3
Church Rd. Frat 70 B1
Church Rd. Gos 42 C4
Church Rd. Gt Tot 116 B1
Church Rd. Gt Y 8 C1
Church Rd. Hadl 188 C1
Church Rd. Hat Pev 114 A2
Church Rd. Hock 177 D4
Church Rd. Kelv 81 E1
Church Rd. Lay H 84 C2
Church Rd. Lit Bad 129 D3
Church Rd. Lit Bro 53 D2
Church Rd. N Fam 167 D4
Church Rd. Peld 103 E3
Church Rd. Rayl 175 E4
Church Rd. Rayl 176 C1
Church Rd. South 200 A4
Church Rd. South 201 E3
Church Rd. Sud 13 D3
Church Rd. T Gr 79 D3
Church Rd. Tend 72 A3
Church Rd. Terl 96 B1
Church Rd. Thor 89 D3
Church Rd. Thund 187 E3
Church Rd. Tipt 100 B3
Church Rd. Toll M 117 F1
Church Rd. Twin 18 B3
Church Rd. Ult 130 B3
Church Rd. W Berg 48 C2
Church Rd. W Han 152 A2
Church Rd. W Mers 121 D3
Church Rd. Walt 94 B4
Church Rd. Wic Bis 115 F3
Church Rd. Wic S P 17 D3
Church Rd. With 80 A1
Church Rd. Worm 29 F3
Church Rd. Wrab 37 F2
Church Sq. Bures 28 C4
Church Sq. St O 108 A2
Church St. Bel S P 5 D2
Church St. Box 32 A4
Church St. Chelm 127 D1
Church St. Cla 4 A4
Church St. Cogg 63 D2
Church St. Col En 27 D1
Church St. Colch 67 F4
Church St. Fee 81 D1
Church St. Gest 10 C1
Church St. Gold 133 F4
Church St. Gt Bad 141 D3
Church St. Gt Map 16 B1
Church St. Harw 40 C3
Church St. Mald 132 A1
Church St. Nay 20 B3
Church St. Pan 59 F4

Church St. Rayl 176 B1
Church St. Rowh 87 D4
Church St. Si Hed 15 E1
Church St. Sud 12 B3
Church St. Toll D 118 B2
Church St. Tolle 119 E1
Church St. With 97 F2
Church View Rd. Thund 187 F3
Church View. Ard 51 F4
Church Wlk. Colch 67 F4
Church Wlk. Mald 131 F2
Church Wlk. Sud 12 C4
Churchfield Cotts. Church 183 D4
Churchfield Rd. Cogg 63 D2
Churchfield Rd. Walt 94 B4
Churchfields. South 192 C1
Churchfields. W Mers 121 D3
Churchill Ave. Hals 26 A2
Churchill Cl. Brigh 106 C4
Churchill Dr. Sud 7 F1
Churchill Rd. Brain 59 F4
Churchill Rd. Tipt 100 C3
Churchill Rise. Sprin 127 F4
Churchill W. South 200 A4
Churchill Way. Colch 68 A2
Churchponds. Ca Hed 15 F2
Churchway. Hadl 188 C1
Churchward Ave. Copf 83 D4
Churnwood Rd. Colch 50 B1
Chuzzlewit Dr. Chelm 126 C4
Cimarron Cl. S Woo F 165 E4
Cinque Port Rd. Brigh 106 C4
Circular Rd E. Colch 67 F3
Circular Rd N. Colch 67 F3
Circular Rd S. Colch 67 F2
Cistern Yd. Colch 67 E3
City Rd. W Mers 121 D3
Clachar Cl. Sprin 128 A2
Clacton Rd. Elmst M 70 B2
Clacton Rd. Gt Oak 55 E1
Clacton Rd. Lit Oak 57 D3
Clacton Rd. Mist 54 A3
Clacton Rd. St O 108 A2
Clacton Rd. Thor 89 E2
Clacton Rd. Weel 91 D3
Clacton Rd. Wiv 69 E3
Clacton Rd. Wiv 55 E3
Claire Cotts. Birch 83 F3
Claire Rd. Walt 93 D3
Clairmont Cl. Brain 59 F1
Clairmont Rd. Colch 66 C3
Clapgate Dr. Lit Cla 91 E1
Clara Reeve Cl. Colch 66 C2
Clare Ave. Runw 163 E1
Clare Cl. Hals 43 E4
Clare Rd. Brain 59 E3
Clare Rd. Thund 187 D3
Clare Way. Clact 109 D3
Claremont Dr. Basil 186 A2
Claremont Rd. Elmst M 87 E4
Claremont Rd. South 190 C1
Clarence Cl. S Ben 187 E2
Clarence Cl. Sprin 128 A2
Clarence Rd N. S Ben 187 F2
Clarence Rd. S Ben 187 E2
Clarence Rd. Cla 4 A4
Clarence Rd. Rayl 177 D1
Clarence Rd. S Ben 187 E2
Clarence Rd. South 200 A4
Clarence Rd. Sud 7 F1
Clarence St. South 200 A4
Clarendon Park. Clact 110 A3
Clarendon Rd. Ashi 166 C1
Clarendon Rd. Basil 186 B4
Clarendon Rd. Canv 197 E2
Clarendon Way. Colch 49 F1
Clarke Rise. Col N 155 F3
Clarke's Rd. Harw 39 F2
Clarkesmead. Tipt 100 B2
Claters Cl. South 190 A1
Clatterfield Gdns. South 190 A1
Claud Ince Ave. T Gr 78 C3
Claudius Rd. Colch 68 A3
Claudius Way. With 114 C4
Clavering Rd. Brain 59 F2
Clavering. Basil 185 F2
Clay Hill Rd. Basil 185 E3
Clay La. St O 108 B4
Clay Lane Gr. Colch 50 B2
Claybrick Ave. Hawk 177 E3
Claydon Cl. Basil 186 C4
Clayburn End. Basil 186 B4
Clayburn Side. Basil 185 E3
Claydon Cres. Basil 185 E3
Claydons La. Hadl 188 B4
Clayhall Rd. Clact 110 A3
Clayhave Ave. Bures 29 D4
Claypits La. Fox 6 B3
Claypits Rd. Bore 112 C1
Clays Rd. Walt 94 A4
Clayspring Cl. Hock 177 E4
Clayton Rd. Harw 39 E1
Clearwater. Colch 66 A3
Clematis Tye. Sprin 127 F4
Clematis Way. Colch 68 C4
Clements Gdns. Hawk 178 A3
Clements Green La. S Woo F 165 E4
Clements Hall Way. Hawk 178 A3

Clements Hall Way. Hawk 178 A2
Clements Pl. S Woo F 165 E4
Cleveland Cl. Colch 50 B2
Cleveland Dr. South 190 B2
Cleveland Rd. Basil 185 E3
Cleveland Rd. Canv 197 D1
Cleves Cl. Bore 112 C1
Clevis Dr. S Woo F 165 F3
Clickett End. Basil 185 E3
Clickett Hill. Basil 185 E3
Clickett Side. Basil 185 E3
Clieveden Rd. South 200 C3
Cliff Ave. South 190 C1
Cliff Gdns. South 199 D4
Cliff Gdns. South 190 C1
Cliff Par. South 198 B4
Cliff Par. Walt 94 C3
Cliff Rd. Clact 110 C3
Cliff Rd. Harw 40 B2
Cliff Rd. South 199 D4
Cliff Way. Frin 94 A3
Cliffsea Gr. South 189 F1
Clifftown Par. South 199 F4
Clifftown Rd. South 200 A4
Clifton Ave. S Ben 187 E2
Clifton Cl. S Ben 187 E2
Clifton Dr. South 199 E4
Clifton Mews. South 200 A4
Clifton Rd. Ashi 178 B4
Clifton Rd. Basil 186 C4
Clifton Rd. Canv 197 D2
Clifton Rd. Wiv 69 E2
Clifton Ter. South 200 A4
Clifton Terr. Wiv 87 D4
Clifton Way. S Ben 187 E2
Climmer Rd. Canv 197 D3
Clinton Cl. E Han 153 E4
Clinton Rd. Canv 196 B2
Clive Rd. Colch 68 A3
Cliveden Cl. Chelm 126 C2
Clobbs Yd. Chelm 127 D4
Clockhouse Way. Brain 60 A3
Clopton Dr. L Mel 7 E3
Clopton Green. Basil 185 D4
Close The. Clact 125 D4
Close The. Frin 93 D2
Close The. Frin 93 F3
Close The. Harw 40 A2
Close The. S Ben 187 E1
Close The. Sud 12 C4
Close The. T Gr 78 C3
Close The. Thund 187 E1
Clova Rd. South 189 F1
Clovelly Gdns. Runw 174 B4
Clover Cl. Basil 185 F2
Clover Cl. Sud 7 F1
Clover Dr. Thor 89 D3
Clover Way. Ard 109 D3
Clover Way. Basil 185 F2
Cloverlands. Colch 50 B1
Cluanie Orch. Cav 1 C1
Cluny Sq. South 191 E2
Clyde Cres. Rayl 176 B2
Clydesdale Rd. Brain 59 F1
Coach La. Mald 131 F2
Coach Rd. Alres 88 A4
Coach Rd. Gt Hor 49 D4
Coan Ave. Clact 109 E1
Coast Rd. W Mers 121 D3
Coats Hutton Rd. Colch 67 D2
Cobbins Chase. Burn 170 A4
Cobbins Cl. Burn 170 A4
Cobbins The. Burn 170 A4
Cobbs Pl. Sprin 128 A2
Cobden Wlk. Basil 186 B4
Cobham Rd. South 199 E4
Cobham Rd. South 190 B2
Cock and Bell La. L Mel 7 E4
Cock Rd. Lit Map 17 D1
Cockaynes La. Alres 88 A4
Cockerell Cl. Basil 174 A1
Cockethurst Cl. South 190 A2
Cockett Wick La. St O 108 B1
Cockrell's Rd. Worm 30 A2
Codenham Green. Basil 185 D4
Codenham Straight. Basil 185 D4
Codham Little Park Dr. Wneth 41 E3
Coggeshall Rd (Feering). Cogg 81 E4
Coggeshall Rd. Ard 51 E4
Coggeshall Rd. Brain 60 B2
Coggeshall Rd. Cogg 62 A1
Coggeshall Rd. Ea Col 45 D4
Coggeshall Rd. Gt T 64 A4
Coggeshall Rd. Mks T 81 D3
Coggeshall Rd. Mks T 64 B2
Coggeshall Rd. Stis 60 B2
Coggeshall Way. Hals 26 A3
Coke St. Harw 40 B3
Cokefield Ave. South 191 E2
Coker Rd. Canv 196 B1
Cokers Cl. Bl Not 78 B3
Colam La. Lit Bad 129 E2
Colbert Ave. South 191 E2
Colchester Cl. South 190 A2
Colchester Rd. Ard 51 D1
Colchester Rd. Ard 51 F4

Colchester Rd. Bore 128 A3
Colchester Rd. Bures 28 C4
Colchester Rd. Clact 110 B3
Colchester Rd. Cogg 63 E1
Colchester Rd. Ded 33 F3
Colchester Rd. Ea Col 45 F3
Colchester Rd. Elmst M 69 F3
Colchester Rd. Gt Ben 71 E2
Colchester Rd. Gt Bro 52 A2
Colchester Rd. Gt Oak 55 D1
Colchester Rd. Gt Tot 116 B3
Colchester Rd. Hals 26 A1
Colchester Rd. Lang 104 A3
Colchester Rd. Lawf 35 D2
Colchester Rd. M Bure 29 D3
Colchester Rd. Mald 132 A3
Colchester Rd. South 190 C1
Colchester Rd. St O 108 A3
Colchester Rd. Tend 72 B1
Colchester Rd. Th L S 73 F3
Colchester Rd. Tipt 100 B4
Colchester Rd. Tolle 119 D3
Colchester Rd. Virl 102 A1
Colchester Rd. W Berg 48 C2
Colchester Rd. W Mers 121 E4
Colchester Rd. Wa Col 46 C3
Colchester Rd. Weel 72 B1
Colchester Rd. With 98 B2
Colchester Rd. Wiv 69 E2
Colchester Rd. Wix 55 D3
Cold Hall Chase. Gt Bro 70 C3
Coldnailhurst Ave. Brain 59 F3
Cole Green. Bel S P 5 D1
Cole Hill. Gt Le 95 D3
Coleman St. South 191 D1
Colemans Ave. South 190 B2
Colemans La. Dan 142 B4
Coleridge Rd. Mald 132 A1
Coles Brook Rd. Gt Ben 69 F2
Coles La. Walt 76 A1
Coles Oak La. Ded 33 E3
College Ct. Lawf 35 E2
College Rd. Brain 59 F1
College Rd. Clact 110 A2
College Way. South 199 F4
Coller Rd. Rams 39 F3
Colletts Chase. Worm 29 F3
Colley Rd. Gt Bad 141 D3
Collier Ct. Brain 59 F1
Colliers The. Mald 132 C2
Collindale Gdns. Clact 110 B3
Collingdale Cl. Canv 197 E2
Collingwood Cl. Brain 59 F1
Collingwood Rd. Basil 185 E2
Collingwood Rd. Clact 109 E1
Collingwood Rd. S Woo F 165 F3
Collingwood Rd. With 98 A1
Collingwood Terr. Basil 185 E3
Collingwood Wlk. Basil 185 E3
Collingwood. S Ben 187 F2
Collins Cl. Brain 59 F1
Collins Rd. Lit Map 17 E1
Collins Way. South 190 A3
Colne Bank Ave. Colch 49 F1
Colne Bank Ave. Colch 97 F1
Colne Chase. With 97 F1
Colne Cl. S Woo F 165 F4
Colne Dr. South 192 C1
Colne Park Rd. Ea Col 45 E4
Colne Pl. Basil 185 E2
Colne Rd. Bures 28 C4
Colne Rd. Clact 109 F1
Colne Rd. Cogg 63 D3
Colne Rd. Hals 26 A1
Colne Rd. Si Hed 24 C4
Colne Rise. Rowh 86 C4
Colne Springs. Ridge 8 A3
Colne St. Brigh 106 C3
Colne Valley Cl. Hals 25 E1
Colne View. St O 107 D1
Colne Way. St O 106 C2
Colneford Hill. Ea Col 45 E4
Colneys Cl. Sud 7 E1
Colthorpe Rd. Clact 110 A2
Coltishall Cl. Wick 175 D3
Columbine Gdns. Walt 94 A4
Columbine Mews. Stanw 66 B4
Columbines The. Cav 1 C1
Colvin Chase. Chelm 140 A1
Colvin Cl. Colch 66 C4
Colworth Cl. Hadl 189 D1
Colyers Reach. Sprin 128 A1
Comet Way. South 190 A3
Commerce Park. Colch 68 B2
Commerce Way. Colch 67 D2
Commercial Rd. South 190 B2
Common App. Thund 188 A4
Common La. Lit Bad 129 F1
Common La. Thund 188 A4
Common La. Woo Wa 130 A2
Common Rd. Gt Wak 193 D2
Common St. Cla 4 A4
Common The. Dan 142 C3
Common The. E Han 153 D4
Common The. Thund 188 A4
Commonhall La. Hadl 188 B2
Commons The. Colch 67 D3
Compasses Rd. Bradw 61 F3

Compasses Rd. Bradw

Compton Ct. Canv 197 E1
Compton Rd. Colch 68 B4
Comyns Pl. Writ 126 A1
Con Way. S Ben 187 E2
Conan Doyle Cl. Brain 78 A4
Concord Ave. Canv 196 C3
Conder Way. Colch 68 B2
Conduit La. Woo Mor 143 F3
Conduit St. Chelm 127 D1
Conies Rd. Hals 43 E4
Conifer Cl. Alres 87 F4
Conifer Cl. Colch 68 B4
Conifers. Hadl 188 C2
Coniston Cl. Bl Not 77 E3
Coniston Cl. Rayl 176 C1
Coniston Rd. Canv 197 D2
Coniston Rd. Thund 187 F4
Coniston. South 190 A4
Connaught Ave. Frin 93 F2
Connaught Cl. Clact 110 A2
Connaught Dr. S Woo F 165 E4
Connaught Gdns E. Clact 110 A2
Connaught Gdns W. Clact 110 A2
Connaught Gdns. Brain 60 A2
Connaught Gdns. South 201 E3
Connaught Rd. Lit Cla 91 E3
Connaught Rd. Rayl 189 D4
Connaught Wlk. Rayl 189 D4
Conquerors Cl. Hat Pev 114 A2
Conrad Rd. With 97 F3
Constable Ave. Clact 109 E3
Constable Cl. Colch 49 F2
Constable Cl. Lawf 35 D2
Constable Cl. S Wers 121 E4
Constable Rd. Sud 12 C4
Constable View. Sprin 127 F3
Constable Way. South 202 A4
Constance Cl. With 115 D4
Constantine Rd. Colch 67 E3
Constantine Rd. With 114 C4
Constitution Hill. S Ben 187 E2
Constitution Hill. Sud 12 C4
Convent Hill. Brain 60 A3
Convent La. Brain 60 A3
Convent Rd. Canv 197 D2
Conway Ave. Gt Wak 193 D2
Conway Cl. Elmst M 87 E4
Conway Cl. Hals 43 E4
Cook Cl. Harw 39 F1
Cook Cres. Colch 68 C4
Cook Pl. Sprin 127 F3
Cook's Hall Rd. W Berg 48 B2
Cook's La. Colch 66 C4
Cookham Ct. South 192 C1
Cooks Cl. Hals 43 F4
Cooks Green. Basil 174 B1
Cooks Hill. Box 32 A3
Coolyne Way. Clact 110 A4
Coombe Rd. Soum 159 E2
Coombe Rise. Chelm 127 D4
Coombes Gr. Roch 179 D1
Coombewood Dr. Thund 187 F3
Cooper Wlk. Colch 68 B4
Cooper's La. Ded 33 F3
Cooper's Row. Chelm 127 D3
Coopers Ave. Mald 132 B3
Coopers La. Clact 109 E3
Coopers Way. South 191 D3
Copdoek. Basil 185 E4
Copelands. Hawk 178 C3
Copford Ave. Rayl 176 C1
Copland Cl. Gt Bad 140 C4
Coppens Green. Wick 174 C3
Copper Beeches. Stanw 66 B3
Copper Beeches. Thund 188 A4
Copperas Rd. Brigh 106 C3
Copperfield Rd. Chelm 126 C4
Coppice End. Colch 50 A2
Coppice Rd. Alres 88 A4
Coppins Cl. Sprin 127 F2
Coppins Rd. Clact 109 E2
Copt Hall La. Gt Wig 103 E2
Copt Hill. Dan 142 C3
Coptfold Cl. South 191 F1
Coral Cl. S Woo F 165 E4
Coralin Wlk. Stanw 66 B3
Corasway. Thund 188 A3
Cordelia Cres. Rayl 176 B2
Cordell Pl. L Mel 7 E4
Cordell Rd. L Mel 7 E4
Cordwainers The. South 191 D3
Coriander Rd. Tipt 100 B2
Cormorant Wlk. Chelm 140 B3
Cornard Rd. Sud 12 C4
Cornec Ave. Rayl 189 D3
Cornec Chase. Rayl 189 D3
Cornel Cl. With 97 E2
Cornerth Cres. Sud 13 D3
Cornfields. S Woo F 165 E4
Cornflower Cl. Stanw 66 B4
Cornflower Dr. Clact 127 F3
Cornflower Rd. Clact 125 D4
Cornford Way. Lawf 35 D2
Cornhill Ave. Hock 177 F4
Cornhill. Chelm 127 D1
Cornish Gr. S Woo F 165 F3
Cornwall Cres. Chelm 127 D4
Cornwall Gdns. Brain 60 A2

Cornwall Gdns. Hawk 178 B3
Cornwall Rd. Basil 186 C4
Cornwallis Dr. S Woo F 165 F4
Cornwalls Dri. Mks T 64 C2
Cornworthy. South 201 E4
Corona Rd. Canv 197 E3
Coronation Ave. Brain 59 F1
Coronation Ave. Colch 68 A1
Coronation Cl. Gt Wak 192 C2
Coronation Rd. Burn 170 A2
Coronation Rd. Clact 109 E2
Coronation Way. T Gr 78 B3
Corporation Rd. Chelm 127 D2
Corsel Rd. Canv 197 F2
Cortoncroft Cl. Walt 93 F4
Cosgrove Ave. Hadl 189 D2
Cossington Rd. South 199 F4
Cotelands. Basil 185 F2
Cotman Ave. Lawf 35 D3
Cotman Rd. Clact 109 E3
Cotman Rd. Colch 67 D3
Cotswold Ave. Rayl 176 B2
Cotswold Cres. Chelm 126 B3
Cotswold Ct. Colch 50 B2
Cotswold Dr. L Mel 7 E3
Cotswold Rd. Clact 109 F3
Cotswold Rd. South 190 B1
Cottage Dr. Colch 68 B2
Cottage Gr. Clact 109 E3
Cottage Green. Clact 109 E3
Cottage Pl. Chelm 127 D2
Cottage Wlk. Clact 109 E3
Cottesmore Cl. Canv 197 D1
Cottesmore Gdns. Hadl 189 D1
Cottonwood Cl. Colch 67 E1
Coulde Dennis. E Han 153 D4
Coulsdon Cl. Clact 109 E3
Court St. Nay 20 A1
Courtauld Cl. Hals 25 F2
Courtauld Homes. Hals 25 F2
Courtauld Rd. Basil 174 B1
Courtauld Rd. Brain 60 A2
Courtenay Cl. Sud 7 E1
Courtland Mews. Mald 144 C4
Courtland Pl. Mald 144 C4
Courtlands. Chelm 127 D3
Courtlands. Hals 43 F4
Courts The. Rayl 176 C2
Coval Ave. Chelm 127 D2
Coval La. Chelm 127 D2
Coventry Cl. Colch 68 A4
Coventry Cl. Hull 165 F1
Coverley Hill. Hull 165 F1
Coverts The. W Mers 121 E3
Coverts The. Writ 126 A1
Cow La. St O 107 E2
Cowdray Ave. Colch 50 A1
Cowdray Cres. Colch 67 F4
Cowell Ave. Chelm 126 C3
Cowpar Mews. Brain 78 A4
Cowslip La. Stanw 66 B4
Cowslip Mead. Basil 185 D3
Cox Rd. Alres 88 A4
Cox's Hill. Lawf 56 B1
Coxs Cl. S Woo F 165 F4
Crabb's Hill. Hat Pev 113 F2
Crabtree La. Lit Hor 30 B1
Crabtree. Walt 93 E4
Cracknell Cl. With 69 D1
Craftsmans Sq. South 191 D3
Craig's Hill. Bures 28 C3
Craigfield Ave. Clact 110 A3
Craigs La. M Bure 28 C3
Craiston Way. Gt Bad 140 C3
Cramphorn Wlk. Chelm 126 C2
Cranbrook Ave. Thund 188 B2
Crane's La. Kelv 80 C1
Crane's La. Kelv 80 C1
Cranes Cl. Basil 185 E4
Cranes Farm Rd. Basil 185 D4
Cranes La. Basil 185 E4
Cranfield Ct. Runw 174 B4
Cranfield Park Rd. Wick 174 C2
Cranford Ct. Frin 93 F3
Cranleigh Cl. Clact 109 D3
Cranleigh Dr. South 189 F1
Cranleigh Gdns. Hull 165 E1
Cranley Ave. South 190 B1
Cranley Gdns. South 201 E3
Credon Cl. Clact 190 B1
Credon Dr. Clact 109 F4
Craylands. Basil 185 F4
Creek Rd. Canv 197 E2
Creek View Ave. Hull 165 E2
Creek View. Basil 185 F2
Creekhurst Cl. Brigh 107 D3
Creeksea La. Burn 169 E1
Creeksea Rd. Cane 169 F1
Creekview Rd. S Woo F 165 F4
Creephedge La. S Woo F 153 F2
Creffield Rd. Colch 67 E3
Crescent Rd. Canv 197 E2
Crescent Rd. Gt Bad 141 D4

Crescent Rd. Hadl 189 D1
Crescent Rd. Mald 131 F3
Crescent Rd. S Ben 187 E1
Crescent Rd. Tolle 119 F1
Crescent Rd. Walt 94 B4
Crescent The. Clact 110 A4
Crescent The. Colch 50 B3
Crescent The. Frin 93 D2
Crescent The. Frin 93 F2
Crescent The. Gt Hor 31 D1
Crescent The. Hadl 188 C2
Crescent The. Mks T 65 D2
Crescent The. Th L S 73 F1
Crescent The. W Berg 48 B3
Cress Croft. Brain 60 B1
Cressing Rd. Brain 60 B1
Cressing Rd. With 97 F3
Crest Ave. Basil 186 B3
Crest The. South 189 E3
Crestlands. Alres 88 A4
Creswick Ave. Rayl 176 B2
Cricketers Cl. Sud 12 C3
Cricketers Way. Wick 174 A1
Cricketfield Gr. South 189 F1
Cricknollow. S Woo F 165 E3
Crina Wlk. Basil 185 F3
Cringle Lock. S Woo F 165 E3
Cripplegate. Soum 159 F3
Crispin Ct. Colch 67 F4
Crittall Dr. Brain 59 E2
Crittall Rd. With 98 A2
Crocklands. Hals 44 A3
Crockleford Hill. Ard 51 E2
Crockleford Rd. Elmst M 69 F3
Crocus Cl. Clact 109 E2
Crocus Way. Sprin 127 F4
Croft Cl. Brain 60 A2
Croft Cl. S Ben 187 D2
Croft Cl. Sprin 127 F4
Croft Rd. Clact 109 E2
Croft Rd. Kelv 81 D1
Croft Rd. S Ben 187 E3
Croft Rd. Sud 12 C4
Croft The. Bures 19 F4
Croft The. Ea Col 45 D3
Croft The. Glems 2 B2
Croft The. Gt Y 9 D1
Croft The. Rayl 188 C4
Crofts The. Barl 192 C2
Crome Cl. Colch 67 D3
Crome Rd. Clact 109 E3
Cromer Rd. Soum 200 A4
Crompton St. Chelm 126 C1
Cromwell Hill. Mald 131 F2
Cromwell La. Mald 131 F2
Cromwell Rd. Colch 67 F3
Cromwell Rd. Hock 177 F3
Cromwell Rd. South 191 D2
Cromwell Way. With 97 F1
Cropenburg Wlk. Canv 197 D3
Crosby Rd. South 199 E4
Cross Ave. Wick 174 B3
Cross Cl. Colch 56 B1
Cross La. W Mers 121 F4
Cross Park Rd. Wick 174 B2
Cross Rd. Clact 109 D2
Cross Rd. Mald 132 A1
Cross Rd. S Ben 188 A2
Cross Rd. With 97 F3
Cross St. Sud 12 B4
Cross Way. W Mers 121 F4
Crossfield Rd. Thund 187 F4
Crossfield Rd. Clact 109 F2
Crossfield Rd. South 191 E1
Crossfield Way. Walt 93 D3
Crossfields. Nay 20 B3
Crossley Ave. Clact 124 C4
Crosstree Wlk. Colch 68 A1
Crossways Hill. Woo Wa 130 A2
Crossways The. South 199 D4
Crossways. Canv 196 C2
Crossways. Chelm 140 B4
Crossways. Clact 124 C4
Crossways. Col En 26 C1
Crouch Ave. Hull 165 F1
Crouch Beck. S Woo F 165 F3
Crouch Dr. With 97 E1
Crouch Dr. With 97 E1
Crouch Meadow. Hull 165 F1
Crouch Rd. Burn 170 B3
Crouch St. Colch 67 F3
Crouch View Cotts. Rett 164 B3
Crouch View Gr. Hull 165 E2
Crouch Way. South 201 D4
Crouchman's Farm Rd. Ult 130 B4
Crouchmans Ave. Gt Wak 193 D2
Crouchview Cl. Wick 174 C4
Crow La. Tend 73 D2
Crow Pond Rd. Terl 96 B2
Crowborough Rd. South 190 C1
Crowhall La. Brad 36 C2
Crowhurst Ct. Colch 67 F4
Crowhurst Rd. Colch 67 F4
Crown Ave. Basil 186 B4
Crown Bay Rd. Colch 68 B4
Crown Gdns. Rayl 176 B1
Crown Hill. Rayl 176 B1
Crown La N. Ard 50 C4

Crown La S. Ard 51 D2
Crown La. Tend 72 B2
Crown Rd. Clact 109 E1
Crown Rd. Col N 155 F3
Crown Rd. Hock 177 D3
Crown St. Ca Hed 15 F2
Crown St. Ded 33 F3
Crown Way. Soum 159 E2
Crownfield Rd. Glems 2 A3
Crows La. S Woo F 154 B3
Crowstone Ave. South 199 E4
Crowstone Cl. South 190 B1
Crowstone Rd. South 199 E4
Croxon Way. Burn 170 A4
Cruce Way. St O 106 C2
Crummock Cl. Bl Not 77 E3
Cuckoo Cnr. South 190 C2
Cuckoo Hill. Bures 19 F1
Cuckoo Hill. Si Hed 24 A4
Culver Par. Colch 67 F4
Culver Rise. S Woo F 165 F4
Culver Sq. Colch 67 F4
Culver St E. Colch 67 F4
Culver St N. Colch 67 F4
Culver St W. Colch 67 F4
Culverdown. Basil 185 D3
Culvert Cl. Cogg 62 C1
Cumberland Ave. Mald 131 F1
Cumberland Ave. S Ben 187 E2
Cumberland Cl. South 191 E1
Cumberland Cl. Brain 60 A2
Cumberland Cres. Chelm 127 D4
Cumming Rd. S Han 163 D1
Cunningham Cl. South 201 D4
Cunnington Rd. Brain 60 B2
Cuppers Cl. With 97 F1
Curds Rd. Ea Col 45 D2
Curlew Ave. May 158 A4
Curlew Cl. Clact 109 F3
Curlew Cl. Kelv 81 E1
Curlew Cl. Mald 132 B3
Curlew Cres. Basil 185 D2
Curlew Dr. S Ben 187 E1
Curling Tye La. Woo Wa 131 D2
Curling Tye. Basil 185 E4
Curling Wlk. Basil 185 E4
Currants Farm Rd. Brain 59 F3
Current's La. Harw 40 C3
Curtisway. Rayl 176 C2
Curzon Rd. Sud 13 D4
Curzon Way. Sprin 128 A1
Curzon Wlk. Basil 186 A3
Cusak Rd. Sprin 128 A1
Custom House La. Harw 40 B3
Cut The. Tipt 100 B3
Cut Throat La. With 98 A2
Cut-a-thwart La. Mald 131 E2
Cuthedge La. Cogg 80 B4
Cutlers Rd. S Woo F 165 F4
Cutmore Pl. Chelm 139 F4
Cuton Hall La. Bore 128 A3
Cutting Dr. Hals 25 E1
Cymbeline Way. Colch 67 D4
Cypress Cl. Clact 109 F4
Cypress Dr. Chelm 140 B3
Cypress Gr. Colch 68 C4
Cypress Mews. S Wers 121 D4
Cypress Rd. With 98 A2
Cyril Child Cl. Colch 68 C4

Damant's Farm La. Th L S 74 B1
Damases La. Bore 113 D1
Damask Rd. Stanw 66 B4
Dampier Rd. Cogg 62 C2
Danbury Cl. Mks T 64 C2
Danbury Cl. South 189 F2
Danbury Down. Basil 185 F4
Danbury Rd. Rayl 176 A2
Danbury Vale. Dan 143 D3
Dancing Dick's La. With 97 D1
Dandies Chase. South 189 F4
Dandies Cl. South 189 E4
Dandies Dr. South 189 E4
Dane Rd. Chelm 126 C1
Dane St. South 202 A3
Dane's Ave. South 201 F3
Danes Cl. Sud 13 D2
Danescroft Cl. South 189 F2
Danescroft Dr. South 189 F2
Danesfield. S Ben 188 A4
Danesleigh Gdns. South 189 E2
Daneum Holt. Cla 4 A3
Daniel Cole Rd. Colch 67 F2
Daniel Dr. Colch 67 D1
Daniel Way. Silv E 79 F2
Daniell Cl. Clact 109 E3
Darcy Rise. Lit Bad 129 F1
Darenth Rd. Hadl 189 D1
Dark La. Thund 188 A3
Darkhouse La. Rowh 87 D4
Darlinghurst Gr. South 190 A1
Darnay Rise. Chelm 126 B3
Darnel Way. Stanw 66 A4
Darnet Rd. Tolle 119 F5
Darrell Cl. Chelm 127 D3
Dart Cl. With 97 E1
Dartmouth Cl. Rayl 176 B3
Dartmouth Rd. Sprin 127 F3
Darwin Cl. Brain 59 F1
Darwin Cl. Kelv 68 A1
Datchet Dr. South 192 C1
Davall Cl. Lit Oak 39 E1
Davenants. Basil 174 A1
Davey Cl. Colch 68 B3
Davey Cl. Harw 163 E1
Davidson Cl. Sud 13 E2
Dawberry Pl. S Woo F 165 E3
Dawes La. W Mers 121 F4
Dawlish Cres. Rayl 176 B3
Dawlish Dr. South 189 F1
Dawnford Cl. Stanw 66 B4
Dawnings The. S Woo F 165 E4
Daws Heath Rd. Hadl 188 C4
Daws Heath Rd. Rayl 188 C4
Days Cl. Chelm 127 D1
Dazeley's La. Str S M 34 C4
De Burgh Rd. Colch 66 C3
De Vere Ave. S Sud 13 E3
De Staunton Cl. Alres 88 A4
De Vere Ave. Mald 132 A1
De Vere Cl. Wiv 87 D4
De Vere Estate. Gt Ben 89 E4
De Vere La. Wiv 87 D4
De Vere Rd. Colch 67 D3
De Vere Rd. Ea Col 44 C4
De Vere Way. Harw 39 F1
De Veres Rd. Hals 25 E1
Dead La. Ard 51 E4
Dead La. Gt Ben 89 F1
Dead La. Lawf 35 D3
Dead La. Lit Cla 91 D3
Deadman's La. Gt Bad 140 B2
Deal Cl. Brain 59 F3
Deal Cl. Clact 125 E4
Dean Rogers Pl. Brain 59 F4
Dean St. Brigh 106 C4
Dean Way. Chelm 126 C1
Deane's Cl. Harw 40 A1
Deanery Gdns. Brain 59 F4
Deanery Hill. Brain 59 F4
Debden Cl. With 97 F1
Debden Dr. Sud 50 C1
Debden Rd. Colch 50 C1
Dedham Ave. Clact 109 D3
Dedham Meade. Ded 33 E1
Dedham Rd. Ard 51 F4
Dedham Rd. Box 32 A3
Dedham Rd. Lawf 34 C2
Dedham Rd. Str S M 22 C1
Deepdale Rd. Harw 40 A2
Deepdale. Thund 187 F3
Deepdene. Rayl 176 B4
Deepdene. Basil 185 D3
Deeping Wlk. St O 108 A1
Deeping. South 200 A4
Deepwater Rd. Canv 196 C2
Deer Park Cl. Ca Hed 15 F2
Deerhurst Chase. S Woo F 142 C1
Deerhurst Cl. Thund 188 A4
Deerhurst. Thund 188 A4
Deerleap Way. Brain 59 F4
Defoe Cres. Colch 49 F2
Deford Rd. With 98 A1
Deirdre Ave. Wick 174 A4
Deirdre Cl. Wick 174 A4

Delamere Rd. Chelm ... 126 C1
Delamere Rd. Colch ... 50 B2
Delaware Cres. South ... 201 E4
Delaware Rd. South ... 201 E4
Delder Ave. Canv ... 197 E1
Delft Rd. Canv ... 197 D2
Delftzul Rd. Canv ... 197 D2
Delgada Rd. Canv ... 197 E2
Delhi Rd. Basil ... 186 B3
Dell The. Basil ... 185 D2
Dell The. Gt Bad ... 140 C3
Dell The. Sud ... 13 D3
Dell The. Wick ... 174 C4
Delmar Gdns. Runw ... 163 E1
Delview. Canv ... 196 C3
Delvins. Basil ... 186 A4
Delvyn's La. Gest ... 50 B4
Dencourt Cres. Basil ... 185 F3
Dene Cl. Rayl ... 176 B2
Dene Ct. Chelm ... 126 B3
Dene Gdns. Rayl ... 176 B2
Dene Gdns. Rayl ... 176 B2
Denesmere. S Ben ... 187 E2
Deneway. Basil ... 185 E3
Dengayne. Basil ... 185 E3
Dengie Cl. With ... 114 C4
Denham Cl. Elmst M ... 87 E4
Denham Rd. Canv ... 197 D2
Denmark St. Colch ... 67 F3
Denten Cl. With ... 115 D4
Denton App. South ... 190 B3
Denton Ave. South ... 190 B3
Denton Cl. South ... 190 B3
Denver Dr. Basil ... 174 B1
Derby Cl. May ... 146 C1
Derby Cl. Steep ... 147 D1
Derbydale. Hawk ... 178 B3
Derek Gdns. South ... 190 C3
Dering Cres. South ... 189 E4
Derventer Ave. Canv ... 197 D3
Derwent Ave. Rayl ... 176 C1
Derwent Gdns. Clact ... 110 B3
Derwent Rd. Colch ... 50 B2
Derwent Way. Bl Not ... 77 E4
Derwent Way. Chelm ... 126 B2
Devereaux Cl. Walt ... 93 F4
Devereox Rd. South ... 200 A4
Devon Gdns. Hawk ... 178 B3
Devon Cl. Colch ... 67 D2
Devon Way. Canv ... 197 D3
Devon Way. Clact ... 110 C4
Devon Way. Harw ... 39 E1
Devonshire Gdns. Brain ... 60 A2
Devonshire Rd. Burn ... 170 B3
Devonshire Rd. Soum ... 159 E3
Dewlands. Basil ... 185 D4
Dewsgreen. Basil ... 185 D4
Dewyk Rd. Canv ... 197 E3
Dial Rd. Gt Ben ... 89 F2
Diana Way. Clact ... 109 E1
Dickens Cl. Brain ... 78 A4
Dickens Cl. South ... 191 D1
Dickens Pl. Chelm ... 126 B4
Dicket's Hill. Gt Y ... 15 D3
Digby Mews. W Mers ... 121 E3
Dilbridge Rd. Colch ... 68 B4
Dilston. Dan ... 143 D3
Dinant Ave. Canv ... 196 C2
Dinants Cres. Mks T ... 64 C2
Dinsdale Cl. Colch ... 68 B4
Dismals The. Terl ... 96 A1
Disraeli Rd. Rayl ... 189 D4
Distillery La. Colch ... 68 B2
Ditton Court Rd. South ... 199 E4
Dixon Ave. Chelm ... 126 C2
Dixon Ave. Clact ... 109 E3
Dixon Cl. Lawf ... 35 D2
Dixon Way. Wiv ... 69 D1
Dobbies La. Mks T ... 64 C2
Dock La. Gt Oak ... 57 D2
Dock Rd. May ... 147 D1
Dockfield Ave. Harw ... 39 F2
Dockwra La. Dan ... 143 D4
Doctor's La. Ashe ... 3 E1
Docwra Rd. Kelv ... 81 E1
Doeshill Dr. Wick ... 174 C4
Doggetts Chase. Roch ... 178 C3
Doggetts Cl. Roch ... 178 C3
Doghouse Rd. Bradw ... 61 F2
Dolby Rise. Sprin ... 127 F1
Dollant Ave. Canv ... 197 D2
Dolphins. South ... 190 B2
Dombey Cl. Chelm ... 126 C4
Doms La. Terl ... 96 A1
Domsey Bank. Mks T ... 84 C2
Domsey Chase. Fee ... 82 C4
Don Ct. With ... 97 E1
Donald Thorn Cl. Wick ... 174 B3
Donald Way. Chelm ... 140 B4
Donard Dr. W Berg ... 48 B2
Doney Chase. Lit Brx ... 115 F3
Donkey La. Str S M ... 22 C1
Donne Dr. Clact ... 125 D4
Donyland Way. Rowh ... 86 C4
Dooley Rd. Hals ... 25 E1
Dorchester End. Colch ... 68 A2
Dorewards Ave. Brain ... 59 F4
Doric Ave. Hawk ... 178 B3
Dorking Cres. Clact ... 109 E3

Dorothy Curtice Ct. Copf ... 65 F3
Dorothy Farm Rd. Rayl ... 177 D1
Dorothy Gdns. Thund ... 187 F3
Dorothy Sayers Dr. With ... 98 A3
Dorset Ave. Gt Bad ... 140 C3
Dorset Cl. Clact ... 110 C3
Dorset Cl. Gt Bad ... 140 C3
Dorset Gdns. Hawk ... 178 B3
Dorset Rd. Burn ... 170 B2
Dorset Rd. Mald ... 144 C4
Dorset Way. Canv ... 197 D3
Douglas Cl. Chelm ... 140 B2
Douglas Dr. Wick ... 174 B3
Douglas Gr. With ... 97 E1
Douglas Rd. Clact ... 109 E2
Douglas Rd. Hadl ... 188 C2
Douglas Rd. Harw ... 40 A2
Douglas Wlk. Chelm ... 140 A4
Doulton Way. Hawk ... 178 B3
Dove Cres. Harw ... 39 E1
Dove Dr. S Ben ... 187 D1
Dove La. Chelm ... 140 A3
Dovecote. South ... 192 C1
Dovedale Gdns. Clact ... 110 B3
Dovedale. Canv ... 197 E3
Dover Cl. Brain ... 59 F3
Dover Cl. Clact ... 125 E4
Dover Rd. Brigh ... 106 C4
Dovercliff Rd. Canv ... 197 F1
Dovervelt Rd. Canv ... 197 E3
Dovesgate. S Ben ... 187 D2
Dow Ct. Soum ... 159 E2
Dowches Dr. Kelv ... 81 E2
Dowches Gdns. Kelv ... 81 E2
Dowling Rd. M Bure ... 28 C2
Down Hall Rd. Rayl ... 176 B2
Downer Rd N. Thund ... 187 F3
Downer Rd. S Ben ... 187 E3
Downesway. S Ben ... 187 E2
Downey Cl. Basil ... 185 E4
Downhall Cl. Rayl ... 176 B2
Downhall Park Way. Rayl ... 176 B3
Downham Rd. Canv ... 197 D2
Downham Rd. Runw ... 163 E4
Downleaze. S Woo F ... 165 F4
Downs Gr. Basil ... 185 F2
Downs Rd. Mald ... 132 A2
Downs The. Nay ... 20 B3
Downsway. Sprin ... 127 E3
Downton Wlk. Tipt ... 100 B3
Dragon Cl. Burn ... 170 A3
Drake Ave. May ... 158 A4
Drake Cl. Thund ... 188 B3
Drake Gdns. Brain ... 60 B2
Drake Rd. South ... 190 B1
Drakes App. Clact ... 109 D1
Drakes La. Lit Wal ... 112 A4
Drakes The. South ... 201 D4
Drakes Way. Rayl ... 176 C2
Drapers Chase. Mald ... 132 B2
Drapers Rd. S Woo F ... 165 F4
Drapery Comm. Glems ... 2 A2
Drays The. L Mel ... 7 D3
Drayton Cl. Mald ... 132 A1
Dreweteignton. South ... 201 E4
Driberg Way. Brain ... 60 A1
Driffield Cl. Fee ... 81 E2
Drift The. Sud ... 13 E3
Driftway. Basil ... 185 F2
Drive The. Chelm ... 127 D3
Drive The. Clact ... 110 A4
Drive The. Harw ... 40 A1
Drive The. Hull ... 165 E2
Drive The. May ... 157 F4
Drive The. Rayl ... 189 D4
Drive The. Roch ... 178 C2
Drive The. South ... 199 D4
Driveway The. Canv ... 197 F2
Droitwich Ave. South ... 191 E1
Drood Cl. Chelm ... 126 C4
Drum Field. Str S M ... 22 B1
Drury La. Brain ... 59 F2
Drury La. Ridge ... 8 A3
Drury Rd. Colch ... 67 E3
Dryden Ave. South ... 191 D1
Dryden Cl. Mald ... 145 D4
Drywoods. S Woo F ... 165 E3
Du Cane Pl. With ... 98 A1
Dubarry Cl. Thund ... 187 F3
Duck La. Ded ... 33 F2
Duckets Mead. Cane ... 168 B1
Dudley Cl. Colch ... 68 A2
Dudley Rd. Clact ... 109 E2
Dudley Rd. Ea Col ... 44 C4
Dudley Rd. Fing ... 86 C2
Duffield Dr. Colch ... 68 C4
Duffield Rd. Gt Bad ... 140 B4
Duffs Hill. Glems ... 2 A3
Dugard Ave. Colch ... 66 C2
Duggers La. Brain ... 60 A1
Dugmore Ave. Walt ... 93 E4
Duke St. Brigh ... 106 C3
Duke St. Chelm ... 127 D2
Dukes Ave. Soum ... 159 E2
Dukes La. Sprin ... 127 F2
Dukes Park Ind Est. Sprin ... 127 F2
Dukes Rd. Brain ... 59 F3
Dulverton Ave. South ... 190 A2
Dulverton Cl. South ... 190 A3

Dulwich Rd. Clact ... 110 B3
Dumont Ave. St O ... 107 D1
Duncan Ave. South ... 190 A1
Duncan Rd. Colch ... 67 D2
Duncan Rise. Gt Y ... 8 C1
Dundee Ave. Hadl ... 189 D1
Dundee Cl. Hadl ... 189 E1
Dundonald Dr. South ... 189 F1
Dungannon Chase. South ... 201 D3
Dungannon Dr. South ... 201 D3
Dunkirk Rd. Burn ... 170 B3
Dunlin Cl. Mald ... 132 B3
Dunlin Cl. S Woo F ... 154 B1
Dunlin Ct. Kelv ... 81 E1
Dunmore Rd. Sprin ... 128 A2
Dunnock Way. Colch ... 69 D4
Dunoon Cl. Brain ... 60 B2
Dunster Ave. South ... 190 A3
Dunthorne Rd. Colch ... 50 C1
Dunthorpe Rd. South ... 189 D1
Dupont Cl. Clact ... 109 E3
Durants Wlk. Wick ... 174 B3
Durham Rd. Hawk ... 178 A3
Durham Rd. Colch ... 191 E1
Durham Sq. Colch ... 68 A4
Durham Way. Rayl ... 176 B3
Durley Cl. S Ben ... 187 F2
Durrington Cl. Basil ... 185 E3
Duxford. Wick ... 175 D3
Dyer's Rd. Mald ... 132 A1
Dyer's Rd. Stanw ... 66 B2
Dyke Cres. Canv ... 196 B2
Dykes Chase. Mald ... 131 E4
Dyne's Hall Rd. Gt Map ... 25 E4
Dynevor Gdns. Hadl ... 189 D1

Eagle Ave. Walt ... 76 B1
Eagle La. Brain ... 59 F3
Eagle Way. South ... 201 F4
Earlhams Cl. Harw ... 39 F1
Earls Colne Rd. Gt T ... 46 A1
Earls Hall Ave. South ... 190 C2
Earls Hall Dr. Clact ... 108 C3
Earls Hall Par. South ... 190 C2
Earlsfield Dr. Sprin ... 127 F2
Earlsmead. S Ben ... 187 F2
Earlswood Way. Colch ... 67 E1
Earlswood. S Ben ... 187 E2
East Bay. Colch ... 68 A4
East Bridge Rd. S Woo F ... 165 F4
East Cres. Canv ... 196 C2
East Dock Rd. Rams ... 39 F3
East Gores Rd. Gt T ... 63 F3
East Hanningfield Rd. Rett ... 153 E1
East Hanningfield Rd. Sand ... 142 A1
East Hill. Colch ... 68 A4
East La. Ded ... 34 A3
East Mayne. Basil ... 174 A1
East Mersea Rd. W Mers ... 104 C1
East Mill. Hals ... 25 F1
East Rd. E Mers ... 105 F1
East Rd. W Mers ... 121 E3
East Sq. Basil ... 185 D3
East St. Brain ... 60 A2
East St. Cogg ... 63 D1
East St. Colch ... 68 A4
East St. Gold ... 134 A1
East St. Harw ... 40 B2
East St. Roch ... 178 C1
East St. South ... 190 C1
East St. Sud ... 12 C4
East St. South ... 198 C4
East St. Tolle ... 119 E1
East St. Wiv ... 87 D4
East Stockwell St. Colch ... 67 F4
East Terr. Walt ... 76 B1
East Thorpe. Basil ... 185 E3
East Wlk. Basil ... 185 D3
Eastbourne Gr. South ... 190 B2
Eastbrooks Mews. Basil ... 186 A4
Eastbrooks Pl. Basil ... 186 A4
Eastbrooks. Basil ... 186 A4
Eastbury Ave. Hawk ... 178 B2
Eastcheap. Rayl ... 176 B2
Eastcliff Ave. Clact ... 110 A2
Eastcote Gr. South ... 191 E2
Eastend Rd. Brad O S ... 137 E2
Easterford Rd. Kelv ... 81 E1
Easterling Cl. Harw ... 40 A2
Eastern App. Sprin ... 127 F3
Eastern Cres. Brain ... 59 F3
Eastern Esp. Canv ... 197 E1
Eastern Espl. South ... 200 B3
Eastern Prom. St O ... 106 C2
Eastern Rd. Brigh ... 106 C4
Eastern Rd. Rayl ... 176 A1
Eastfield Rd. Canv ... 197 E3
Eastgate St. Harw ... 40 B3
Eastgate. Basil ... 185 D3
Easthorpe Rd. Copf ... 82 B4
Eastleigh Rd. S Ben ... 187 F1
Easton Rd. With ... 98 A2
Easton Way. Frin ... 94 A3
Eastview Dr. Rayl ... 176 B3
Eastways. Canv ... 196 C3
Eastways. With ... 98 A2

Eastwood Bvd. South ... 190 A2
Eastwood Dr. Colch ... 50 A2
Eastwood La S. South ... 190 A1
Eastwood Old Rd. Hadl ... 189 D1
Eastwood Old Rd. South ... 189 D1
Eastwood Park Cl. South ... 189 F3
Eastwood Park Dr. South ... 189 F4
Eastwood Rd N. South ... 189 F2
Eastwood Rd. Rayl ... 188 C4
Eastwood Rd. South ... 189 E1
Eastwood Rise. Rayl ... 189 E4
Eastwoodbury Cl. South ... 190 C3
Eastwoodbury La. South ... 190 B3
Eaton Mews. Colch ... 68 A2
Eaton Rd. Hadl ... 189 E1
Eaton Way. Gt Tot ... 116 C4
Ebenezer Cl. With ... 97 F3
Ebony Cl. Colch ... 67 E1
Eckersley Rd. Chelm ... 127 E2
Eden Cl. With ... 97 F2
Eden Way. Chelm ... 126 B3
Edenside. Walt ... 93 F4
Edgefield Ave. Lawf ... 35 D2
Edgware Rd. Clact ... 109 E3
Edgworth Rd. Sud ... 12 C4
Edinburgh Ave. Hadl ... 189 D1
Edinburgh Cl. With ... 115 D4
Edinburgh Gdns. Brain ... 60 B2
Edison Cl. Brain ... 59 F1
Edison Gdns. Colch ... 50 B1
Edison Rd. Clact ... 110 C3
Edith Cl. Canv ... 196 B2
Edith Rd. Canv ... 196 B2
Edith Rd. Clact ... 109 F1
Edith Rd. South ... 190 C1
Edith Rd. Walt ... 93 E4
Edmund Green. Gos ... 42 C4
Edmund Rd. With ... 114 C4
Edward Ave. Brigh ... 106 C4
Edward Cl. Ashi ... 178 B3
Edward Cl. Lit Cla ... 91 F3
Edward Dr. Chelm ... 140 B4
Edward Gdns. Runw ... 174 B4
Edward Rd. Th L S ... 91 F4
Edward St. Rams ... 39 F3
Edwin Hall View. S Woo F ... 154 B1
Edwin's Hall La. S Woo F ... 154 B2
Egbert Gdns. Runw ... 163 E1
Egerton-Green Rd. Colch ... 67 D2
Eglinton Dr. South ... 191 D3
Egremont St. Glems ... 2 A2
Egremont Way. Stanw ... 66 B2
Egret Cres. Colch ... 69 D4
Eight Acre La. Colch ... 67 E4
Eld La. Colch ... 67 F4
Eldbert Cl. South ... 191 F1
Elder Ave. Wick ... 174 B4
Elder Tree Rd. Canv ... 197 E2
Elder Way. Wick ... 174 B3
Elderberry Gdns. With ... 98 A2
Elderstep Ave. Canv ... 197 F2
Elderton Rd. South ... 190 B1
Eldon Cl. Colch ... 50 C1
Eldon Way. Hock ... 177 F3
Eldred Cl. Colch ... 67 D2
Eldred Dr. Sud ... 12 C4
Eleanor Chase. Wick ... 174 B4
Eleanor Cl. Tipt ... 100 B3
Eleanor Wlk. Tipt ... 100 B3
Electric Ave. South ... 190 B1
Elgar Cl. Thund ... 187 D3
Elham Dr. Chelm ... 127 D1
Elham Dr. Basil ... 186 B3
Elianore Rd. Colch ... 67 D3
Eliot Cl. Wick ... 174 B3
Eliot Mews. South ... 191 D1
Eliot Way. Mald ... 132 A1
Elizabeth Ave. Rayl ... 176 B1
Elizabeth Ave. With ... 115 D4
Elizabeth Cl. Clact ... 109 F2
Elizabeth Cl. Hawk ... 177 F2
Elizabeth Dr. Wick ... 174 A4
Elizabeth Rd. Harw ... 40 A2
Elizabeth Rd. South ... 200 B3
Elizabeth Way. Brigh ... 106 B4
Elizabeth Way. Hat Pev ... 114 A2
Elizabeth Way. Mald ... 132 A3
Elizabeth Way. Sud ... 12 C3
Elizabeth Way. Thund ... 188 B2
Elizabeth Way. With ... 98 A2
Ellen Way. Bl Not ... 77 E4
Ellenbrook Cl. South ... 189 F2
Ellesmere Rd. Ashi ... 167 E3
Ellesmere Rd. Canv ... 196 C2
Elliot Cl. S Woo F ... 165 F3
Elliots Dr. Walt ... 94 A4
Ellis Rd. Box ... 31 F2
Ellis Rd. Brad ... 54 A3
Ellis Rd. Clact ... 109 F1
Elliston Way. Sud ... 12 B3
Elm Ave. Mald ... 132 B3
Elm Bungalows. Brain ... 59 E2
Elm Cl. Gdns ... 88 A4
Elm Cl. Broom ... 127 D4
Elm Cl. Gt Bad ... 140 C3
Elm Cl. Rayl ... 176 B2
Elm Cl. Si Hed ... 15 E1
Elm Cl. South ... 201 F4
Elm Cl. Tipt ... 100 B4

Elm Cres. Colch ... 68 B4
Elm Dr. Hals ... 25 F1
Elm Dr. Rayl ... 176 B2
Elm Drive. Brigh ... 106 B4
Elm Gr. Clact ... 109 F3
Elm Gr. Hull ... 165 E1
Elm Gr. South ... 201 D4
Elm Gr. Walt ... 93 E3
Elm Gr. Wiv ... 69 D1
Elm Green La. Dan ... 142 B4
Elm Green. Basil ... 186 A3
Elm La. Fee ... 64 A1
Elm Rd. Basil ... 174 C1
Elm Rd. Canv ... 197 E2
Elm Rd. Chelm ... 140 A4
Elm Rd. Hadl ... 188 B1
Elm Rd. Lit Cla ... 91 E2
Elm Rd. Runw ... 174 B4
Elm Rd. S Ben ... 187 E4
Elm Rd. S Ben ... 189 F1
Elm Rd. South ... 201 F4
Elm Rd. Sud ... 13 D4
Elm Rise. With ... 98 A3
Elm Tree Ave. Walt ... 93 F4
Elm Tree Cl. Walt ... 93 F4
Elm View Rd. S Ben ... 187 D2
Elm Way. Bore ... 112 C1
Elmden Cl. Clact ... 109 F3
Elmfield Cl. Clact ... 110 C4
Elmhurst Ave. S Ben ... 187 D2
Elmhurst Rd. Harw ... 40 B2
Elms Dr. Chelm ... 126 B3
Elms Hall Rd. Col En ... 44 C4
Elmsleigh Dr. South ... 189 F2
Elmstead Rd. Colch ... 68 C3
Elmstead Rd. Wiv ... 69 E2
Elmtree Rd. Basil ... 186 A2
Elmwood Ave. Colch ... 67 E1
Elmwood Ave. Hawk ... 177 F2
Elmwood Dr. W Mers ... 121 E4
Elounda Ct. S Ben ... 187 E2
Elronds Rest. S Woo F ... 165 E3
Elsden Chase. Soum ... 159 E2
Elsenham Cres. Basil ... 185 F3
Elsinor Ave. Canv ... 196 C3
Elthorne Park. Clact ... 109 E2
Elton Wlk. Tipt ... 100 B3
Elwes Cl. Colch ... 50 B1
Elwin Rd. Tipt ... 100 B3
Ely Cl. Soum ... 159 E2
Ely Rd. South ... 191 D1
Elysian Gdns. Tolle ... 119 E1
Ember Way. Burn ... 170 A3
Emberson Ct. Sprin ... 127 F2
Empire Rd. Harw ... 40 B2
Empress Ave. W Mers ... 121 F3
Endean Ct. Wiv ... 69 D1
Endeavour Cl. Tolle ... 119 E1
Endsleigh Ct. Colch ... 67 E4
Endway The. May ... 158 B1
Endway. Hadl ... 188 C1
Enfield Rd. Wick ... 175 E4
Englefield Cl. Hawk ... 178 A2
Enid Way. Colch ... 49 E1
Ennerdale Ave. Bl Not ... 77 E3
Ennismore Gdns. South ... 191 D2
Enterprise Ct. Brain ... 60 A1
Enterprise Way. Wick ... 174 C3
Enville Way. Colch ... 50 A2
Epping Cl. Chelm ... 126 C4
Epping Cl. Clact ... 109 F4
Epsom Cl. Clact ... 109 E3
Erbury Pl. Cla ... 4 A4
Eric Rd. Basil ... 186 C3
Erica Wlk. Colch ... 68 C4
Erick Ave. Chelm ... 127 E4
Eridge Cl. Brain ... 60 B2
Erle Havard Rd. W Berg ... 48 C2
Ernalds Cl. Ea Col ... 45 D4
Ernest Rd. Wiv ... 69 E1
Ernulph Wlk. Colch ... 68 A4
Errington Rd. Colch ... 67 E3
Esplanade Gdns. South ... 199 D4
Esplanade The. Clact ... 111 D3
Esplanade The. Hull ... 165 E2
Esplanade. Frin ... 94 A1
Esplanade. Harw ... 40 B3
Esplanade. May ... 146 C1
Essex Ave. Chelm ... 127 D4
Essex Ave. Clact ... 124 C3
Essex Ave. Sud ... 7 F1
Essex Cl. Canv ... 197 D1
Essex Cl. Rayl ... 176 C1
Essex Gdns. South ... 189 F2
Essex Hall Rd. Colch ... 67 F4
Essex Knowle. Bures ... 19 F1
Essex Rd. Basil ... 186 C3
Essex Rd. Burn ... 170 B3
Essex Rd. Clact ... 109 F1
Essex Rd. Mald ... 131 F1
Essex Rd. Mald ... 144 C4
Essex Regiment Way. Broom ... 127 E4
Essex St. South ... 200 A4
Essex Way. S Ben ... 187 E3
Essex Yeomanry Way. Colch ... 66 A3
Estate Rd. Hadl ... 188 C2

Estella Mead. Chelm 126 C4
Estuary Cres. Sho G 40 A4
Estuary Gdns. Gt Wak 193 E1
Estuary Mews. Tolle 119 E1
Estuary Park Rd. W Mers 121 F3
Estuary Rd. Sho G 40 A4
Ethel Rd. Rayl 189 D4
Ethelbert Rd. Ashi 167 E1
Etheldore Ave. Hock 177 F4
Ethelred Gdns. Runw 163 E1
Eton Cl. Canv 197 D3
Eton Rd. Clact 109 F2
Eton Rd. Frin 94 A3
Eudo Rd. Colch 67 E2
Europa Way. Rams 39 F2
Evelyn Rd. Hock 177 F3
Evelyn Wood Rd. T Gr 78 C3
Everard Rd. Basil 186 A4
Everest Way. Mald 132 A3
Everest. Rayl 176 B3
Evergreen Dr. Colch 50 B2
Everitt Way. Si Hed 15 F1
Eversley Rd. Basil 185 E3
Eversley Rd. Thund 187 E4
Eves Crn. Burn 170 A4
Eves Cres. Chelm 127 D3
Eves Ct. Harw 39 E1
Ewan Cl. Hadl 189 D2
Ewan Cl. Stanw 66 B3
Ewan Way. Hadl 189 D2
Ewan Way. Stanw 66 B4
Ewell Hall Chase. Kelv 81 E1
Exchange Way. Chelm 127 D1
Exeter Cl. Basil 185 F4
Exeter Cl. Brain 60 A3
Exeter Cl. Gt Hor 49 D4
Exeter Cl. South 192 C1
Exeter Dr. Colch 68 A4
Exeter Rd. Sprin 127 F3
Exford Ave. South 190 A2
Exhibition La. Gt Wak 192 C3
Exmoor Cl. Chelm 126 B1
Exmouth Dr. Rayl 176 B3
Eynesham Way. Basil 174 A1

Faber Rd. With 114 C4
Fabians Cl. Cogg 63 D2
Factory Hill. Tipt 100 C2
Factory La E. Hals 25 F1
Factory La W. Hals 25 F1
Factory Terr. Hals 25 F1
Faggots Yd. Brain 59 F3
Fair Cl. Brigh 107 D3
Fair Green. Glems 2 A3
Fair Mead. Basil 185 D4
Fairfax Ave. Basil 186 B4
Fairfax Dr. South 190 B1
Fairfax Mead. Sprin 127 F1
Fairfax Rd. Colch 67 F3
Fairfield Cres. South 189 F3
Fairfield Gdns. South 189 F3
Fairfield Rd. Brain 59 F1
Fairfield Rd. Chelm 127 D2
Fairfield Rd. Clact 110 B3
Fairfield Rd. S Ben 188 B2
Fairfield. Gt Wak 193 D2
Fairhaven Ave. W Mers 121 F3
Fairhead Rd. Colch 68 B4
Fairhouse Ct. Basil 185 E3
Fairland Cl. Rayl 176 C3
Fairlawn Gdns. South 190 C3
Fairleads. Dan 142 C4
Fairleigh Ave. Basil 186 B3
Fairleigh Dr. Basil 189 E1
Fairleigh Rd. Basil 186 B3
Fairlight Rd. S Ben 188 B2
Fairlop Cl. Clact 109 F4
Fairlop Cres. Canv 197 D2
Fairlop Gdns. South 189 E3
Fairmead Ave. Hadl 188 C3
Fairmead Ave. South 190 B1
Fairmead. Rayl 176 C4
Fairstead Hall Rd. Fair 96 A3
Fairstead Rd. Fair 96 B3
Fairstead Rd. Terl 96 B2
Fairstead. Basil 185 D3
Fairview Cl. Thund 187 E4
Fairview Cres. Thund 187 E4
Fairview Dr. South 190 B2
Fairview Gdns. Hadl 189 D4
Fairview Rd. Basil 185 F3
Fairview Wlk. Thund 187 E4
Fairview. Canv 196 C3
Fairway Dr. Burn 170 A3
Fairway Gdns Cl. South 189 E3
Fairway Gdns. South 189 E3
Fairway The. South 189 E3
Fairway The. Thund 187 E4
Fairway. Gt Bad 140 B4
Fairway. Wick 174 B2
Fairways The. Col N 155 F3
Fairy Hall La. Rayl 59 D1
Fal Dr. With 97 F1
Falbro Cres. Hadl 188 B2
Falcon Cl. South 189 F3
Falcon Cres. Colch 68 A2
Falcon Fields. Mald 144 C4
Falcon Mews. Mald 144 C4

Falcon Rd. Soum 159 E2
Falcon Sq. Ca Hed 15 F2
Falcon Way. Basil 185 E2
Falcon Way. Clact 109 F3
Falcon Way. South 192 C1
Falcon Yd. Wiv 87 D4
Falkenham End. Basil 185 E4
Falkenham Path. Basil 185 E4
Falkenham Rise. Basil 185 E4
Falkenham Row. Basil 185 E4
Falkland Cl. Bore 128 C4
Falklands Dr. Harw 35 E2
Falklands Rd. Burn 170 A3
Fallowfield Cl. Harw 39 F2
Fallowfield Rd. Colch 67 E1
Fallows The. Canv 196 C3
Falmouth Rd. Sprin 127 F3
Fambridge Chase. Wh Not 78 C1
Fambridge Cl. Mald 132 A1
Fambridge Dr. Wick 174 C3
Fambridge Rd. Alth 157 F1
Fambridge Rd. Ashi 167 E3
Fambridge Rd. Col N 156 A2
Fambridge Rd. Mald 156 A2
Fambridge Rd. N Fam 156 A2
Fambridge Rd. Purl 156 A2
Fane Rd. Thund 187 E4
Fanny's La. St O 90 B1
Fanton Ave. Wick 174 C2
Fanton Chase. Wick 175 D3
Fanton Wlk. Wick 175 D3
Faraday Cl. Brain 59 F1
Faraday Cl. Clact 110 A4
Faraday Rd. South 189 E3
Farford Field. Sud 13 E3
Farm Cres. Rett 164 C2
Farm Rd. Canv 197 D3
Farm Rd. Gt Oak 56 B2
Farm View. Rayl 176 B3
Farm Way. Thund 187 E4
Farm Wlk. Brigh 106 C4
Farmers End. Stanw 66 B3
Farmfield Rd. Gt T 46 A1
Farmleigh Ave. Clact 109 F4
Farnes Ave. Wick 174 B4
Farriers End. Stanw 66 B3
Farriers Way. South 190 C3
Farrington Way. Lawf 35 D2
Farthing Centre The. Chelm ... 127 D1
Fastnet. South 190 A4
Faulkbourne Rd. Faulk 97 E2
Faulkbourne Rd. With 97 E2
Fauners. Basil 185 D3
Fawkner Ct. Sprin 127 F1
Featherby Way. Roch 179 D1
Feeches Rd. South 190 B3
Feedhams Cl. Wiv 69 E2
Feering Dr. Basil 185 F3
Feering Hill. Fee 81 E2
Feering Rd. Fee 63 D1
Feering Row. Basil 185 F3
Felixstowe Cl. Clact 109 D2
Fellcroft. Basil 186 B3
Felmores. Basil 186 A4
Felstead Cl. Colch 86 A4
Felstead Cl. S Ben 187 E2
Felstead Rd. S Ben 187 E3
Fen La. Ard 33 E1
Fen St. Nay 20 A1
Fenn Cl. S Woo F 165 F4
Fenn Rd. Hals 26 A1
Fennel Cl. Tipt 100 B3
Fennings Chase. Colch 68 A4
Fenno Cl. Colch 66 C2
Fenwick Way. Canv 197 D3
Ferdinand Wlk. Colch 68 C4
Fermoy Rd. South 201 D4
Fern Hill. Glems 2 A4
Fern Way. Clact 124 C4
Fernbrook Ave. South 200 B4
Ferndale Cl. Clact 109 D2
Ferndale Cres. Canv 197 D1
Ferndale Rd. Harw 40 B2
Ferndale Rd. Rayl 176 C3
Ferndale Rd. South 191 E1
Ferndown Rd. Frin 93 F3
Ferndown Way. Hat Pev 114 A2
Fernie Rd. Brain 170 A3
Fernlea Rd. Burn 170 A3
Fernlea Rd. Harw 40 B2
Fernlea Rd. S Ben 187 F2
Fernlea. Colch 49 E1
Fernleigh Dr. South 190 A1
Fernwood Ave. Clact 110 C3
Fernwood. Hadl 188 C2
Ferrers Rd. S Woo F 165 E3
Ferry Rd. Brain 169 F3
Ferry Rd. Canv 196 B4
Ferry Rd. Fing 87 D3
Ferry Rd. Hull 165 E1
Ferry Rd. N Fam 167 D3
Ferrymead. Canv 196 C3
Festival Gdns. Toll D 118 B2

Feverills Rd. Lit Cla 91 E2
Fiat Ave. Clact 124 B3
Fiddlers Folly. E A Gr 47 F1
Fiddlers Hill. E A Gr 47 F1
Field Way. Wiv 69 E1
Field Wlk. Walt 94 A4
Fields Cl. Weel 90 C3
Fields Farm Rd. Lay H 85 D2
Fieldway. Basil 186 B2
Fieldway. Wick 174 C3
Fifth Ave. Canv 196 C2
Fifth Ave. Chelm 127 D3
Fifth Ave. Frin 93 F3
Fifth Ave. Wick 175 D3
Filey Rd. Soum 159 D2
Fillebrook Ave. South 190 A1
Filliol Cl. E Han 153 D3
Finch Dr. Gt Ben 71 E1
Finchdale. Clact 109 F3
Finches The. Thund 188 A4
Finchfield. Rayl 176 B1
Finchingfield Way. Colch 86 A4
Finchingfield Way. Wick 174 B3
Finchland View. S Woo F 165 E3
Finchley Rd. Chelm 140 A4
Finchley Rd. South 199 E4
Finer Cl. Clact 109 E3
Fingringhoe Rd. Colch 68 B1
Fingringhoe Rd. Lang 86 A2
Finham Cl. Colch 68 C4
Fir Tree Cl. Colch 50 A2
Fir Tree La. Lit Bad 129 F1
Fir Tree Rise. Colch 140 A3
Fir Tree Wlk. Mald 132 B3
Fir Way. Clact 125 D3
Fir Wlk. Canv 196 C3
Firecrest Rd. Chelm 140 B3
Firecrest Rd. Gt Bad 140 B3
Firfield Rd. Thund 188 B3
Firle Wlk. Colch 68 C4
Firs Chase. W Mers 121 D3
Firs Dr. Writ 126 A1
Firs Hamlet. W Mers 121 D3
Firs Rd. Tipt 100 B2
Firs Rd. W Mers 121 D4
Firs The. Canv 196 C3
Firs The. Lay H 85 D3
First Ave. Canv 196 C2
First Ave. Chelm 127 D3
First Ave. Clact 110 A2
First Ave. Frin 93 F2
First Ave. Glems 2 B3
First Ave. Hals 26 A1
First Ave. Harw 40 B2
First Ave. Hull 165 F1
First Ave. South 199 D4
First Ave. Walt 76 B2
First Ave. Weel 72 C1
First Ave. Wick 175 D3
Firstore Dr. Colch 66 C4
Firwood's Rd. Hals 43 F4
Fish St. Gold 133 F3
Fisher Way. Brain 60 B2
Fishponds Hill. Lit Hor 30 C2
Fisin Wlk. Colch 66 C2
Fitch's Cres. Mald 132 A1
Fitzgerald Cl. Lawf 35 D2
Fitzgilbert Rd. Colch 67 E2
Fitzwalter La. Dan 142 B3
Fitzwalter Pl. Chelm 126 C2
Fitzwalter Rd. Bore 128 C4
Fitzwalter Rd. Colch 67 D3
Fitzwilliam Manor. Chelm 126 C4
Fitzwilliam Rd. Colch 67 D4
Five Acres. S Woo F 142 C2
Five Acres. Walt 94 A4
Fiveash La. Bradw 61 F1
Flag Hill. St O 89 F1
Flagstaff Rd. Colch 67 F3
Flail Cl. Elmst M 69 F3
Flambird's Chase. Purl 154 C4
Flamboro Cl. South 189 E3
Flamboro Wlk. South 189 E3
Flanders Cl. Brain 59 F3
Flanders Field. Colch 68 A2
Flatford Dr. Clact 109 D2
Flatford Rd. Str S M 34 B4
Flax La. Glems 2 B2
Fleet Rd. S Ben 187 E1
Fleetway. Basil 185 F2
Fleetwood Ave. Clact 110 C4
Fleetwood Ave. South 189 F1
Fleetwood Cl. South 189 F1
Fleming Cl. Brain 59 F1
Flemings Farm Rd. Rayl 189 E4
Flemming Ave. South 189 F1
Flemming Cres. South 189 F1
Fletchers Sq. South 191 D3
Flinstich Manor. Chelm 126 C4
Flixton Cl. Clact 109 D2
Flora Rd. With 97 E2
Florence Cl. Hadl 188 B2
Florence Gdns. Hadl 188 B2
Florence Neale House. Canv . 197 D2
Florence Rd. Canv 197 E2
Florence Rd. Walt 76 C1

Florie's Rd. Gt T 63 F4
Flowers Way. Clact 125 D4
Fobbing Farm Cl. Basil 185 D2
Fobbing Rd. Basil 185 D3
Foksville Rd. Canv 197 E2
Fold The. Basil 185 D3
Folkards La. Brigh 106 C4
Folley The. Lay H 85 D3
Folley The. Stanw 66 B3
Folly Chase. Hock 177 F3
Folly La. Hock 177 D3
Folly The. Toll K 100 C1
Folly The. Wiv 87 D4
Ford La. Alres 88 A3
Ford La. Colch 49 E3
Ford Rd. Clact 109 E2
Ford St. Ald 47 F1
Fordham Rd. M Bure 29 F1
Fordham Rd. Worm 29 F1
Fordson Rd. Bore 128 A3
Fordstreet Hill. Ald 47 E1
Forefield Green. Sprin 127 F4
Foregate Rd. Colch 68 B1
Forest Dr. Chelm 126 C1
Forest Park Ave. Clact 109 F4
Forest Rd. Colch 68 B4
Forest Rd. With 98 A3
Forest View Dr. Hadl 189 D2
Forfar Cl. Hadl 189 E1
Forfields Way. T Gr 78 C3
Forge Cres. Bradw 61 E2
Forge St. Ded 34 A3
Forrest Cl. S Woo F 165 E4
Forsythia Cl. Chelm 140 A4
Fort William Rd. Basil 185 D1
Fortescue Chase. South 191 F1
Fortune Cl. Gt Le 95 D4
Fossetts La. Ford 47 F2
Fostal Cl. South 189 F2
Foster Rd. Canv 197 E2
Foster Rd. Gt Tot 116 A2
Foster Rd. Rams 39 F3
Foulgar Cl. S Woo F 165 E4
Foundry La. Burn 170 A3
Foundry La. Copf 65 E3
Foundry La. Ea Col 45 D3
Fountain Cl. Copf 83 F4
Fountain La. Hock 177 E3
Fourth Ave. Canv 196 C2
Fourth Ave. Chelm 127 D3
Fourth Ave. Clact 110 B2
Fourth Ave. Frin 93 F2
Fourth Ave. Glems 2 B3
Fourth Ave. Hals 26 A1
Fourth Ave. Wick 175 D3
Fox Burrows La. Writ 126 A1
Fox Cl. Thund 187 F3
Fox Cres. Chelm 126 C2
Fox's Rd. Ashe 3 F1
Foxborough Rd. Gt Bad 140 C4
Foxes La. E A Gr 47 E1
Foxfield Cl. Hock 178 A3
Foxglove Cl. With 97 E2
Foxglove Way. Sprin 127 F3
Foxhall Rd. Steep 159 D4
Foxhatch. Wick 174 C3
Foxmead. With 98 B3
Foxmeadows. Thund 187 F3
Foxwood Pl. Hadl 189 E1
Frampton Rd. Basil 174 A1
Frances Cl. Wiv 69 D1
Francis Cl. Tipt 100 B2
Francis Cl. Silv E 79 E2
Francis Mews. Mald 145 D4
Francis Rd. Brain 59 E1
Francis Rd. Sud 12 C4
Francis St. Brigh 106 C3
Francis Way. Silv E 79 E2
Francis Wlk. Rayl 176 B1
Frank Clater Cl. Colch 68 A4
Franklin Rd. N Fam 167 D4
Franklins Way. Wick 174 C4
Fraser Cl. Chelm 140 B4
Fraser Cl. South 201 F4
Frating Hill. Frat 72 A2
Frating Rd. Ard 52 A2
Frating Rd. Gt Bro 70 C3
Fratting Abbey Farm Rd. Thor 89 E3
Freebournes Rd. With 98 A1
Freeland Rd. Clact 110 A4
Freelands. Brigh 107 D3
Fremantle Cl. S Woo F 154 B1
Fremantle Rd. Colch 68 A1
Fremantle. South 201 E3
Fremnells The. Basil 185 E4
French Rd. Stow M 155 F1
Frensham Cl. Stanw 66 B3
Frere Way. Fing 87 E4
Freshwater Dr. Basil 185 F2
Frettons. Basil 185 F3
Friars Cl. Clact 109 F3
Friars Cl. South 50 B1
Friars Cl. Elmst M 87 E4
Friars Ct. Colch 68 B2

Friars La. Brain 60 A2
Friars La. Mald 131 F1
Friars St. South 201 F4
Friars St. Sud 12 C4
Friars Wlk. Chelm 127 D1
Friday Wood Green. Colch 85 F4
Friends Field. Bures 19 F1
Friern Gdns. Wick 174 A4
Friern Pl. Wick 174 A3
Friern Wlk. Wick 174 A4
Frieslana Rd. Walt 93 F3
Frinton Cl. Clact 110 B3
Frinton Rd. Th L S 92 B4
Frinton Rd. Walt 93 E3
Frobisher Dr. Clact 108 C1
Frobisher La. Harw 39 F1
Frobisher Way. Brain 60 B2
Frobisher Way. South 192 C1
Frog Hall Cl. Fing 87 D3
Fronk's Ave. Harw 40 B1
Fronk's Rd. Harw 40 A1
Frowick La. St O 90 A1
Fryatt Ave. Harw 40 A2
Fryth The. Basil 185 F4
Fulford Dr. South 190 A3
Fulbridge. Mald 132 A2
Fuller's Cl. Kelv 81 D1
Fuller's Rd. Colch 68 B1
Fulmar Cl. Colch 69 D4
Fulmar Way. Wick 175 D3
Fulton Rd. Thund 187 E4
Furlongs. Basil 185 E2
Furrow Cl. Colch 66 C3
Furrowfelde. Basil 185 D2
Further Meadow. Writ 139 D4
Furtherwick Rd. Canv 197 E2
Furze Cres. Alres 88 A4
Furze La. Gt Bro 71 D3
Fyfield Ave. Wick 174 B3
Fyfield Path. Rayl 176 A2
Fyfields. Basil 186 B4

Gablefields. Sand 141 E3
Gables The. Basil 186 A4
Gables The. Hadl 189 D3
Gadwall Reach. Kelv 81 E1
Gafzelle Dr. Canv 197 E1
Gage's Rd. Bel S P 4 C1
Gainsborough Ave. Canv 197 F2
Gainsborough Cl. Clact 100 C3
Gainsborough Cl. W Mers 121 F3
Gainsborough Dr. Lawf 35 D2
Gainsborough Dr. South 190 C1
Gainsborough Rd. Colch 67 D3
Gainsborough Rd. Sud 12 C4
Gainsford Ave. Clact 110 A2
Gainsford End Rd. Topp 14 B3
Galahad Cl. Burn 170 A3
Galleydene Ave. Chelm 140 B2
Galleydene. Hadl 189 D3
Galleywood Rd. Chelm 140 A3
Galleywood Rd. Gt Bad 140 C2
Gallford Rd. Mald 132 A2
Galloway Dr. Lit Cla 91 E2
Galsworthy Cl. Brain 78 A4
Galton Rd. South 199 E4
Gambleside. Basil 185 F2
Gandalf's Ride. S Woo F 165 E3
Ganges Rd. Sho G 40 A4
Gaol La. Sud 12 C4
Garden Cl. Clact 111 D3
Garden Cl. Alth 157 F2
Garden Farm. W Mers 121 E4
Garden Field. Hat Pev 113 F2
Garden Fields. Gt T 64 B4
Garden Fields. Steep 147 E2
Garden Pl. Sud 12 C4
Garden Rd. Clact 125 D4
Garden Rd. Walt 94 B4
Garden. Alth 157 F2
Gardeners La. Cane 168 C1
Gardeners Rd. Hals 25 F1
Gardeners. Gt Bad 140 B3
Gardens Pl. Clact 109 D2
Gardenia Wlk. Colch 68 C4
Garland Rd. Rams 39 F3
Garners The. Roch 178 C1
Garnons Chase. Worm 30 A3
Garrettlands. Sand 141 F3
Garrod Ct. Roum .... ? (blank)
Garrodwood Cl. W Berg 48 C2
Gascoigne Rd. Colch 68 A3
Gate St. Mald 131 F2
Gatefield Cl. Walt 93 F4
Gateway. Basil 185 D3
Gatscombe Cl. Hock 177 E3
Gattens The. Rayl 176 C2
Gauden Rd. Brain 59 F1
Gay Bowers La. Dan 142 C2
Gay Bowers Rd. Dan 142 C2
Gay Bowers Way. With 185 E4
Gay Bowers. Basil 185 E4
Gay Bowers. Hock 177 D3
Gay Links. Basil 185 D4
Gayleighs. Rayl 176 B2

Gays La. Cane 168 C1
Gayton Rd. South 191 D1
Gazelle Ct. Colch 50 B2
Geesh Rd. Canv 197 E3
Generals La. Bore 112 A1
Genesta Cl. Tolle 119 E1
Genesta Rd. South 199 E4
Genk Cl. Canv 197 D3
Gennep Rd. Canv 197 D3
George Ave. Brigh 106 C4
George Cardnell Way. May ... 146 C1
George Cl. Clact 109 E1
George Cut. Brigh 106 C3
George La. Glems 2 A2
George Rd. Brain 59 E1
George St. Chelm 127 D1
George St. Colch 67 F4
George St. Harw 40 B3
George St. South 202 A3
George Yd. Brain 59 F2
Geranium Cl. Clact 109 E2
Geranium Wlk. Colch 68 B4
Gerard Rd. Clact 109 E3
Gernon Rd. Ard 51 F4
Gestingthorpe Rd. Bel W ... 10 C3
Geylen Rd. Canv 197 F2
Ghyllgrove. Basil 185 D4
Gibcracks. Basil 185 F3
Gibson Rd. Si Hed 24 B4
Giffins Cl. Brain 59 F1
Gifford Green. Basil 186 A3
Gifford Rd. S Ben 187 E3
Gifhorn Rd. Canv 197 F2
Gilbert Rd. Colch 68 A2
Gilbert Cl. Rayl 176 C1
Gilbert Rd. Cla 4 A4
Gilbert Way. Brain 60 B3
Gilchrist Way. Brain 59 F2
Gilda Terr. Brain 59 D1
Gilderdale Cl. Colch 50 B2
Gilders Way. Clact 109 E3
Gill The. Hadl 188 B3
Gills Ave. Canv 197 E2
Gilman Dr. South 201 E4
Gilmore Way. Gt Bad 141 D3
Gilpin Way. Bl Not 77 E4
Gilson Cl. Sprin 127 F1
Gilwell Park Cl. Colch 67 D2
Gimson Cl. With 97 F1
Gippeswyck. Basil 185 E4
Gipson Park Cl. South 189 E3
Girling St. Sud 12 B4
Gladden Fields. S Woo F 165 E3
Glade The. Basil 185 E2
Glade The. Colch 50 C1
Gladeview. Clact 109 F4
Gladstone Ct. Chelm 127 D1
Gladstone Gdns. Rayl 176 B1
Gladstone Rd. Colch 68 A3
Gladstone Rd. Hock 177 F3
Gladstone Rd. Tipt 100 B2
Gladwin Rd. Colch 67 E2
Glasseys La. Rayl 188 B4
Glastonbury Chase. South .. 190 A3
Glebe Ave. Brain 59 F3
Glebe Cl. Elmst M 70 A3
Glebe Cl. Gt Wak 193 E2
Glebe Cl. Rayl 176 B2
Glebe Cl. South 200 C4
Glebe Cl. Wix 55 E3
Glebe Cres. With 97 F2
Glebe Dr. Rayl 176 B2
Glebe Field. Basil 185 E4
Glebe Gdns. Fee 81 F3
Glebe La. Deng 149 E1
Glebe Rd. Chelm 127 D2
Glebe Rd. Colch 67 E1
Glebe Rd. Kelv 81 D1
Glebe Rd. Mald 132 B3
Glebe Rd. Tipt 100 B3
Glebe Rd. Wick 174 C4
Glebe The. Purl 144 B1
Glebe Way. Burn 170 B3
Glebe Way. Clact 125 D4
Glebe Way. Frin 93 F3
Glebe Way. Hadl 188 C2
Glebefield Rd. Hat Pev 114 A2
Glebelands. Thund 187 D4
Glen Ave. Colch 67 F2
Glen Rd. Basil 185 F2
Glen Rd. S Ben 187 F3
Glen Rd. South 199 D4
Glen The. Rayl 188 C4
Glenbervie Dr. South 189 F1
Glencoe Dr. Wick 175 D4
Glendale Gdns. South 189 E1
Glendale Gr. Colch 50 B2
Glendale Rd. Burn 170 B3
Glendale. S Woo F 154 C1
Gleneagles Rd. South 191 D1
Gleneagles Way. Hat Pev .. 114 A2
Gleneagles. S Ben 187 D3
Glenhurst Rd. South 191 E1
Glenmere Park Ave. S Ben .. 188 A2
Glenmere. Basil 185 E1
Glenmore St. South 191 E1
Glenridding. S Ben 187 E3
Glenside. Sud 13 D3
Glentress Cl. Colch 50 B2

Glenwood Ave. Hawk 177 F3
Glenwood Ave. Rayl 189 D4
Glenwood Ave. South 190 B1
Glenwood. Canv 196 C3
Glisson Sq. Colch 67 D2
Globe Cl. Tipt 100 B3
Globe Wlk. Tipt 100 B3
Gloucester Ave. Chelm 140 B3
Gloucester Ave. Colch 67 E2
Gloucester Ave. May 158 B4
Gloucester Ave. Rayl 189 D4
Gloucester Cres. Chelm 127 D3
Gloucester Gdns. Brain 60 A2
Gloucester Terr. South 201 D3
Gloucester Way. Sud 7 E1
Glyders The. S Ben 187 F1
Glynde Way. South 191 F1
Goat Hall La. Chelm 140 A2
Goat House La. Haze 143 F2
Goat House La. Purl 143 F2
Goat Lodge Rd. Gt Tot 116 A3
Gobions. Basil 185 D2
Goda Cl. With 114 C4
Goddard Way. Sprin 127 F1
Godfrey's Mews. Chelm 127 D1
Godlings Way. Brain 59 F1
Godmans La. Mks T 64 C2
Godric Rd. With 114 C4
Godwin Cl. Hals 25 E1
Godwit Cl. Kelv 81 E1
Goff's La. Beau 73 F4
Goings La. W Mers 121 E3
Goirle Ave. Canv 197 E2
Goldberry Mead. S Woo F ... 165 E3
Goldcrest Cl. Colch 69 D4
Golden Cross Rd. Ashi 178 B3
Golden Dawn Way. Colch ... 49 F1
Golden La. Th L S 73 F2
Golden Lion La. Harw 40 C3
Golden Manor Dr. Thund ... 187 F3
Golden Noble Hill. Colch ... 68 A3
Goldenacres. Sprin 127 F4
Goldenlond. Nay 20 B3
Goldfinch Cl. Colch 69 D4
Goldfinch La. Thund 188 A4
Goldhanger Cl. Brain 78 B4
Goldhanger Cross. Basil 185 F4
Goldhanger Ct. Brain 78 B4
Goldhanger Rd. Gold 132 B2
Goldhanger Rd. Mald 132 B2
Golding Thoroughfare. Sprin . 127 F2
Golding Way. St O 108 A3
Goldingham Dr. Brain 59 F4
Goldings Cres. Basil 185 F2
Goldings Way. Glems 2 A2
Golday Ave. Chelm 127 E1
Golday Gdns. Chelm 127 E1
Golday Rd. Chelm 127 E1
Goldmer Cl. South 201 E4
Goldsands Rd. South 159 F1
Goldsmith Dr. Rayl 176 B4
Goldsworthy Dr. Gt Wak ... 193 E1
Golf Green Rd. Clact 125 D4
Goodchild Way. Gt Y 9 D1
Goodey Cl. Colch 68 A4
Goodlake Cl. Harw 39 F1
Goodmayes Wlk. Wick 174 B3
Goodwood Cl. Thund 188 A4
Goojerat Rd. Colch 67 E3
Goor Ave. Canv 197 E2
Goose Cotts. Rayl 164 C1
Gordon Pl. South 199 F4
Gordon Rd. Basil 185 E3
Gordon Rd. Chelm 140 A3
Gordon Rd. Hadl 189 D1
Gordon Rd. Harw 40 A1
Gordon Rd. South 199 F4
Gordon Way. Harw 40 A1
Gordons. Basil 186 A3
Gore La. Brain 59 D1
Gore The. Basil 185 D4
Goring Rd. Colch 50 B3
Gorse La. Clact 110 A4
Gorse La. Tipt 100 B2
Gorse Way. Clact 124 C4
Gorse Way. Stanw 66 B2
Gorse Wlk. Colch 68 B4
Gosbecks Rd. Colch 67 D1
Gosfield Cl. Rayl 176 A2
Gosfield Hall Dr. Gos 42 B4
Gosfield Rd. Colch 46 B2
Gosfield Rd. Gos 42 B2
Gosford Cl. Cla 4 A4
Goshawk Dr. Chelm 140 A3
Goslings. The. Silv E 79 E3
Goslings The. South 202 A4
Gouldings Ave. Walt 94 A4
Goulds Rd. Alph 18 C1
Gowan Brae. S Ben 187 D3
Gowan Cl. S Ben 187 D3
Gowers Ave. Gt Bad 140 C3
Gowers End. Glems 2 B3
Goya Rise. South 192 B1
Graces Cl. With 115 D4
Graces La. Lit Bad 129 E1
Graces Wlk. Frin 94 A3
Grafton Pl. Sprin 128 A2
Grafton Rd. Canv 197 E1
Grafton Rd. Harw 40 B2

Graham Cl. Hock 177 F4
Grainger Cl. South 191 D1
Grainger Rd. South 191 D1
Grampian Gr. Chelm 126 B3
Granary Cl. Latch 157 D3
Grand Dr. South 198 C4
Grand Par. South 198 C4
Grandview Rd. Thund 187 F4
Grange Ave. Hadl 189 D3
Grange Ave. May 158 B4
Grange Ave. Wick 174 B3
Grange Cl. Hals 43 F4
Grange Cl. South 189 F2
Grange Cl. Walt 94 A4
Grange Farm Rd. Colch 68 B2
Grange Gdns. Rayl 176 A2
Grange Gdns. South 200 A4
Grange Hill. Cogg 62 C1
Grange Park Dr. South 189 F1
Grange Rd. Basil 186 C4
Grange Rd. Gt Hor 49 D4
Grange Rd. Harw 40 A2
Grange Rd. Lane 52 C4
Grange Rd. Runw 163 E1
Grange Rd. South 189 E1
Grange Rd. Thund 187 F4
Grange Rd. Till 150 A1
Grange Rd. Tipt 99 F2
Grange Way. Col Wic Bis 115 F2
Grange Way. Colch 68 B2
Granger Ave. Mald 131 F1
Grangeway. Thund 188 A3
Grantham Ct. Colch 68 A4
Grantham Rd. Gt Hor 49 D4
Grantley Cl. Copf 65 E3
Granville Cl. S Ben 187 F2
Granville Cl. W Berg 48 C2
Granville Rd. Ashi 166 C1
Granville Rd. Clact 109 E2
Granville Rd. Colch 68 A3
Granville Terr. Burn 170 B2
Granville Way. Brigh 107 D4
Grapnells. Basil 185 F2
Grasby Cl. Wiv 69 D1
Grasmead Ave. South 189 F1
Grasmere Ave. Hull 165 E2
Grasmere Cl. Bl Not 77 E3
Grasmere Cl. S Ben 187 F2
Grasmere Rd. Canv 196 C2
Grasmere Rd. Thund 187 F3
Grassfields. Walt 93 F3
Grassmere. Colch 50 A3
Gratmore Green. Basil 185 F2
Gravel Hill Way. Harw 39 F1
Gravel Rd. Rayl 189 E4
Gravel The. Cogg 62 C1
Gray Rd. Colch 68 A4
Grayling Dr. Colch 50 A3
Grays Cl. W Mers 121 E3
Grays Mead. Si Hed 15 E1
Graysons Cl. Rayl 176 C1
Great Bentley Rd. Frat 71 D1
Great Burches Rd. Thund ... 188 A4
Great Cob. Sprin 127 F3
Great Eastern Ave. South ... 191 D1
Great Eastern Rd. Hock 177 F3
Great Eastern Rd. Sud 12 C4
Great Gibcracks Chase. Sand 142 A1
Great Harrods. Walt 94 A4
Great Hays. South 189 F2
Great Holland Common Rd.
  Clact 92 B1
Great Leighs Way. Basil 174 B3
Great Mistley. Basil 185 E3
Great Oaks. Basil 185 E3
Great Ranton. Basil 186 B4
Great Saling. Wick 175 D3
Great Smials. S Woo F 165 E3
Great Spenders. Basil 185 F4
Great Sq. Brain 59 F2
Great Tey Rd. Ald 64 B2
Great Totham Rd. Lit Brx ... 115 F3
Great Wheatley Rd. Rayl ... 176 A1
Great Yd. Hals 43 F4
Great Yeldham Rd. Topp 14 B4
Greene House Farm Rd. Nay W .. 8 C3
Grebe Cl. May 158 A4
Green Acres Rd. Lay H 85 D3
Green Ave. Canv 196 C2
Green Cl. Hat Pev 114 B2
Green Cl. Sprin 127 E2
Green Cl. With 98 A2
Green End La. Frin 93 D3
Green Farm Rd. Col En 27 D1
Green La. Ald 47 E1
Green La. Ard 51 E1
Green La. Ard 51 E4
Green La. Burn 170 A4
Green La. Canv 196 C2
Green La. Colch 50 B3
Green La. Gt Hor 31 E3
Green La. High 22 B2
Green La. Latch 158 A3
Green La. Lit Tot 117 E2
Green La. S Woo F 165 E4

Green La. South 189 F4
Green La. T Gr 78 A1
Green La. Tipt 100 B3
Green La. Walt 76 B1
Green La. Weel 91 D3
Green Man La. Lit Brx 115 F4
Green Mead. S Woo F 165 E4
Green Meadows. Dan 143 D3
Green Oaks Cl. S Ben 187 F2
Green Rd. S Ben 187 E1
Green The. Chelm 126 C2
Green The. Cla 3 E2
Green The. Clact 109 D1
Green The. Mist 35 F2
Green The. South 189 F4
Green The. Writ 126 A1
Green Trees Ave. Col N 155 F3
Green Way. Col En 27 D1
Green's Yd. Colch 67 F4
Greenacre Mews. South 189 E1
Greenacres. Clact 110 A3
Greenacres. Cogg 62 C1
Greenacres. Colch 49 F2
Greenacres. Hadl 188 C2
Greenbanks. South 190 A1
Greendyke. Canv 196 C3
Greenfield Dr. Gt T 46 B1
Greenfield. With 98 A1
Greenfields. Chelm 140 B1
Greenfields. Gos 42 C4
Greenfinch End. Colch 68 C4
Greenford Rd. Clact 109 E2
Greenhurst Rd. Brigh 107 D3
Greenland Gr. St O 107 E2
Greenlands. Hawk 178 B2
Greenleas. Thund 188 A3
Greenmill. Lawf 35 E3
Greenstead Ct. Colch 68 B3
Greenstead Rd. Colch 68 B4
Greensted The. Basil 185 F3
Greensward La. Hock 177 F4
Greenview. Canv 196 C3
Greenway Cl. Clact 110 A4
Greenway Gdns. Bl Not 77 E4
Greenway The. Clact 110 A4
Greenway The. Runw 163 E2
Greenway. Frin 93 F3
Greenways The. Cogg 63 D2
Greenways. Canv 196 C3
Greenways. Chelm 127 D3
Greenways. Fee 81 E2
Greenways. Gos 42 C4
Greenways. Mald 131 F1
Greenways. Roch 178 C1
Greenways. S Ben 187 E1
Greenways. South 200 C4
Greenwood Ave. S Ben 187 F1
Greenwood Gr. Colch 50 B2
Gregory Cl. Hawk 177 F2
Gregory St. Sud 12 C4
Grendel Way. Clact 110 C3
Grenfell Ave. Clact 110 B2
Grenfell Cl. Colch 50 B1
Grenville Cl. Walt 76 C1
Grenville Rd. Brain 59 F1
Grey Ladys. Chelm 140 A1
Grey's Paddock. Kelv 81 E1
Greyhound Hill. Langh 32 C3
Greyhound Rd. Glems 2 A2
Greyhound Way. South 191 D1
Greys Cl. Cav 1 B1
Greystones Cl. Colch 67 D2
Grieves Ct. Stanw 66 B2
Griffin Ave. Canv 197 E3
Grimston Rd. Colch 68 A2
Grimston Way. Walt 94 A4
Groom Pk. Clact 109 F2
Grooms La. Silv E 79 F2
Grosvenor Cl. Gt Bad 140 B4
Grosvenor Cl. Tipt 100 B3
Grosvenor Mews. South 199 F2
Grosvenor Rd. S Ben 196 C4
Grosvenor Rd. South 199 E4
Grove Ave. W Mers 121 E3
Grove Ave. Walt 94 A4
Grove Cl. Rayl 176 C1
Grove Ct. Rayl 177 D1
Grove Hill. Ded 33 E2
Grove Hill. Langh 32 C3
Grove Hill. Rayl 189 D4
Grove Orch. Brain 42 B1
Grove Rd. Brain 59 F3
Grove Rd. Cant 35 E4
Grove Rd. Chelm 127 D1
Grove Rd. Lit Cla 91 E3
Grove Rd. Rayl 176 C1
Grove Rd. S Ben 187 E2
Grove Rd. South 200 A4
Grove Ter. Clact 109 F1
Grove The. Clact 109 E1
Grove The. Ea Col 45 D3
Grove The. S Woo F 129 F2
Grove The. South 191 E1
Grove The. With 98 A1
Grove Wlk. South 201 F3
Grove Rd. Wick 174 B3
Grovelands Rd. Wick 174 B3
Grover St. South 200 A4

Grovewood Ave. Rayl 189 D4
Grovewood Cl. Rayl 189 D4
Gryme's Dyke Way. Stanw ... 66 C2
Guernsey Cl. Mald 131 F1
Guernsey Gdns. Runw 163 E1
Guernsey Way. Brain 59 E1
Guild Way. S Woo F 165 E4
Guildford Rd. Colch 68 A4
Guildford Rd. South 191 D1
Guithavon Rd. With 97 F1
Guithavon Rise. With 97 F1
Guithavon St. With 97 F1
Guithavon Valley. With 97 F1
Gun Hill Pl. Basil 185 E3
Gun Hill. Langh 33 D4
Gunfleet Cl. W Mers 121 D4
Gunfleet. South 201 E4
Gunners Rd. South 202 A4
Gurton Rd. Cogg 63 D2
Gurney Benham Cl. Colch ... 67 D2
Guy Cook Cl. Sud 13 E3
Guys Farm Rd. S Woo F 165 E4
Gwendalen Ave. Canv 197 E2
Gwyn Cl. Bore 112 C1
Gwynne Rd. Harw 40 B2
Gypsy La. Copf 82 B3

Haarle Rd. Canv 197 E1
Haarlem Rd. Canv 196 B3
Hackamore. Thund 188 A3
Hackmans La. Col N 155 D4
Hackmans La. Purl 155 D4
Hacks Dr. Thund 188 A4
Haddon Cl. Rayl 176 A2
Haddon Mead. S Woo F 165 E3
Hadfelda Sq. Hat Pev 114 A2
Hadleigh Park Ave. S Ben .. 188 B2
Hadleigh Rd. Clact 109 E2
Hadleigh Rd. Frin 94 A3
Hadleigh Rd. High 22 A3
Hadleigh Rd. South 189 E1
Hadleigh Rd. South 199 F4
Hadley Cl. Brain 42 A1
Hadrians Cl. With 114 C4
Haggars La. Frat 70 C2
Haig Cl. Chelm 127 D1
Hainault Ave. Hawk 178 B2
Hainault Ave. South 190 B1
Hainault Cl. Hadl 188 C2
Hainault Gr. Chelm 126 C3
Hainault Rd. N Fam 156 A1
Halfacres. With 115 D4
Halks Rd. With 97 F2
Hall Chase. Mks T 65 D2
Hall Cl. Gt Bad 141 D3
Hall Cres. Clact 110 C3
Hall Cres. Hadl 188 B2
Hall Cut. Brigh 106 C3
Hall Estate. Gold 133 F4
Hall Farm Cl. Fee 81 F2
Hall Farm Cl. S Ben 187 E1
Hall Farm Rd. S Ben 187 E1
Hall La. Harw 40 A1
Hall La. Ridge 6 A3
Hall La. Sand 141 E3
Hall La. Th L S 74 A1
Hall La. Walt 76 B1
Hall Park Ave. South 199 D4
Hall Park Way. South 199 D4
Hall Rd. Ashel 160 B4
Hall Rd. Bel W 11 D3
Hall Rd. Copf 65 F2
Hall Rd. Deng 160 B4
Hall Rd. Ford 47 E3
Hall Rd. Fox 7 D2
Hall Rd. Gt Bro 52 B1
Hall Rd. Gt Tot 116 B2
Hall Rd. Mk Ture 35 D2
Hall Rd. Mald 132 A2
Hall Rd. Pan 59 D3
Hall Rd. Roch 178 B1
Hall Rd. Soum 159 F2
Hall Rd. Tolle 119 E1
Hall Rd. W Berg 48 B3
Hall Rise. Sud 12 B3
Hall Rd. With 114 C4
Hall St. Chelm 127 D1
Hall St. L Mel 7 F3
Hall View Rd. Gt Ben 89 F4
Haller Rd. Canv 197 F2
Hallowell Down. S Woo F .. 165 F3
Halstead Ct. Wick 174 B3
Halstead Rd. E A Gr 47 F1
Halstead Rd. Ea Col 45 D3
Halstead Rd. Gos 42 B2
Halstead Rd. Gos 24 C1
Halstead Rd. Gos 42 C2
Halstead Rd. Si Hed 25 D3
Halstead Rd. Stanw 66 B4
Halstock Wall 93 D4
Halstow Way. Basil 186 B4
Halthwhite Rd. S Woo F 165 E4
Halyard Reach. S Woo F ... 165 F3
Hamberts Rd. S Woo F 154 C1

Hamble Cl. With ... 97 F1
Hamble Way. Burn ... 170 A3
Hamboro Gdns. Hadl ... 189 D1
Hambro Cl. Rayl ... 176 C2
Hambro Hill. Rayl ... 176 C2
Hambro' Ave. Rayl ... 176 B2
Hamford Cl. Walt ... 76 B1
Hamford Dr. Gt Oak ... 56 B2
Hamilton Cl. Hadl ... 189 D1
Hamilton Gdns. Hock ... 177 F4
Hamilton Rd. Basil ... 186 C4
Hamilton Rd. Colch ... 67 E3
Hamilton Rd. Frin ... 93 D3
Hamilton Rd. Sud ... 12 C4
Hamilton Rd. Wiv ... 87 D4
Hamilton St. Rams ... 39 F3
Hamlet Court Rd. South ... 199 E4
Hamlet Ct. Law ... 28 C4
Hamlet Dr. Colch ... 68 C4
Hamlet Rd. Chelm ... 127 D1
Hamlet Rd. South ... 199 F4
Hamley Cl. Thund ... 187 D3
Hammonds Rd. Lit Bad ... 128 C2
Hammonds Rd. Sand ... 128 C2
Hampstead Ave. Clact ... 109 E3
Hampstead Gdns. Hock ... 177 F4
Hampton Cl. South ... 190 C2
Hampton Ct. Hock ... 177 E3
Hampton Gdns. South ... 190 C2
Hampton Rd. Gt Bad ... 140 C4
Hamstel Rd. South ... 191 E1
Hanbury Gdns. Colch ... 50 A3
Hanbury Rd. Chelm ... 139 F4
Handel Rd. Canv ... 197 E1
Handley's La. Lit Brx ... 115 F3
Hankin Ave. Harw ... 39 E1
Hannah Cl. Canv ... 197 D3
Hannett Rd. Canv ... 197 F2
Hanningfield Cl. Rayl ... 176 A2
Hanover Cl. Basil ... 185 F3
Hanover Ct. Walt ... 94 A4
Hanover Dr. Basil ... 185 F3
Hanover Mews. Hock ... 177 E3
Hanwell Cl. Clact ... 109 E3
Harborough Hall Rd. Mess ... 82 C1
Harbour Cres. Harw ... 40 C2
Harcourt Ave. Harw ... 40 A2
Harcourt Ave. South ... 190 C1
Hardings Reach. Burn ... 170 B2
Hardwick Cl. Rayl ... 176 B1
Hardy Cl. Brain ... 78 A4
Hardy Cl. Catt ... 35 E4
Hardys Way. Canv ... 196 C3
Harebell Cl. Colch ... 50 A3
Harebell Dr. With ... 97 F2
Haresland Cl. Hadl ... 188 C3
Harewood Ave. Hawk ... 178 B3
Harewood Rd. Colch ... 66 C3
Harfred Ave. Mald ... 132 C2
Harkilees Way. Brain ... 59 F3
Harley St. Hadl ... 189 E1
Harley Wlk. Basil ... 186 A3
Harlings Gr. Chelm ... 127 E2
Harman Wlk. Clact ... 109 E3
Harness Cl. Sprin ... 127 F4
Harold Gdns. Runw ... 163 F1
Harold Gr. Frin ... 93 F2
Harold Rd. Brain ... 59 F1
Harold Rd. Clact ... 109 F1
Harold Rd. Frin ... 93 F2
Harold Way. Frin ... 93 F2
Haron Cl. Canv ... 197 D2
Harpclose Rd. Sud ... 12 C4
Harper Way. Rayl ... 176 B2
Harpur's Rd. Glems ... 2 A2
Harrington Cl. South ... 189 F2
Harridge Rd. South ... 189 F2
Harrison Dr. Brain ... 60 A1
Harrison Gdns. Hull ... 165 E1
Harrison Rd. Colch ... 67 E2
Harrogate Dr. Hock ... 177 F4
Harrogate Rd. Hock ... 177 F4
Harrow Cl. Hawk ... 178 A3
Harrow Gdns. Hawk ... 178 A3
Harrow Rd. Basil ... 175 D1
Harrow Rd. Canv ... 197 D3
Harrow Rd. Clact ... 109 F2
Harrow Way. Gt Bad ... 141 D3
Harrsett Rd. Colch ... 68 A3
Hart Cl. Thund ... 188 A3
Hart Rd. Thund ... 188 A3
Hart St. Chelm ... 127 D1
Hart's La. Ard ... 33 D1
Hartest Way. Sud ... 13 D3
Hartford Cl. Rayl ... 176 A2
Hartford End. Basil ... 186 A3
Hartington Pl. South ... 200 A4
Hartington Rd. South ... 200 A4
Hartland Cl. South ... 189 E4
Hartley Cl. Sprin ... 128 A2
Harvard Ct. Colch ... 50 A2
Harvard Cl. S Woo F ... 165 E4
Harvest End. Stanw ... 66 B3
Harvest Rd. Canv ... 197 D3
Harvesters Way. Gt T ... 64 A4
Harvest Way. Elmst M ... 69 F3
Harvey Cres. Stanw ... 66 B2
Harvey Rd. Basil ... 174 B1

Harvey Rd. Colch ... 67 D1
Harvey Rd. Gt Tot ... 116 A2
Harvey Rd. Wiv ... 69 E1
Harvey St. Hals ... 25 F1
Harwich Rd. Ard ... 51 E3
Harwich Rd. Ard ... 51 F4
Harwich Rd. Beau ... 74 A4
Harwich Rd. Brad ... 36 C1
Harwich Rd. Colch ... 68 B4
Harwich Rd. Gt Bro ... 70 C3
Harwich Rd. Gt Oak ... 56 B2
Harwich Rd. Lawf ... 34 B1
Harwich Rd. Lit Ben ... 53 F2
Harwich Rd. Lit Ben ... 71 E4
Harwich Rd. Lit Cla ... 91 F3
Harwich Rd. Lit Oak ... 57 E4
Harwich Rd. Mist ... 36 A2
Harwich Rd. Rams ... 56 A4
Harwich Rd. Wix ... 37 E1
Harwich Rd. Wix ... 55 F3
Harwich Rd. Wrab ... 37 E1
Haselfoot Rd. Bore ... 128 A4
Haskell Mews. Brain ... 78 A4
Haslemere Gdns. Walt ... 93 F4
Haslemere Rd. Runw ... 163 E1
Hasler Rd. Tolle ... 119 E1
Hassel Rd. Canv ... 197 D2
Hastings Ave. Clact ... 125 E4
Hastings Pl. Brigh ... 106 C3
Hastings Rd. Colch ... 67 D2
Hastings Rd. South ... 200 A4
Hastings The. Runw ... 163 E1
Hatchcroft Gdns. Elmst M ... 70 A3
Hatfield Gr. Chelm ... 126 B1
Hatfield Rd. Hat Pev ... 114 C2
Hatfield Rd. Langf ... 131 D4
Hatfield Rd. Rayl ... 176 A2
Hatfield Rd. Terl ... 96 B1
Hatfield Rd. With ... 114 C4
Hatherley The. Hawk ... 185 E4
Hatley Gdns. S Ben ... 187 E3
Havanna Dr. Rayl ... 176 A4
Haven Ave. Clact ... 111 D3
Haven Cl. Basil ... 185 F2
Haven Cl. Canv ... 196 C2
Haven Rd. Canv ... 196 B1
Haven Rd. Colch ... 68 B2
Haven The. Harw ... 39 F2
Havengore. Basil ... 186 B4
Havengore. Sprin ... 127 F3
Havenside. Barl ... 192 C3
Havering Cl. Clact ... 109 F4
Havering Cl. South ... 50 A1
Havering Cl. Gt Wak ... 193 D2
Havisham Way. Chelm ... 126 C4
Hawbush Green. T Gr ... 78 C3
Hawfinch Rd. Lay H ... 85 D3
Hawfinch Wlk. Chelm ... 140 A3
Hawk Hill. Rett ... 164 B1
Hawk La. Runw ... 164 B1
Hawkbush Green. Basil ... 174 A1
Hawkendon Rd. Clact ... 109 D2
Hawkes Rd. Cogg ... 62 C2
Hawkesbury Bush La. Basil ... 185 D1
Hawkesbury Cl. Canv ... 196 C1
Hawkesbury Rd. Canv ... 196 C1
Hawkesway. Clact ... 109 F3
Hawkhurst Cl. Chelm ... 126 C1
Hawkins Cl. Purl ... 143 F1
Hawkins Rd. Alres ... 88 A4
Hawkins Rd. Colch ... 68 B3
Hawkins Way. Brain ... 60 B2
Hawkridge. South ... 201 E4
Hawks Cl. Dan ... 143 D3
Hawksway. Basil ... 185 D2
Hawkwood Rd. S Han ... 163 D3
Hawkwell Chase. Hawk ... 177 F2
Hawkwell Park Dr. Hawk ... 177 F1
Hawkwell Rd. Hock ... 177 F3
Hawkwood Cl. S Woo F ... 154 C1
Hawkwood Rd. Si Hed ... 24 B4
Hawthorn Ave. Colch ... 68 C4
Hawthorn Cl. Chelm ... 140 B3
Hawthorn Cl. Hawk ... 177 F3
Hawthorn Rd. Canv ... 197 E2
Hawthorn Rd. Clact ... 109 F3
Hawthorn Rd. Hat Pev ... 114 B2
Hawthorn Rd. Sud ... 13 D4
Hawthorn Rise. With ... 98 A3
Hawthorn Way. Rayl ... 176 C1
Hawthorne Gdns. Hock ... 177 D3
Hawthornes. Purl ... 144 A3
Hawthornes. The. Dan ... 142 C4
Hawthorns. S Ben ... 187 E2
Hawthorns. Si Hed ... 15 E1
Hawthorns. Walt ... 93 F4
Hawtree Cl. South ... 200 B4
Hay Green. Dan ... 142 B4
Hay La. Brain ... 60 B2
Haycocks La. W Mers ... 104 C1
Haye La. Fing ... 86 B2
Hayes Barton. South ... 201 E4
Hayes Chase. Rett ... 164 C3
Hayes Cl. Chelm ... 127 D1
Hayes La. Canv ... 196 C2
Hayes Rd. Clact ... 109 F2

Hayhouse Rd. Ea Col ... 45 D3
Haynes Green Rd. Lay M ... 101 D4
Haytor Cl. Brain ... 60 B1
Haywain The. Stanw ... 66 B3
Hayward Ct. Colch ... 66 B3
Haze Park Rd. Walt ... 76 C1
Hazel Cl. Hadl ... 188 C2
Hazel Cl. South ... 189 E1
Hazel Cl. Thor ... 89 D3
Hazel Cl. With ... 98 A2
Hazel Gr. Brain ... 59 F1
Hazeldene. Rayl ... 176 B2
Hazleigh Hall La. Haze ... 144 B3
Hazell Ave. Colch ... 67 D1
Hazelton Rd. Colch ... 50 B1
Hazelville Cl. Harw ... 39 F1
Hazelwood Cres. Lit Cla ... 91 E1
Hazelwood Gr. South ... 189 F3
Hazelwood. Hawk ... 177 F2
Hazelwood. Thund ... 187 D4
Hazlemere Rd. Clact ... 110 B2
Head La. Sud ... 13 D3
Head St. Gold ... 133 F3
Head St. Hals ... 25 F1
Head St. Rowh ... 86 C4
Headcorn Cl. Basil ... 186 B3
Headgate Cl. Colch ... 67 F4
Headgate. Colch ... 67 F3
Hearsall Ave. Chelm ... 127 D4
Heath Dr. Chelm ... 140 A3
Heath Dr. Alres ... 88 A4
Heath Rd. Brad ... 54 B4
Heath Rd. Colch ... 66 C3
Heath Rd. E A Gr ... 48 A1
Heath Rd. Mist ... 36 A3
Heath Rd. Rowh ... 86 C4
Heath Rd. St O ... 90 C1
Heath Rd. Stanw ... 66 B2
Heath Rd. Tend ... 54 B1
Heath Rd. Tend ... 72 C4
Heath Rd. Wiv ... 69 D1
Heath The. Ded ... 33 F2
Heath The. Lay H ... 85 D3
Heather Cl. Clact ... 110 A4
Heather Cl. Lay H ... 84 C3
Heather Ct. Sprin ... 127 F3
Heather Dr. Colch ... 49 E1
Heather Dr. Hadl ... 189 D1
Heathercroft Rd. Wick ... 175 D3
Heathfield Rd. Chelm ... 127 D4
Heathfield. Rayl ... 176 B1
Heathfield. Thund ... 188 B3
Heathfields. E A Gr ... 66 A4
Heathgate. Wic Bis ... 115 E3
Heathlands. Thor ... 89 D3
Heaton Way. Tipt ... 100 B3
Heckfords Rd. Gt Ben ... 71 F1
Hedge Dr. Colch ... 67 D2
Hedge La. Hadl ... 188 B2
Hedge Lands. Cogg ... 65 E3
Hedgehope Ave. Rayl ... 176 B2
Hedgerow The. Basil ... 185 F2
Hedgerows. Bore ... 128 A3
Hedingham Rd. Bul ... 11 E1
Hedingham Rd. Gos ... 24 C1
Hedingham Rd. Hals ... 25 F2
Heeswyk Rd. Canv ... 197 D4
Heidelburg Rd. Canv ... 197 E3
Heights The. Dan ... 142 B4
Heilsburg Rd. Canv ... 197 E3
Helden Ave. Canv ... 197 D3
Helena Cl. Hawk ... 177 F3
Helena Cl. S Woo F ... 165 E3
Helena Rd. Rayl ... 176 C2
Helford Ct. With ... 97 E1
Hellendoorn Rd. Canv ... 197 E1
Helm Cl. Gt Hor ... 49 E4
Helmons La. W Han ... 152 A2
Helmsdale. Canv ... 196 C3
Helpeston. Basil ... 185 E3
Helston Rd. Sprin ... 127 F3
Hemingway Rd. With ... 97 F3
Hemlock Cl. With ... 98 A2
Hemmings Ct. Mald ... 144 C3
Hendon Cl. Clact ... 109 D3
Hendon Cl. Wick ... 174 B3
Hengist Gdns. Runw ... 163 E1
Henley Cres. South ... 190 B2
Henley Ct. Colch ... 66 C4
Henniker Gate. Sprin ... 128 A2
Henny Back Rd. Alph ... 18 C2
Henny Rd. Lam ... 19 D3
Henrietta Cl. Wiv ... 69 E2
Henry Dixon Rd. With ... 98 B3
Henry Dr. Hadl ... 189 D1
Henry Rd. Chelm ... 127 D2
Henson Ave. Canv ... 197 E3
Heralds Way. S Woo F ... 165 F4
Herbage Park Rd. Woo Wa ... 130 B1
Herbert Gr. South ... 200 A4
Herbert Rd. Canv ... 197 D2
Herbert Rd. Clact ... 109 F2
Herbert Rd. South ... 201 E3
Herberts Way. Rayl ... 176 B3
Hereford Rd. Clact ... 110 C3
Hereford Rd. Colch ... 68 A4

Hereford Wlk. Basil ... 185 F4
Hereward Cl. Wiv ... 69 E2
Hereward Gdns. Runw ... 163 E1
Hermes Dr. Burn ... 170 A3
Hermes Way. South ... 191 E4
Hermitage Ave. S Ben ... 188 A2
Hermitage Rd. South ... 199 F4
Hernen Rd. Canv ... 197 E3
Heron Dale. Basil ... 185 E3
Heron Glade. Clact ... 109 F4
Heron Rd. Kelv ... 81 E1
Heron Way. Mald ... 132 B3
Heron Way. May ... 158 A4
Herongate. S Ben ... 187 D2
Herongate. South ... 201 F4
Heronsgate. Walt ... 93 F3
Herrick Cl. Colch ... 67 D3
Herring's Way. Ford ... 47 E3
Herschell Rd. Hadl ... 189 E1
Hertford Dr. Basil ... 185 E1
Hertford Rd. Canv ... 196 C2
Hervilly Way. Walt ... 94 A4
Hester Pl. Burn ... 170 B3
Hetherington Cl. Colch ... 86 A4
Hetzand Rd. Canv ... 197 F2
Hever Cl. Hock ... 177 E3
Hewes Cl. Colch ... 68 C4
Hewitt Rd. Lit Oak ... 39 E1
Heybridge Dr. Wick ... 174 C4
Heybridge House Ind Est. Mald132 A2
Heybridge St. Mald ... 132 A3
Heycroft Dr. T Gr ... 78 C3
Heycroft Rd. Hawk ... 177 F3
Heycroft Rd. South ... 189 F3
Heycroft Rd. Wick ... 174 B4
Heycroft Way. Tipt ... 100 B3
Heygate Ave. South ... 200 A4
Heythrop The. Sprin ... 127 E2
Heywood Way. Mald ... 132 A3
Hickford Hill. Bel S P ... 4 C3
Hickling Cl. Walt ... 94 A4
Hickory Ave. Colch ... 68 B4
High Barretts. Basil ... 186 A3
High Beeches. S Ben ... 187 D2
High Bridge Rd. Sprin ... 127 E1
High Chelmer. Chelm ... 127 D1
High Cliff Dr. South ... 198 C4
High Croft. Col En ... 27 D1
High Elms Rd. Hull ... 165 F1
High Garrett. Brain ... 42 B1
High Lift Villas. Box ... 32 B4
High Mead. Hawk ... 177 F3
High Pasture. Lit Bad ... 129 E2
High Rd. Basil ... 186 A3
High Rd. Hock ... 177 D3
High Rd. Lay H ... 85 D3
High Rd. Rayl ... 176 B1
High Rd. S Ben ... 187 E2
High Ridge. Gt Bro ... 116 B4
High St N. W Mers ... 121 E4
High St. Brad O S ... 137 D1
High St. Brain ... 59 F1
High St. Brigh ... 106 C3
High St. Bures ... 19 F1
High St. Burn ... 170 B2
High St. Cane ... 168 B1
High St. Canv ... 196 C3
High St. Cav ... 1 B1
High St. Chelm ... 127 D1
High St. Cla ... 4 A4
High St. Clact ... 109 F1
High St. Colch ... 67 F4
High St. Ded ... 33 F4
High St. Gt Bad ... 140 C4
High St. Gt Wak ... 193 D2
High St. Gt Y ... 9 D1
High St. Hadl ... 188 B2
High St. Hals ... 198 B4
High St. Hals ... 25 F1
High St. harw ... 40 B2
High St. Kelv ... 81 E1
High St. Langh ... 32 B2
High St. Mald ... 132 A1
High St. Mann ... 35 E2
High St. Mist ... 36 A3
High St. Nay ... 20 A1
High St. Rayl ... 176 B1
High St. Rowh ... 87 D4
High St. S Ben ... 187 E1
High St. South ... 159 E2
High St. South ... 200 A4
High St. T H L S ... 73 F1
High St. Tolle ... 119 E1
High St. W Mers ... 121 D3
High St. Walt ... 94 B4
High St. Wick ... 174 B4
High St. Wiv ... 87 D4
High Tree La. Walt ... 76 B1
High View Ave. Clact ... 109 F3
High View Cl. Clact ... 109 F3
High View. St L ... 148 B4
High Ham. High ... 22 A4
Higham Rd. High ... 22 A4
Higham Rd. Str S M ... 22 B2
Highams Chase. Gold ... 134 A4

Highams Rd. Hock ... 177 F3
Highbank Cl. South ... 189 F3
Highbirch Rd. St O ... 90 B2
Highbury Terr. Hals ... 25 F1
Highbury Way. Sud ... 13 D3
Highclere Rd. Colch ... 50 A2
Highcliff Cres. Ashi ... 178 B4
Highcliff Rd. S Ben ... 196 C4
Highcliffe Cl. Wick ... 174 C4
Highcliffe Rd. Wick ... 174 C4
Highcliffe Way. Wick ... 174 C4
Highfield Ave. Harw ... 40 A2
Highfield Cl. S Ben ... 188 B2
Highfield Cl. Brain ... 60 A3
Highfield Cl. Dan ... 142 B3
Highfield Cl. South ... 190 B1
Highfield Cres. Rayl ... 176 B3
Highfield Cres. South ... 190 B1
Highfield Dr. Colch ... 67 E4
Highfield Dr. South ... 190 B1
Highfield Gdns. South ... 190 B2
Highfield Mead. E Ham ... 153 D4
Highfield Rd. Chelm ... 126 C2
Highfield Rd. Frin ... 93 F3
Highfield Stile Rd. Brain ... 60 A3
Highfield Way. South ... 190 B2
Highfield. Cla ... 4 B4
Highfields La. Mess ... 99 F4
Highfields Rd. With ... 97 F1
Highfields. Gt Y ... 9 D1
Highfields. Hals ... 43 F4
Highland Rd. Corr ... 185 D1
Highlands Ave. Basil ... 185 E2
Highlands Blvd. Hadl ... 189 D1
Highlands Chalet Pk. Clact ... 110 A4
Highlands Cres. Basil ... 185 E2
Highlands Dr. Mald ... 131 F1
Highlands Hill. May ... 158 B3
Highlands Rd. Basil ... 186 C3
Highlands Rd. Rayl ... 165 D1
Highlands. Gos ... 24 C1
Highlands. Rayl ... 176 B1
Highmead. Rayl ... 176 B1
Highview Cl. Sud ... 7 F1
Highview Rd. Thund ... 188 A4
Highwood Cl. South ... 189 F2
Highwoods App. Colch ... 50 B2
Highwoods Sq. Colch ... 50 A2
Hilary Cl. Roch ... 178 C3
Hilary Cres. Rayl ... 176 C1
Hilbery Rd. Canv ... 197 E2
Hildavalle Dr. South ... 190 B1
Hill Ave. Wick ... 174 C4
Hill Cl. L Mel ... 7 F3
Hill Cl. S Ben ... 187 F2
Hill Cotts. Gt Ben ... 89 F1
Hill Cres. Chelm ... 127 E1
Hill Ct. Basil ... 185 E3
Hill La. Hawk ... 177 F3
Hill Rd. Chelm ... 127 E1
Hill Rd. Clact ... 110 B3
Hill Rd. Cogg ... 62 C4
Hill Rd. Harw ... 40 B2
Hill Rd. S Ben ... 187 F2
Hill Rd. South ... 190 C1
Hill Rd. South ... 200 A3
Hill Top Ave. S Ben ... 187 F1
Hill View Rd. Sprin ... 127 E2
Hill View. S Woo F ... 142 C1
Hillary Cl. Mald ... 132 A3
Hillary Cl. Sprin ... 127 E2
Hillborough Rd. South ... 190 B2
Hillcrest Cotts. Langh ... 32 C3
Hillcrest Rd. Hock ... 177 F3
Hillcrest Rd. S Woo F ... 165 E4
Hillcrest Rd. South ... 200 A4
Hillcrest Rd. Sud ... 7 F1
Hillcrest View. Basil ... 185 E2
Hillcrest. Clact ... 110 A3
Hillcrest. Steep ... 147 D1
Hillcrest. Walt ... 93 E4
Hillhouse La. Tend ... 73 D2
Hillhouse La. Th L S ... 73 D2
Hilliards Rd. Gt Brx ... 115 F2
Hillie Bunnies. Ea Col ... 45 D4
Hillman Ave. Clact ... 124 C3
Hillridge. Colch ... 50 A2
Hills Cl. Brain ... 59 F1
Hills Cres. Colch ... 67 D3
Hills Rd. Si Hed ... 24 B4
Hillside Ave. Hawk ... 177 F3
Hillside Cres. Clact ... 110 B3
Hillside Cres. South ... 199 D4
Hillside Gdns. Brain ... 59 F1
Hillside Mews. Chelm ... 140 A4
Hillside Rd. Burn ... 170 A3
Hillside Rd. Frin ... 93 E3
Hillside Rd. Rayl ... 189 E4
Hillside Rd. S Ben ... 187 F2
Hillside Rd. South ... 198 C4
Hillside Rd. Sud ... 12 C4
Hillside. Frin ... 93 F2
Hilston Cl. Colch ... 68 B4
Hilltop Ave. Hull ... 165 F1
Hilltop Cres. Weel ... 72 C1
Hilltop Rise. Weel ... 72 C1

Hillview Cl. Rowh 86 C4
Hillview Rd. Rayl 176 B2
Hillway. South 199 D4
Hillwood Gr. Wick 174 C4
Hilton Cl. Mann 35 E2
Hilton Rd. Canv 197 D3
Hilton Way. Si Hed 24 C4
Hilton Wlk. Canv 197 D3
Hilton Wlk. Si Hed 24 C4
Hilversum Wlk. Canv 197 D3
Hindles Rd. Canv 197 E2
Hines Cl. Ald 65 D4
Hinguar St. South 201 F3
Hitcham Rd. Cogg 62 C2
Hitchcock Pl. Sud 7 F1
Hitchin Mews. Brain 78 A4
Hither Blakers. S Woo F 165 E4
Hitherwood Rd. Colch 67 E1
Hobart Cl. Chelm 126 C3
Hobbiton Hill. S Woo F 165 E3
Hobbs Dr. Box 32 A3
Hobbs La. Glems 2 B1
Hobleythick La. South 190 B2
Hockley Cl. Basil 185 E3
Hockley Cl. Brad O S 137 E1
Hockley Green. Basil 185 E3
Hockley Rd. Basil 185 E3
Hockley Rd. Brad O S 137 E1
Hockley Rd. Rayl 176 C2
Hockley Rise. Hock 177 F3
Hodges Holt. With 115 D4
Hodgson Ct. Wick 175 D3
Hodgson Way. Wick 175 D3
Hoe Dr. Colch 67 D3
Hoe La. Pent 5 F4
Hoe La. Rett 164 A3
Hoe Mill Rd. Woo Wa 130 C2
Hog's La. Str S M 34 C4
Hogarth Cl. W Mers 121 E3
Hogarth Dr. South 202 A4
Hogarth End. Walt 93 F4
Hogwell Chase. Stow M 166 A4
Holbech Rd. Basil 185 E3
Holbek Rd. Canv 197 F2
Holborough Cl. Colch 68 C4
Holbrook Cl. Colch 109 D2
Holbrook Cl. S Woo F 165 E4
Holdsworth Cl. Glems 2 A2
Holgate. Basil 186 B4
Holkham Ave. S Woo F 165 E4
Holland Ave. Canv 196 B3
Holland Park. Clact 110 A2
Holland Rd. Clact 110 A2
Holland Rd. Frin 93 F2
Holland Rd. Lit Cla 91 F1
Holland Rd. South 199 E4
Holland Rd. Walt 93 D3
Hollands Wlk. Basil 185 E1
Holledge Cres. Walt 93 F3
Hollies Rd. Bradw 61 D1
Hollliland Croft. Gt T 64 B4
Hollis Lock. Sprin 128 A2
Hollow La. Broom 126 C4
Hollow La. Bures 19 F2
Hollow La. Ashe 3 F2
Hollow Rd. Kelv 80 C1
Hollow Rd. Mald 132 A3
Holly Bank. With 97 F3
Holly Cl. Burn 170 A3
Holly Cl. Colch 67 E1
Holly La. Gt Hor 31 E2
Holly Oaks. Worm 29 F2
Holly Rd. Stanw 66 B3
Holly View Cl. Tend 72 C3
Holly Way. Chelm 140 B4
Holly Way. Elmst M 70 A3
Holly Way. Tipt 100 B3
Holly Wlk. Canv 196 C2
Holly Wlk. With 98 A3
Hollybush Hill. Gt Ben 89 F1
Hollymead Cl. Colch 49 F2
Hollytree Gdns. Rayl 188 B4
Hollywood Cl. Gt Bad 140 C3
Holm Oak. Colch 68 A2
Holman Cres. Colch 67 D2
Holman Rd. Hals 43 F4
Holmbrook Way. Frin 93 F3
Holmes Rd. Hals 43 F4
Holmsdale Cl. 190 B2
Holmswood. South 197 F3
Holmwood Cl. Clact 109 D3
Holsworthy. South 201 E4
Holt Dr. Rowh 86 A4
Holt Dr. Wic Bis 115 F3
Holt Farm Way. Hawk 178 B2
Holt's Rd. Lit Hor 30 A2
Holton Rd. Canv 197 F2
Holton Rd. Rayl 177 D1
Holtynge. S Ben 187 E2
Holybread La. Lit Bad 129 E4
Holyoak La. Hawk 177 F2
Holyrood Dr. South 190 A1
Holyrood. Harw 39 F1
Home Farm Cl. Gt Wak 193 D2
Home Farm La. Ard 52 A4
Home Mead. Chelm 140 B1
Home Mead. With 126 A1
Homefield Cl. Chelm 126 B3
Homefield Rd. Colch 67 E1

Homefield Rd. With 98 A2
Homefield Way. Ea Col 45 D4
Homefield Way. T Gr 78 B4
Homefield. South 59 F3
Homefields Ave. S Ben 187 D3
Homerton Cl. Clact 109 F4
Homestead Gdns. Hadl 188 B1
Homestead Rd. Basil 186 C4
Homestead Rd. Hadl 188 B1
Homestead Way. Hadl 188 B2
Homestead. Sprin 127 D4
Homing Rd. Lit Cla 91 E2
Honey Bridge Rd. Nay 20 B4
Honey Cl. Gt Bad 140 B3
Honey Pot La. Stow M 155 E2
Honeypot La. Basil 185 D4
Honeypot La. St O 91 D2
Honeypot La. Wix 101 D1
Honeypot La. Wix 54 C2
Honeysuckle Way. Colch 68 C4
Honeysuckle Way. Thor 89 D3
Honeysuckle Way. With 97 E2
Honeywood Ave. Cogg 63 D2
Honeywood Rd. Hals 26 A2
Honiley Ave. Wick 174 B2
Honington Cl. Wick 175 D3
Honiton Rd. South 200 B4
Honywood Cl. Mks T 64 C2
Honywood Rd. Colch 67 E4
Honywood Way. Walt 93 F4
Hood Gdns. Brain 60 B2
Hooley Dr. Rayl 176 B4
Hop Gardens La. Woo Wa 130 C2
Hope Rd. Canv 197 E2
Hope Rd. S Ben 187 E1
Hopkin's La. Harw 40 B3
Hopkins Cl. Walt 93 F3
Hopkins Mead. Sprin 128 A1
Hopkirk Cl. Dan 142 C4
Hopper Wlk. Colch 68 B3
Hopping Jacks La. Dan 142 C4
Hoppit Mead. Brain 59 F1
Horace Rd. South 200 A4
Hordle Pl. Harw 40 B2
Hordle St. Harw 40 B2
Horkesley Hill. Gt Hor 31 D4
Horkesley Rd. Box 49 F4
Horkesley Way. Wick 174 C3
Horley Cl. Clact 109 E3
Horn La. Cogg 63 D1
Hornbeam Cl. Colch 140 A3
Hornbeam Cl. Colch 67 E1
Hornbeam Wlk. With 98 A2
Hornbeams The. Lit Oak 57 D4
Hornbeams. Thund 187 D4
Hornby Ave. South 190 B3
Hornby Cl. South 190 B3
Hornchurch Cl. Wick 175 D3
Horne Row. Dan 142 B3
Horner Pl. With 98 A1
Hornet Way. Burn 170 A3
Hornsland Rd. Canv 197 F2
Horrocks Cl. Colch 68 A4
Horse and Groom La. Chelm 140 A2
Horsey Rd. Walt 93 E4
Horsley Cross. Basil 185 D4
Hospital La. Colch 67 E3
Hospital Rd. Colch 67 E3
Hospital Rd. South 201 F3
Houblon Dr. Chelm 140 B1
Houchin's La. Cogg 63 D2
Hovefields Ave. Wick 174 B2
Hovefields Dr. Wick 174 B2
Howard Ave. Harw 39 F1
Howard Chase. Basil 185 D3
Howard Cl. Brain 60 B2
Howard Cres. Basil 186 B3
Howard Dr. Sprin 128 A1
Howard Pl. Canv 197 D1
Howard Rd. Clact 110 B2
Howard Vyse Cl. Clact 109 D4
Howards Chase. South 190 C1
Howards Cl. Bore 128 C4
Howbridge Hall Rd. With 114 C4
Howbridge Rd. With 114 C4
Howe Chase. Hals 25 F2
Howe Cl. Colch 68 B4
Howe Green Rd. Purl 155 F4
Hoxton Cl. Clact 109 E2
Hoyners. Dan 143 D4
Hubbards Chase. Walt 94 A4
Hubert Rd. Colch 67 D4
Hucklesbury Ave. Clact 110 C4
Hudson Cl. Clact 110 C4
Hudson Cl. Harw 40 A1
Hudson Cres. South 189 F3
Hudson Rd. South 189 E3
Hudson Way. Canv 197 D3
Hudsons La. High 21 D3
Hull La. Terl 96 A1
Hull's La. Sand 141 F4
Hullbridge Rd. Rayl 176 B4
Hullbridge Rd. S Woo F 154 C3
Hullbridge Rd. S Woo F 165 E4
Hulton Cl. Bore 128 C4
Humber Ave. Clact 124 C3
Humber Cl. Rayl 176 B1

Humber Rd. Sprin 127 E3
Humber Rd. With 97 E1
Humphry Rd. Sud 32 B3
Hundred La. Bour 32 B2
Hundred La. Langh 32 B2
Hungerdown La. Lawf 34 C1
Hunnable Rd. Brain 59 F1
Hunt Ave. Mald 132 A3
Hunt Cl. Fee 81 E2
Hunt Dr. Clact 109 E3
Hunt Rd. Ea Col 45 D3
Hunt Way. Walt 93 F3
Hunt's Cl. Writ 139 D4
Hunt's Dr. Writ 139 D4
Hunter Dr. Lawf 35 D2
Hunter Rd. Brain 60 B1
Hunter's Chase. Ard 33 F1
Hunters Ridge. Colch 50 A2
Hunters Way. Sprin 127 F4
Huntingdon Rd. South 200 B4
Huntingdon Way. Clact 109 F3
Hunts Farm Cl. Tolle 119 E1
Hunts Hill. Glems 2 A2
Hunwicke Rd. Colch 68 C4
Hurnard Dr. Colch 67 D4
Hurrell Down. Bore 112 C1
Hurrell Down. Colch 50 A2
Hurrells La. Lit Bad 128 C2
Hurricane Way. Wick 175 D3
Hurst Cl. Brigh 107 D3
Hurst Way. South 189 F2
Hurst Way. Sprin 127 F1
Hyacinth Cl. Clact 109 E2
Hyacinth Cl. Tolle 119 D1
Hyacinth Ct. Sprin 127 F4
Hyde Chase. Purl 143 E2
Hyde Farm Chase. Dan 143 D2
Hyde Green. Dan 143 D4
Hyde La. Dan 143 D4
Hyde Rd. Sud 12 C4
Hyde Way. Wick 174 B3
Hyde Wood La. Ashi 178 C4
Hydeway. Thund 187 F3
Hydewood Rd. Lit Y 9 D2
Hylands The. Hock 177 E3
Hythe Cl. Brain 59 F3
Hythe Cl. Clact 125 E4
Hythe Cl. Brigh 88 C1
Hythe Hill. Colch 68 A3
Hythe Quay. Colch 68 B3
Hythe Station Rd. Colch 68 B3
Hythe The. Mald 132 A1

Iceni Way. Colch 67 D2
Ifracombe Ave. South 200 B4
Ilex Cl. Colch 67 E1
Ilfracombe Ave. Basil 186 B3
Ilfracombe Rd. South 191 E1
Ilgars Rd. Runw 163 F1
Ilmington Dr. Basil 174 A1
Imogen Cl. Colch 68 C4
Imperial Ave. May 146 C1
Imperial Ave. South 198 C4
Imphal Cl. Colch 67 E1
Inchbonnie Rd. S Woo F 165 F3
Ingarfield Rd. Clact 110 C3
Ingelrica Ave. Hat Pev 114 A2
Ingestre St. Harw 40 B3
Inglenook. Clact 110 A4
Inglis Rd. Colch 67 E3
Ingram Mews. Brain 78 A4
Ingram's Piece. Ard 11 E4
Ingram's Well Rd. Sud 12 C4
Ingrave Cl. Wick 174 C3
Inkerpole Pl. Sprin 127 E4
Inverness Ave. South 190 B1
Inverness Cl. Colch 68 B1
Inworth La. Wa Col 28 B1
Inworth Rd. Fee 81 F2
Inworth Wlk. Colch 68 A1
Inworth Wlk. Wick 175 D4
Ipswich Rd. Clact 110 B3
Ipswich Rd. Colch 50 B2
Ipswich Rd. Langh 32 C1
Ipswich Rd. Str S M 22 C2
Ireton Rd. Colch 67 E3
Iris Cl. Sprin 127 F3
Iron Latch La. E A Gr 66 B4
Iron Latch La. Stanw 66 B4
Ironwell La. Hawk 178 B2
Ironwell La. Roch 178 B2
Irvine Rd. Colch 67 E3
Irvington Cl. South 189 E2
Irvon Hill Rd. Wick 174 C4
Isbourne Rd. Colch 68 C4
Ishams Chase. With 115 D4
Island La. Walt 75 F1
Island La. Walt 75 F1
Ivy La. E Mers 106 A2
Ivy Lodge Rd. Gt Hor 45 E4
Ivy Rd. Thund 187 D3
Ivy Wlk. Canv 196 C2

Jacaranda Cl. Sprin 127 F3
Jack Hatch Way. Wiv 69 D2
Jackdaw Cl. South 201 F4
Jacklin Cl. Wick 174 C4
Jackson Cl. Gt Bad 140 B3
Jackson Rd. Clact 109 F1

Jaggards Rd. Cogg 63 D2
James Carter Rd. Colch 66 C2
James Cl. Wiv 69 E2
James Gdns. St O 108 A3
James Rd. Clact 109 E1
James St. Brigh 106 C3
James St. Colch 68 A3
Jameson Pl. Sud 12 C4
Jameson Rd. Clact 109 E2
Jameson Rd. Sud 12 C4
Janette Ave. Canv 196 C2
Janmead. With 98 A2
Jaques Cl. Glems 2 B3
Jardine Rd. Basil 186 B4
Jarmin Rd. Colch 67 F4
Jarvis Field. Lit Bad 129 E3
Jarvis Rd. Canv 197 D3
Jarvis Rd. S Ben 187 E2
Jasmine Cl. Clact 68 C4
Jasmine Cl. Sprin 127 F4
Jasmine Way. Clact 125 D4
Jason Cl. Canv 197 D3
Jason Ct. Canv 197 D3
Jays La. Mks T 64 C2
Jays The. Colch 50 A2
Jaywick La. Clact 109 D1
Jeffcut Rd. Sprin 127 F1
Jefferson Cl. Colch 66 C3
Jeffery Rd. Gt Bad 141 E4
Jeffery Cl. Colch 66 C3
Jeffrey's Rd. T Gr 78 C3
Jellicoe Way. Brain 60 B2
Jenkin's Hill. Brad 36 B2
Jenner Cl. Brain 59 F1
Jenner Mead. Sprin 128 A2
Jersey Gdns. Runw 174 B4
Jersey Rd. Mald 132 A1
Jersey Way. Brain 59 F1
Jesmond Rd. Canv 197 D1
Jessica Cl. Colch 68 C4
Joes Rd. Sud 13 F4
John Ball Wlk. Colch 67 F4
John English Ave. Brain 59 F2
John Harper St. Colch 67 F4
John Henry Keene Meml Hms.
Chelm 127 D2
John Kent Ave. Colch 67 D1
John Raven Ct. Fee 81 E2
John Ray Gdns. Bl Not 78 A3
John Ray St. Brain 60 A2
John St. Brigh 106 C3
John St. South 202 A3
Johnson Cl. Brain 78 A4
Johnson Cl. Roch 178 B3
Johnson Rd. Gt Bad 141 D3
Johnson Rd. St O 108 A2
Johnson's Dr. Elmst M 70 A3
Johnston Cl. Clact 110 C3
Johnston Cl. Hals 43 F4
Johnstone Rd. South 201 D4
Jones Cl. South 190 C2
Jonquil Way. Colch 49 E1
Joseph Gdns. Silv E 79 F2
Josselin Cl. Ea Col 45 D4
Josselin Ct. Basil 174 B1
Josselin Rd. Basil 174 B1
Jotmans La. S Ben 187 D2
Journeymans Way. South 191 D3
Joyce's Chase. Gold 134 A4
Jubilee Ave. Clact 109 F4
Jubilee Cl. Rayl 89 F1
Jubilee Cotts. Pag Ch 180 B3
Jubilee Ct. Si Hed 24 C4
Jubilee Dr. Runw 174 A4
Jubilee End. Lawf 35 E3
Jubilee La. And 51 E2
Jubilee Rd. Rayl 176 C1
Jubilee Rd. Sud 12 C4
Jubilee Rise. Dan 143 D3
Jubilee Way. Walt 93 F3
Julien Court Rd. Brain 60 A2
Juliers Cl. Canv 197 E2
Juliers Rd. Canv 197 E2
Junction Rd. Basil 186 A2
Junction Rd. Col N 156 A3
Juniper Cl. Hals 25 F2
Juniper Cres. With 98 A3
Juniper Dr. Chelm 140 A3
Juniper Rd. Bore 128 C4
Juniper Rd. South 189 F2
Juniper Rd. Stanw 66 B3
Juniper Way. Colch 68 C4
Jupe's Hill. Wa Col 28 B1
Jupes Hill. Ded 34 B2
Juvina St. With 114 C4

Kale Croft. Stanw 66 B3
Kale Rd. S Ben 187 E2
Kamerwyk Ave. Canv 197 E2
Karen Cl. S Ben 196 C4
Karen Cl. Wick 174 C4
Katherine Cl. Rayl 177 D1
Katherine Rd. Basil 186 C4
Kathleen Dr. South 190 B2
Katonia Ave. May 146 C1
Kay Cl. Gt Le 95 D2
Keable Rd. Mks T 64 C2
Keating Cl. Lawf 35 D2
Keats Ave. Brain 77 F4
Keats Cl. Mald 145 D4

Keats Rd. Colch 66 C3
Keats Sq. S Woo F 165 F3
Keats Way. Wick 174 B4
Keats Wlk. Rayl 177 D1
Kebbles. Glems 2 A3
Keble Cl. Colch 67 E3
Keddington Hill. Sud 13 D1
Keeble Cl. Tipt 100 C3
Keeble Park. Mald 144 C4
Keegan Pl. Canv 197 E2
Keelars La. Elmst M 69 F1
Keelers Way. Gt Hor 49 D4
Keelings La. Deng 160 C4
Keelings Rd. Deng 160 C4
Keene Way. Chelm 140 A2
Keer Ave. Canv 197 E1
Keighley Mews. South 192 B1
Keith Ave. Runw 163 E1
Keith Cl. Clact 110 A4
Keith Way. South 190 C3
Kellington Rd. Canv 197 E2
Kelly Rd. Basil 186 C3
Kelredon Rd. Mess 82 B1
Kelso Cl. Gt Hor 49 E3
Kelvedon Cl. Chelm 127 D3
Kelvedon Cl. Rayl 176 A2
Kelvedon Hall La. Gt Brx 99 F2
Kelvedon Rd. Cogg 81 D4
Kelvedon Rd. Lit Bry 115 F3
Kelvedon Rd. Toll D 100 A4
Kelvedon Rd. Toll D 118 B3
Kembles. Rayl 176 C2
Kempson Dr. Sud 13 E3
Kempster Rd. Canv 188 A4
Kemsley Rd. Ea Col 45 D3
Ken Cooke Ct. Colch 67 F4
Kendal Cl. Hull 165 F1
Kendal Cl. Rayl 176 C1
Kendal Cl. Wick 175 D3
Kendal Rd. Colch 68 A3
Kendal Road Folley. Colch 68 A3
Kendal Way. South 189 F4
Kenholme. South 189 F2
Kenilworth Gdns. South 190 A2
Kenilworth Gr. Th L S 74 A1
Kenilworth Rd. Clact 109 E4
Kenley Cl. Wick 175 D3
Kenmore Cl. Canv 197 F1
Kennedy Cl. Rayl 189 D4
Kennedy Cl. Thund 187 D4
Kennedy Way. Clact 110 A3
Kennet Way. Chelm 126 B3
Kenneth Rd. Basil 186 B4
Kenneth Rd. Thund 187 F3
Kensington Ave. South 200 B4
Kensington Way. Hock 177 E3
Kent Ave. Canv 197 D3
Kent Ave. South 198 C4
Kent Cl. Brigh 106 C4
Kent Elms Cl. South 189 F3
Kent Gdns. Brain 60 A2
Kent Green Cl. Hock 177 F3
Kent View Ave. South 199 D4
Kent View Rd. Basil 185 D2
Kent's Ave. Clact 110 C3
Kentings The. Brain 59 F1
Kents Grass. Tolle 119 E1
Kents Hill Rd N. Thund 187 E4
Kents Hill Rd. S Ben 187 E2
Kenway. South 190 C3
Kenworthy Rd. Brain 59 F1
Kenyon Cl. Str S M 22 B1
Kerby Rise. Sprin 127 F1
Kerridge's Cut. Mist 36 A2
Kerry Ct. Colch 68 B4
Kersey Ave. Sud 13 D3
Kersey Dr. Clact 109 D3
Kestrel Way. Clact 109 F4
Kestrel Wlk. Chelm 140 A2
Keswick Ave. Clact 110 B3
Keswick Ave. Hull 165 F1
Keswick Cl. Clact 110 B3
Keswick Cl. Walt 93 E4
Keswick Rd. Thund 187 F4
Ketleys View. Pan 59 D4
Ketleys. Chelm 140 B2
Kew La. Frin 93 D2
Key Rd. Clact 109 F2
Keyes Way. Brain 60 B2
Keymer Way. Colch 66 B2
Keynes Way. Harw 39 F1
Keysland. Thund 188 A3
Kilburn Gdns. Clact 109 E3
Kildermorie Cl. Colch 50 B2
Kilmaine Rd. Harw 39 F1
Kiln Barn Ave. Clact 110 C4
Kiln Dr. Sud 13 D3
Kiln Rd. Thund 188 A2
Kiln Rd. Colch 62 C3
Kilns Hill. Cogg 62 C3
Kilnwood Ave. Hock 177 E3
Kilworth Ave. South 200 A4
Kimberley Rd. Basil 192 C3
Kimberley Rd. Colch 68 A3
Kimberley Rd. S Ben 187 E2
Kincaid Rd. St O 108 A2
King Charles Rd. W Mers 121 E3

King Coel Rd. Colch ... 66 B4
King Edward Ave. Burn ... 170 A3
King Edward Quay. Colch ... 68 B3
King Edward VII Dr. Sho G ... 40 A4
King Edward Way. With ... 114 C4
King George's Rd. S Woo F ... 165 E4
King George's Ave. Harw ... 40 A2
King George's Cl. Rayl ... 176 B1
King Harold Rd. Colch ... 67 D2
King Henry's Dr. Roch ... 190 C4
King St. Brad ... 54 B4
King St. Ca Hed ... 15 F2
King St. Mald ... 132 A1
King St. Sud ... 12 C4
King Stephen Rd. Colch ... 68 A3
King's Cl. St O ... 108 A2
King's Head St. Harw ... 40 C3
King's La. L Mel ... 7 F4
King's Quay St. Harw ... 40 C3
King's Rd. Brain ... 59 F3
King's Rd. Burn ... 170 A2
King's Rd. Clact ... 109 E1
King's Rd. Harw ... 40 A2
King's Rd. S Ben ... 187 F1
King's Rd. South ... 190 A1
Kingfisher Cl. Colch ... 50 A2
Kingfisher Cl. Mald ... 132 B3
Kingfisher Cl. South ... 201 F4
Kingfisher Dr. S Ben ... 187 E1
Kingfisher Way. Kelv ... 81 E1
Kingfishers. Basil ... 185 E2
Kingfishers. Clact ... 109 F3
Kingley Cl. Wick ... 174 A4
Kingley Dr. Wick ... 174 A4
Kings Ave. Clact ... 110 B3
Kings Chase. With ... 98 A1
Kings Cl. Canv ... 196 B2
Kings Cl. Lawf ... 35 E2
Kings Cl. Rayl ... 176 C1
Kings Ct. Burn ... 170 A2
Kings Ct. Harw ... 40 A2
Kings Farm. Rayl ... 176 C3
Kings Head Ct. Colch ... 67 F4
Kings Hill. Sud ... 13 D3
Kings La. Stis ... 60 C2
Kings Mead. Peb ... 27 D4
Kings Meadow Rd. Colch ... 67 F4
Kings Meadow. Sud ... 13 D3
Kings Mews. Wiv ... 69 E2
Kings Par. Clact ... 110 C3
Kings Park. Thund ... 187 F3
Kings Rd. Canv ... 196 B2
Kings Rd. Chelm ... 126 C2
Kings Rd. Glems ... 2 B3
Kings Rd. Gt Tot ... 116 B4
Kings Rd. Hals ... 25 F1
Kings Rd. Rayl ... 176 B1
Kings Rd. Soum ... 159 E2
Kings Way. S Woo F ... 154 B1
Kings Wlk. Tolle ... 119 F1
Kingsbridge Cl. Brain ... 59 F4
Kingsbury Cl. Mks T ... 64 C2
Kingsbury Wlk. Sud ... 13 E3
Kingsdown Cl. Basil ... 186 B3
Kingsdown Wlk. Canv ... 197 D3
Kingshawes. Thund ... 188 A3
Kingsland Beach. W Mers ... 121 E3
Kingsland Cl. W Mers ... 121 E3
Kingsland Rd. W Mers ... 121 E3
Kingsley Cres. Thund ... 188 B4
Kingsley La. Thund ... 188 A4
Kingsman Dr. Clact ... 109 E3
Kingsmans Farm Rd. Hull ... 166 A2
Kingsmere Cl. W Mers ... 121 E4
Kingsmere. Thund ... 188 A3
Kingsteignton. South ... 201 E4
Kingston Ave. Sprin ... 127 F2
Kingston Cres. Sprin ... 127 F2
Kingston Way. Thund ... 187 F3
Kingsway. Colch ... 67 F4
Kingsway. Harw ... 40 A2
Kingsway. Hull ... 165 E1
Kingsway. South ... 190 A1
Kingsway. Tipt ... 100 B3
Kingswood Chase. South ... 189 E4
Kingswood Cres. Rayl ... 176 A1
Kingswood Rd. Basil ... 185 F3
Kingswood Rd. Basil ... 185 E3
Kingswood Rd. Colch ... 49 F2
Kingwell Ave. Clact ... 109 F3
Kinlett Gdns. Colch ... 50 A2
Kinloch Chase. With ... 114 C4
Kino Rd. Walt ... 94 B4
Kipling Cl. Chelm ... 127 D3
Kipling Mews. Sud ... 191 D1
Kipling Way. Brain ... 78 A4
Kirby Hall Rd. Ca Hed ... 15 E3
Kirby Rd. Basil ... 185 F3
Kirby Rd. Walt ... 94 A4
Kirk Pl. Sprin ... 127 F2
Kirkbaye. Walt ... 93 F3
Kirkby Rd. Frin ... 93 D3
Kirkhurst Cl. Brigh ... 107 D3
Kirklees. Chelm ... 127 D2
Kirkmans Rd. Chelm ... 140 B2
Kirkton Cl. Sho G ... 40 A4
Kitchen Hill. Bul ... 12 A3
Kitchener Rd. N Fam ... 156 A1

Kitchener Way. Sho G ... 40 A4
Kitkatts Rd. Canv ... 197 D2
Kittiwake Dr. Mald ... 132 B3
Klondyke Ave. Rayl ... 176 A2
Knapton Cl. Sprin ... 127 E4
Knight St. S Woo F ... 165 F4
Knights Cl. Tipt ... 100 C2
Knights Rd. Brain ... 60 B1
Knights Rd. Clgg ... 62 C1
Knightsbridge Cl. Colch ... 67 E2
Knightswick Rd. Canv ... 197 D2
Knivet Cl. Rayl ... 176 C1
Knoll The. Rayl ... 176 B1
Knollcroft. South ... 201 E3
Knowle The. Basil ... 185 E2
Knowles Cl. Hals ... 25 F1
Knox Gdns. Clact ... 109 F3
Knox Rd. Clact ... 109 F3
Kohima Rd. Colch ... 67 D1
Kolburg Rd. Canv ... 197 E2
Kollum Rd. Canv ... 197 F2
Koln Cl. Canv ... 196 B2
Komberg Cres. Canv ... 197 E3
Konnybrook. Thund ... 188 A2
Korndyk Ave. Canv ... 197 E2
Kreswell Gr. Harw ... 40 A1
Kursaal Way. South ... 200 B4
Kynaston Pl. With ... 98 A1
Kynaston Rd. Pan ... 59 D4

Laars Ave. Canv ... 197 E3
Laburnum Ave. Wick ... 174 B3
Laburnum Cl. Clact ... 109 E2
Laburnum Cl. Gt Ben ... 89 F4
Laburnum Cl. Hock ... 177 E3
Laburnum Cl. Wick ... 174 B4
Laburnum Cres. Walt ... 93 E3
Laburnum Dr. Chelm ... 140 B3
Laburnum Gr. Canv ... 196 B2
Laburnum Gr. Colch ... 68 C4
Laburnum Gr. Hock ... 177 D3
Laburnum Way. Hat Pev ... 114 A2
Laburnum Way. With ... 98 A3
Labworth La. Canv ... 197 E1
Labworth Rd. Canv ... 197 E1
Ladbrook Dr. Colch ... 68 A4
Ladbrooke Rd. Clact ... 109 E3
Ladell Cl. Colch ... 66 C2
Ladram Cl. South ... 201 E4
Ladram Rd. South ... 201 E4
Ladram Way. South ... 201 E4
Lady La. Chelm ... 140 B4
Ladygate Centre. Wick ... 174 B4
Ladysmith Ave. Brigh ... 106 C4
Laing Rd. Colch ... 68 C3
Lake Ave. Clact ... 109 E2
Lake Dri. Thund ... 187 F3
Lake Way. Clact ... 124 C3
Lake Wlk. Clact ... 109 E2
Lakeside Cres. Canv ... 197 F3
Lakeside. Rayl ... 176 B2
Lakeview. Canv ... 197 D3
Lakin Cl. Sprin ... 128 A2
Lamarsh Hill. Bures ... 19 F1
Lamarsh Hill. Gt H ... 19 D3
Lamarsh Rd. Alph ... 19 D2
Lamb La. Si Hed ... 24 B4
Lambert's Rd. Gt T ... 45 F1
Lambeth Mews. Hock ... 177 E3
Lambeth Rd. South ... 189 F3
Lambeth Rd. Thund ... 187 E3
Lambeth Wlk. Clact ... 109 F3
Lambourne Cl. Clact ... 109 E3
Lambourne Cl. Stanw ... 66 B2
Lambourne Cres. Basil ... 185 F3
Lambourne Gr. Mald ... 144 C4
Lambourne Hall Rd. Cane ... 168 C1
Lammas Way. Wiv ... 69 E1
Lancaster Gdns E. Clact ... 110 A2
Lancaster Gdns W. Clact ... 110 A2
Lancaster Gdns. Rayl ... 189 D4
Lancaster Gdns. South ... 200 A4
Lancaster Rd. Rayl ... 189 D4
Lancaster Rd. Sud ... 7 E1
Lancaster Way. Brain ... 59 F2
Lancaster Way. Ea Col ... 44 C1
Lanchester Ave. Clact ... 124 B3
Lancia Ave. Clact ... 124 B3
Land Cl. Clact ... 109 E3
Land La. Colch ... 68 A4
Landale Dr. Colch ... 50 A2
Landermere Rd. Th L S ... 74 A3
Landermere. Basil ... 185 D4
Landsburg Rd. Canv ... 197 E3
Landsdown Rd. Sud ... 13 D4
Landseer Rd. Colch ... 67 D3
Landwick La. Deng ... 160 C4
Lane Rd. Wa Col ... 46 B4
Lane The. Clact ... 141 D3
Lane The. Mist ... 35 F2
Lane The. W Mers ... 121 D4
Langdale Gdns. Chelm ... 140 B4
Langdale. Bl Not ... 77 E4
Langdon Rd. Rayl ... 176 A2
Langenhoe Hall La. Lang ... 104 B4
Langenhoe. Wick ... 174 C3
Langford Cres. Thund ... 187 F3
Langford Gr. Basil ... 186 B4

Langford Rd. Mald ... 131 F3
Langford Rd. Wic Bis ... 115 E1
Langham Dr. Clact ... 109 D2
Langham Dr. Rayl ... 175 F2
Langham Dr. Rayl ... 176 A2
Langham La. Langh ... 32 B1
Langham Rd. Box ... 31 F1
Langley Cl. Rayl ... 189 D4
Langley Hill. Lam ... 19 D2
Langleys. Basil ... 185 D2
Langport Dr. South ... 190 A2
Langton Ave. Chelm ... 126 C3
Langwood. W Mers ... 121 E4
Lanham Green Rd. T Gr ... 79 D4
Lanhams. Basil ... 186 B4
Lansdale. Dan ... 143 D4
Lansdown Ave. Hadl ... 188 C3
Lansdowne Ave. South ... 190 A1
Lansdowne Cl. Tipt ... 100 B3
Lansdowne Rd. Clact ... 124 C3
Lanvalley Rd. Colch ... 66 C3
Lappmark Rd. Canv ... 197 E2
Lapwater Cl. South ... 189 E1
Lapwing Dr. Kelv ... 81 E1
Lapwing Dr. Mald ... 132 B3
Lapwing Rd. Runw ... 163 E1
Larch Cl. Colch ... 68 B4
Larch Gr. Chelm ... 140 B3
Larch Gr. Mald ... 20 A1
Larch Gr. With ... 98 A3
Larch Wlk. Hat Pev ... 114 A3
Larch Wlk. Mald ... 132 B3
Larches The. Bore ... 128 C4
Larches The. Thund ... 187 E4
Larchwood Cl. Hadl ... 189 D3
Lark Hill Rd. Cane ... 168 A1
Lark Rise. Sud ... 12 B3
Larkfield Cl. Hawk ... 178 B2
Larkfield Rd. Gt Ben ... 71 E1
Larksfield Cres. Harw ... 40 A2
Larkspur Cl. With ... 97 F3
Larkswood Wlk. Wick ... 174 B3
Larkway. Walt ... 93 F4
Larneys The. Walt ... 93 F4
Larup Ave. Canv ... 197 E2
Larup Gdns. Canv ... 197 E2
Lascelles Gdns. Hawk ... 178 B3
Latchetts Shaw. Basil ... 185 D2
Latchingdon Cl. Rayl ... 176 A2
Latchingdon Rd. Col N ... 156 B3
Latchingdon Rd. Latch ... 156 B3
Latchingdon Rd. Purl ... 156 B3
Lathcoates Cres. Gt Bad ... 140 C4
Launceston Cl. Colch ... 68 A1
Laundry Gdns. Sud ... 12 B3
Laurel Ave. Wick ... 174 B4
Laurel Cl. Clact ... 110 A4
Laurel Cl. Clact ... 198 B4
Laurel Dr. L Mel ... 7 E4
Laurel Gr. Chelm ... 140 A4
Laurels The. Rayl ... 188 C4
Laurels The. S Woo F ... 165 E4
Laurence Ave. With ... 115 D4
Laurence Cl. Wmnet M ... 69 F3
Laurence Croft. Writ ... 126 A1
Lavender Cl. Tipt ... 100 B2
Lavender Cl. With ... 97 F2
Lavender Ct. Sprin ... 127 F3
Lavender Gr. South ... 190 B2
Lavender Way. Colch ... 49 E1
Lavender Wlk. Harw ... 174 B4
Lavender Wlk. Clact ... 125 D4
Lavenham Cl. Clact ... 109 D2
Lavenham Cl. South ... 67 E2
Lawford La. Writ ... 126 B1
Lawling Ave. Mald ... 132 B3
Lawlinge Rd. Latch ... 157 D3
Lawn Ave. South ... 191 D1
Lawn Chase. With ... 97 F2
Lawns Cl. W Mers ... 121 E4
Lawns The. Sprin ... 127 E3
Lawns The. Thund ... 187 D4
Lawnscourt. Thund ... 187 D4
Lawrence Rd. Basil ... 186 C4
Lawshall's Hill. Wa Col ... 27 E1
Laxton Cl. Colch ... 67 D2
Laxton Gr. Frin ... 93 D2
Laxton Rd. Alres ... 88 A4
Laxtons The. Hawk ... 178 B3
Layer Breton Hill. Lay Br ... 84 A1
Layer Rd. Bould ... 60 B1
Layer Rd. Gt Wig ... 102 C3
Layer Rd. Lang ... 85 F2
Layer Rd. Lay H ... 85 F2
Layer Rd. Stanw ... 85 D4
Layzell Croft. Sud ... 13 E3
Le Cateau Rd. Colch ... 67 F3
Lea Cl. Brain ... 60 B1
Lea Gr. Hat Pev ... 114 C1
Lea La. Gt Brx ... 98 C1
Lea Rd. S Ben ... 187 E3
Leach Cl. Gt Bad ... 141 D4
Leam Cl. Colch ... 68 B2
Leamington Rd. Hock ... 177 F4
Leamington Rd. South ... 200 B4
Leapingwell Cl. Sprin ... 127 F4
Leas Cl. South ... 199 D4

Leas Gdns. South ... 199 D4
Leas Rd. Clact ... 109 E1
Leas Rd. Colch ... 67 E1
Leas The. Burn ... 170 B3
Leas The. Frin ... 94 A3
Leas The. South ... 199 E4
Leaside. Thund ... 187 D3
Leasway The. South ... 199 D4
Leasway The. Wick ... 174 A3
Leasway. Rayl ... 176 C1
Leasway. Wick ... 174 A3
Leather La. Brain ... 59 F2
Leather La. Gt Y ... 9 D1
Leather La. South ... 200 A4
Lede Rd. Canv ... 197 D2
Lee Lotts. Gt Wak ... 193 D2
Lee Rd. Basil ... 186 C2
Lee Rd. Harw ... 40 B2
Lee Wick La. St O ... 107 E1
Lee Wootens La. Basil ... 185 D2
Leech's La. Colch ... 49 E2
Leeches Way. Hawk ... 178 B2
Leeward Rd. S Woo F ... 165 F3
Leeway The. Dan ... 142 C4
Legerton Cotts. Wa Col ... 28 B1
Legg St. Chelm ... 127 D2
Leicester Cl. Clact ... 108 C1
Leicester Cl. Colch ... 68 A4
Leicester Ct. Silv E ... 79 E2
Leige Ave. Canv ... 197 D3
Leigh Beck La. Canv ... 197 F1
Leigh Beck Rd. Canv ... 197 F2
Leigh Cliff Rd. South ... 198 C4
Leigh Dr. Wic Bis ... 115 E3
Leigh Fells. Basil ... 186 B3
Leigh Gdns. Hadl ... 189 E1
Leigh Hall Rd. South ... 189 E1
Leigh Hill. South ... 198 B4
Leigh Hts. Hadl ... 188 C2
Leigh Park Cl. South ... 198 C4
Leigh Park Rd. South ... 198 B4
Leigh Rd. Canv ... 197 D1
Leigh Rd. South ... 190 A1
Leigh View Dr. South ... 189 D1
Leigham Court Dr. South ... 189 F1
Leighams Rd. E Han ... 153 F4
Leighcroft Gdns. South ... 189 E1
Leighfields Ave. South ... 189 D3
Leighfields Rd. South ... 189 D3
Leighfields. Thund ... 188 A3
Leighlands Rd. S Woo F ... 165 E4
Leighton Ave. South ... 189 F1
Leighton Rd. Thund ... 187 F2
Leighville Gr. South ... 189 E1
Leighwood Ave. South ... 189 D1
Leitrim Ave. South ... 201 E3
Lekoe Rd. Canv ... 196 C3
Lenham Way. Basil ... 186 B3
Leon Dr. Basil ... 185 E2
Leonard Dr. Rayl ... 176 A2
Leonard Mews. Brain ... 78 A4
Leonard Rd. Basil ... 185 D1
Leonard Rd. South ... 199 E4
Les Bois. Lay H ... 85 D3
Leslie Cl. South ... 189 E3
Leslie Gdns. Rayl ... 176 C1
Leslie Park. Burn ... 170 B2
Leslie Rd. Rayl ... 176 C1
Lesley Gdns. Hawk ... 178 B2
Lethe Grove. Colch ... 85 F4
Lettons Chase. S Woo F ... 165 E3
Levens Way. Clact ... 109 F4
Levens Way. Bl Not ... 77 E3
Lever La. Roch ... 178 C1
Lewes Rd. South ... 191 E2
Lewes Way. Thund ... 188 A4
Lewis Dr. Chelm ... 140 A3
Lexden Cl. South ... 189 F2
Lexden Gr. Colch ... 66 C4
Lexden Rd. Colch ... 66 C4
Lexden Rd. W Berg ... 48 B2
Ley Field. Mks T ... 64 C2
Ley The. Brain ... 60 B1
Leybourne Dr. Sprin ... 127 F4
Leys Rd. Wiv ... 69 E2
Leys The. Basil ... 185 E2
Leys The. Sprin ... 127 F3
Leyton Ct. Clact ... 109 F4
Leywood Cl. Brain ... 60 B1
Licac Ct. Wiv ... 69 D1
Lichfield Cl. Chelm ... 126 C3
Lichfield Cl. Colch ... 68 A4
Lichfields The. Basil ... 185 F4
Lilac Cl. With ... 115 D4
Lifstan Way. South ... 200 C4
Lilac Ave. Canv ... 197 E2
Lilac Ave. Wick ... 174 B4
Lilac Cl. Chelm ... 140 B3
Lilian Rd. Burn ... 170 B3
Lilian's La. Gt Bro ... 52 C2
Lillies The. Brain ... 42 A1
Lillput Cl. South ... 177 D2
Lily Cl. Sprin ... 127 F4
Limbourne Dr. Mald ... 132 B3
Limburg Rd. Canv ... 196 B2
Lime Ave. Colch ... 68 B4

Lime Ave. Hadl ... 189 E1
Lime Ave. Harw ... 40 A2
Lime Cl. Clact ... 109 E2
Lime Cl. With ... 98 A3
Lime Gr. Sud ... 12 B3
Lime Rd. S Ben ... 187 F2
Lime St. Brigh ... 106 C3
Lime Way. Brain ... 170 A3
Lime Wlk. Chelm ... 140 B3
Limebrook Way. Mald ... 144 C4
Limes The. Chelm ... 140 A1
Limes The. Gos ... 42 C4
Limes The. L Mel ... 7 F4
Limes The. Rayl ... 176 C1
Limetree Rd. Canv ... 187 D2
Limetree Rd. Canv ... 197 F2
Lincoln Ave. Clact ... 124 B3
Lincoln Chase. South ... 191 F2
Lincoln La. Gt Hor ... 31 E1
Lincoln Rd. Basil ... 185 F4
Lincoln Rd. Colch ... 68 A4
Lincoln Way. Canv ... 196 C2
Lincoln Way. Colch ... 68 A4
Lincoln Way. Rayl ... 176 B3
Linde Rd. Canv ... 197 D2
Linden Cl. Chelm ... 140 B4
Linden Cl. Colch ... 50 C1
Linden Cl. Lawf ... 35 D2
Linden Cl. Rayl ... 176 C1
Linden Cl. Thund ... 187 E3
Linden Dr. Clact ... 109 F4
Linden Leas. Thund ... 187 E3
Linden Rd. Thund ... 187 E3
Lindens The. Brain ... 60 A1
Lindford Dr. Basil ... 185 F3
Lindisfarne Ave. South ... 190 A1
Lindisfarne Ct. Mald ... 144 C4
Lindon Rd. Runw ... 163 E2
Lindsell Green. Basil ... 185 F3
Lindsell La. Basil ... 185 F3
Lindsey Ave. Sud ... 13 D3
Lindsey Rd. Gt Wak ... 193 D2
Lingcroft. Basil ... 185 F2
Lingfield Dr. Roch ... 179 D2
Lingwood Cl. Dan ... 142 C4
Link Cl. Colch ... 49 F2
Link Rd. Brigh ... 107 D3
Link Rd. Canv ... 196 C2
Link Rd. Clact ... 109 E1
Link Rd. Hals ... 43 E4
Link Rd. Rayl ... 176 B2
Links Dr. Chelm ... 139 F4
Links Rd. Bradw ... 79 D4
Links Way. Hadl ... 188 C2
Linksway. Hadl ... 185 D3
Linkway. Basil ... 185 D3
Linley Gdns. Clact ... 109 E1
Linne Rd. Canv ... 197 E3
Linnet Cl. Chelm ... 140 A3
Linnet Dr. Chelm ... 140 A3
Linnet Dr. S Ben ... 187 E1
Linnet Way. Gt Ben ... 89 E4
Linnets. Basil ... 185 D2
Linnets. Clact ... 109 F3
Linroping Ave. Canv ... 197 F2
Linstead Cl. Clact ... 109 D2
Lion Rd. Glems ... 2 C3
Lion Wlk. Colch ... 67 F4
Lionel Hurst Cl. Sud ... 13 E3
Lionel Rd. Canv ... 197 D2
Lionfield Terr. Sprin ... 127 E2
Lisle Rd. Colch ... 68 A3
Lister Rd. Brain ... 77 F4
Liston La. Fox ... 7 D4
Liston La. L Mel ... 7 E4
Listonhall Chase. Si Hed ... 24 B4
Litchfield Cl. Clact ... 109 F3
Litchfield. Harw ... 39 E1
Littell Tweed. Sprin ... 128 A2
Little and Great Sir Hughes La.
  W Han ... 141 D1
Little Baddow Rd. Dan ... 142 C4
Little Baddow Rd. Woo Wa ... 130 B2
Little Bakers. Walt ... 94 A4
Little Bentley Rd. Tend ... 54 A1
Little Bentley. Basil ... 185 D4
Little Braxted La. With ... 98 B2
Little Bromley Rd. Ard ... 52 A4
Little Bromley Rd. Gt Bro ... 52 C2
Little Bromley Rd. Lit Ben ... 53 F1
Little Charlton. Basil ... 185 F3
Little Chittock. Basil ... 185 F3
Little Church St. Harw ... 40 C3
Little Clacton Rd. Frin ... 92 C1
Little Clacton Rd. Lit Cla ... 109 F3
Little Dorrit. Chelm ... 126 C4
Little Fretches. South ... 189 F2
Little Garth. Basil ... 186 A3
Little Gypps Cl. Canv ... 196 C2
Little Gypps Rd. Canv ... 196 C2
Little Harrods. Walt ... 94 A4
Little Hayes Chase. Stow ... 155 E1
Little Hays. South ... 189 E2
Little Horkesley Rd. Worm ... 30 A2
Little Hyde Cl. Gt Y ... 9 D1
Little Hyde Rd. Gt Y ... 9 D1
Little London La. Woo Wa ... 130 B2

Little Meadow. Writ 126 A1
Little Nell. Chelm 126 C4
Little Oaks. Basil 185 D3
Little Searles. Basil 186 A4
Little Spenders. Basil 185 E2
Little Sq. Brain 59 F2
Little St Mary's. L Mel 7 E4
Little Stambridge Hall Rd.
  Gt Stam 179 E2
Little Stile. Writ 139 D4
Little Tey Rd. Fee 81 F3
Little Thorpe. South 192 A1
Little Totham Rd. Gold 117 E1
Little Totham Rd. Lit Tot 117 E1
Little Wakering Hall La. Gt Wak 193 D2
Little Wakering Rd. Barl 192 C3
Little Wheatley Chase. Rayl .. 176 A2
Little Wood. Walt 93 F3
Little Yeldham Rd. Lit Y 9 E2
Littlebury Ct. Basil 186 A4
Littlebury Gdns. Colch 68 B2
Littlebury Green. Basil 186 A4
Littlecotes. Colch 49 E2
Littlecroft. S Woo F 165 E3
Littlefield Rd. Colch 67 E1
Littlethorpe. Basil 185 F2
Llewellyn Cl. Sprin 127 E2
Lloyd Rd. Sho G 40 A4
Lloyd Wise Cl. South 191 E2
Loamy Hill Rd. Toll M 117 D4
Lobelia Cl. Bore 128 A3
Locarno Ave. Runw 163 F1
Lock Rd. Hals 43 F4
Lockhart Ave. Colch 67 E4
Lockram La. With 97 F1
Lockram La. With 98 A1
Locks Hill. Roch 178 C1
Lodge Ave. Gt Bad 140 C4
Lodge Cl. Clact 109 F2
Lodge Cl. Lit Oak 57 E4
Lodge Cl. South 176 C1
Lodge Cl. Thund 188 A3
Lodge Cres. Bore 128 C4
Lodge Ct. W Berg 48 C2
Lodge Farm Cl. South 189 E3
Lodge Farm La. St O 108 B2
Lodge Farm Rd. Glems 2 B2
Lodge La. Ard 51 E3
Lodge La. Bril 51 E3
Lodge La. Brigh 106 C4
Lodge La. Lang 86 B1
Lodge La. Langh 50 B4
Lodge La. Pele 103 E4
Lodge La. Purl 104 C4
Lodge La. Tend 72 C3
Lodge La. Tend 59 F1
Lodge Rd. Haze 144 A3
Lodge Rd. Lit Bad 92 A2
Lodge Rd. Lit Oak 57 E4
Lodge Rd. Mald 131 F2
Lodge Rd. Mess 82 B2
Lodge Rd. S Woo F 153 F3
Lodge Rd. With 139 D4
Lodgelands Cl. Rayl 176 C1
Lodwick. South 201 E3
Loftin Way. Gt Bad 140 B4
Lombardy Cl. Basil 186 B3
Lombardy Pl. Chelm 127 D2
London Hill. Chelm 139 F1
London Hill. Rayl 176 B2
London Land Cotts. Worm .. 29 F2
London Rd. Basil 185 E2
London Rd. Basil 187 D3
London Rd. Bl Not 77 E3
London Rd. Brain 59 F2
London Rd. Chelm 139 F4
London Rd. Clact 109 F4
London Rd. Copf 65 E2
London Rd. Fee 81 F2
London Rd. Gt Hor 30 C2
London Rd. Gt Le 77 E3
London Rd. Hadl 189 E1
London Rd. Kelv 81 D1
London Rd. Mald 131 E2
London Rd. Mks T 64 C1
London Rd. Rayl 176 B2
London Rd. South 190 B1
London Rd. Stanw 66 C4
London Rd. Thund 187 D3
London Rd. Wick 174 A4
London Rd. Wick 174 A4
London Rd. Wick 175 E3
Long Acres. Fee 81 F2
Long Brancks. Writ 126 A1
Long Gages. Basil 185 D4
Long Green. T Gr 78 C4
Long La. Frin 93 D2
Long La. Hull 165 F1
Long Meadow. Dr. Wick 174 C4
Long Meadows. Harw 39 F1
Long Melford By-Ps. L Mel 7 F3
Long Pastures. Glems 2 B2
Long Rd W. Ded 33 F2
Long Rd. Canv 196 C2
Long Rd. Lawf 35 D2
Long Rd. Mist 35 D2
Long Riding. Basil 185 E3
Long Wyre St. Colch 67 F4
Longacre. Basil 185 E4

Longacre. Chelm 139 E4
Longacres Rd. T Gr 78 C3
Longacres. Brain 60 A1
Longbarn Hill. Brad 37 D1
Longborough Cl. Basil 174 A1
Longcroft Rd. Colch 68 B4
Longfellow Rd. Mald 132 A1
Longfield Cl. Wick 175 D4
Longfield Rd. Gt Bad 140 C4
Longfield Rd. S Woo F 165 E4
Longfield Rd. Wick 175 D4
Longfield. With 97 F3
Longfields. St O 108 A2
Longhams Dr. S Woo F 165 E4
Longleat Dr. Brain 77 F4
Longleat Cl. Chelm 140 C4
Longmead Ave. Gt Bad 140 C4
Longmeads Cl. Writ 126 A1
Longmeads. Wic Bis 115 F3
Longmore Ave. Gt Bad 140 C4
Longridge. Colch 68 C4
Longsands. South 201 E4
Longship Way. Mald 144 C4
Longstomps Ave. Chelm 140 A4
Lonsdale Rd. South 191 E1
Lord Holland Rd. Colch 67 F2
Lord Roberts Ave. South 189 F1
Lordship Rd. Writ 126 A1
Lordswood Rd. Colch 67 E1
Lorien Gdns. S Woo F 165 E3
Lorkin's La. Twin 18 B2
Lornes Cl. South 191 E2
Loten Rd. S Ben 187 D1
Lott's La. Brad 54 B4
Lott's Rd. Clact 91 D2
Lottern Rd. Canv 197 E1
Lotts Yd. Colch 68 A3
Louis Dr E. Rayl 176 A2
Louis Dr W. Rayl 176 A2
Louisa Ave. Thund 187 D3
Louise Cl. Walt 76 C4
Louise Rd. Rayl 176 C1
Louvaine Ave. Wick 174 A4
Love La. Brad 106 C4
Love La. Rayl 176 B1
Love Way. Clact 109 E3
Lovelace Ave. South 200 B4
Lovelace Gdns. South 191 E1
Lovell Rise. South 190 A3
Lovens Cl. Canv 197 E1
Lover's La. Gt Ben 90 A4
Loves Wlk. Gt Bad 140 C4
Loves Wlk. Writ 139 D4
Lovibond Pl. Sprin 127 F2
Low Rd. Harw 39 F1
Low St. South 201 F3
Low St. Glems 2 B3
Lowe Chase. Walt 94 A4
Lowefields. La Col 45 E3
Lower Anchor Rd. Chelm 127 D1
Lower Ave. Basil 186 B2
Lower Burnham Rd. Purl 156 B1
Lower Chase. Alth 157 F2
Lower Church Rd. Thund 187 D3
Lower Farm Rd. Box 21 D1
Lower Green. Chelm 140 B1
Lower Green. Wa Col 28 B1
Lower Harlings. Sho G 40 A4
Lower Holt St. Ea Col 45 E3
Lower Lambricks. Rayl 176 B2
Lower Langley. Gt T 46 B1
Lower Marine Par. Harw 40 B1
Lower Park Rd. Brigh 106 C4
Lower Park Rd. Wick 174 B2
Lower Rd. Ashi 166 B1
Lower Rd. Ashi 167 D1
Lower Rd. Birch 84 A3
Lower Rd. Fox 7 D2
Lower Rd. Hull 166 B1
Lower Rd. Lay B 102 A4
Lower Rd. M Bure 29 D3
Lower Rd. Peld 103 E3
Lower Southend Rd. Wick ... 174 B4
Lower St. Cav 1 B1
Lower St. Glems 2 C3
Lower St. Str S M 33 F4
Loxford. Basil 186 A4
Luard Way. Birch 84 A2
Luard Way. With 97 F1
Lubbards Cl. Rayl 176 B3
Lucas Ave. Chelm 140 B3
Lucas Ave. Ford 47 E3
Lucas Rd. Colch 67 F3
Lucas Rd. Sud 12 C4
Lucas's La. Beau 73 E3
Lucerne Dr. Wick 175 D4
Lucerne Rd. Elmst M 70 A3
Lucerne Wlk. Wick 175 D4
Luces La. Ca Hed 15 F3
Lucksfield Way. Gt Bad 140 C3
Lucy Cl. Stanw 66 B3
Lucy La N. Stanw 66 A4
Lucy La S. Stanw 66 B4
Lucy Rd. South 200 A4
Ludgores La. Dan 142 B3
Ludgrove. Latch 157 D3
Ludham Hall La. Bl Not 77 E4
Luff Way. Walt 93 F4
Lufkin Rd. Colch 49 F2

Lugar Cl. Colch 68 C3
Luker Rd. South 200 A4
Lumber Leys. Walt 94 A4
Luncies Rd. Basil 185 F3
Lundy Cl. South 190 A3
Lunnish Hill. Rams 38 C1
Lupin Dr. Sprin 127 F3
Lupin Mews. Sprin 127 F3
Lupin Way. Clact 109 E2
Lushington Ave. Walt 93 F3
Lushington Rd. Lawf 35 D2
Lutus Cl. Cla 4 A3
Lydford Rd. South 199 F4
Lydgate Cl. Lawf 35 D2
Lydia Dr. St O 107 D1
Lyfl Rd. Canv 197 D2
Lyme Rd. South 191 E1
Lymington Ave. Clact 110 A4
Lymington Ave. South 189 F1
Lympstone Cl. South 190 A3
Lyndale Ave. South 191 D1
Lyndene. Thund 187 D3
Lyndhurst Dr. S Woo F 142 C1
Lyndhurst Rd. Ashi 167 E1
Lyndhurst Rd. Clact 110 B2
Lynfords Ave. Runw 164 A2
Lynfords Dr. Runw 163 F1
Lynfords Dr. Runw 164 A2
Lynmouth Ave. Chelm 140 B4
Lynmouth Gdns. Chelm 187 E3
Lynn View Cl. S Ben 187 E3
Lynne Cl. Walt 93 E3
Lynstede. Basil 186 A3
Lynton Cl. Harw 40 A2
Lynton Dr. Sprin 127 F3
Lynton Rd. S Ben 188 B2
Lynwood Green. Rayl 189 D4
Lyon Cl. Chelm 140 A2
Lyon Cl. Clact 110 A2
Lyons Hall Rd. Brain 60 B4
Lyster Ave. Gt Bad 141 D4
Lyth Ave. South 201 E4

Macbeth Cl. Colch 68 C4
Macdonald Ave. South 190 C1
Macintyres Wlk. Hawk 178 B3
Mackay Ct. Colch 68 A1
Maclarens. Gt Tot 116 A3
Macmurdo Cl. South 189 E4
Macmurdo Rd. South 189 E4
Madeira Ave. South 189 F1
Madeira Rd. Clact 110 B2
Madeline Pl. Chelm 126 C3
Madgements Rd. Stis 61 D4
Madrid Ave. Rayl 176 A4
Magazine Farm Way. Colch .. 67 D3
Magazine Rd. South 201 F3
Magdalen Cl. Clact 109 F2
Magdalen St. Colch 68 A3
Magdalene Cres. Silv E 79 E2
Magna Mead. Barl 192 B4
Magnolia Cl. Chelm 140 A3
Magnolia Cl. With 98 A4
Magnolia Dr. Colch 68 C4
Magnolia Rd. Hawk 178 A3
Magnolia Way. Roch 191 D4
Magwitch Cl. Chelm 126 C4
Maidenburgh St. Colch 67 F4
Maidment Cres. With 114 C4
Main Rd. Alth 157 F2
Main Rd. Bore 128 B4
Main Rd. Dun 142 B4
Main Rd. E Han 153 E3
Main Rd. Frat 70 C2
Main Rd. Frin 93 D2
Main Rd. Harw 40 A3
Main Rd. Harw 177 F2
Main Rd. Hawk 177 E3
Main Rd. Rams 39 D1
Main Rd. Rett 164 A3
Main Rd. S Woo F 154 A3
Main Rd. St L 148 B4
Main Rd. Worm 29 F2
Maine Cres. Rayl 176 A2
Maitland Pl. South 192 C1
Makins Rd. Rams 39 F3
Malard Cl. Tolle 119 E1
Maldon Cl. Sud 13 D4
Maldon Rd. Brad 83 F2
Maldon Rd. Brad O S 149 E4
Maldon Rd. Burn 169 F4
Maldon Rd. Colch 67 E2
Maldon Rd. Dan 143 D3
Maldon Rd. Dan 143 D3
Maldon Rd. Gold 133 E3
Maldon Rd. Gt Bad 141 E4
Maldon Rd. Gt Tot 116 B4
Maldon Rd. Gt Brx 99 F1
Maldon Rd. Hat Pev 114 A2
Maldon Rd. Kelv 81 E1
Maldon Rd. Langf 131 E3
Maldon Rd. Marg 139 E3
Maldon Rd. Sand 141 E4
Maldon Rd. South 191 D1
Maldon Rd. Stanw 66 B1

Maldon Rd. Steep 147 E1
Maldon Rd. Tipt 100 B2
Maldon Rd. Toll D 118 B1
Maldon Rd. Toll M 118 B1
Maldon Rd. With 115 D4
Maldon Rd. Woo Mor 144 A4
Maldon Way. Clact 109 D2
Malgraves Pl. Basil 186 A4
Malgraves. Basil 186 A4
Mallard Cl. Kelv 81 E2
Mallard Cl. Lay H 85 D3
Mallard Rd. Chelm 140 A3
Mallard Way. Sud 13 E3
Mallards. May 158 A4
Mallards. South 192 C1
Mallow Field. Hals 25 F1
Malmsmead. South 201 E4
Maltese Rd. Chelm 127 D2
Malthouse Rd. Mann 35 E2
Malting Farm La. Ard 33 E1
Malting Green Rd. Lay H 85 D3
Malting La. Cla 4 A4
Malting La. Walt 75 E1
Malting Rd. Colch 67 E1
Malting Rd. Peld 103 E3
Malting Villas Rd. Roch 178 C1
Malting Yd. Wiv 87 D4
Maltings Cl. Bures 19 F1
Maltings Cl. With 114 C4
Maltings La. With 114 B4
Maltings Rd. Brigh 88 C1
Maltings Rd. Gt Bad 141 D3
Maltings Rd. Rett 164 C1
Maltings The. Ray 59 D1
Maltings The. South 159 F2
Malvern Ave. Canv 196 B2
Malvern Cl. Chelm 126 B3
Malvern Cl. Rayl 176 B2
Malvern Rd. Hock 177 F1
Malvern Way. Gt Hor 49 D4
Malwood Dr. S Ben 187 D3
Malwood Rd. S Ben 187 D3
Malyon Court Cl. S Ben 188 A2
Malyon Rd. With 114 C4
Malyons Cl. Basil 186 A4
Malyons Green. Basil 186 A4
Malyons La. Hull 165 E1
Malyons Mews. Basil 186 A4
Malyons Pl. Basil 186 A4
Malyons The. S Ben 188 A2
Malyons. Basil 186 A4
Manchester Dr. South 189 E1
Manchester Dr. South 189 E1
Manchester Rd. Clact 110 C3
Mandeville Rd. Mks T 64 C2
Mandeville Way. Thund 187 E4
Mandeville Way. Walt 93 F3
Manfield Gdns. St O 108 A3
Manfield. Hals 25 F1
Mangapp Chase. Burn 170 A3
Manilla Rd. South 200 B4
Mannering Gdns. South 190 A2
Manners Way. South 190 C3
Manningtree Rd. Ded 34 A3
Manningtree Rd. Lit Ben 71 F4
Manningtree Rd. Str S M 35 F4
Manns Way. Rayl 176 B3
Manor Ave. Basil 186 B3
Manor Cl. Cav 1 B1
Manor Cl. Gt Hor 49 E4
Manor Cl. Rayl 188 B4
Manor Dr. Gt Bad 140 C4
Manor House Way. Brigh 106 C4
Manor La. Harw 40 A1
Manor Rd. Chelm 127 E1
Manor Rd. Colch 67 F4
Manor Rd. Deng 149 E3
Manor Rd. Frin 93 D2
Manor Rd. Hadl 189 D1
Manor Rd. Hat Pev 114 B1
Manor Rd. Hock 177 E3
Manor Rd. S Woo F 165 E3
Manor Rd. South 199 E4
Manor Rd. Sud 7 F1
Manor Rd. Thund 187 E3
Manor Rd. W Berg 48 C3
Manor Rd. Wiv 87 D4
Manor Rd. Woo Wa 131 D2
Manor St. Brain 60 A3
Manor Way. Clact 111 D3
Manors Way. Silv E 79 E2
Manse Chase. Mald 132 A1
Mansel Cl. South 189 F3
Mansted Gdns. Hawk 178 B3
Maple Ave. Brain 59 E1
Maple Ave. Mald 132 A3
Maple Ave. South 198 C4
Maple Cl. Clact 109 E2
Maple Cl. Harw 40 A2
Maple Dr. Chelm 140 A3
Maple Dr. Rayl 176 B4
Maple Dr. With 98 A3
Maple Leaf. Tipt 100 B4
Maple Rd. Sud 13 D3
Maple Sq. South 191 D1
Maple Way. Burn 170 A3
Maple Way. Canv 196 C2

Maple Way. Colch 68 A2
Maplebene Ave. Hull 165 F1
Mapledene Sweep. Basil 185 E2
Mapleleaf Cl. Hock 177 F4
Mapleleaf Gdns. Wick 174 A3
Maples The. Wick 174 A3
Maplesfield. Hadl 188 B2
Maplestead. Basil 185 E4
Maplin Cl. Thund 187 E4
Maplin Gdns. Basil 185 F3
Maplin Way N. South 192 B1
Maplin Way. South 201 E3
Marasca End. Rowh 86 A4
Maraschino Cres. Rowh 86 A4
Marconi Rd. Chelm 127 D2
Marcos Rd. Canv 197 E2
Marcus Ave. South 201 D4
Marcus Chase. South 201 D4
Marcus Gdns. South 201 D4
Marennes Cres. Brigh 106 C4
Mareth Rd. Colch 67 D2
Margaret Cl. Brigh 106 C3
Margaret Rd. Colch 67 F4
Margaretting Rd. Chelm 139 F1
Margaretting Rd. Writ 139 D3
Margarite Way. Wick 174 A4
Margraten Ave. Canv 197 E1
Marguerite Dr. South 189 F1
Maria St. Harw 40 B3
Marigold Ave. Clact 109 E3
Marigold Cl. Sprin 127 F3
Marigold Cl. Colch 68 C4
Marina Ave. Rayl 176 B2
Marina Cl. South 190 C2
Marina Gdns. Clact 110 B3
Marina Mews. Walt 94 B4
Marina Rd. Hat Pev 114 A2
Marine App. Canv 197 D1
Marine Ave. Canv 197 F1
Marine Ave. South 189 E1
Marine Cl. South 199 F4
Marine Cl. Hadl 189 D1
Marine Par E. Clact 110 A2
Marine Par W. Clact 109 F1
Marine Par. Canv 197 F1
Marine Par. Harw 40 B2
Marine Par. May 146 C1
Marine Par. South 200 A4
Mariners Ct. Gt Wak 193 E2
Mariners Way. Mald 145 D4
Marion Ave. Clact 109 F3
Mariskals. Basil 186 A3
Mark Rd. Till 149 F2
Market Ave. Runw 174 B4
Market End. Cogg 62 C1
Market Hill. Cla 4 A4
Market Hill. Cogg 63 D2
Market Hill. Hals 25 F1
Market Hill. Sud 12 C4
Market Pavement. Basil 185 D3
Market Pl. Brain 59 F2
Market Pl. Mald 131 F1
Market Pl. South 200 A4
Market Rd. Chelm 127 D1
Market Sq. Basil 185 D3
Market Sq. S Woo F 165 E4
Market St. Harw 40 C3
Markland Cl. Chelm 140 B2
Marks Dr. S Woo F 165 F4
Marks Gdns. Brain 60 B1
Marks Hall Rd. Cogg 62 C3
Marks La. Rett 163 F4
Marland Dr. Mald 131 F1
Marlborough Ave. Till 149 F2
Marlborough Cl. Clact 109 E2
Marlborough Cl. Thund 187 E4
Marlborough Dr. Sud 12 C4
Marlborough Rd. Brain 60 A2
Marlborough Rd. Chelm 127 D1
Marlborough Wlk. Hock 177 E3
Marlin Cl. Hadl 188 C4
Marlowe Gdns. South 190 C2
Marlowe Cl. Brain 78 A4
Marlowe Cl. Mald 145 D4
Marlowe Rd. Clact 109 D1
Marlowe Way. Colch 66 C3
Marlpits Rd. Purl 154 C3
Marmaduke Ave. Rayl 176 A2
Marne Rd. Colch 67 F2
Marney Cl. Gt Bad 140 C4
Marney Dr. Basil 185 F3
Marney Way. Frin 94 A3
Marram Cl. Colch 66 A4
Marsh Cres. Rowh 86 B4
Marsh Farm La. Thor 89 E1
Marsh Farm Rd. S Woo F 165 E3
Marsh Rd. Burn 171 E3
Marsh Rd. High 21 F3
Marsh Rd. South 201 F3
Marsh Rd. Till 150 A2
Marshall Cl. Hadl 188 C3
Marshalls Cl. Rayl 176 C1

Marshalls Rd. Brain 59 F1
Marshalls. Hawk 178 B2
Marston Beck. Sprin 128 A1
Martello Rd. Walt 94 B4
Marten's La. Nay 20 C4
Martin End. Lay H 85 D3
Martin Mews. S Ben 187 E2
Martin Mews. S Woo F 165 F4
Martin Wlk. Hawk 177 F2
Martin's Rd. Hals 25 F1
Martingale Dr. Sprin 127 F4
Martingale. Thund 188 A3
Martinsdale. Clact 109 F3
Martock Ave. South 190 A3
Martyns Gr. South 190 A1
Martyns Rise. L Mel 7 E3
Marvens. Chelm 140 B2
Mary La N. Gt Bro 71 D4
Mary La S. Gt Bro 71 D3
Mary Warner Rd. Ard 51 F4
Maryborough Gr. Colch 68 A1
Marylands Ave. Hock 177 E4
Mascalls The. Gt Bad 140 C4
Mascalls Way. Gt Bad 140 C4
Masefield Dr. Colch 66 C3
Masefield Rd. Brain 78 A4
Masefield Rd. Mald 145 D4
Mashey Rd. Lit Y 9 E3
Mason Cl. Colch 67 D2
Mason Ct. Clact 109 D2
Mason Rd. Colch 49 F1
Matching Green. Basil 185 F4
Matfield Cl. Sprin 127 E4
Mathews Cl. Str S M 22 B1
Matlock Rd. Canv 196 C2
Matthews Cl. Hals 26 A2
Maugham Cl. Wick 174 B3
Maurice Rd. Canv 197 E2
May Ave. Canv 197 E1
May Ave. Canv 197 E2
May Wlk. Chelm 140 B4
May's La. Ded 33 F2
Mayberry Wlk. Colch 68 A2
Maybury Cl. Mks T 64 C2
Mayda Cl. Hals 25 E1
Maydells. Basil 186 A3
Maydene. S Woo F 165 E4
Mayes La. Dan 142 C4
Mayes La. Lit Oak 39 E1
Mayes La. Sand 141 F3
Mayfair Ave. Basil 186 B4
Mayfield Ave. Hull 165 F1
Mayfield Ave. South 190 C2
Mayfield Cl. Colch 50 B1
Mayfield Rd. Writ 126 A1
Mayflower Ave. Harw 40 C3
Mayflower Cl. South 190 A3
Mayflowers. Thund 187 D4
Mayford Way. Clact 109 D3
Mayland Ave. Canv 197 D1
Mayland Cl. Mald 132 B2
Mayland Cl. May 158 A4
Mayland Green. May 158 A4
Mayland Hill. May 158 B3
Mayland Rd. With 98 A1
Maylands Dr. Bl Not 77 E4
Mayling Rd. Brain 59 E1
Mayne Crest. Sprin 127 F3
Mayors Wlk. Colch 67 F4
Maypole Dr. St O 108 A2
Maypole Green Rd. Colch 67 E1
Maypole Rd. Gt Tot 131 F4
Maypole Rd. Tipt 100 B4
Maysent Ave. Brain 59 F3
Maytree Wlk. Thund 187 D4
Maze The. South 189 E4
McCalmont Dr. Rayl 176 B4
McDivitt Wlk. South 190 A3
Mead Pastures. Woo Wa 130 B2
Mead Path. Chelm 139 F4
Mead The. Sud 13 D2
Meadgate Ave. Gt Bad 140 C4
Meadow Cl. Basil 186 B4
Meadow Cl. Clact 110 A4
Meadow Cl. Gt Bro 71 D3
Meadow Cl. Hals 43 F4
Meadow Cl. Pan 59 D4
Meadow Cl. Wick 174 B3
Meadow Cl. South 200 C4
Meadow Grass Cl. Colch 66 A3
Meadow La. Runw 163 F2
Meadow La. Sud 12 C4
Meadow La. W Mers 121 E3
Meadow Mews. S Woo F 165 D4
Meadow Rd. Colch 67 E1
Meadow Rd. Hadl 188 C1
Meadow Rd. Hull 165 F1
Meadow Rd. Rett 164 B3
Meadow Side. Chelm 127 D2
Meadow View Cl. Colch 66 C3
Meadow View Rd. Sud 12 B3
Meadow View Wlk. Canv 196 C2
Meadow Way. Bl Not 78 B3
Meadow Way. Clact 125 D4
Meadow Way. Hock 177 F3
Meadow Way. Lang 86 A1
Meadow Way. Latch 157 D3
Meadow Way. Wick 174 B2
Meadowclose. Thund 188 A3

Meadowcroft Way. Walt 93 F4
Meadowland Rd. Wick 175 D3
Meadowside. Brain 59 F3
Meadowside. Chelm 127 E2
Meadowside. Rayl 176 B1
Meadway The. Basil 186 A2
Meadway The. South 199 D4
Meadway. Canv 197 E1
Meadway. Gos 42 C4
Meadway. Lawf 35 D2
Meadway. Mald 132 A1
Meadway. Rayl 176 C1
Meadway. Thund 187 E4
Meakins Cl. South 189 F4
Mearns Pl. Sprin 127 F2
Mede Way. Wiv 69 E2
Medlar Cl. With 98 A2
Medoc Cl. Basil 186 B4
Medway Ave. With 97 E1
Medway Cl. Chelm 126 B2
Medway Cres. Hadl 189 D1
Medway. Burn 170 A3
Meekings Rd. Sud 13 D4
Meers The. Walt 93 F3
Meesons Mead. Hawk 178 B2
Meesons Meadows. Mald 144 C4
Meeting Field. L Mel 7 E4
Meeting La. E Mers 105 E1
Meeting La. Ridge 8 A4
Meggison Way. S Ben 187 E2
Melba Ct. Writ 126 B1
Melbourne Ave. Chelm 126 C3
Melbourne Chase. Colch 68 A1
Melbourne Rd. Clact 109 F2
Melcombe Rd. S Ben 187 E2
Melford Rd. Cav 1 C1
Melford Rd. Sud 12 C2
Mell Rd. Tolle 119 F1
Mellor Chase. Colch 66 C4
Melrose Gdns. Clact 110 B3
Melrose Rd. W Mers 121 E3
Melton Cl. Clact 109 D2
Melville Heath. S Woo F 165 F3
Mendip Cl. Rayl 176 C2
Mendip Cres. South 190 A2
Mendip Rd./Chelm 126 B3
Mendip Rd. South 190 A2
Mendlesham Cl. Clact 109 D2
Menish Way. Sprin 128 A2
Meon Cl. Sprin 127 E3
Meppel Ave. Canv 197 D3
Mercer Ave. Gt Wak 193 D2
Mercers Way. Colch 67 F4
Merchant St. S Woo F 165 F4
Mercia Cl. Gt Bad 141 D4
Mercury Cl. Wick 174 C4
Meredene. Basil 185 F3
Meredith Rd. Clact 109 F2
Meriadoc Dr. S Woo F 165 E3
Merilies Cl. South 190 A2
Merilies Gdns. South 190 A2
Merivale Cl. Lawf 35 E2
Merivale Rd. Lawf 35 D2
Merlin Cl. Canv 197 D2
Merlin End. Colch 50 C1
Merlin Pl. Chelm 126 C3
Merlin Way. Runw 163 E1
Merricks La. Basil 185 F1
Merrilees Cres. Clact 110 B3
Merrivale. S Ben 187 E1
Merryfield App. South 189 F2
Merryfields Ave. Hock 177 E4
Merrymount Gdns. Clact 110 A3
Mersea Ave. W Mers 121 D3
Mersea Cl. Hock 68 A2
Mersea Rd. Peld 103 F3
Mersea Rd. Rowh 86 B3
Mersea View. St O 107 D2
Mersey Fleet Way. Brain 60 B1
Mersey Rd. With 97 F1
Mersey Way. Chelm 126 B3
Merstham Dr. Clact 109 E3
Merton Cl. Rowh 86 A4
Merton Pl. S Woo F 165 F3
Merton Rd. Hock 177 D4
Merton Rd. South 190 C3
Mess Rd. South 201 F3
Messines Rd. Colch 67 E2
Meteor Rd. South 199 E4
Methersgate. Basil 185 E4
Metz Ave. Canv 197 D2
Mews Ct. Chelm 127 D1
Mews The. Frin 93 F3
Mews The. Hock 177 E3
Mey Wlk. Hock 177 E3
Meyel Ave. Canv 197 E3
Meynell Ave. Canv 197 E1
Meyrick Cres. Colch 67 F3
Michaelmas Way. Chelm 126 B4
Michaelstowe Cl. Harw 39 F1
Michaelstowe Dr. Harw 39 E1
Mid Colne. Basil 185 E2
Middle Crockerford. Basil 185 F2
Middle Green. Wa Col 28 B1
Middle Mead. Roch 178 C1
Middle Mead. Wick 174 C4

Middle Mill Rd. Colch 67 F4
Middle Way. L Mel 7 E4
Middleborough. Colch 67 F4
Middleborough. Colch 67 F4
Middleburgh Rd. Canv 196 C3
Middlefield Rd. Mal 36 A2
Middlehall. Hals 25 F1
Middlemead. S Han 152 B2
Middlemead. W Han 152 B2
Middlesex Ave. South 189 F2
Middleton Cl. Clact 109 E3
Middleton Row. S Woo F 165 F3
Middleton Rd. Sud 13 D2
Middlewick Cl. Colch 68 A1
Midguard Way. Mald 144 C4
Midhurst Ave. South 190 B2
Midland Cl. Colch 67 E1
Midsummer Meadow. South 192 C1
Midway Rd. Colch 67 E1
Midway. Clact 124 C3
Milburn Cres. Chelm 126 B1
Mildmay Rd. Burn 170 B3
Mildmay Rd. Chelm 127 D1
Mildmays. Dan 142 C4
Mile End Rd. Colch 49 F2
Miles Cl. Stanw 66 B3
Milford Cl. Elmst M 69 E1
Military Rd. Colch 68 A3
Mill Chase. Hals 25 F1
Mill Cl. Till 149 F2
Mill Cl. Tipt 100 B3
Mill Fields. Dan 143 D3
Mill Green Cl. Basil 186 A4
Mill Green Pl. Basil 186 A4
Mill Green. Basil 186 A4
Mill Green. Burn 170 A2
Mill Hill. Brain 60 A1
Mill Hill. Chelm 139 F1
Mill Hill. Lawf 34 B2
Mill Hill. Mann 35 E2
Mill Hill. Purl 144 B1
Mill Hill. S Ben 196 C4
Mill Hill. Sud 12 B4
Mill Hill. Worm 29 F3
Mill La. Ard 52 A2
Mill La. Birch 83 F2
Mill La. Brad 36 B1
Mill La. Cav 5 D4
Mill La. Col En 45 D4
Mill La. Dan 143 D3
Mill La. Ded 33 F4
Mill La. Frin 92 C2
Mill La. Gt Le 95 D4
Mill La. Gt Map 25 F4
Mill La. Gt Stam 179 D1
Mill La. Gt Y 9 D2
Mill La. Harw 40 B2
Mill La. Lay H 85 D3
Mill La. Lit Bad 129 F2
Mill La. Mald 132 A2
Mill La. Nay 20 B4
Mill La. Peb 26 C4
Mill La. S Ben 12 B4
Mill La. T Gr 78 B3
Mill La. Terl 96 A1
Mill La. Th L S 73 F1
Mill La. Toll M 117 F2
Mill La. Viri 119 D4
Mill La. Walt 94 B4
Mill La. Weel 91 D3
Mill La. With 97 F1
Mill Lane Cl. Weel 91 D3
Mill Rd. Box 31 F2
Mill Rd. Burn 170 B4
Mill Rd. Cla 4 B4
Mill Rd. Colch 49 F3
Mill Rd. Fing 87 D4
Mill Rd. Fox 6 B3
Mill Rd. Gt Tot 116 B4
Mill Rd. Mald 132 A1
Mill Rd. May 158 A4
Mill Rd. Rayl 176 C3
Mill Rd. Ridge 8 A3
Mill Rd. Till 149 F2
Mill Rd. W Mers 121 E4
Mill St. Brigh 107 D3
Mill St. Colch 68 A3
Mill St. Nay 20 A1
Mill St. St O 107 F2
Mill Tye. Sud 13 D2
Mill Vue Rd. Sprin 127 F1
Mill Wlk. Tipt 100 B3
Millars Cl. S Woo F 165 F4
Millbridge Rd. With 97 F1
Miller's Barn Rd. Clact 109 D1
Millers Cl. Brain 60 A4
Millers Cl. Gt Hor 49 D4
Millers Cl. Gt Hor 49 D4
Millers Croft. Gt Bad 140 C3
Millers Gdns. Kelv 81 D1
Millers La. Stanw 66 B3
Millers Mead. Fee 81 F2
Millfield. Burn 170 A3
Millfields. Writ 126 A1
Mills La. L Mel 7 E2
Millson Bank. Sprin 128 A2
Millview Meadows. Roch 178 C1
Millways. Gt Tot 116 A2

Millwrights. Tipt 100 B3
Milner Pl. Sud 13 D4
Milton Ave. Brain 78 A4
Milton Ave. South 199 F4
Milton Cl. Colch 66 C3
Milton Cl. Rayl 177 D1
Milton Pl. Chelm 127 D3
Milton Pl. South 199 F4
Milton Rd. Harw 40 B2
Milton Rd. Hals 35 D1
Milton Rd. Mald 145 D4
Milton Rd. South 199 E4
Milton Rd. With 97 F3
Milton St. South 191 D1
Miltsin Ave. Canv 197 E3
Mimosa Cl. Sprin 127 F1
Minden Rd. Sud 12 C4
Minerva Cl. Harw 39 F1
Minsmere Way. Sud 13 E3
Minster Cl. Rayl 177 D1
Minster Way. Mald 144 C4
Minton Hts. Hawk 178 B3
Miramar Ave. Canv 196 C2
Mistley End. Basil 185 E3
Mistley Path. Basil 185 E3
Mistley Side. Basil 185 E3
Mitchell Ave. Hals 25 F1
Mitchell Way. S Woo F 165 E4
Michells Ave. Canv 197 E2
Mitton Vale. Sprin 127 F1
Moat End. South 192 A1
Moat Farm Chase. With 97 F2
Moat Field. Basil 185 E4
Moat La. Alph 19 D2
Moat Rd. Ford 47 E3
Moat Rise. Rayl 176 B1
Modlen Rd. Walt 94 A4
Mollands. Basil 185 F2
Molrams La. Gt Bad 141 D3
Monk's La. Ded 33 E3
Monkdowns Rd. Cogg 63 D2
Monklands Ct. Hals 25 E1
Monks Cl. With 97 F2
Monks Lodge Rd. Gt Map 16 B2
Monks Mead. S Woo F 142 C1
Monks Rd. Ea Col 45 D4
Monksford Dr. Hull 165 E1
Monkside. Basil 185 E4
Monkwick Ave. Colch 67 E2
Monks Rd. Colch 67 E2
Montague Ave. Hadl 189 D1
Montague Pl. Canv 196 C2
Montbretia Cl. Stanw 66 B3
Montbretia Cl. Clact 109 E2
Montgomery Ave. South 176 B4
Montgomery Cl. Colch 67 E1
Montgomery Cl. Sprin 127 F4
Montgomery Ct. South 192 C1
Montrose Rd. Sprin 127 F2
Montsale. Basil 186 B4
Moor Hall La. S Woo F 142 C2
Moor Park Cl. South 189 E3
Moor Park Gdns. South 189 E3
Moor Rd. Gt T 64 A4
Moor Rd. Langh 32 B2
Moor's Farm Chase. Lit Tot 117 D2
Moorcroft Ave. Hadl 188 C3
Moorcroft. Hawk 178 B3
Moores Ave. Basil 185 E1
Moorhen Ave. St L 148 B4
Moors Cl. Fee 81 F3
Moors Cl. Gt Ben 71 F1
Moorsfield. Sud 13 D2
Moorside. Colch 68 B4
Mope La. Wic Bis 115 E3
Moran Ave. Chelm 127 D4
Morant Rd. Colch 68 A3
Morebarn Rd. Gt Bro 52 C2
Moreland Ave. Thund 187 E4
Moreland Rd. Runw 163 E1
Moreland Cl. W'dham 193 D2
Moreland Rd. Thund 187 E4
Morella Cl. Gt Ben 89 F4
Morello Ct. Rowh 86 A4
Moretons. Basil 186 A3
Moretons. Chelm 140 A1
Morley Rd. Hals 25 F1
Morley Rd. Tipt 100 B2
Morleys Rd. Ea Col 45 D3
Mornington Ave. Roch 179 D1
Mornington Cres. Canv 197 E2
Mornington Rd. Canv 197 E2
Mornington Rd. Canv 197 E2
Morris Cl. Gt Wak 193 D1
Morris Ave. Clact 124 C3
Morris Rd. Chelm 127 D1
Morrow La. Ard 52 A3
Morse Cl. Str S M 22 B1
Morses La. Brigh 88 C1
Morten Rd. Colch 67 F4
Mortimer Rd. Hat Pev 114 A2
Mortimer Rd. Rayl 176 C3
Morton Rd. Gt Tot 116 A2
Morton Way. Hals 26 A2
Moss Cl. Basil 186 B2
Moss Dr. Basil 185 F2
Moss Path. Chelm 140 B2

Moss Rd. Stanw 66 C2
Moss Rd. With 98 A2
Moss Way. W Berg 48 C2
Moss Wlk. Chelm 140 A3
Mossfield Cl. Colch 67 E3
Mott's La. Mks T 64 B2
Motts La. With 98 A2
Moulsham Chase. Chelm 140 B4
Moulsham Dr. Chelm 140 A4
Moulsham St. Chelm 127 D1
Moulsham Thrift. Chelm 140 A4
Mount Ave. Hock 177 F3
Mount Ave. Rayl 176 B2
Mount Ave. South 199 D4
Mount Bovers La. Hawk 177 F2
Mount Cl. Rayl 176 B1
Mount Cl. Wick 174 C4
Mount Cres. Hock 177 E3
Mount Cres. S Ben 187 F2
Mount Hill. Hals 25 E1
Mount Lodge Chase. Gt Tot 116 B3
Mount Pleasant Rd. S Woo F 165 E4
Mount Pleasant. Hals 25 F1
Mount Pleasant. Mald 131 F1
Mount Rd. Brain 60 A2
Mount Rd. Cogg 63 D1
Mount Rd. S Ben 187 F2
Mount Rd. Wick 174 C4
Mount Rise. Hals 25 E1
Mount The. Colch 66 C3
Mount The. Tolle 119 E1
Mount Way. Wick 174 C4
Mountain Ash Ave. South 189 D3
Mountain Ash Cl. Colch 50 B1
Mountain Ash Cl. South 189 D3
Mountains Rd. Gt Tot 116 B4
Mountbatten Cl. Sud 7 F1
Mountbatten Dr. Colch 68 A2
Mountbatten Dr. South 192 C1
Mountbatten Rd. Brain 60 B2
Mountbatten Rd. Sud 7 F1
Mountbatten Way. Sprin 127 F4
Mountdale Gdns. South 189 F2
Mountfields. Basil 186 B2
Mounthill Ave. Sprin 127 E2
Mountnessing. Hadl 188 B1
Mountview Cres. St L 148 B4
Mountview Rd. Clact 110 A3
Moverons La. Brigh 88 B1
Mowden Hall La. Hat Pev 113 F3
Moy Rd. Colch 68 A1
Mucking Hall Rd. Barl 192 B4
Muirway. Thund 187 D4
Mulberry Ave. Colch 66 A2
Mulberry Gdns. With 98 A2
Mulberry Rd. Canv 196 B2
Mulberry Way. Sprin 127 E3
Mullins Rd. Brain 59 F3
Mumford Cl. W Berg 48 C2
Mumford Rd. W Berg 48 B2
Mundon Rd. Brain 60 B1
Mundon Rd. Mald 145 E4
Munnings Dr. Clact 109 E3
Munnings Rd. Colch 50 A2
Munnings Way. Lawf 35 D3
Munro Rd. With 97 F3
Munsons Alley. South 159 E2
Munsterburg Rd. Canv 197 E3
Murchison Cl. Chelm 126 C3
Murray Cl. Brain 59 F3
Murrell Lock. Sprin 128 A2
Murrels La. Hock 177 D4
Muscade Cl. Tipt 100 B3
Museum St. Colch 67 F4
Musk Cl. Stanw 66 B4
Musket Gr. Rayl 176 B3
Muswell Wlk. Clact 109 E3
Mychett Cl. Clact 109 E3
Myland Hall Chase. Colch 50 B2
Myrtle Gr. Colch 68 A3

Nabbott Rd. Chelm 126 C1
Nalla Gdns. Chelm 127 D4
Namur Ave. Canv 197 E3
Nancy Smith Cl. Colch 67 F3
Nansen Ave. Ashi 178 B3
Nansen Rd. Clact 110 B3
Napier Ave. Colch 67 F3
Napier Ave. South 200 A4
Napier Ct. Chelm 126 C1
Napier Gdns. Thund 188 B3
Napier Rd. Rayl 176 C2
Narvik Cl. Mald 144 C4
Nash Cl. Colch 67 D2
Nash Cl. Lawf 35 D3
Nassau Rd. St O 108 A2
Navestock Cl. Rayl 176 A2
Navestock Rd. Clact 109 F4
Nayland Cl. Wick 174 C4
Nayland Dr. Clact 109 D2
Nayland Rd. Bures 28 C4
Nayland Rd. Colch 49 E3
Nayland Rd. Colch 49 E3
Nayland Rd. Gt Hor 49 E3
Nayland Rd. Lit Hor 30 C3
Nayland Rd. W Berg 48 B4

Nayling Rd. Brain 59 E1
Naze Park Rd. Walt 76 C2
Nazeing The. Basil 185 F3
Neale Rd. Hals 25 F1
Neasden Ave. Clact 109 E3
Neil Armstrong Way. South .. 190 A3
Nelson Cl. Rayl 176 C2
Nelson Ct. Burn 170 B2
Nelson Gdns. Brain 60 B2
Nelson Gdns. Rayl 176 C2
Nelson Mews. South 200 A4
Nelson Pl. S Woo F 165 F3
Nelson Rd. Ashi 178 B3
Nelson Rd. Basil 185 F3
Nelson Rd. Clact 109 F1
Nelson Rd. Colch 66 C3
Nelson Rd. Harw 40 B2
Nelson Rd. Rayl 176 C2
Nelson Rd. South 190 A1
Nelson St. Brigh 106 C3
Nelson St. South 200 A4
Nelson Rd. South 201 F3
Ness Wlk. With 97 E1
Nether Ct. Hals 26 A1
Nether Hill. Gest 10 C2
Nether Mayne. Basil 185 D2
Nether Priors. Basil 185 E3
Nether Rd. Cav 1 B1
Netherfield. S Ben 188 A2
Nethergate St. Cla 4 A4
Nevada Rd. Canv 197 E3
Nevendon Rd. Basil 174 A1
Nevendon Rd. Wick 174 B3
Nevern Cl. Rayl 188 C4
Nevern St. Rayl 188 C4
Neville Shaw. Basil 185 D3
New Bowers Way. Sprin 127 F3
New Captains Rd. W Mers .. 121 D3
New Cut. Bures 28 C4
New Cut. Glems 2 A2
New Cut. Gt Ben 89 F4
New Cut. Lay H 84 C3
New Dukes Way. Sprin 127 F3
New England Cres. Gt Wak . 193 E1
New Farm Rd. Stanw 66 B3
New Hall La. Mund 145 F2
New Hall Rd. Ashi 167 D1
New Kiln Rd. Colch 67 E4
New La. Fee 61 F3
New Lodge Chase. Lit Bad .. 129 D1
New London Rd. Chelm 127 D1
New Meadgate Terr. Gt Bad . 140 B4
New Moor Cl. Soum 159 F2
New Moor Cres. Soum 159 F2
New Nabbots Way. Sprin 127 E4
New Park Rd. Ashi 167 D1
New Park Rd. S Ben 187 E3
New Park St. Colch 68 A3
New Park. Ca Hed 15 F2
New Pier St. Walt 94 B4
New Queens Rd. Sud 7 F1
New Rd. Ald 02 D1
New Rd. Burn 170 B3
New Rd. Canv 196 C2
New Rd. Gos 42 C3
New Rd. Gt Bad 141 D3
New Rd. Gt Wak 193 E2
New Rd. Hadl 188 B2
New Rd. Hat Pev 114 A2
New Rd. Kelv 81 E1
New Rd. L Mel 7 D4
New Rd. Mann 35 E2
New Rd. Mess 82 B1
New Rd. Mist 35 F2
New Rd. Stanw 66 B3
New Rd. Terl 96 B2
New Rd. Tipt 100 B3
New Rd. Tolle 119 E1
New St. Brain 59 F1
New St. Brigh 106 C3
New St. Chelm 127 D2
New St. Glems 2 A3
New St. Hals 25 F1
New St. Mald 131 F1
New St. Sud 12 C4
New Thorpe Ave. Th L S 74 A1
New Town Rd. Colch 68 A3
New Town Rd. Th L S 73 F1
New Village. Catt 35 E4
New Way. St O 106 C2
New Writtle St. Chelm 127 D1
Newbarn Rd. Gt T 46 A1
Newbridge Hill. W Berg 48 B2
Newbridge Rd. Tipt 100 C3
Newcastle Ave. Colch 66 C2
Newcomen Way. Colch 50 B3
Newcourt Rd. Sprin 127 E2
Newell Ave. South 202 A4
Newgate St. Walt 94 B4
Newhall. Hawk 178 B3
Newhaven La. Harw 40 B3
Newhouse Rd. Ea Col 44 C2
Newington Ave. South 191 F1
Newington Cl. South 191 F1
Newington Gdns. Clact 109 F4
Newland Pl. With 98 A1
Newland Precinct. With 98 A1
Newland St. With 98 A1
Newlands Dr. With 98 A1

Newlands La. Nay 20 A1
Newlands Rd. Canv 197 E3
Newlands Rd. Wick 174 B2
Newman's Rd. Sud 12 C4
Newmill La. Catt 36 A4
Newnham La. Brain 59 F1
Newnham Green. Mald 131 F2
Newport Ave. Col N 156 A3
Newport Cl. Basil 141 D3
Newport Ct. Harw 40 A1
Newport Dr. Clact 110 A4
Newport Way. Walt 94 A3
Newpots Cl. Peld 103 E3
Newpots La. Peld 103 E3
Newstead Rd. Gt Wak 193 D2
Newsum Gdns. Rayl 176 A2
Newton Cl. Brain 60 B2
Newton Croft. Sud 13 D4
Newton Hall Gdns. Ashi 178 B3
Newton Park Rd. Thund 188 A4
Newton Rd. Harw 40 A2
Newton Rd. Sud 13 D4
Newton Way. St O 108 A3
Nicholas Cl. Writ 126 A1
Nicholas Ct. Chelm 126 C3
Nicholas Ct. With 97 F1
Nichols Cl. Lawf 35 D2
Nicholsons Cres. S Ben 188 A2
Nicholson Pl. E Han 153 D4
Nicholson Rd. S Ben 188 A2
Nicholsons Gr. Colch 68 A3
Nickleby Rd. Chelm 126 B3
Nien - Oord. Clact 109 E2
Nightingale Cl. Clact 109 F3
Nightingale Cl. Colch 69 D4
Nightingale Cl. Harw 39 F1
Nightingale Cl. South 190 C3
Nightingale Hill. Langh 32 C3
Nightingale La. Canv 197 E2
Nightingale Way. Clact 109 F3
Nineacres. Brain 60 A1
Nipsells Chase. May 147 D1
Nipsells Chase. Steep 147 D1
Noakes Ave. Gt Bad 140 C3
Noaks Rd. High 22 B4
Nobles Green Cl. South 189 F4
Nobles Green Rd. South 189 F4
Nook The. Wiv 69 D2
Norbury Cl. Mks T 64 C2
Nordland Rd. Canv 197 E2
Nore Rd. Rayl 189 E4
Noredale. South 201 E3
Norfolk Ave. Clact 110 C4
Norfolk Ave. South 189 F2
Norfolk Ave. W Mers 121 E4
Norfolk Cl. Canv 197 D3
Norfolk Cl. Mald 131 F1
Norfolk Cres. Colch 50 A1
Norfolk Dr. Chelm 127 D4
Norfolk Gdns. Brain 60 A2
Norfolk Rd. Mald 131 F1
Norfolk Way. Canv 196 C3
Norman Cl. Mks T 64 C2
Norman Cl. St O 108 A2
Norman Cres. Rayl 176 C3
Norman Hill. Terl 96 A1
Norman Rd. Clact 110 C3
Norman Rd. Mann 35 E2
Norman Way. Colch 67 D2
Norman Way. St O 106 C2
Normandie Way. Burn 170 B3
Normandy Ave. Colch 68 A2
Normans Rd. Canv 197 E2
Norris Cl. Brain 60 B3
North Ave. Chelm 126 C3
North Ave. South 191 E1
North Benfleet Hall Rd. Wick 174 C1
North Colne. Basil 185 E2
North Cres. South 190 B3
North Cres. Wick 174 B4
North Crockerford. Basil 185 F2
North Dell. Sprin 127 F4
North Dr. Gt Bad 140 C4
North Dr. May 146 C1
North End Rd. Gest 10 B1
North End Rd. Lit Y 9 F2
North End Soum 159 F3
North Gunnels. Basil 185 D3
North Hill. Colch 67 F4
North Hill. Lit Bad 129 E3
North La. Copf 65 D3
North Rd. Bel W 10 C3
North Rd. Brigh 106 C4
North Rd. Clact 109 F3
North Rd. Gt Y 9 D1
North Rd. South 190 C1
North Rise. Sud 13 D3
North Shoebury Rd. South . 192 B1
North St. Gt Wak 193 D2
North St. Mald 132 A1
North St. Mann 35 E2
North St. Roch 178 C1
North St. South 159 E2
North St. South 198 C4
North St. Sud 12 C4
North St. Till 149 F2

North St. Toll D 118 C3
North St. Tolle 119 E1
North St. Walt 76 B1
North St. Walt 94 B4
North Station Rd. Colch 67 F4
North Weald Cl. Wick 175 D3
Northbourne Rd. Clact 109 F2
Northcroft. Sud 12 C4
Northcroft. Ave. S Ben 187 E3
Northern Rd. Sud 13 D4
Northfield Cres. Gt Wak 193 D2
Northfield Gdns. Colch 50 A2
Northgate St. Colch 67 F4
Northlands Pavement. Basil 186 A3
Northumberland Ave. South 200 B4
Northumberland Cl. Brain 60 A2
Northumberland Cres. South 200 B4
Northumberland Ct. Sprin .. 127 E2
Northview Dr. South 190 B1
Northville Dr. South 190 B2
Northwick Rd. Canv 196 A2
Norton Ave. Canv 197 F2
Norton Rd. Chelm 127 D2
Norway Cres. Harw 39 F2
Norwich Ave. South 191 E1
Norwich Cl. Colch 68 A4
Norwich Cl. South 191 E1
Norwich Cres. Rayl 176 B3
Norwich Wlk. Basil 185 F4
Norwood Ave. Clact 110 A3
Norwood Dr. S Ben 187 F1
Norwood End. Basil 185 E4
Norwood Way. Walt 94 A4
Notley Rd. Brain 59 F1
Nottingham Rd. Clact 110 C3
Nounsley Rd. Hat Pev 114 A1
Nunn's Rd. Colch 67 F4
Nunnery St. Ca Hed 15 E2
Nuns Meadow. Gos 42 C4
Nunty's La. Cogg 44 A1
Nursery Cl. Rayl 176 B1
Nursery Cl. Stanw 66 B3
Nursery Dr. Brain 60 A3
Nursery La. Dan 142 C4
Nursery Rd. Chelm 140 A4
Nursery Rd. Sud 13 D3
Nutcombe Cres. Hawk 178 B2

Oak Ave. Wick 175 E4
Oak Bungalows. Brain 59 F2
Oak Chase. Wick 174 A4
Oak Cl. Th L S 74 A1
Oak Cl. W Berg 48 C2
Oak Fall. With 98 A3
Oak Farm Rd. Woo Wa 130 C1
Oak Hill. Wketh 145 D4
Oak Lodge Tye. Bore 128 A3
Oak Rd N. Hadl 188 C1
Oak Rd S. Hadl 188 C1
Oak Rd. Canv 197 E2
Oak Rd. Hals 43 E4
Oak Rd. Lit Map 26 A4
Oak Rd. Mald 132 B3
Oak Rd. Peb 26 C4
Oak Rd. Roch 178 C1
Oak Rd. Sud 13 D3
Oak Rd. Tipt 100 B4
Oak Rd. Wa Col 46 B2
Oak Rd. With 98 B3
Oak Ridge. Lit Oak 57 D4
Oak Tree Rd. Alres 88 A4
Oak Wlk. Hock 177 F4
Oak Wlk. Si Hed 15 E1
Oak Wlk. Thund 187 E4
Oak Wlk. Thund 187 E4
Oak Wood Gr. Basil 186 A3
Oakapple Cl. Colch 67 E1
Oakdene Rd. Basil 186 B4
Oaken Grange Dr. South 190 C3
Oakfield Cl. S Ben 187 E2
Oakfield Rd. Ashi 167 E4
Oakfield Rd. Ben 187 E2
Oakhurst Cl. Wick 174 B3
Oakhurst Dr. Wick 174 B3
Oakhurst Rd. Rayl 188 C4
Oakhurst Rd. South 191 D1
Oakland Rd. Harw 40 B2
Oakland Way. Lit Bad 129 E4
Oaklands Ave. Colch 66 C3
Oaklands Cl. Bl Not 77 E4
Oaklands Cres. Chelm 140 A4
Oaklea Ave. Sprin 127 F2
Oakleigh Ave. Hull 165 F1
Oakleigh Ave. South 200 A4
Oakleigh Park Dr. South 189 F1
Oakleigh Rd. Clact 109 F4
Oakleighs. S Ben 187 E2
Oakley Ave. Rayl 175 F2
Oakley Rd. Brain 59 F4
Oakley Rd. Harw 39 F2
Oakley Rd. Wix 55 F3
Oakmead Rd. St O 107 D2
Oaks Dr. Colch 67 E3
Oaks Pl. Colch 49 F2
Oaks The. Walt 93 F3
Oakview. Harw 39 F1
Oakwood Ave. Clact 110 C4
Oakwood Ave. South 199 F3
Oakwood Ave. W Mers 121 E4

Orchard Side. South 189 D3
Orchard Cl. Chelm 127 D1
Orchard The. Wick 174 A4
Orchard Way. Glems 2 A2
Orchards. With 97 F1
Orchid Pl. S Woo F 165 E4
Orchill Dr. Hadl 188 C2
Orford Cres. Sprin 127 E3
Oriel Cl. Sud 13 D3
Orion Cl. Basil 174 A1
Orion Way. Brain 60 A2
Orlando Cl. Walt 94 B4
Orlando Dr. Basil 174 B1
Ormesby Chine. S Woo F .. 165 E3
Ormonde Ave. Hadl 189 D1
Ormonde Ave. Roch 178 C2
Ormonde Gdns. Hadl 189 D1
Ormonds Cres. S Woo F 154 A2
Ormsby Rd. Canv 196 B2
Orpen Cl. W Berg 48 B2
Orpen's Hill. Birch 84 A3
Orrmo Rd. Canv 197 D3
Orsett Ave. Hadl 189 E3
Orsett End. Basil 185 E4
Orsino Wlk. Colch 68 C4
Orvis La. Str S M 34 C4
Orwell Cl. Wick 175 D3
Orwell Ct. Colch 50 C1
Orwell Rd. Clact 109 F1
Orwell Rd. Harw 40 B2
Orwell Way. Burn 170 A3
Orwell Wlk. With 97 F2
Osbert Rd. With 114 C4
Osborne Ave. Hock 177 E3
Osborne Cl. Clact 110 A4
Osborne Rd. Basil 185 E3
Osborne Rd. South 186 C4
Osborne Rd. South 190 C1
Osborne Rd. W Mers 121 F3
Osborne St. Colch 67 F3
Osea Rd. Gold 133 D2
Osea Way. Sprin 127 F3
Osprey Cl. South 192 C1
Osprey Way. Chelm 140 A3
Ospreys. Clact 109 F3
Osterley Pl. S Woo F 165 E3
Othello Cl. Colch 68 C4
Otten Rd. Bel S P 5 D1
Ottershaw Way. Clact 109 D3
Ouida Rd. Canv 197 E2
Oulton Ave. Canv 196 C3
Oulton Cl. Harw 39 F1
Ouse Chase. With 97 E1
Outing Cl. South 200 B3
Outpart Eastward. Harw 40 C3
Overhall Hill. Col En 27 E1
Overmead Dr. S Woo F 165 F4
Overton Cl. Thund 187 E3
Overton Dr. Thund 187 D3
Overton Rd. Thund 187 D3
Overton Way. Thund 187 E3
Owen Ward Cl. Colch 67 D2
Owl's Hill. Terl 96 A2
Owls Retreat. Colch 68 C4
Oxenford Cl. Harw 39 F1
Oxford Cl. South 13 D3
Oxford Cres. Clact 109 D2
Oxford Ct. Ea Col 45 D3
Oxford Ct. Sprin 127 F3
Oxford Meadow. Si Hed 15 E1
Oxford Rd. Canv 197 E2
Oxford Rd. Clact 109 F2
Oxford Rd. Hals 25 E1
Oxford Rd. Mann 35 E2
Oxford Rd. Roch 178 C2
Oxley Hill. Lang 85 F2
Oxley Hill. Toll D 118 A4
Oxlip Rd. With 97 F2
Oyster Tank Rd. Brigh 106 C3
Ozonia Cl. Wick 174 B3
Ozonia Cl. Wick 174 B3
Ozonia Way. Wick 174 B3

Paarl Rd. Canv 197 D2
Packards La. Ford 29 F1
Packe Cl. Fee 81 D4
Paddock Cl. Harw 40 B2
Paddock Cl. South 189 F4
Paddock Dr. Clact 109 D2
Paddocks The. Bures 28 C4
Paddocks The. Gt Tot 116 A2
Paddocks The. Gt Tot 116 A2
Paddocks The. Rayl 176 C1
Paddocks The. With 98 B2
Paddocks. Hull 165 E2
Page Cl. With 114 B4
Page Rd. Basil 186 C4
Page Rd. Clact 110 B3
Pagel Mead. Basil 185 D3
Pages La. Toll D 118 C1
Paget Rd. Rowh 86 C4
Paget Rd. Wiv 87 E3
Pagesham Rd. Pag Ch 180 B3
Paignton Ave. Sprin 127 E3

Paignton Cl. Rayl 176 B3
Palfrey Hts. Catt 35 E4
Pall Mall. South 189 F1
Pallister Rd. Clact 109 F1
Palm Cl. Chelm 140 B3
Palm Cl. With 98 A4
Palm Rd. Corr 185 D1
Palmeira Ave. South 199 E4
Palmers Croft. Sprin 128 A1
Palmerston Rd. South 199 E4
Palmerston Rd. Th L S 74 A1
Palmerstone Rd. Canv 196 B2
Pampas Cl. Colch 50 A2
Pan La. E Han 153 D3
Pan La. E Han 153 D3
Pan Wlk. Chelm 126 B3
Panfield La. Brain 59 F3
Pannels Cl. Glems 2 A2
Pantile Ave. South 191 E2
Pantile Hill. Sour 159 E2
Pantling's La. Kelv 81 D3
Panton Cres. Colch 68 C4
Panton Mews. Brain 78 A4
Papenburg Rd. Canv 197 D3
Papillon Rd. Colch 67 F4
Parade The. Walt 94 B4
Paradise Rd. Writ 139 E4
Pargat Dr. Rayl 189 E4
Pargetters Hyam. Hock .. 177 F3
Park Ave. Canv 197 F1
Park Ave. Chelm 126 C2
Park Ave. South 189 F3
Park Boulevard. Clact 110 C3
Park Chase. Hadl 188 C1
Park Chase. St O 108 B3
Park Cl. Sud 13 D4
Park Cl. Wick 174 B3
Park Cotts. Gos 42 C4
Park Dr. Brain 78 A4
Park Dr. Brigh 106 C4
Park Dr. Hals 25 F1
Park Dr. Mald 132 A1
Park Dr. Wick 174 B3
Park Drive Par. Brigh 106 C4
Park Gdns. Hawk 177 F3
Park La. Bul 1 D1
Park La. Canv 197 F2
Park La. Ea Col 45 D3
Park La. Glems 2 B2
Park La. Gos 42 C4
Park La. Langh 32 C2
Park La. South 199 F4
Park La. South 201 D4
Park La. Toll K 101 D2
Park La. Topp 14 A4
Park Lane Cl. Ea Col 45 D3
Park Rd. Ard 51 F2
Park Rd. Burn 170 A3
Park Rd. Canv 197 F1
Park Rd. Chelm 127 D1
Park Rd. Clact 109 E1
Park Rd. Colch 67 E3
Park Rd. Colch 69 D2
Park Rd. Gt Bro 71 E4
Park Rd. Gt Hor 31 D4
Park Rd. Hadl 189 D1
Park Rd. Haw 41 F4
Park Rd. Mald 131 F1
Park Rd. Nay 20 C2
Park Rd. Silv E 80 A1
Park Rd. South 199 F4
Park Rd. Sud 13 D4
Park Rd. Th'l 187 F3
Park Rd. Wiv 87 E4
Park Side. Basil 186 A4
Park Side. South 190 A1
Park Sq E. Clact 125 D4
Park Sq W. Clact 124 C4
Park St. Nay 20 B3
Park St. South 199 F4
Park Terr. South 199 F4
Park The. Mann 35 E2
Park Vale Cl. Ca Hed 15 F2
Park View Cres. Gt Bad .. 140 C3
Park View Dr. Hadl 189 D1
Park Way. South 190 A1
Park Wood La. Lit Tot 117 D2
Parkanaur Ave. South 201 D4
Parkdale. Dan 142 B4
Parker Ct. Brad O S 136 C2
Parker Rd. Chelm 127 E1
Parker Way. Hals 43 F4
Parker's Way. Harw 20 A1
Parkeston Rd. Harw 40 A2
Parkeston Rd. Rams 39 F3
Parkfield St. Rowh 86 C4
Parkfields. Si Hed 15 E1
Parkfields. Thund 188 A2
Parkgate Rd. Silv E 80 A2
Parkgate. Canv 199 E4
Parkhall Rd. Gos 41 F4
Parkhurst Dr. Rayl 176 B4
Parkhurst Rd. Basil 186 A3
Parklands Ave. Rayl 176 C3
Parklands Cl. Glems 2 B3
Parklands Dr. Sprin 127 E2
Parklands. Canv 197 D3
Parklands. Hawk 178 B2

Parklards Way. Chelm 140 B1
Parkstone Ave. S Ben 188 A2
Parkstone Dr. South 190 C2
Parkway Cl. South 189 F4
Parkway The. Canv 197 D1
Parkway. Chelm 127 D1
Parkway. Rayl 188 C4
Parkway. Wiv 69 D1
Parkwood Dr. Sud 7 F1
Parmenter Dr. Sud 13 E3
Parnell Cl. Colch 68 A1
Parr Dr. Colch 66 C2
Parry Dr. Clact 109 E3
Parson's Field. Ded 34 A3
Parson's Heath. Colch 50 C1
Parson's Hill. Colch 67 D3
Parsonage La. Lit Bad 129 E1
Parsonage La. Rams 38 A1
Parsonage La. Tend 72 C4
Parsonage St. Hals 25 F1
Parsons Hill. Gt Bro 70 C4
Parsons Rd. Thund 187 E3
Parsonson Wlk. Colch 68 C3
Partridge Ave. Chelm 126 C3
Partridge Cl. Gt Oak 56 B2
Partridge Dr. Ford 47 E3
Partridge Green. Basil ... 186 A3
Paschal Way. Gt Bad 140 C4
Paslowes. Basil 186 A4
Paston Cl. S Woo F 154 C1
Patching Hall La. Chelm 127 D2
Paternoster Row. Walt 94 B4
Path The. Gt Ben 89 F4
Pathfields Rd. Clact 109 E2
Pathway The. Walt 93 F3
Pathways. Basil 185 F3
Patmore Rd. Colch 50 B1
Patten Cl. Mks T 64 C2
Patterdale. Thund 187 D4
Pattern Bush Cl. Catt 35 E4
Patticroft. Glems 2 A3
Pattison Cl. With 115 D4
Pattiswick Cnr. Basil 185 F4
Pattiswick Sq. Basil 185 F4
Pattock's La. Gt T 46 B1
Pattocks. Basil 185 F3
Patrick's La. Harw 40 B2
Pauline Cl. Clact 110 A3
Pauls Cres. Elmst M 69 F3
Pauls Ct. Canv 197 D3
Pauls Way. Clact 109 D1
Pavilion Cl. South 191 F1
Pavilion Dr. South 189 F1
Pawle Cl. Gt Bad 141 D4
Paxman Ave. Colch 67 D2
Paxton Rd. Clact 110 A4
Paycocke Way. Cogg 63 D2
Payne Pl. E Han 153 D3
Payne's La. Lit Bro 53 E2
Paynters Hill. Basil 185 F2
Paynters Mead. Basil 185 F2
Peace Rd. Stanw 66 B4
Peach Ave. Hock 177 F4
Peacocks Cl. Cav 1 B1
Peacocks Rd. Cav 1 B1
Peakes Cl. Tipt 100 A4
Pear Trees. Thund 187 F2
Pearce Manor. Chelm 139 F4
Pearmain Cl. Runw 163 E1
Pearmain Way. Stanw 66 B4
Pearsons Ave. Harw 176 A2
Peartree Bsns Centre. Stanw .. 66 C2
Peartree Cl. South 191 E2
Peartree Cl. Brain 60 A1
Peartree Hill. M Bure 29 D3
Peartree La. S Woo F 142 C2
Peartree Rd. Stanw 66 C2
Peartree Way. Lit Cla 91 E1
Pease Pl. E Han 153 D3
Pebmarsh Cl. Colch 86 A4
Pebmarsh Dr. Wick 174 C3
Pebmarsh Rd. Alph 18 C1
Pebmarsh Rd. Col En 26 C1
Pebmarsh Rd. Peb 18 C1
Pecocks Cl. Sud 13 E3
Pedder's Cl. Colch 66 C2
Pedlars Cl. Dan 143 D3
Pedlars Path. Dan 143 D3
Peel Ave. South 202 A4
Peel Cres. Sprin 59 F2
Peel Rd. Sprin 127 F2
Peersword Rd. Colch 67 E1
Peg Millar's La. Far 96 C3
Peg Millar's La. Terl 96 C3
Pegasus Way. Brain 59 F3
Pegasus Way. Colch 50 B1
Peggotty Cl. Chelm 126 C1
Peldon Pavement. Basil 185 E4
Peldon Rd. Gt Wig 103 D2
Peldon Rd. Lang 86 A1
Peldon Rd. Peld 103 F4
Pelham Cl. Harw 40 A3
Pelham Rd. South 191 F1
Pelham's La. Colch 67 F4
Pelly Ave. With 115 D4
Pembroke Ave. Mald 131 F1
Pembroke Cl. Colch 68 B2

Pembroke Gdns. Clact 110 C3
Pembroke Mews. Basil .. 186 B4
Pembroke Pl. Chelm 127 D4
Pembury Rd. South 199 E4
Pendle Cl. Basil 174 A1
Pendlestone. Thund 188 B2
Pendower. Rayl 176 A1
Penfold Rd. Clact 109 F2
Penhurst Ave. South 190 C1
Penlan Hall La. Ford 47 D3
Penn Mews. Brain 78 A4
Pennial Rd. Canv 197 D2
Pennine Rd. Chelm 126 B3
Pennsylvania La. Tipt 100 B3
Penny Royal Rd. Dan 142 C3
Pennyroyal Cres. With 97 F2
Penrice Cl. Colch 68 C3
Penshurst Dr. S Woo F .. 165 E3
Penticton Rd. Brain 59 F1
Pentland Ave. Chelm 127 D3
Pentland Ave. South 201 E3
Pentlow Dr. Cav 1 C1
Pentlow Hill. Pent 6 A4
Pentlow La. Cav 1 C1
Penzance Cl. Sprin 127 F3
Pepper's Rd. Box 31 F1
Pepys St. Harw 40 B3
Percival Rd. Walt 75 E1
Percival Rd. Walt 76 B1
Percy Cottis Rd. Roch ... 178 C2
Percy Rd. South 189 E1
Percys. Basil 185 F3
Peregrine Cl. Basil 185 D2
Peregrine Cl. Clact 109 F4
Peregrine Cl. Colch 68 C4
Peregrine Dr. Chelm 140 A2
Peregrine Dr. S Ben 187 E1
Perriclose. Sprin 127 D1
Perri Pl. Chelm 127 D1
Perry Green. Basil 185 D4
Perry Hill. Sprin 127 E2
Perry La. Langh 33 D2
Perry Rd. S Ben 187 D2
Perry Rd. Tipt 100 B3
Perry Spring. Basil 185 E3
Perry Way. With 98 A1
Perryfield. Sud 13 D2
Persardi Ct. Rowh 86 A4
Pershore End. Colch 66 C3
Perth Cl. Clact 68 A1
Perwenham Ct. Elmst M .. 87 E4
Petworth Cl. Elmst M 87 E4
Petworth Gdns. South ... 191 E1
Pevensey Gdns. Hull 165 F1
Peverel Ave. Hat Pev 114 B1
Pharos La. W Mers 121 E3
Philbrick Cres E. Rayl ... 176 B2
Philbrick Cres W. Rayl .. 176 B2
Philip Cl. Walt 94 A3
Philip Rd. With 114 C4
Phillip Rd. Wiv 87 D4
Phillips Chase. Brain 60 A3
Phillips Field Rd. Sud 13 D3
Philmead Rd. S Ben 187 D1
Philpott Ave. South 191 E1
Phoenix Gr. Chelm 140 A4
Phoenix Way. Hadl 188 B4
Picasso Way. South 193 D1
Pickers Way. Clact 110 C4
Picketts Ave. South 189 F2
Picketts Cl. South 189 F2
Picketts. Canv 196 B2
Pickford Wlk. Colch 50 B1
Pickwick Ave. Chelm 126 B3
Picton Cl. Rayl 176 C1
Picton Gdns. Rayl 176 C1
Pier App. Walt 94 B4
Pier Ave. Clact 109 F1
Pier Gap. Clact 109 F1
Pier Hill. South 200 A4
Pierce Glade. Tipt 100 B3
Pierrefitte Way. Brain 59 F2
Pightle Way. Walt 94 A4
Pilborough Way. Colch 66 C2
Pilcox Hall La. Tend 72 A4
Pilgrim Cl. Brain 59 F3
Pilgrims Cl. South 191 F1
Pilgrims Way. Hadl 188 C2
Pine Cl. Canv 196 C2
Pine Cl. Catt 35 E4
Pine Cl. Gt Ben 89 F4
Pine Cl. Hadl 188 C3
Pine Cl. Wick 174 B3
Pine Gr. W Mers 121 D4
Pine Gr. With 98 A3
Pine Rd. Hadl 188 B1
Pinecroft Gdns. Colch 50 A2

Pinecroft Rise. Sud 12 B3
Pines Rd. Chelm 126 B3
Pines The. Hat Pev 114 A3
Pinetrees. S Ben 188 B2
Pinewood Ave. South 189 E3
Pinewood Cl. Clact 109 E3
Pinewood Cl. Hull 165 F1
Pinewood Cl. Walt 93 E3
Pinkham Dr. With 114 C4
Pinmill. Basil 185 E3
Pinners Cl. Burn 169 F4
Pintails. Basil 186 B4
Pintolis. S Woo F 165 E3
Pipchin Rd. Chelm 126 C3
Piper Rd. Colch 67 D4
Piper's Tye. Chelm 140 B2
Pippins Rd. Burn 170 B3
Pippins The. Glems 2 B3
Pirie Rd. W Berg 48 C2
Pit La. Tipt 100 B3
Pitmans Cl. South 200 A4
Pitmire La. Lam 19 D3
Pitsea Rd. Basil 186 A3
Pitseaville Gr. Basil 185 F3
Pitt Ave. Chelm 140 C3
Pitt Chase. Gt Bad 140 C3
Pitt Green. With 115 D4
Plains Farm Cl. Colch 50 B3
Plains Field. Brain 60 B1
Plains Rd. Gt Tot 116 C3
Plains Rd. Lit Tot 116 C3
Plaistow Green Rd. Hals 25 E3
Plane Tree Cl. Brain 170 A3
Plane Tree Cl. Chelm 140 A3
Plantation Rd. Bore 112 C1
Planton Way. Brigh 106 B4
Plas Newydd Cl. South . 200 C3
Plas Newydd. South 200 C3
Plashetts. Basil 185 E4
Playle Chase. Gt Tot 116 A2
Pleasant Rd. South 200 A4
Pleshey Cl. South 200 A4
Pleshey Cl. Wick 174 C3
Plough Cl. Colch 67 D3
Plough Green. Bul 11 F1
Plough La. Sud 12 B4
Ploughmans Headland. Stanw 66 B3
Plover Wlk. Chelm 140 A2
Plovers The. St L 148 B4
Plowmans. Rayl 176 C2
Plum St. Glems 2 A3
Plumberow Ave. Hock ... 177 F4
Plumberow Mount Ave. Hock 177 F4
Plume Ave. Colch 67 D2
Plume Ave. Mald 131 F1
Plumleys. Basil 186 A4
Plummers Rd. Ford 47 F4
Plumptre La. Dan 142 B3
Plumtree Ave. Gt Bad ... 140 C3
Plymouth Rd. Clact 125 E4
Plymouth Rd. Sprin 127 F3
Plymtree. South 192 B1
Pocklington Cl. Sprin 128 A2
Point Cl. Canv 197 F2
Point Clear Rd. St O 107 F2
Point Rd. Canv 197 F2
Pointer Pl. Walt 93 F4
Pointwell La. Cogg 81 D4
Pole Barn La. Frin 94 A3
Pole La. Wh Not 78 B2
Polead Rd. T Gr 79 D3
Pollard Wlk. Clact 109 E3
Pollards Green. Sprin ... 127 F1
Polley Cl. Walt 93 F4
Polstead St. Nay 20 B3
Polstead Way. Clact 109 D2
Polsteads. Basil 185 F2
Pomfret Mead. Basil 185 D3
Pond Chase. Colch 67 D2
Ponders Rd. Ford 47 E2
Pondfield Rd. Colch 50 B1
Pondholton Dr. With 115 D4
Ponds Rd. Chelm 140 A1
Poole St. Cav 1 B1
Poole St. Gt Y 15 D4
Pooles La. S Woo F 165 F2
Poondfield Cl. Alres 88 A4
Poors La. N. Hadl 189 D3
Poors La. Hadl 189 D3
Pope's Rd. Wa Col 46 B2
Poperinghe Rd. Colch 67 F2
Popes Cres. Basil 186 A3
Popes Wlk. Rayl 177 D1
Poplar Cl. Chelm 140 B3
Poplar Cl. S Woo F 165 E4
Poplar Cl. With 98 A4
Poplar Cl. With 98 A4
Poplar Gr. Mers 121 D4
Poplar Rd. Canv 197 E2
Poplar Rd. Rayl 188 A3
Poplar Rd. Sud 13 D4
Poplar Way. Walt 93 E3
Poplars Ave. Hawk 177 F2
Poplars Cl. Alres 88 A4

Poppy Gdns. Colch 68 B2
Poppy Green. Bore 128 A3
Poppyfield Cl. South 189 E3
Pork Hall La. Gt Le 95 D3
Pork La. Frin 92 C3
Porlock Ave. South 190 A2
Port La. Colch 68 A3
Porter Way. Clact 109 D2
Porter's La. E A Gr 47 F1
Porters Brook Wlk. Colch 50 B1
Porters Cl. E A Gr 47 F1
Porters Cotts. E A Gr 47 F1
Porters Pk. Bore 113 D1
Porters. Basil 186 B4
Portland Ave. Harw 40 B2
Portland Ave. South 200 A4
Portland Cl. Brain 60 A2
Portland Cres. Harw 40 B2
Portland Rd. South 200 A4
Portlight Cl. Mist 36 A2
Portobello Rd. Walt 94 B4
Portreath Pl. Chelm 127 D4
Portsmouth Rd. Clact ... 125 E4
Portway Ct. Hals 25 F2
Post Office La. Glems 2 A3
Post Office La. Lit Tot ... 117 D2
Post Office Rd. Chelm ... 127 D4
Post Office Rd. Woo Mor 143 F3
Postman's La. Lit Bad ... 129 F1
Pot Kiln Chase. Gest 10 C1
Pot Kiln Rd. Sud 7 F1
Pot Kilns The. Sud 13 E3
Potter St. Si Hed 24 C4
Potters Cl. Dan 143 D3
Potters Way. South 190 C3
Pottery La. Ea Hed 15 F2
Pottery La. Chelm 127 D3
Poulton Pl. Gt Bad 140 C4
Pound Farm Dr. Harw 40 A2
Pound Fields. Writ 139 D4
Pound La. Basil 186 C4
Powers Hall End. With 97 F2
Pownall Cres. Colch 67 F2
Poynings Ave. South 191 F1
Poyntens. Rayl 176 B1
Poynters La. Gt Wak 192 C1
Poynters La. South 192 C1
Prentice Cl. Roch 178 C1
Prentice Hall La. Tolle .. 119 D1
Prentice Hall La. Tolle .. 135 D4
President Rd. Colch 66 C3
Preston Gdns. Rayl 176 B2
Preston Rd. Clact 110 B3
Preston Rd. South 199 E4
Prestwood Cl. Thund 188 A4
Prestwood Dr. Thund ... 188 A3
Pretoria Rd. Hals 25 F1
Prettygate Rd. Colch 67 D2
Prettygate Rd. Colch 67 E2
Pricres The. Hull 165 E1
Primrose Cl. Canv 197 D3
Primrose Hill. Chelm 126 C2
Primrose La. Rams 56 A4
Primrose Pl. Tipt 100 B3
Primrose Pl. With 97 F2
Primrose Rd. Clact 110 C3
Primrose Wlk. Colch 68 C4
Primrose Wlk. Mald 132 A1
Primula Cl. Clact 109 E2
Primula Way. Bore 128 A3
Prince Albert Rd. W Mers 121 E3
Prince Ave. South 190 B2
Prince Charles Cl. Clact 109 F1
Prince Charles Cl. Sud ... 12 C4
Prince Charles Rd. Colch 68 A1
Prince Cl. South 190 B3
Prince of Wales Rd. Gt Tot 116 C2
Prince Philip Ave. Clact 109 F1
Prince Philip Rd. Colch ... 68 A1
Prince St. Sud 12 C4
Prince William Ave. Canv 196 C3
Prince's Espl. Walt 76 B1
Princel La. Ded 33 F4
Princes Ave. Sud 158 A4
Princes Ave. South 159 E2
Princes Ave. Thund 187 F3
Princes Rd. Burn 170 A4
Princes Rd. Canv 196 C2
Princes The. Chelm 140 A4
Princes St. Colch 110 B3
Princes St. Harw 40 B3
Princes St. Mald 131 F2
Princes St. South 200 A4
Princess Anne Cl. Clact 109 E1
Princess Ct. South 199 D4
Princess Dr. Colch 66 C3
Princess Gdns. Hawk 178 B3
Princess Rd. Rayl 39 F3
Princess St. Rams 39 F3
Princeton Mews. Colch ... 50 A2
Prior Cl. Hals 43 E4
Priors Cl. Colch 68 C2
Priors Green. Sils 15 F2
Priors East. Basil 185 E3
Priory Ave. South 190 C2
Priory Cl. Chelm 126 C2
Priory Cl. Hat Pev 114 A1
Priory Cotts. Birch 83 F3

Priory Cres. South

Priory Cres. South 190 C2
Priory Ct. Hat Pev 114 A2
Priory Farm Rd. Hat Pev 114 A1
Priory La. S Woo F 142 C1
Priory Mews. Hat Pev 114 B1
Priory Rd. Clact 109 F2
Priory Rd. Sud 7 F1
Priory Rd. Tipt 100 B2
Priory Rd. Wa Col 46 A2
Priory St. Colch 68 A4
Priory St. Ea Col 45 D4
Priory The. Writ 126 A1
Priory View Rd. South 189 F3
Priory Way. South 159 F2
Priory Wlk. Sud 12 C3
Priory Wood Cres. South 189 F3
Priorywood Dr. South 189 F3
Prittle Cl. Thund 188 B3
Prittlewell Chase. South 190 B2
Prittlewell Sq. South 199 F4
Prittlewell St. South 191 D1
Proctor Way. Mks T 64 C2
Progress Ct. Brain 59 F2
Progress Rd. South 189 E3
Promenade The. Burn 170 B2
Promenade The. South 201 E3
Promenade Way. Brigh 106 C3
Promenade. Harw 40 B2
Promenade. May 146 C1
Promenade. Walt 76 C1
Prospect Cl. Hat Pev 114 A2
Prospect Cl. South 200 B4
Prospect Park. Frin 93 D3
Prospero Cl. Colch 68 C4
Provence Cl. Stanw 66 B4
Providence. Burn 170 B2
Provident Sq. Chelm 127 E1
Prunus Ct. Rowh 86 A4
Prykes Dr. Chelm 127 D1
Pryor Cl. With 98 A1
Pryors Rd. Chelm 140 B1
Pudding La. Birch 84 A2
Pudsey Hall La. Cane 168 A1
Puffin Pl. South 192 C1
Puffinsdale. Clact 109 F3
Pulpitfield Cl. Walt 94 A4
Pulpits Cl. Hock 177 F4
Pump Hill. Gt Bad 140 C4
Pump Hill. St O 108 B2
Pump La. Dan 142 B3
Pump La. Sprin 127 F3
Pump Mead Cl. South 159 E2
Pump Rd. Purl 144 B2
Purbeck Ct. Gt Bad 140 C3
Purcell Cl. Colch 68 C3
Purdeys Way. Roch 191 D4
Purleigh Cl. Basil 174 B1
Purleigh Dr. Col N 156 A3
Purleigh Rd. Rayl 176 A2
Purleigh St. Purl 144 C1
Purley Way. Clact 109 D3
Purley Way. South 190 B3
Pye Cnr. Ca Hed 15 F2
Pyefleet Cl. Brigh 106 C4
Pyefleet Cl. Fing 87 E2
Pyefleet View. Lang 86 A2
Pyesand. Walt 93 E4
Pygot Pl. South 59 F2
Pyms Rd. Chelm 140 A2
Pyne Gate. Chelm 140 A1

Quakers' Alley. Colch 67 F4
Quarter Gate. S Woo F 165 F3
Quay La. Beau 74 A3
Quay La. Sud 12 C3
Quay La. Walt 75 E1
Quay St. Mann 35 E2
Quay The. Burn 170 B2
Quay The. Harw 40 C3
Quebec Ave. South 200 A4
Queech La. Catt 36 A4
Queen Anne Dr. W Mers 121 E3
Queen Anne Gdns. W Mers ... 121 E3
Queen Anne Rd. W Mers 121 E3
Queen Annes Dr. South 190 B2
Queen Anns Gr. Hull 176 B4
Queen Elizabeth Ave. Clact .. 109 F1
Queen Elizabeth II Sq.
    S Woo F 165 F4
Queen Elizabeth Way. Colch .. 68 A1
Queen Mary Ave. Colch 67 F2
Queen St. Brigh 106 C3
Queen St. Ca Hed, ... 15 F2
Queen St. Chelm 127 D1
Queen St. Cogg 63 D2
Queen St. Colch 67 F4
Queen St. Gt Oak 56 B2
Queen St. Mald 132 A1
Queen St. Si Hed 24 C3
Queen St. South 159 E2
Queen Victoria Dr. Sho G 40 A4
Queen's Ave. Mald 132 A1
Queen's Ave. South 189 F1
Queen's Cnr. W Mers 121 E4
Queen's Gdns. Pan 59 D4
Queen's Head Rd. Box 31 F2
Queen's Rd. Chelm 127 E1

Queen's Rd. Clact 109 E1
Queen's Rd. Colch 67 E3
Queen's Rd. Ea Col 45 D4
Queen's Rd. Frin 93 F2
Queen's Rd. Harw 40 A1
Queen's S Ben 187 E1
Queen's St. South 198 C4
Queen's Rd. South 199 F4
Queen's Rd. W Berg 48 B2
Queen's Rd. Wiv 87 E4
Queenborough La. Brain 77 E4
Queenborough Rd. South 159 E2
Queenbury Cl. W Mers 121 F3
Queens Cl. Sud 12 C4
Queens Ct. Burn 170 A2
Queens Mews. W Mers 121 D3
Queens Rd. Brain 59 F3
Queens Rd. Burn 170 B3
Queens Rd. Rayl 176 B1
Queens Rd. Sud 12 C4
Queensbury Ave. Copf 65 E3
Queensland Ave. Rock 190 C4
Queensland Cres. Chelm 126 C3
Queensland Dr. Colch 68 A1
Queensmere. Thund 188 A3
Queensway. Clact 110 B3
Queensway. Lawf 35 E2
Queensway. South 200 A4
Queensway. Sud 13 D3
Queensway. Tipt 100 B3
Quendon Rd. Basil 185 F4
Quendon Way. Frin 94 A3
Quilp Dr. Chelm 126 C4
Quilters Cl. Basil 185 E4
Quilters Cl. Clact 110 C3
Quilters Straight. Basil 185 E4
Quinion Cl. Chelm 126 B4
Quorn Gdns. Hadl 189 D1

Rachael Gdns. Silv E 79 F2
Rackenford. South 201 E4
Radiator Rd. Sud 13 D3
Radnor Rd. Ashi 167 E1
Radwinter Ave. Wick 174 B3
Raeburn Cl. Walt 93 F4
Ragian Rd. Frin 94 A3
Raile Wlk. L Mel 7 E4
Railway Sq. Chelm 127 D2
Railway St. Brain 60 A2
Railway St. Chelm 127 D2
Railway St. Mann 35 E2
Railway Terr. Clact 109 F2
Railway Terr. South 191 D2
Rainbow Ave. Canv 197 E2
Rainbow Mead. Hat Pev 114 A3
Rainbow Rd. Canv 197 E2
Rainbow Rd. W Mers 121 E3
Rainham Way. Frin 94 A3
Rainsborowe Rd. Colch 67 E2
Rainsford Ave. Chelm 126 C2
Rainsford La. Chelm 126 C2
Rainsford Rd. Chelm 126 C2
Rambler Cl. Stanw 66 B4
Ramblers Way. Burn 170 B2
Rampart St. South 202 A3
Rampart Terr. South 202 A3
Ramplings Ave. Clact 109 F3
Ramsay Dr. Basil 185 F2
Ramsey Chase. Latch 157 D3
Ramsey Cl. Mald 132 B2
Ramsey Rd. Hals 43 E4
Ramsey Rd. Harw 39 E1
Ramshaw Dr. Sprin 127 F2
Ramuz Dr. South 190 B1
Rana Cl. Brain 59 F2
Rana Dr. Brain 59 F2
Randolph Cl. South 189 F2
Randulph Terr. Sprin 127 E2
Randway. Rayl 176 B1
Ranger Wlk. Colch 68 A2
Rangoon Cl. Colch 67 D1
Ransom Rd. Tipt 100 B3
Ranulph Way. Hat Pev 114 A2
Raphael Dr. South 193 D1
Raphael Dr. Sprin 127 F4
Rat La. Hadl 188 B4
Ratcliffe Rd. Colch 66 C3
Ratsborough Chase. Soum 159 E1
Rattwick Dr. Canv 197 F2
Raven Dr. S Ben 187 E1
Raven Way. Colch 49 F2
Ravendale Way. South 192 B1
Ravens Ave. Hals 43 F4
Ravensbourne Dr. Chelm 126 B3
Ravenscourt Dr. Basil 185 F3
Ravensdale. Basil 185 D2
Ravensdale. Clact 109 F3
Ravensfield. Basil 185 D2
Ravenswood Chase. Roch 190 C4
Rawden Cl. Harw 40 A2
Rawreth La. Rayl 176 A3
Rawston Rd. Colch 67 F4
Ray Ave. Harw 40 A2
Ray Cl. Canv 197 D1
Ray Cl. Hadl 189 D1

Ray La. Rams 39 D2
Ray The. Sprin 127 F3
Ray Wlk. Hadl 189 D1
Raycliff Ave. Clact 109 F4
Raydon Way. Sud 13 E3
Rayleigh Ave. Rayl 189 E4
Rayleigh Ave. South 190 C1
Rayleigh Cl. Brain 60 B2
Rayleigh Cl. Colch 50 A1
Rayleigh Downs Rd. Ray 189 F4
Rayleigh Dr. South 189 E2
Rayleigh Rd. Rayl 189 E3
Rayleigh Rd. South 189 E3
Rayleigh Rd. Thund 188 A3
Rayleigh Rd. Thund 188 A3
Rayment Ave. Canv 197 E2
Raymonds Cl. S Woo F 165 E4
Raymonds Dr. Thund 187 F3
Rayne Rd. Brain 59 E2
Rayner Rd. Colch 67 D2
Rayner Way. Hals 25 F1
Rayside. Basil 185 E3
Read Cl. Hawk 178 A2
Readers Ct. Gt Bad 140 C3
Reaper Rd. Colch 67 D3
Rebecca Gdns. Silv E 79 F2
Rebow Rd. Harw 40 A1
Rebow Rd. Wiv 87 D4
Rebow St. Colch 68 A3
Recreation Ave. South 189 F1
Recreation Rd. Clact 110 A3
Recreation Rd. Colch 68 A3
Recreation Rd. Si Hed 24 B4
Recreation Way. Brigh 106 C4
Recreation Wlk. Sud 13 D3
Rectory Ave. Hawk 178 B3
Rectory Cl. Colch 49 F1
Rectory Cl. Glems 2 A3
Rectory Cl. Hadl 188 C2
Rectory Cl. Basil 186 B4
Rectory Garth. Rayl 176 B1
Rectory Gdns. Basil 186 B3
Rectory Gr. South 198 B4
Rectory Gr. Wick 174 C4
Rectory Hill. Nay 20 B4
Rectory Hill. Wiv 69 E1
Rectory La. Chelm 127 D2
Rectory La. Lang 86 A1
Rectory La. Latch 157 D2
Rectory La. Rams 39 D1
Rectory La. Rett 164 C3
Rectory La. Sible 17 E3
Rectory La. Woo Mor 143 F3
Rectory Meadow. Bradw 61 E1
Rectory Park Dr. Basil 186 A3
Rectory Rd. Ald 64 A4
Rectory Rd. Basil 186 B3
Rectory Rd. Copf 65 E1
Rectory Rd. Frat 70 C1
Rectory Rd. Hadl 188 C2
Rectory Rd. Hawk 178 A2
Rectory Rd. Langh 32 C4
Rectory Rd. Lit Ben 71 F4
Rectory Rd. Midd 12 C2
Rectory Rd. N Fam 56 C3
Rectory Rd. Rams 56 C3
Rectory Rd. Rowh 86 C4
Rectory Rd. Si Hed 15 E1
Rectory Rd. St O 90 C2
Rectory Rd. Stis 61 D4
Rectory Rd. Tipt 100 B3
Rectory Rd. Toll K 101 E1
Rectory Rd. Weel 91 D3
Rectory Rd. Wiv 69 E1
Rectory Rd. Woo Wa 130 B2
Rectory Rd. Wrab 38 A2
Rectory Rd. Writ 139 D4
Rectory Terr. Hawk 178 A2
Red Barn La. Gt Oak 56 A1
Red Barn Rd. Brigh 106 C4
Red House La. Sud 12 C4
Red Lion Yd. Colch 67 F4
Redbridge Rd. Clact 109 F4
Redcliff Dr. South 190 B1
Redcliff Rd. Chelm 127 D1
Reddings La. Till 149 E2
Rede Way. Sud 13 E3
Redgate Cl. Wick 175 D4
Redgate Ct. Rayl 187 F2
Redgrave Rd. Basil 185 F2
Redhills Rd. S Woo F 165 E4
Redhouse La. Box 31 E1
Redmayne Dr. Chelm 140 A4
Redmayne Dr. Chelm 139 F4
Rednell Cl. Colch 50 A1
Redrose Wlk. Clact 109 E2
Redruth Cl. Sprin 127 F4
Redshank Cres. S Woo F 154 B1
Redshank Dr. Mald 132 B3
Redstock Rd. South 191 D1
Redwood Cl. Colch 68 C4
Redwood Cl. Hadl 189 D1
Red Cl. Clact 109 E2
Reed Hall Ave. Colch 67 E2
Reeds Way. Wick 174 B4
Reeves Way. S Woo F 165 F4
Refinery Rd. Rams 39 F3

Regency Cl. Runw 163 E1
Regency Cl. Sprin 127 E2
Regency Green. Colch 67 D2
Regency Green. South 190 C2
Regent Cl. Brigh 106 C4
Regent Cl. Rayl 176 A2
Regent Rd. Brigh 106 C4
Regent St. Mann 35 E2
Regent St. Rowh 87 D4
Regents Ct. Burn 170 A2
Regina Rd. Chelm 127 E2
Reigate Ave. Clact 109 F3
Rembrandt Cl. South 202 A4
Rembrandt Gr. Sprin 127 F3
Rembrandt Way. Colch 67 D3
Remembrance Ave. Burn 170 A2
Remembrance Ave. Hat Pev .. 114 A2
Remercie Rd. Mist 36 A2
Remus Cl. Colch 49 F3
Renée Rd. Chelm 127 F4
Renoir Pl. Sprin 127 F4
Repton Cl. Basil 174 A1
Repton Gr. South 190 A4
Retreat Rd. Hock 177 F3
Retreat The. South 199 F4
Retreat The. With 98 A1
Rettendon Cl. Rayl 176 A2
Rettendon Gdns. Runw 163 F1
Rettendon Turnpike. Rett 164 B4
Rettendon View. Wick 174 C4
Reymead Cl. W Mers 121 E4
Reynard Ct. Gt Bad 140 C3
Reynards Cl. Walt 93 E3
Reynards Copse. Colch 50 A2
Reynolds Ave. Colch 67 D3
Reynolds Gate. S Woo F 165 F3
Rhoda Rd N. Thund 187 F3
Rhoda Rd. S Ben 187 F2
Richard Ave. Brigh 106 C3
Richard Ave. Wiv 69 E2
Richards Wlk. Clact 109 F3
Richardson Wlk. Colch 66 C3
Richmond Ave. S Ben 187 E1
Richmond Ave. South 199 F4
Richmond Ave. South 200 A4
Richmond Cr. Brigh 106 C4
Richmond Cres. Harw 40 A1
Richmond Dr. Clact 109 D1
Richmond Rd. South 190 B2
Richmond Rd. Rayl 188 B4
Richmond Rd. W Mers 121 E3
Richmond St. South 191 E1
Rickling. Basil 185 D2
Ricksones Rd. With 98 A3
Ridge The. Lit Bad 129 E1
Ridge The. Walt 94 A4
Ridgemount S Ben 187 F2
Ridgeway Gdns. South 199 D4
Ridgeway The. Brain 60 A1
Ridgeway The. Harw 40 A2
Ridgeway The. South 199 D4
Ridgeway. Colch 50 A2
Ridgewell Ave. Rayl 176 B1
Ridgewell Gr. Gt Y 8 C2
Ridgewell Way. Colch 67 F4
Ridings The. Canv 197 D3
Ridings The. Gt Bad 140 B4
Ridings The. Roch 178 C1
Ridlands Cl. T Gr 78 C3
Ridley Rd. Basil 174 B1
Ridley Rd. Chelm 127 D4
Riffams Cl. Basil 186 B4
Riffams Dr. Basil 186 B4
Riffhams Chase. Lit Bad 129 E1
Riffhams Dr. Gt Bad 141 D4
Riffhams La. Dan 142 B3
Rifle Hill. Brain 59 F1
Rigby Ave. Mist 36 A2
Rigby Rd. Mist 36 A2
Rignals La. Chelm 140 B2
Riley Ave. Clact 124 C3
Rimini Cl. Colch 49 F3
Ringwood Dr. Rayl 189 E4
Ripley Cl. Clact 109 D3
Ripple Way. Colch 50 A1
Rippleside. Basil 185 F3
Risby Cl. Colch 109 D2
Rise The. E & Gr 66 A4
Riven dell Vale. S Woo F 165 E3
Rivenhall Wick 175 D3
River Cl. Hals 25 F1
River Cotts. Bore 128 C4
River Hill. Terl 96 A2
River View Rd. S Ben 187 F1
River View. Alth 157 F1
River View. Brain 59 F2
River View. With 115 D4
Riverbank Cl. Ca 4 B4
Riverdale. South 189 E4
Rivermead. Chelm 127 D2
Riverside Ave E. Lawf 35 E2
Riverside Rd. Burn 170 B2
Riverside Way. Kelv 81 E1
Riverside Wlk. Colch 67 F4
Riverside Wlk. Wick 174 A4

Roper's Chase. Writ

Riverside. Bradw 61 E2
Riverton Dr. St L 135 D1
Rivertons. Basil 185 F2
Riverview Ct. Basil 185 F2
Riverview Gdns. Hull 165 E1
Riverview. Basil 186 A2
Riverview. Lawf 35 E2
Riviera Dr. South 200 B4
Rivish La. L Mel 7 E4
Roach Ave. Rayl 176 B1
Roach Vale. Colch 50 C1
Roach Vale. South 189 F4
Robert Way. Wick 174 C3
Robert Way. Wiv 69 E2
Robert's Hill. M Bure 28 C2
Roberts Rd. Colch 68 A3
Roberts Rd. N Fam 167 D4
Robin Cl. Gt Ben 89 E4
Robin Way. Chelm 140 A3
Robin Way. Sud 12 B3
Robinsbridge Rd. Cogg 62 C1
Robinsdale. Clact 109 F3
Robinson Rd. Brigh 107 D4
Robjohns Rd. Chelm 139 F4
Robletts Way. Worm 29 F2
Rochdale Way. Colch 68 C3
Roche Ave. Hawk 178 C1
Rochefort Dr. Roch 190 C4
Rochehall Way. Roch 191 D4
Rochester Dr. South 190 B2
Rochester Mews. South 190 B2
Rochester Way. Basil 185 D2
Rochester Way. Sud 7 E1
Rocheway. Roch 179 D1
Rochford Ave. South 190 C1
Rochford Cl. Wick 74 C4
Rochford Garden Way. Roch . 178 C2
Rochford Hall Cl. Roch 178 C1
Rochford Rd. Canv 197 E2
Rochford Rd. Chelm 127 E1
Rochford Rd. South 190 B3
Rochford Rd. St O 108 A2
Rochford Way. Walt 94 A4
Rockall. South 190 A4
Rockingham Cl. Colch 50 B2
Rocklands Rd. South 190 A1
Rodbridge Dr. South 7 D3
Rodbridge Hill. L Mel 7 D3
Roddam Cl. Colch 67 E3
Roding Cl. Gt Wak 193 D2
Roding Leigh. S Woo F 165 F4
Roding Way. Wick 174 C3
Rodings The. South 189 E4
Rodney Gdns. Brain 60 B2
Rodney Pl. Sud 7 F1
Rodney Way. Chelm 139 F4
Roedean Cl. South 191 F1
Roedean Gdns. South 191 F1
Rogation Cl. Stanw 66 B3
Roggel Rd. Canv 197 E1
Rokell Way. Walt 93 F3
Rokells. Basil 185 D4
Rokescroft. Basil 186 A3
Roland La. Canv 197 D2
Rolands Cl. Chelm 126 C4
Rolley La. Kelv 81 E1
Rolph Cl. Th L S 74 A1
Romainville Way. Canv 196 B2
Roman Hill. Rowh 86 A4
Roman Rd. Chelm 127 D1
Roman Rd. Colch 68 A4
Roman Way. L Mel 7 E3
Roman Way. St O 107 D2
Romans Pl. Writ 126 A1
Romans Way. Writ 126 A1
Romford Cl. Colch 68 A4
Romney Cl. Brain 59 F3
Romney Cl. Brigh 106 C4
Romney Cl. Clact 109 E3
Romney Cl. Walt 93 F4
Romney Way. Hock 177 E3
Romsey Cres. S Ben 187 D3
Romsey Rd. S Ben 187 D3
Romsey Rd. S Ben 187 D3
Ronald Dr. Rayl 176 A2
Ronald Hill Gr. South 190 B1
Ronald Park Ave. South 190 B1
Ronald Rd. Hals 43 F4
Roodegate. Basil 185 D2
Rookeries The. Mks T 65 D2
Rookery Chase. Ard 33 F1
Rookery Cl. Hat Pev 114 A3
Rookery La. Gt Tot 116 C4
Rookery La. Tipt 100 B4
Rookery Mead. S Woo F 165 E4
Rookery The. Lawf 35 E2
Rookwood Cl. Clact 109 E4
Rookyards. Basil 185 F3
Roosevel Ave. Canv 197 D2
Roosevelt Way. Colch 68 A2
Roots Hall Ave. South 190 B1
Roots Hall Rd. South 190 C1
Roots La. Wic Bis 115 F3
Rope Wlk. Brigh 107 D3
Rope Wlk. Mald 132 A1
Roper's Chase. Writ 139 D4

225

Ropers La. L Mel

School St. Nay

Ropers La. L Mel 7 D2
Rosabelle Ave. Wiv 69 D1
Rosalind Cl. Colch 68 C4
Rosary Gdns. South 190 A2
Rosbach Rd. Canv 197 E2
Rosberg Rd. Canv 197 F2
Rose Acre. Basil 185 F3
Rose Acre. High 22 C3
Rose Ave. Stanw 66 B2
Rose Cres. Colch 49 E1
Rose Glen. Chelm 140 B4
Rose Hill. Brain 60 A1
Rose La. Virl 119 D4
Rose La. Wiv 87 D4
Rose Rd. Canv 197 D2
Rose Way. Roch 191 D4
Rosebank Rd. W Mers 121 D3
Rosebank. Harw 40 A2
Rosebay Cl. With 97 E2
Roseberry Ave. Thund 187 E4
Rosebery Ave. Colch 68 A4
Rosebery Rd. Chelm 140 A4
Rosecroft Cl. Clact 109 F3
Roselaine. Basil 185 D4
Rosemary Ave. Brain 59 F2
Rosemary Cres. Clact 109 F1
Rosemary Cres. Tipt 100 B3
Rosemary La. Ca Hed 16 A3
Rosemary La. Hals 25 F1
Rosemary La. Thor 89 D3
Rosemary Rd W. Clact 109 F1
Rosemary Rd. Clact 109 F1
Rosemary Way. Clact 125 D4
Rosemead. Thund 187 E4
Roserna Rd. Canv 197 E2
Rosewood Cl. Colch 50 A2
Rosewood La. South 201 F3
Rosilian Dr. Hull 166 B1
Roslings Cl. Chelm 126 B3
Rossendale Cl. Colch 50 B2
Rossendale. Chelm 126 C1
Rossetta Cl. Wiv 69 D1
Rosshill Ind Park. Stobr 191 D2
Rossiter Rd. South 202 A4
Rosslyn Cl. Hock 177 F4
Rosslyn Rd. Hock 177 F4
Rothbury Rd. Chelm 126 B1
Rothchilds Ave. Rayl 176 B2
Rothesay Ave. Chelm 140 A4
Rothmans Ave. Gt Bad 140 C3
Rothwell Cl. Hadl 189 E3
Roughtons. Chelm 140 B2
Round Bush Corner. Birch 83 E2
Round Cl. Colch 67 D4
Round Hill Rd. S Ben 188 A1
Roundacre. Basil 185 D3
Roundacre. Hals 43 F4
Roundbush Rd. Lay M 83 E1
Roundbush Rd. Purl 156 A4
Rous Chase. Chelm 140 A1
Rouses La. Clact 108 C2
Rover Ave. Clact 124 C4
Row The. Str S M 22 B1
Rowallan Cl. Colch 67 D2
Rowan Chase. Tipt 100 B3
Rowan Cl. Clact 109 E2
Rowan Cl. Gt Ben 89 F4
Rowan Cl. Harw 40 A2
Rowan Cl. Stanw 66 B2
Rowan Dr. Mald 132 B3
Rowan Way. Cane 168 C1
Rowan Way. Hat Pev 114 A2
Rowan Way. With 98 A3
Rowan Wlk. South 189 E3
Rowhedge Cl. Basil 174 B1
Rowhedge Ferry Rd. Wiv 87 D4
Rowhedge Rd. Colch 68 C1
Rowherns La. Lit Ben 71 F2
Rowland's Yd. Harw 39 F1
Rowlands The. S Ben 187 F2
Rowley Cl. Catt 35 E4
Roxburghe Rd. Weel 90 C3
Roxwell Ave. Chelm 126 B2
Roxwell Rd. Chelm 126 B2
Roxwell Rd. Writ 126 B2
Royal Cl. Hawk 178 B3
Royal Mews. South 200 A4
Royal Oak Dr. Wick 175 D4
Royal Sq. Ded 33 F4
Royal Terr. South 200 A4
Roydon Bridge. Basil 185 E4
Roydon Way. Walt 93 F3
Royer Cl. Hawk 178 A2
Royston Ave. South 191 D2
Ruaton Dr. Clact 109 E2
Rubens Cl. South 202 A4
Rubens Gate. Sprin 127 F4
Rubicon Ave. Wick 174 C4
Rudd Ct. Colch 50 C1
Rudkin Rd. Colch 49 F3
Rudsdale Way. Colch 66 C3
Ruffles Cl. Rayl 176 C2
Rugby Rd. Sud 13 D2
Rugosa Cl. Stanw 66 B4
Rumseys Fields. Dan 142 C4
Rundells Wlk. Basil 185 F4
Rundels The. Thund 188 A3
Runnacles St. Silv E 79 E3
Running Mare La. Chelm 140 A2
Runnymeade Rd. Canv 197 D2
Runnymede Chase. Thund 188 A3
Runsell La. Dan 143 D4
Runsell View. Dan 143 D4
Runwell Gdns. Runw 163 E1
Runwell Rd. Runw 163 F1
Runwell Rd. Runw 164 A2
Runwell Terr. South 199 F4
Runwood Rd. Canv 196 B2
Rupert Rd. Soum 159 E2
Rurik Ct. Mald 144 C4
Rush Cl. Thund 187 D3
Rush Green Rd. Clact 109 D2
Rushbottom La. Basil 175 D1
Rushes La. Ashel 149 D1
Rushley Cl. Gt Wak 193 D2
Rushley. Basil 174 B1
Rushleydale. Sprin 127 F3
Rushmere Cl. W Mers 121 E3
Ruskin Ave. South 191 D1
Ruskin Cl. Walt 93 F4
Ruskin Path. Wick 174 B3
Ruskin Rd. Chelm 127 F1
Ruskoi Rd. Canv 196 C3
Russell Gdns. Chelm 140 A2
Russell Gdns. Wick 174 C4
Russell Gr. Roch 179 D1
Russell Rd. Clact 110 A2
Russell Rd. N Fam 156 A1
Russell Way. Chelm 139 F4
Russell's Rd. Hals 43 D4
Russet Cl. Brain 60 A1
Russet Way. Burn 170 B3
Russet Way. Hock 177 F4
Russets. Clelm 140 B2
Russets The. Hawk 178 B3
Rutherford Cl. Rayl 189 E3
Rutland Ave. Colch 67 D2
Rutland Ave. South 200 C4
Rutland Dr. Rayl 176 A4
Rutland Gdns. Brain 60 A2
Rutland Gdns. Hawk 178 B3
Rutland Rd. Chelm 127 D4
Rutland Rd. N Fam 167 D4
Rydal Cl. Hull 165 E2
Rydal Cl. Rayl 176 C1
Rydal Way. Bl Not 77 E3
Ryde Ave. Clact 110 A4
Ryde Cl. Hadl 189 D3
Ryde The. Hadl 189 D3
Ryder Way. Basil 174 B1
Rye Cl. Brigh 88 C1
Rye Cl. Colch 66 C3
Rye Cl. Hat Pev 114 A2
Rye Field The. Lit Bad 129 E2
Rye La. Lay H 85 D2
Rye Mill La. Fee 81 F2
Ryedene Cl. Basil 185 F2
Ryedene Pl. Basil 185 F2
Ryedene. Basil 185 F2
Ryegate Rd. Colch 67 F4
Ryes La. Bul 12 A1
Rylands Rd. South 191 E1
Ryle The. Writ 139 D4
Rysley. Lit Bad 129 E2
Sackville Cl. Chelm 126 C2
Sackville Rd. South 191 F1
Sackville Way. W Berg 48 B2
Saddle Rise. Sprin 127 F4
Sadler Cl. Colch 68 A2
Sadlers Cl. Walt 93 E3
Sadlers. Thund 187 D3
Saffory Cl. Rayl 189 E4
Saffron Way. Tipt 100 B2
Sage Rd. Colch 68 A1
Sage Wlk. Tipt 100 B2
St Agnes Dr. Canv 196 B2
St Alban's Rd. Clact 110 A2
St Alban's Rd. Colch 67 E4
St Andrew's Ave. Colch 68 B3
St Andrew's Gdns. Colch 68 B4
St Andrew's Rd. Clact 109 F2
St Andrew's Rd. Hat Pev 114 A2
St Andrew's Rd. Roch 178 C1
St Andrew's Rd. Weel 72 C1
St Andrew's Rise. Bul 11 F3
St Andrews Cl. Alres 88 A4
St Andrews Cl. Canv 196 B2
St Andrews Pl. Brigh 88 C1
St Andrews Rd. Bore 112 C1
St Andrews Rd. Hals 25 F1
St Andrews Rd. South 201 E3
St Andrews Rd. Sud 13 D3
St Ann's Rd. South 191 D1
St Anne's Rd. Colch 68 B4
St Annes Cl. Cogg 63 D1
St Annes Rd. Canv 197 F2
St Anns Rd. Clact 109 F2
St Anthony's Dr. Chelm 140 B4
St Augustine's Ave. South 201 D3
St Austell Rd. Colch 50 B1
St Austin's La. Harw 40 C3
St Barbara's Rd. Colch 67 E2
St Bartholomew Cl. Colch 50 B2
St Bartholomews La. Sud 7 E1
St Benet's Rd. South 190 C1
St Bernard Rd. Colch 50 B1
St Botolph's Circus. Colch 67 F3
St Botolph's St. Colch 67 F3
St Botolph's Terr. Walt 94 B4
St Botolphs Church Wlk. Colch 67 F3
St Bridge Ct. Colch 50 B1
St Catharines Cl. Colch 67 E1
St Catherine Rd. L Mel 7 E4
St Catherine's Rd. Chelm 126 C1
St Catherines Cl. Wick 174 C4
St Charles Dr. Wick 174 C4
St Christopher Rd. Colch 50 B1
St Christophers Cl. Canv 196 B2
St Christophers Way. Clact 125 D4
St Clair Cl. Clact 109 F4
St Clair's Dr. St O 108 A3
St Clair's Rd. St O 108 A3
St Clare Dr. Colch 67 D4
St Clare Meadow. Roch 178 C2
St Clare Rd. Colch 67 D3
St Clement Rd. Colch 50 B1
St Clement's Ave. South 189 F1
St Clement's Cl. S Ben 187 E3
St Clement's Cres. S Ben 187 E3
St Clement's Dr. South 189 F2
St Clement's Rd. S Ben 187 E3
St Clements Cl. Hawk 178 A2
St Clere's Hall La. St O 108 A2
St Cleres Cres. Wick 174 C4
St Cleres Way. Dan 142 B4
St Columb Ct. Colch 50 B1
St Cyrus Rd. Colch 50 B2
St David's Cl. Colch 68 B4
St David's Way. Wick 174 C4
St Davids Dr. Hadl 189 D2
St Davids Terr. Hadl 189 D2
St Davids Wlk. Canv 196 B2
St Dominic Rd. Colch 50 B1
St Edmund's Cl. South 191 E2
St Edmund's Ct. Colch 68 B4
St Edmund's Hill. Bures 19 E3
St Edmund's Hill. Sud 19 E3
St Edmunds La. Bures 19 F1
St Fabian's Dr. Chelm 126 C2
St Faith Rd. Colch 50 B1
St Fillan Rd. Colch 50 B1
St Gabriels Ct. Basil 186 A3
St George's Ave. Harw 40 B1
St George's Dr. South 190 C2
St George's La. South 201 F3
St George's Park Ave. South 190 A1
St Georges Cl. Gt Bro 52 C1
St Georges Wlk. Canv 196 B2
St Georges Wlk. Thund 187 D3
St Giles Cl. Mald 131 F1
St Giles Cres. Mald 131 F1
St Gregory's Ct. Sud 12 B4
St Guiberts Rd. Canv 196 C3
St Helen's Green. Harw 40 C3
St Helen's La. Colch 67 F4
St Helen's Rd. South 199 F4
St Helena Rd. Colch 67 E3
St Helens Ave. Clact 110 A4
St Ives Cl. Clact 109 D2
St Ives Rd. Peld 103 F3
St Jame's St. Ca Hed 15 F2
St James Ave. South 201 D4
St James Cl. Canv 196 B2
St James Cl. South 190 A2
St James Gdns. South 190 A2
St James Park. Chelm 126 B2
St James Rd. Basil 185 E3
St James Rd. Brain 59 F3
St James's Wlk. Hock 177 E3
St Jean Wlk. Tipt 100 B3
St John Ave. Brain 59 F1
St John's Ave. Chelm 140 A4
St John's Ave. Colch 67 F3
St John's Cres. Gt Hor 49 D4
St John's Ct. Tolle 119 E1
St John's Green. Colch 67 F3
St John's Green. Writ 126 A1
St John's Rd. Chelm 140 A4
St John's Rd. Clact 109 D3
St John's Rd. Colch 50 B2
St John's Rd. Gt Wak 193 D2
St John's Rd. S Ben 188 B2
St John's Rd. South 199 F4
St John's Rd. Wiv 87 E4
St John's Rd. Writ 126 A1
St John's St. Colch 67 F3
St Johns Cl. Gt Wak 193 D2
St Johns Cres. Canv 196 B2
St Johns Dr. Rayl 175 F2
St Joseph Rd. Colch 50 B2
St Jude Gdns. Colch 50 B1
St Judes Cl. Colch 50 B1
St Julian Gr. Colch 68 A3
St Lawrence Dr. St L 135 D1
St Lawrence Gdns. South 189 F3
St Lawrence Hill. St L 148 C3
St Lawrence Rd. Colch 50 B1
St Lawrence Rd. Till 149 E3
St Leonard's Rd. South 200 A4
St Leonards Rd. Colch 68 B3
St Luke's Chase. Tipt 100 B3
St Luke's Cl. Colch 50 B1
St Luke's Rd. South 191 E1
St Lukes Cl. Canv 196 B2
St Margaret's Rd. Sprin 127 F2
St Mark Dr. Colch 50 B1
St Mark's Rd. S Ben 188 B2
St Marks Rd. Canv 196 B2
St Marks Rd. Clact 109 F2
St Martin's Cl. Rayl 188 B4
St Martin's Cl. Thund 187 D4
St Martins Cl. Clact 109 F2
St Mary's Cl. Gt Bad 140 C3
St Mary's Cl. Pan 59 D4
St Mary's Cl. S Ben 187 E1
St Mary's Cres. Basil 186 B3
St Mary's Dr. S Ben 187 F1
St Mary's La. Mald 132 A1
St Mary's Path. Basil 186 B4
St Mary's Rd. Brain 60 A2
St Mary's Rd. Burn 170 B3
St Mary's Rd. Clact 109 F2
St Mary's Rd. Frin 94 A3
St Mary's Rd. Gt Ben 89 F3
St Mary's Rd. Kelv 81 E1
St Mary's Rd. S Ben 196 C4
St Mary's Rd. South 190 C1
St Mary's Rd. With 98 A4
St Marys Cl. South 192 B1
St Marys Mews. Tolle 119 E1
St Michael's La. Brain 59 F1
St Michael's Rd. Brain 59 F1
St Michael's Rd. Chelm 140 A4
St Michael's Rd. Harw 40 A1
St Michael's Rd. Rayl 188 C4
St Michael's Rd. Th L S 73 F1
St Michaels Ave. Basil 186 B2
St Michaels Cl. Latch 157 D3
St Michaels Ct. Mann 35 E2
St Michaels Rd. Canv 196 B2
St Michaels Rd. Colch 67 E1
St Michaels Wlk. Chelm 140 B1
St Mildreds Rd. Chelm 140 A4
St Monance Way. Colch 50 B1
St Nazaire Rd. Chelm 126 C3
St Neots Cl. Colch 50 B1
St Nicholas Cl. With 97 F2
St Nicholas Pass. Colch 67 F4
St Nicholas Rd. Till 149 F2
St Nicholas Rd. With 97 F2
St Nicholas St. Colch 67 F4
St Nicholas Way. Cogg 63 D2
St Osyth Rd. Alres 88 B4
St Osyth Rd. Clact 109 E2
St Osyth Rd. Lit Cla 91 E1
St Paul's Rd. Clact 110 A2
St Paul's Rd. Colch 67 F4
St Pauls Rd. Canv 196 B2
St Peter's Ave. Mald 131 F1
St Peter's Cl. Brain 59 F2
St Peter's Rd. Brain 59 F2
St Peter's Rd. Chelm 126 C1
St Peter's Rd. Cogg 63 D1
St Peter's Rd. W Mers 121 D3
St Peter's St. Colch 67 F4
St Peter's Terr. Wick 174 B4
St Peter's Wlk. Brain 59 F2
St Peters Ct. Sud 12 C4
St Peters Field. Burn 170 A3
St Peters Rd. Canv 196 B2
St Peters Rd. Hock 177 D4
St Peters's-in-the-Fields. Brain 59 F2
St Runwald St. Colch 67 F4
St Saviour Cl. Colch 50 B1
St Stephens Rd. Col N 156 A2
St Thomas Cl. Colch 50 C1
St Thomas Rd. Ashi 167 D2
St Vincent Chase. Brain 60 A3
St Vincent Rd. Clact 109 E1
St Vincent's Rd. South 199 F4
St Vincents Rd. Chelm 140 A4
Sairard Cl. South 189 E4
Sairard Gdns. South 189 E4
Salary Cl. Colch 50 C1
Salcombe Rd. Brain 60 B1
Salcott Cres. Wick 174 C3
Salem Wlk. Rayl 176 A2
Salerno Cres. Colch 67 E1
Salerno Way. Chelm 126 C3
Salforal Cl. Rett 153 D1
Salisbury Ave. Colch 67 F3
Salisbury Ave. South 190 C1
Salisbury Rd. Clact 110 B3
Salisbury Rd. South 189 E1
Salmon Cl. Colch 66 C2
Salmon's La. Gt T 64 A2
Saltcoats Hill. Stow M 155 D1
Saltcoats. S Woo F 165 E4
Salter Pl. Sprin 127 F1
Salter's Meadow. Toll D 118 B2
Saltings The. Hadl 188 B2
Salvia Cl. Clact 109 E2
Samphire Cl. With 97 E2
Sampson's La. Peld 103 F2
Samson's Rd. Brigh 88 C1
Samsons Cl. Brigh 106 C4
Samuel Manor. Sprin 127 F2
Samuels Dr. South 201 D4
San Remo Par. South 199 F4
San Remo Rd. Canv 197 E2
Sanctuary Rd. Hadl 189 D2
Sandbanks. Hadl 188 B1
Sanderling Gdns. Mald 132 B3
Sanderlings. S Ben 187 E1
Sanders Dr. Colch 67 D4
Sanders Rd. Canv 197 D3
Sanderson Ct. Colch 67 F4
Sandford Cl. Wiv 87 E4
Sandford Mill Rd. Sprin 127 F1
Sandford Mill Rd. Sprin 128 A1
Sandford Rd. Chelm 127 F2
Sandhill Rd. Rayl 189 E4
Sandhurst Cl. South 189 F2
Sandhurst Cres. South 189 F2
Sandhurst. Canv 196 B2
Sandleigh Rd. South 190 A1
Sandon Cl. Gt Hor 49 E4
Sandon Cl. Hawk 178 B2
Sandon Hall Bridleway. Sand 141 E2
Sandon Rd. Basil 185 F3
Sandown Ave. South 190 A1
Sandown Cl. Clact 110 A4
Sandown Cl. Wick 175 D4
Sandown Rd. Thund 188 A4
Sandown Rd. Wick 175 D4
Sandpiper Cl. Colch 69 D4
Sandpiper Cl. Mald 132 B3
Sandpiper Cl. South 201 F4
Sandpiper Wlk. Chelm 140 B3
Sandpit La. Burn 170 B3
Sandpit Rd. Brain 59 F2
Sandpit Rd. South 202 A4
Sandringham Ave. Hock 177 E3
Sandringham Ct. Sud 13 D4
Sandringham Rd. South 200 B4
Sandwich Cl. Brain 59 F3
Sandwich Rd. Brigh 106 C4
Sandwich Rd. Clact 125 E4
Sandy Hill. M Bure 29 E3
Sandy La. Bul 12 A3
Sandy La. Sud 12 A3
Santour Rd. Canv 196 C3
Saran Ct. Wiv 69 D1
Sarcel. Stis 61 E3
Sargeant Cl. Colch 68 A2
Sarre Way. Brigh 106 C4
Sassoon Way. Mald 145 D4
Satanita Rd. South 199 E4
Saul's Ave. With 115 D4
Sauls Bridge Cl. With 115 D4
Saunders Ave. Brain 59 F2
Savill Rd. Colch 68 B1
Saville St. Walt 76 B1
Sawkins Ave. Gt Bad 140 B3
Sawkins Cl. Gt Bad 140 B3
Sawkins Gdns. Gt Bad 140 B3
Sawney Brook. Writ 126 A1
Sawyer's Rd. Toll D 117 E3
Saxmunden Way. Clact 109 D2
Saxon Cl. Colch 66 C2
Saxon Cl. Rayl 176 C3
Saxon Cl. Runw 163 F1
Saxon Dr. With 97 F2
Saxon Way. Chelm 127 D4
Saxon Way. Clact 110 C3
Saxon Way. Mald 132 A1
Saxon Way. S Ben 187 E1
Saxonville. S Ben 187 D2
Saxted Dr. Clact 109 D2
Sayers. Thund 188 A3
Saywell Brook. Sprin 128 A1
Scalby Rd. Soum 159 D2
Scaldhurst. Basil 186 B4
Scarborough Dr. South 189 F1
Scarborough Rd. Soum 159 D2
Scarfe Way. Colch 68 C3
Scarletts Cl. With 115 D4
Scarletts Rd. Colch 68 B3
Scarletts. Basil 185 E4
Sceptre Rd. Tolle 119 E1
School Chase. Hals 43 F4
School Hill. Birch 84 A2
School La. Basil 175 D1
School La. Birch 84 A2
School La. Ded 33 F4
School La. Frat 71 D1
School La. Gt Hor 31 D1
School La. Gt Wig 102 C2
School La. Lawf 35 D1
School La. Lit Hor 30 B3
School La. Mist 35 F2
School La. S Ben 196 B4
School La. Str S M 22 B1
School La. W Berg 48 C2
School Rd. Colch 68 A1
School Rd. Copf 65 E2
School Rd. Elmst M 70 A2
School Rd. Frin 93 F3
School Rd. Gt Oak 56 B2
School Rd. Gt Tot 116 A2
School Rd. Langh 32 C2
School Rd. Lit Hor 30 B2
School Rd. Lit Map 26 A4
School Rd. Lit Tot 117 D2
School Rd. Lit Y 9 E2
School Rd. Mess 82 B1
School Rd. Pent 5 F3
School Rd. Sho G 40 A4
School Rd. Si Hed 24 B4
School Rd. Silv E 79 F2
School Rd. Tend 72 C3
School Rd. Wic Bis 115 F3
School Rd. Wic S P 17 E3
School St. Nay 20 B3

School St. Sud 12 C4
School View Rd. Chelm ... 126 C2
School Way. South 189 F2
School Wlk. Brain 59 F2
Schoolfield. Glems 2 A3
Scofield Ct. Sud 13 D3
Scotland St. Nay 20 C3
Scott Cl. Brain 78 A4
Scott Dr. Colch 66 C3
Scotts Hall Cotts. Cane ... 179 E4
Scotts Hall Rd. Cane 179 E4
Scotts Hill. Soum 159 D2
Scotts Wlk. Chelm 126 B3
Scotts Wlk. Rayl 177 D1
Scraley Rd. Gt Tot 132 B3
Scraley Rd. Mald 132 B3
Scratton Rd. South 199 F4
Scrip's Rd. Cogg 81 D4
Scrub La. Hadl 188 C2
Scylla Cl. Mald 132 E3
Scythe Way. Colch 66 C2
Scythe Way. Colch 67 D2
Sea Cornflower Way. Clact .. 125 D4
Sea Cres. Clact 124 C3
Sea Flowers Way. Clact .. 125 D4
Sea Glebe Way. Clact 125 D4
Sea Holly Way. Clact 125 D3
Sea King Cres. Colch 50 A2
Sea Lavender Way. Clact .. 125 D4
Sea Pink Way. Clact 125 D4
Sea Reach. South 198 C4
Sea Rosemary Way. Clact .. 125 D4
Sea Shell Way. Clact 125 D3
Sea Thistle Way. Clact ... 125 D4
Sea View Par. May 146 C1
Sea View Par. St L 135 E1
Sea View Prom. Tolle 135 D1
Sea Way. Clact 124 C3
Seabrook Gdns. Bore 112 C1
Seabrook Rd. Gt Bad 141 D3
Seaden Cl. Clact 110 A4
Seafield Ave. Mist 36 A2
Seafield Rd. Harw 40 A1
Seafields Gdns. Clact 110 B3
Seafields Rd. Clact 110 B3
Seaforth Ave. South 191 E1
Seaforth Gr. South 191 E1
Seaforth Rd. South 199 E4
Seagers. Gt Tot 116 A2
Seamer Rd. Soum 159 D2
Seamore Ave. Thund 187 E4
Seamore Cl. Thund 187 E3
Seamore Ct. Lawf 35 D2
Seaview Ave. Basil 185 E2
Seaview Ave. Lit Oak 57 E4
Seaview Ave. W Mers 121 F3
Seaview Dr. Gt Wak 193 E2
Seaview Hts. Walt 94 B4
Seaview Rd. Brigh 106 C4
Seaview Rd. Canv 197 F1
Seaview Rd. South 198 C4
Seaview Rd. South 201 F3
Seaview St O 124 A4
Seaview Terr. Hadl 188 B1
Seaview Terr. St O 107 D2
Seaway. Canv 197 D1
Seaway. St L 148 B4
Seawick Rd. St O 124 A3
Sebastian Cl. Colch 68 C4
Second Ave. Canv 196 C2
Second Ave. Chelm 127 D3
Second Ave. Clact 110 A2
Second Ave. Frin 93 F2
Second Ave. Glems 2 B3
Second Ave. Hals 26 A1
Second Ave. Harw 40 B2
Second Ave. Hull 165 F1
Second Ave. South 199 D4
Second Ave. Sud 7 F1
Second Ave. Walt 76 B2
Second Ave. Weel 90 C4
Second Ave. Wick 175 D3
Seddons Wlk. Hock 177 F3
Sedem Ct. Clact 92 A1
Sedgemoor. South 192 B2
Selbourne Rd. Hock 177 F3
Selbourne Rd. South 191 E2
Selbourne Rd. Thund 187 E3
Seldon Cl. South 190 A2
Seldon Rd. Tipt 100 B3
Selworth Cl. South 190 B3
Selwyn Rd. South 191 E1
Serpentine Wlk. Colch 49 F1
Seven Acres. Wick 174 C4
Seven Ash Green. Sprin .. 127 E3
Seventh Ave. Canv 196 C2
Seventh Ave. Chelm 127 D3
Severalls La. Colch 50 B3
Severn Rd. Clact 109 F3
Sewards End. Wick 174 C3
Sewell's La. Bel S P 5 D1
Sexton Cl. Rowh 86 A4
Seymour Rd. Clact 108 C1
Seymour Rd. Hadl 188 C2
Seymour Rd. South 190 B1
Seymour St. Chelm 127 D1
Shackleton Cl. Harw 39 F1
Shaftesbury Ave. Harw 40 A2
Shaftesbury Ave. South .. 200 C3
Shair La. Tend 72 A1
Shakespeare Ave. Rayl .. 177 D1
Shakespeare Ave. South .. 190 C1
Shakespeare Cl. Brain 78 A4
Shakespeare Dr. Mald 132 A1
Shakespeare Dr. South .. 190 C1
Shakespeare Rd. Colch ... 66 C3
Shakleston Cl. Writ 139 D4
Shamrock Cl. Tolle 119 E1
Shanklin Cl. Clact 110 A4
Shanklin Dr. South 190 A1
Shannon Ave. Rayl 176 B1
Shannon Cl. South 189 F2
Shannon Way. Canv 196 B2
Sharlands Cl. Wick 174 C4
Sharnbrook. South 192 B1
Sharpington Cl. Chelm ... 140 B2
Shatters Rd. Lay Br 84 A1
Shaw Cl. Walt 93 F4
Shaw Rd. L Mel 7 E4
Shaw Rd. With 97 F3
Shearers Way. Bore 112 C1
Shears Cres. W Mers 121 E3
Sheepcotes La. Gt Tot ... 116 C1
Sheepcot Rd. Ca Hed 15 F2
Sheepcotes La. Silv E 79 F3
Sheepcotes La. Soum 159 E3
Sheepen Pl. Colch 67 F4
Sheepen Rd. Colch 67 F4
Sheepgate La. Cla 4 A4
Sheepshead Hill. Sud 13 E3
Sheepslye Mews. Colch .. 67 F4
Sheerwater Mews. Colch .. 66 A4
Sheldon Rd. Canv 197 F2
Shellbeach Rd. Canv 197 E1
Shellcroft. Col En 26 C1
Shelley Ave. Sud 13 D3
Shelley Cl. Mald 145 D4
Shelley Rd. Chelm 127 E1
Shelley Rd. Colch 66 C3
Shelley Sq. South 191 D1
Shelley Wlk. Brain 78 A4
Shelleys La. T Gr 78 C4
Shepard Cl. South 190 A3
Shepherds Cl. Hadl 188 C2
Shepherds Croft. Stanw .. 66 B3
Shepherds La. Glems 2 A3
Shepherds Wlk. Hadl 188 C2
Sheppard Cl. Clact 109 E3
Sheppard Dr. Sprin 128 A2
Sherborne Rd. Sprin 127 E3
Sherbourne Cl. Roch 190 C3
Sherbourne Cl. Walt 93 F4
Sherbourne Dr. Basil 174 A1
Sherbourne Gdns. Roch .. 190 C3
Sherbourne Rd. Colch 68 C4
Sheridan Ave. S Ben 188 A2
Sheridan Cl. Rayl 176 C1
Sheridan Wlk. Colch 66 C3
Sheriffs Way. Clact 109 F4
Sheriton Sq. Rayl 176 B2
Sherry Way. Hadl 188 C3
Sherwood Cl. Colch 68 B4
Sherwood Cres. Hadl 188 C2
Sherwood Dr. Chelm 126 B1
Sherwood Dr. Clact 109 F3
Sherwood Way. Fee 81 E2
Sherwood Way. South ... 191 F1
Shewell Wlk. Colch 67 F4
Shewsbury Dri. Thund ... 187 E4
Shillingstone. South 192 B1
Shillitoe Cl. Colch 66 C2
Ship Hill. Brad 36 C2
Ship Rd. Burn 170 B2
Shipwrights Cl. S Ben ... 188 A1
Shipwrights Dr. S Ben ... 188 A2
Shire Cl. Sprin 127 F4
Shirebourn Vale. S Woo F .. 165 E3
Shirley Ct. Clact 109 D1
Shirley Gdns. Basil 186 A4
Shirley Rd. South 189 F3
Shoebridge's Hill. Ded 33 F3
Shoebury Ave. South 201 F4
Shoebury Common Rd. South .. 201 F4
Shoebury Rd. Gt Wak ... 193 F2
Shoebury Rd. South 192 A1
Shop La. E Mers 105 F2
Shop Rd. Lit Bro 53 D3
Shopland Hall Rd. Stobr .. 191 E3
Shopland Rd. Stobr 191 E4
Shore La. Brad 36 C2
Shore Rd. Burn 170 B2
Shorefield Gdns. South .. 199 F4
Shorefield Rd. South 199 E4
Shorefield. S Ben 187 D2
Short Cut Rd. Colch 67 F4
Short Cut Rd. Colch 67 F4
Short Rd. Hadl 188 B1
Short St. South 191 D1
Short Wyre St. Colch 67 F4
Shortacre. Basil 185 E3
Shortlands. Basil 185 D3
Shortridge Ct. With 114 C4
Shrub End Rd. Colch 66 C2
Shrubland Ct. Clact 110 A3
Shrubland Rd. Colch 68 A3
Shrubland Rd. Mist 36 A2
Shrublands Cl. Chelm ... 127 E1
Shums Hill. Walt 93 E4
Shut La. Ea Col 45 D3
Siam Pl. Sud 12 C4
Sidmouth Ave. South 190 B3
Sidmouth Rd. Sprin 127 F3
Sidwell Ave. S Ben 187 F1
Sidwell Chase. S Ben ... 187 F1
Sidwell La. S Ben 187 F1
Sidwell Park. S Ben 187 F1
Siena Mews. Colch 68 A2
Silcock Cl. Colch 50 B1
Silcott St. Brigh 106 C3
Sillett Cl. Clact 109 E3
Silvanus Cl. Colch 67 E3
Silver Rd. Burn 170 B2
Silver St. Mald 131 F2
Silver St. Silv E 79 E2
Silver Way. Runw 174 B4
Silverdale Ave. South ... 190 C1
Silverdale. Rayl 188 C4
Silverdale. Thund 187 F4
Silverpoint Marine. South .. 198 A2
Silversea Dr. South 190 A1
Silverthorn Cl. Hawk 178 B2
Silverthorn Cl. Colch 68 A2
Silverthorne. Canv 196 C2
Silvertree Cl. Hock 177 D3
Simmonds La. Purl 145 D1
Simmonds Way. Dan 142 C4
Simons La. Colch 68 A3
Simpsons La. Tipt 100 A2
Sims Cl. Ea Col 45 D4
Singer Ave. Clact 124 C4
Singleton Ct. Sud 13 D3
Sinnington End. Colch 50 B2
Sioux Cl. Colch 50 A2
Sir Isaac's Wlk. Colch 67 F4
Sir Walter Raleigh Dr. Rayl .. 176 B3
Sirdar Rd. Rayl 188 C4
Siskin Cl. Colch 68 C4
Sittang Cl. Colch 50 A2
Sitwell Cl. Lawf 35 D2
Siward Rd. With 114 B4
Six Bells Ct. Brain 59 F3
Sixth Ave. Canv 196 C2
Sixth Ave. Chelm 127 D3
Skate's Hill. Glems 2 A1
Skelmersdale Rd. Clact .. 109 F2
Skerry Rise. Chelm 127 D4
Skiddaw Cl. Bl Not 77 E4
Skinner's La. Chelm 140 A2
Skitts Hill. Brain 60 A1
Skreens Ct. Chelm 126 B2
Sky Hall Hill. Box 32 B4
Skylark Wlk. Chelm 140 A3
Skymans Fee. Walt 93 F3
Sladbury's La. Clact 110 B4
Slade Rd. Clact 110 B3
Slade's La. Chelm 140 A2
Slades Cl. Glems 2 B3
Slades The. Basil 185 F2
Sloe Hill. Hals 25 E1
Slough Farm Rd. Hals 25 E1
Slough La. Ard 51 E3
Slough La. Purl 143 E2
Slough La. Wiv 69 D3
Slough Rd. Dan 143 E2
Smaley La. L Mel 7 E4
Smallbridge Entry. Bures .. 29 E4
Smallgains Ave. Canv ... 197 F2
Smallwood Cl. Basil 186 B4
Smallwood Rd. Colch 67 D2
Smart Ave. Canv 197 D2
Smeaton Cl. Colch 50 B3
Smeetham Hall La. Bul ... 11 F4
Smith St. South 201 F3
Smither's Chase. Stobr .. 191 D3
Smithers Dr. Gt Bad 141 D3
Smiths Ave. May 158 A4
Smiths Field. Colch 68 B3
Smythe Cl. Clact 109 E3
Smythies Ave. Colch 68 A4
Snakes La. South 190 A3
Snape Cl. Clact 109 D2
Snape Way. Walt 93 F4
Sneating Hall La. Th L S .. 92 C4
Snelling Gr. Gt Bad 140 C3
Sniveller's La. Kelv 80 B2
Snoreham Gdns. Latch .. 157 D3
Snowberry Gr. Colch 68 A2
Snowdonia Cl. Basil 186 B4
Snowdrop Cl. Sprin 127 F4
Snowdrop Cl. With 97 F2
Soane St. Basil 174 A1
Soft Rd. Bel W 10 C3
Softwater La. Hadl 188 C2
Soils The. Rams 56 C3
Solbys La. Hadl 188 C2
Somerdean. Basil 186 B3
Somers Rd. Colch 67 D2
Somerset Ave. Roch 178 C2
Somerset Cl. Colch 67 D2
Somerset Cres. South ... 190 A2
Somerset Cres. Walt 94 A4
Somerset Pl. Chelm 127 D1
Somerset Way. Clact 108 C1
Somerton Ave. South ... 190 A2
Somerville Gdns. South .. 198 C4
Somme Rd. Colch 67 F2
Somnes Ave. Canv 196 C3
Sonell Ct. Wiv 69 D1
Sonning Way. Soum 192 B1
Sonters Down. Rett 164 B3
Sorrel Cl. Clact 49 E1
Sorrell Ct. Gold 133 F4
Sorrell The. Thund 187 E4
Sorrell Rd. Colch 165 F1
South Ave. South 191 E1
South Beech Ave. Wick .. 174 B4
South Cl. Hals 43 F4
South Cl. St O 108 A2
South Colne. Basil 185 E2
South Cres. South 190 B3
South Crockerford. Basil .. 185 F2
South Green Rd. Fing 86 C2
South Gunnels. Basil 185 D3
South Hanningfield Rd. Rett .. 153 D1
South Hanningfield Way. Runw .. 163E2
South Heath Rd. Gt Ben .. 89 F2
South Hill Cl. Dan 142 B3
South House Chase. Mald .. 145 E4
South Mayne. Basil 186 A3
South Par. Canv 197 F1
South Primrose Hill. Chelm .. 126 C2
South Riding. Basil 185 F3
South St. Brad O S 137 D1
South St. Brain 59 F1
South St. Colch 67 F3
South St. Mann 35 E2
South St. Roch 178 C1
South St. Till 149 F2
South St. Toll D 118 B2
Southbourne Gr. Hock ... 178 A3
Southbourne Gr. Wick .. 174 A4
Southbourne Gr. Hock ... 177 F3
Southchard Ave. South .. 202 A4
Southchurch Ave. South .. 200 A4
Southchurch Blvd. South .. 191 F1
Southchurch Hall Cl. South .. 200 B4
Southchurch Rd. South .. 200 B4
Southchurch Rectory Chase.
South 191 F1
Southcliff Park. Clact ... 110 A3
Southcliff. S Ben 187 E2
Southcliff. Walt 94 B4
Southcote Cres. Basil ... 185 F4
Southcote Row. Basil ... 185 F4
Southcroft Cl. Walt 93 E3
Southend Arterial Rd. Rayl .. 188 B4
Southend Arterial Rd. Thund .. 188 B4
Southend Rd. Bark 192 B2
Southend Rd. Gt Bad 141 E2
Southend Rd. Hock 177 F3
Southend Rd. Roch 190 C4
Southend Rd. W Han 141 E2
Southend Rd. Wick 175 D4
Southend Rd. Woo Mor .. 143 E3
Southernhay. Basil 185 D3
Southernhay. South 189 E3
Southey Cl. Mald 132 B2
Southfalls Rd. Canv 197 F2
Southfield Cl. Hadl 188 C2
Southfield Dr. Hadl 188 C2
Southfield. Ded 33 F3
Southgate St. L Mel 7 E3
Southgreen Gdns. Clact .. 109 E2
Southland Cl. Colch 50 B1
Southlands Chase. Sand .. 141 F1
Southminster Rd. Ashel .. 160 A4
Southminster Rd. Burn .. 170 A4
Southminster Rd. St L ... 148 C2
Southminster Rd. St L ... 148 C2
Southsea Ave. South 189 E1
Southview Cl. S Woo F .. 165 F4
Southview Dr. Clact 110 C3
Southview Dr. South 190 B1
Southview Dr. Walt 93 F4
Southview Rd. Basil 185 F3
Southview Rd. Dan 142 B3
Southview Rd. Hock 177 F4
Southwalters. Canv 196 C2
Southwark Path. Basil .. 185 F4
Southway. Brigh 106 C4
Southway. Colch 67 F3
Southwell Rd. S Ben 187 F2
Southwick Gdns. Canv .. 196 C2
Southwick Rd. Canv 196 C2
Southwold Cres. S Ben .. 187 E3
Southwold Way. Clact .. 109 D3
Southwood Chase. Dan .. 143 D2
Southwood Gdns. Rayl .. 189 D4
Sowerberry Cl. Chelm ... 126 C4
Spa Cl. Hock 177 F3
Spa Dr. St L 135 D1
Spa Rd. Fee 81 F2
Spa Rd. Hock 177 F3
Spa Rd. With 97 F1
Spains Hall Pl. Basil 185 E3
Spalding Ave. Chelm 126 C3
Spalding Way. Gt Bad ... 140 C4
Spanbeek Rd. Canv 197 D3
Spanbies Rd. Str S M 22 B1
Spansey Ct. Hals 25 E1
Sparkey Cl. With 115 D4
Sparks La. Ridge 8 A3
Sparling Cl. Colch 67 E1
Sparlings The. Walt 93 E4
Sparrow Cl. Si Hed 24 B4
Sparrow Rd. Sud 13 D3
Sparrows Herne. Basil ... 185 D2
Sparrows Herne. Clact .. 109 F3
Speedwell Cl. With 97 E2
Speedwell Rd. Colch 68 B1
Spencer Cl. Mald 145 D4
Spencer Ct. S Woo F 165 F4
Spencer Gdns. Roch 178 B3
Spencer Rd. Th L S 74 A1
Spencer Rd. Thund 187 E3
Spencer Sq. Brain 59 F4
Spencers. Hawk 177 F2
Spendells Cl. Walt 76 B1
Spenders Cl. Basil 185 E4
Spenlow Dr. Chelm 126 B4
Spennells The. Th L S 74 A1
Spenser Way. Clact 108 C1
Spicers La. L Mel 7 F4
Spinaker Cl. Clact 125 E4
Spindle Wood. Colch 50 A2
Spinks La. With 97 F1
Spinnaker The. S Woo F .. 165 F3
Spinnakers The. S Ben .. 187 D2
Spinnel's Hill. Wix 37 D1
Spinnel's La. Wix 54 C4
Spinney Cl. Wick 174 C4
Spinney The. Brain 60 B1
Spinneys The. Hock 177 E3
Spinneys The. Rayl 177 D1
Spinneys The. South 189 F4
Spires The. Gt Bad 140 C3
Spital Rd. Mald 131 F1
Sporehams La. Dan 142 B2
Sportsmans La. Hat Pev .. 114 A1
Sportsway. Colch 67 F4
Spots Wlk. Chelm 140 B2
Spout La. Sud 19 E4
Spratts La. Lit Bro 53 E1
Spring Chase. Brigh 106 C4
Spring Chase. Wiv 69 D1
Spring Cl. Clact 109 E3
Spring Cl. Lit Bad 129 E3
Spring Elms La. Lit Bad .. 129 F2
Spring Gardens Rd. Wa Col .. 46 C3
Spring Gdns. Rayl 176 B1
Spring La. Colch 67 D4
Spring La. E A Gr 66 A4
Spring La. Gt Tot 116 B4
Spring La. Hat Pev 114 C1
Spring La. W Berg 48 C2
Spring La. Wiv 69 D1
Spring Meadow. Glems 2 A3
Spring Pond Cl. Gt Bad .. 140 C4
Spring Sedge Cl. Stanw .. 66 B4
Spring Way. Si Hed 15 F1
Springbank Ave. Lawf 35 D2
Springett's Hill. Lam 19 E1
Springfield Cotts. Mald .. 132 A3
Springfield Park Ave. Chelm .. 127 D2
Springfield Park Hill. Chelm .. 127 E1
Springfield Park La. Chelm .. 127 E1
Springfield Park Par. Chelm .. 127 E1
Springfield Park Rd. Chelm .. 127 E1
Springfield Pl. Sprin 127 E3
Springfield Rd. Burn 170 A4
Springfield Rd. Chelm ... 127 D1
Springfield Rd. Sprin 127 E2
Springfield Rd. Wick 174 C4
Springfields. Basil 185 F2
Springfields. Brigh 106 C3
Springfields. Colch 67 D2
Springfields. Gt Bro 70 C4
Springlands Way. Sud 7 F1
Springmead. Si Hed 24 B4
Springvalley La. Ard 77 E4
Springvater Cl. Rayl 189 E4
Springwater Gr. Rayl ... 189 E4
Springwater Rd. Rayl ... 189 E4
Springwood Ct. Brain 59 E2
Spruce Ave. Colch 50 A4
Spruce Cl. W Mers 121 D4
Spruce Cl. With 98 A2
Sprundel Ave. Canv 197 E1
Spurgeon Cl. Si Hed 15 F1
Spurgeon Pl. Kelv 81 E1

227

Spurgeon St. Colch Terling Hall Rd. Hat Pev

Spurgeon St. Colch 68 B3
Square The. Colch 67 D2
Square The. Mald 132 A3
Square The. Till 149 F2
Squire St. S Woo F 165 F4
Squirrells Ct. Chelm 126 C3
Squirrels Field. Colch 49 F3
Stabbings Ct. Burn 170 B2
Stable Cl. Colch 66 C3
Stable Ct. W Mers 121 F4
Stablecroft. Sprin 127 F4
Stablefield Rd. Walt 94 A4
Stadium Rd. South 191 D1
Stadium Way. Hadl 188 B4
Stafford Cl. South 190 A3
Stafford Cl. Walt 93 F3
Stafford Wlk. Canv 197 D3
Stagden Cross. Basil 185 F3
Stairs Rd. Gt Wak 193 F2
Stalin Rd. Colch 68 A2
Stallards Cres. Walt 93 F3
Stambourne Rd. Gt Y 8 B2
Stambourne Rd. Topp 14 A4
Stambridge Rd. Clact 109 E2
Stambridge Rd. Gt Stam 179 E1
Stammers Rd. Colch 49 F2
Standard Ave. Clact 124 B3
Standard Rd. Colch 68 B3
Standley Rd. Walt 76 B1
Stane Field. Mks T 64 C2
Stanes Rd. Brain 59 F3
Stanfield Cl. Stanw 66 C2
Stanfield Rd. South 191 D1
Stanford Rd. Canv 197 D2
Stanley Ave. Brigh 107 D4
Stanley Rd. Ashi 178 B4
Stanley Rd. Canv 197 E2
Stanley Rd. Clact 109 E1
Stanley Rd. Hals 25 E1
Stanley Rd. South 200 A4
Stanley Rd. Sud 12 C4
Stanley Rd. Thund 187 E3
Stanley Rd. Wiv 69 E1
Stanley Rise. Sprin 127 F2
Stanley Wood Ave. Sud 7 F1
Stanley Wooster Way. Colch 68 C4
Stanmore Cl. Clact 109 E3
Stanmore Rd. Wick 175 D3
Stanmore Way. St O 108 A2
Stannard Way. Sud 13 D3
Stansfield Rd. Thund 187 D4
Stansgate Rd. Steep 147 F3
Stanstead Rd. Hals 43 F4
Stansted Cl. Chelm 126 C1
Stansted Rd. Colch 68 A1
Stansted Way. Walt 94 A3
Stanway Cl. Glems 2 B3
Stanway Rd. S Ben 187 E3
Stanwell St. Colch 67 F3
Stanwyn Ave. Clact 109 F2
Stapleford End. Wick 175 D3
Staplegrove. South 201 E4
Staplers Heath. Gt Tot 116 A2
Star La. Gt Wak 192 C2
Starboard View. S Woo F 165 F3
Starling's Hill. Si Hed 24 C2
Station App. Basil 186 A2
Station App. Brain 60 A1
Station App. Canv 196 B3
Station App. Frin 93 F3
Station App. Hock 177 F3
Station App. Runw 174 B4
Station App. S Woo F 165 E4
Station App. South 190 C2
Station App. South 200 A4
Station Ave. Rayl 176 B2
Station Ave. Runw 174 B4
Station Ave. South 191 D2
Station Cres. Col N 155 F3
Station Cres. Rayl 176 B2
Station Hill. Bures 19 F1
Station La. Basil 186 A2
Station La. Harw 40 B2
Station Rd. Alres 88 A4
Station Rd. Alth 157 F1
Station Rd. Ard 51 F4
Station Rd. Brad 36 C1
Station Rd. Brain 59 F1
Station Rd. Brigh 106 C3
Station Rd. Burn 170 A2
Station Rd. Canv 197 F1
Station Rd. Cla 4 B4
Station Rd. Clact 109 F1
Station Rd. Col En 26 C1
Station Rd. Col N 156 A3
Station Rd. Ea Col 45 D4
Station Rd. Frat 89 D4
Station Rd. Gt Ben 89 F4
Station Rd. Harw 40 B2
Station Rd. Harw 40 C3
Station Rd. Hat Pev 113 F3
Station Rd. Hock 177 F3
Station Rd. Kelv 81 E2
Station Rd. L Mel 7 E3
Station Rd. Lawf 35 E3
Station Rd. Mald 132 A2
Station Rd. Mks T 65 D2
Station Rd. Rams 39 F3
Station Rd. Rayl 176 B2
Station Rd. Runw 163 E1
Station Rd. S Ben 196 B4
Station Rd. Si Hed 15 F1
Station Rd. Soum 159 E2
Station Rd. South 189 F1
Station Rd. South 189 F2
Station Rd. South 199 E4
Station Rd. South 201 D4
Station Rd. Sud 12 C4
Station Rd. Sud 12 C4
Station Rd. Th L S 91 F4
Station Rd. Thor 89 D3
Station Rd. Tipt 100 B2
Station Rd. Toll D 118 C3
Station Rd. Tolle 119 E1
Station Rd. Wa Col 45 F4
Station Rd. Wa Col 46 B3
Station Rd. Walt 93 D3
Station Rd. Wh Not 78 C1
Station Rd. Wic Bis 115 D2
Station Rd. With 98 A2
Station Rd. Wiv 87 D4
Station Rd. Wrab 37 F2
Station St. Walt 94 B4
Station Way. Basil 185 D3
Steam Mill Rd. Brad 54 A4
Steele Cl. Mks T 64 C2
Steeple Cl. Hawk 178 B2
Steeple Cl. Mald 132 B3
Steeple Hts. Thund 187 D3
Steeple Rd. Latch 157 E3
Steeple Rd. Soum 159 D3
Steeple Rd. St L 148 B2
Steeplefield. South 189 F3
Steeplehall. Basil 186 A3
Steerforth Cl. Chelm 126 B4
Steli Ave. Canv 196 C3
Stella Maris Cl. Canv 197 F2
Stepfield. With 98 A1
Stephan Cranfield Cl. Rowh 87 D4
Stephen Cl. L Mel 7 D3
Stephenson Rd W. Clact 92 A1
Stephenson Rd. Brain 60 A1
Stephenson Rd. Clact 110 A4
Stephenson Rd. Colch 50 B3
Stephenson Rd. N Fam 167 D4
Stephenson Rd. South 189 E3
Sterling Cl. Colch 66 C3
Stevens Cl. Canv 197 E2
Stevens Rd. With 97 F1
Stevens Wlk. Colch 68 C4
Stevenson Way. Wick 174 B3
Stewards Cl. Walt 93 F4
Stewart Rd. Chelm 140 A4
Steyning Ave. South 191 F1
Stile La. Rayl 176 B1
Stilemans. Wick 174 B4
Stiles The. Mald 132 C2
Stirling Ave. Hadl 189 D1
Stirling Pl. Basil 186 A4
Stirrup Cl. Sprin 127 F4
Stivvy's Rd. Woo Wa 130 B2
Stock Chase. Mald 132 A3
Stock Cl. South 190 C2
Stock Rd. South 190 C2
Stock Terr. Mald 132 A3
Stockhouse Cl. Toll K 101 D1
Stockhouse Rd. Lay M 101 D4
Stockwell. Colch 67 F4
Stockwood. Thund 188 A4
Stoke Ash Cl. Clact 109 D2
Stoke Rd. Cla 4 A3
Stoke Rd. Nay 20 A1
Stokefelde. Basil 186 A4
Stokes The. Walt 94 A4
Stone Green Rd. Gt Oak 55 F1
Stone La. Wrab 37 F3
Stone Path Dr. Hat Pev 113 F2
Stone Rd. Gt Bro 53 D1
Stonebridge Hill. Col En 44 C4
Stonebridge Wlk. Chelm 127 D1
Stonecrop. Colch 49 E1
Stonehall Dr. Lit Cla 91 E1
Stonehall La. Gt Oak 55 D1
Stoneham Ave. Clact 109 D2
Stoneham St. Cogg 62 C1
Stonehill Cl. South 189 F2
Stonehill Rd. South 189 F3
Stonehill Way. W Mers 121 D3
Stoneleigh Park. Colch 66 C2
Stoneleighs. Thund 187 F3
Stoney Hills. Burn 170 B4
Stoney La. Brigh 107 D4
Stores La. Tipt 100 B3
Stornoway Rd. South 191 E1
Stour Cl. Glems 2 B1
Stour Cl. Harw 39 E1
Stour Gdns. Sud 13 D2
Stour Green. Cla 4 A3
Stour Rd. Harw 40 B3
Stour St. Cav 5 E4
Stour St. Mann 35 E2
Stour St. Sud 12 C4
Stour Vale. Cla 4 A3
Stourdale Cl. Lawf 35 D2
Stourside. Sho G 40 A4
Stourton Rd. With 97 F2
Stourview Ave. Mist 36 A2
Stourview Cl. Mist 36 A2
Stow Rd. Col N 155 E3
Stowe's La. Till 149 E2
Straight Rd. Box 31 F1
Straight Rd. Brad 36 B1
Straight Rd. Colch 66 C3
Straight Rd. Gt Ben 90 A2
Straight Way. Birch 84 A1
Stranger's Chr. Brigh 88 C1
Strangman Ave. S Ben 188 A2
Strasbourg Rd. Canv 197 E3
Stratford Pl. Walt 94 B4
Stratford Rd. Clact 110 B3
Stratford Rd. Ded 33 E3
Strathmore Rd. N Fam 167 D4
Straw La. Sud 12 C4
Strawberry Cl. Brain 60 A1
Strawberry La. Tipt 100 C2
Street The. Ard 51 F4
Street The. Ashe 3 E1
Street The. Brad 36 C1
Street The. Bradw 61 E2
Street The. Bul 11 F3
Street The. Chelm 140 A1
Street The. Cla 3 E2
Street The. Fee 81 F3
Street The. Gos 42 C4
Street The. Gt T 64 A4
Street The. Hat Pev 114 A2
Street The. Latch 157 D3
Street The. Lit Cla 91 E2
Street The. Mess 82 B1
Street The. Midd 12 C2
Street The. Peb 27 D4
Street The. Rams 39 D1
Street The. S Woo F 154 A2
Street The. Steep 147 F1
Street The. Stis 61 D3
Street The. Stow M 155 E2
Street The. T Gr 79 D3
Street The. Tend 72 C3
Street The. Terl 96 B2
Street The. Toll M 117 D3
Street The. Topp 14 A4
Street The. Virl 119 D4
Street The. Wa Col 46 B3
Street The. Walt 75 D1
Street The. Weel 72 C1
Street The. Wh Not 78 C1
Street The. Wic Bis 115 F3
Street The. Woo Wa 130 B1
Stretford Ct. Silv E 79 E2
Strickmere. Str S M 22 B1
Stroma Ave. Canv 196 C3
Stroma Gdns. South 201 E3
Stromburg Rd. Canv 196 C3
Stromness Pl. South 191 E1
Stromness Rd. South 191 E1
Strood Cl. W Mers 121 D4
Strood The. W Mers 104 B2
Strudwick Cl. Brain 59 F1
Strutt Cl. Hat Pev 114 A2
Stuart Cl. Canv 197 D2
Stuart Cl. Gt Bad 141 D4
Stuart Cl. Gt Wak 192 C2
Stuart Cl. South 191 D1
Stuart Rd. South 191 D1
Stuarts Way. Brain 60 A1
Stubbs Cl. Lawf 35 D2
Stubbs Cl. Walt 93 F4
Stubbs La. Brain 60 B1
Stublands. Basil 185 F3
Studd's La. Colch 49 E2
Stump La. Sprin 127 E2
Sturrick La. Gt Ben 89 E4
Sturrocks. Basil 185 F2
Sudbourne Ave. Clact 109 D2
Sudbrook Cl. Wick 174 B3
Sudbury Cl. Hawk 177 F2
Sudbury Hill. Ca Hed 15 F2
Sudbury Rd. Bul 11 F3
Sudbury Rd. Bures 19 F1
Sudbury Rd. Ca Hed 16 A2
Sudbury Rd. Canv 196 C3
Sudbury Rd. Gest 10 C1
Sudbury Rd. Hals 25 F2
Sudbury Rd. L Mel 7 E2
Sudbury Rd. Lit Map 17 E1
Sudbury Rd. Nay 20 B3
Sudbury Rd. S Han 163 D3
Sudeley Gdns. Hock 177 E3
Suffolk Ave. South 189 F2
Suffolk Ave. W Mers 121 E4
Suffolk Cl. Clact 110 C4
Suffolk Cl. Colch 50 A1
Suffolk Dr. Sprin 128 A2
Suffolk Knowle. Bures 19 F1
Suffolk Rd. Mald 131 F1
Suffolk Rd. Sud 12 C4
Suffolk Sq. Sud 12 C4
Suffolk St. Walt 94 B4
Suffolk Way. Canv 196 C2
Suffolk Wlk. Canv 196 C2
Sugar La. Si Hed 23 F4
Sugden Ave. Wick 174 A4
Sulleys Hill. High 22 A4
Sullivan Cl. Colch 68 C3
Summercourt Rd. South 199 F4
Summerdale. Alth 158 A2
Summerfields. Si Hed 15 F1
Summerhill. Alth 157 F2
Sumpters Way. South 190 C3
Sunbeam Ave. Clact 124 C3
Sunbury Ct. South 192 C1
Sundale Cl. Clact 110 C3
Sunflower Cl. Sprin 127 F3
Sunnedon. Basil 185 E3
Sunningdale Ave. South 190 A1
Sunningdale Fall. Hat Pev 114 A2
Sunningdale Rd. Alth 157 F1
Sunningdale Rd. Chelm 126 C2
Sunningdale Way. Walt 93 F4
Sunningdale. Canv 197 E2
Sunny Point. Walt 76 B2
Sunny Rd. Hawk 177 F3
Sunnybank Cl. South 189 F3
Sunnyfield Gdns. Hock 177 D3
Sunnyfields Rd. Brain 42 B1
Sunnymede Cl. Thund 188 A3
Sunnyside Ave. Basil 186 B2
Sunnyside Rd. Ford 47 E3
Sunnyside Way. Lit Cla 91 E1
Sunnyside. Brain 59 F2
Sunnyway. St L 148 B4
Sunrise Ave. Chelm 127 D3
Surbiton Ave. South 200 B4
Surbiton Rd. South 191 E1
Surig Rd. Canv 197 D2
Surrey Ave. South 189 F2
Surrey La. Tipt 100 B2
Sussex Cl. Bore 128 C4
Sussex Cl. Canv 197 D3
Sussex Gdns. Clact 110 C3
Sussex Rd. Colch 67 E4
Sussex Way. Canv 197 D3
Sutcliffe Cl. Wick 174 B3
Sutherland Bvd. Hadl 189 D1
Sutherland Pl. Wick 174 B3
Sutor Cl. With 97 F1
Sutton Court Dr. Roch 190 C4
Sutton Mead. Sprin 128 A2
Sutton Park Ave. Colch 67 D2
Sutton Rd. Roch 190 C4
Sutton Rd. South 191 D1
Sutton Rd. Stobr 191 D3
Suttons Rd. Gt Wak 193 E1
Swale Rd. Thund 188 A3
Swallow Cl. Lay H 85 D3
Swallow Dale. Basil 185 E2
Swallow Dr. S Ben 187 E1
Swallow Field. Ea Col 45 D3
Swallow Path. Chelm 140 A2
Swallow Rd. Runw 163 E1
Swallow's Row. Gt Ben 72 A1
Swallowcliffe. South 192 B1
Swallowdale. Clact 109 F4
Swallowdale. Colch 68 B2
Swan Chase. Si Hed 24 C4
Swan Cl. Hat Pev 114 A2
Swan Dale. Clact 109 F4
Swan Gr. Wa Col 46 B3
Swan La. Runw 163 E1
Swan Mead. Basil 185 E2
Swan Pass. Colch 67 F4
Swan Rd. Beau 73 E3
Swan Side. Brain 59 F2
Swan St. Kelv 81 E2
Swan St. Si Hed 15 F1
Swan St. Wa Col 46 B2
Swan Yd. Cogg 63 D1
Swanage Rd. South 191 D1
Swanfield. L Mel 7 E4
Swans Green Cl. Thund 188 A3
Swanscomb Rd. Wa Col 45 F2
Swanstead. Basil 185 F2
Swaynes. Str S M 22 B1
Sweden Cl. Harw 39 F2
Sweet Briar Ave. S Ben 187 E1
Sweet Briar Rd. Stanw 66 B4
Sweetbriar Lodge. Canv 196 C2
Sweyne Ave. Hawk 178 A2
Sweyne Ave. South 190 C1
Sweyne Cl. Rayl 176 A2
Swift Ave. Clact 124 C3
Swift Cl. Brain 78 A4
Swinborne Ct. Basil 174 A1
Swinborne Rd. Basil 174 B1
Swinbourne Dr. Brain 59 E2
Swiss Ave. Chelm 127 D2
Sycamore Cl. Canv 196 C2
Sycamore Cl. With 98 A4
Sycamore Gr. Brain 59 E1
Sycamore Gr. South 191 D1
Sycamore Pl. Gt Ben 89 F4
Sycamore Rd. Colch 68 B4
Sycamore Rd. Mald 132 B3
Sycamore Rd. Sud 13 D4
Sycamore Way. Cane 168 B1
Sycamore Way. Catt 35 E4
Sycamore Way. Chelm 140 B3
Sycamore Way. Clact 109 E2
Sycamore Way. Walt 93 E3
Sycamores The. Basil 186 B3
Sydervelt Rd. Canv 197 D2
Sydner Cl. Gt Bad 141 D3
Sydney Rd. Hadl 189 D1
Sydney Rd. S Ben 187 E2
Sydney St. Brigh 106 C3
Sydney St. Colch 68 A1
Syers Field. Weth 23 D1
Sykes Mead. Rayl 176 B1
Sylvan Cl. Canv 197 D1
Sylvan Cl. Chelm 140 A3
Sylvan Way. Hadl 189 D2
Symons Ave. South 189 F4

Tabor Ave. Brain 59 F2
Tabor Cl. Brigh 106 C4
Tabor Rd. Colch 68 B4
Tabor's Hill. Gt Bad 140 C4
Tabora Ave. Canv 196 C3
Tabors Ave. Gt Bad 140 C4
Tabrum's La. Rett 165 D3
Tabrums The. 154 B1
Taffrail Gdns 165 F3
Tailors Way. South 190 C3
Takely End. Basil 185 D3
Takely Ride. Basil 185 D3
Talbot Ave. Clact 124 C3
Talbot Ave. Rayl 176 B2
Talbot Rd. Lit Cla 91 E2
Talbot Rd. Sud 7 F1
Talbot St. Harw 40 B3
Talcott Rd. Colch 68 A1
Talisman Cl. Tipt 100 B3
Talisman Wlk. Tipt 100 B3
Tall Trees. Colch 49 F2
Tallow Gate. S Woo F 165 F3
Tally Ho. Colch 50 A2
Tallyho Cnr. Str S M 22 B1
Tamar Ave. With 97 F1
Tamar Rise. Sprin 127 E3
Tamarisk Way. Clact 124 C3
Tamarisk Way. Colch 68 C4
Tambour Cl. Gt T 64 B4
Tamworth Cha. Colch 68 A1
Tan La. Lit Cla 91 F2
Tangerine Cl. Colch 68 B3
Tangmere Cl. Wick 175 D3
Tankerville Dr. South 189 E1
Tanner Cl. Clact 109 D2
Tanners Way. S Woo F 165 E4
Tanswell Ave. Basil 186 A3
Tanswell Cl. Basil 186 A3
Tantelen Rd. Canv 196 C3
Tapley Rd. Chelm 126 C4
Tapsworth Cl. Clact 109 E3
Tapwoods. Colch 67 D4
Tara Cl. Colch 50 B1
Taragona Mews. Colch 68 A2
Taranto Rd. Canv 197 E2
Tarragon Cl. Tipt 100 B2
Tasman Ct. Chelm 126 C3
Tattersal Gdns. Hadl 189 D1
Tattersall Way. Chelm 139 F4
Tattersalls Chase. Soum 159 F2
Taunton Dr. South 190 A2
Taunton Rd. Sprin 127 F3
Taverners Green Pl. Wick 174 C3
Taverners Wlk. With 97 F2
Tavistock Rd. Sprin 127 F3
Tawney's Ride. Bures 29 D4
Taylor Ave. Chelm 126 C3
Taylor Ct. Colch 67 F4
Taylor Dr. Mann 35 E2
Taylor's Rd. Rowh 86 C4
Teak Wlk. With 98 A2
Teal Ave. May 158 A4
Teal Way. Kelv 81 E1
Tees Cl. With 97 F1
Tees Rd. Sprin 127 E3
Teign Dr. With 97 E1
Teigngrace. South 201 E4
Teignmouth Dr. Rayl 176 B3
Telese Ave. Canv 197 E2
Telford Rd. Brain 60 A1
Telford Rd. Clact 110 B4
Telford Way. Colch 50 B3
Temperance Yd. Ea Col 45 D3
Templars Cl. With 97 F2
Temple Cl. Hadl 188 C2
Temple Cl. Walt 94 A3
Temple Ct. Colch 50 B1
Temple La. Silv E 79 E2
Temple La. T Gr 79 E2
Temple Pattle. Catt 35 E4
Templewood Ct. Hadl 188 B2
Templewood Rd. Basil 186 A3
Templewood Rd. Colch 50 C1
Templewood Rd. Hadl 188 B2
Temptin Ave. Canv 197 F2
Tendring Ave. Rayl 176 A2
Tendring Rd. Tend 54 C1
Tendring Rd. Tend 72 A4
Tendring Rd. Th L S 73 E2
Tennyson Ave. South 191 D1
Tennyson Cl. Brain 77 F4
Tennyson Cl. Hadl 189 D1
Tennyson Dr. Basil 186 A3
Tennyson Rd. Chelm 126 C3
Tennyson Rd. Mald 145 D4
Tenpenny Hill. Alres 88 C3
Tenter Field. Str S M 22 B1
Tenterfield Rd. Mald 132 A1
Tenterfields. Basil 186 B4
Teramo Rd. Canv 197 E2
Terling Cl. Colch 68 A1
Terling Hall Rd. Hat Pev 113 E3

Terling Rd. Hat Pev

Terling Rd. Hat Pev 113 F3
Terling. Rd. With 97 E2
Terling. Basil 185 D3
Terminal Cl. South 201 E4
Terminus Dr. Basil 186 A2
Termitts Chase. Hat Pev 113 F4
Terni Ave. Canv 197 D3
Tern Cl. Kelv 81 E2
Terndale. Clact 109 F3
Terni Rd. Lawf 197 E2
Terra-Cotta Pl. Glems 2 C4
Terrace Hall Chase. Gt Hor ... 49 E3
Terrace The. South 201 F3
Tewkes Rd. Canv 197 E3
Tewkesbury Rd. Clact 109 F2
Tey Rd Cl. Ea Col 45 E3
Tey Rd. Ald 64 C4
Tey Rd. Ald 65 D4
Tey Rd. Cogg 63 D3
Tey Rd. Ea Col 45 E2
Thackeray Cl. Brain 78 A4
Thackeray Row. Wick 174 B3
Thames Ave. Chelm 126 B2
Thames Cl. Brain 60 B1
Thames Cl. Hadl 189 D1
Thames Cl. Rayl 176 B1
Thames Dr. Hadl 189 D1
Thames Rd. Canv 196 C2
Thames Way. Burn 170 A3
Thameside Cres. Canv 196 C3
Thatchers Croft. Lach 156 C3
Thatchers Dr. Elmst M 69 F3
Thaxted Wlk. Colch 86 A4
Thear Cl. South 190 B2
Thelma Ave. Canv 197 D2
Thelsford Wlk. Colch 68 C4
Theobalds Rd. Hadl 189 E1
Thielen Rd. Canv 197 D2
Third Ave. Canv 196 C2
Third Ave. Clact 127 D3
Third Ave. Clact 110 B2
Third Ave. Frin 93 F2
Third Ave. Glems 2 B3
Third Ave. Hals 26 A1
Third Ave. Harw 40 B2
Third Ave. Walt 94 C4
Third Ave. Wick 175 D3
Third Wlk. Canv 196 C2
Thirlmere Cl. Bl Not 77 E4
Thirlmere Rd. Thund 187 F4
Thirslet Dr. Mald 132 B2
Thistle Cl. Gold 133 F3
Thistledown. Basil 185 E3
Thistledown. Colch 50 A2
Thistledown. Pan 59 D4
Thistley Cl. Gold 133 F3
Thistley Green Rd. Brain 60 A4
Thomas Bell Rd. Ea Col 45 D3
Thomas Dr. Canv 196 C3
Thomas Rd. Basil 186 C4
Thomas Rd. Clact 109 E2
Thomas St. S. Brigh 106 C3
Thomas Wakley Cl. Colch ... 49 F3
Thomasin Rd. Basil 174 B1
Thompson Ave. Canv 197 F2
Thompson Ave. Colch 66 C3
Thorin's Gate. S Woo F 165 E3
Thorington Ave. Hadl 188 B3
Thorington Rd. Rayl 177 D1
Thornberry Ave. Weel 72 C1
Thornborough Ave. S Woo F 165 F4
Thornbury Rd. Clact 109 F2
Thorndale. Thund 188 A4
Thorndon Cl. Clact 109 D2
Thorndon Park Cl. Hadl 189 E3
Thorndon Park Cres. Hadl .. 189 D3
Thorndon Park Dr. Hadl 189 D3
Thorne Rd. Kelv 81 D1
Thorney Bay Rd. Canv 197 D1
Thornford Gdns. South 190 C3
Thornhill Cl. Walt 93 F4
Thornhill. Purl 144 B4
Thornhill. South 189 F2
Thorns Way. Walt 94 A4
Thornwood Cl. W Mers 121 E3
Thornwood. Colch 49 F2
Thorolds. Basil 185 F2
Thoughgood Rd. Clact 109 F2
Thorp Leas. Canv 197 D1
Thorpe Bay Gdns. South 201 D3
Thorpe Cl. Hawk 177 F2
Thorpe Espl. South 201 D3
Thorpe Hall Ave. South 201 D4
Thorpe Hall Cl. South 201 D4
Thorpe Park La. Th L S 92 B4
Thorpe Rd. Beau 74 A3
Thorpe Rd. Clact 109 F4
Thorpe Rd. Hawk 177 F2
Thorpe Rd. Th L S 92 C4
Thorpe Rd. Walt 92 C4
Thorpedene Ave. Hull 165 F1
Thorpedene Gdns. South ... 201 E3
Thorrington Cross. Basil 185 E3
Thorrington Rd. Gt Ben 89 E4
Thorrington Rd. Lit Cla 91 E2

Threadneedle St. Ded 33 F4
Three Crowns Rd. Colch 49 F1
Three Gates Cl. Hals 43 E4
Three Mile Hill. Chelm 139 E1
Thrift Wood. S Woo F 142 C1
Throwley Cl. Basil 186 B3
Thrushdale. Clact 109 F3
Thundersley Church Rd.
    Thund 187 F3
Thundersley Gr. Thund 187 F3
Thundersley Park Rd. S Ben 187 F2
Thurlow Dr. South 200 C4
Thurstan Cl. Colch 50 B1
Thurstone. Thund 188 B3
Thurstable Cl. Tolle 119 F1
Thurstable Rd. Tolle 119 F1
Thurstable Way. Tolle 119 F1
Thurston Ave. South 191 F1
Thyme Mews. With 97 F2
Thyme Mews. With 97 F2
Thyme Rd. Tipt 100 B3
Tiberius Gdns. With 114 C4
Tickfield Ave. South 190 C1
Tidings Hill. Hals 43 F4
Tidworth Ave. Runw 163 F1
Tighfield Wlk. S Woo F 165 E3
Tilburg Rd. Canv 197 D2
Tilbury Rd. Gt Y 9 D2
Tilbury Rd. Ridge 8 B4
Tile Barn La. Lawf 34 B1
Tile House Rd. Gt Hor 49 D4
Tilkey Rd. Cogg 62 C2
Tillingham Rd. Ashel 160 A4
Tillingham Rd. South 159 F3
Tillingham Rd. Till 149 E1
Tillingham Way. Rayl 176 A2
Tillwicks Cl. Ea Col 45 D4
Tilney Turn. Basil 185 F2
Timberlog Cl. Basil 185 F3
Timberlog La. Basil 185 F3
Timbermans View. Basil 185 F2
Timpsons La. Sprin 127 F2
Tindal Sq. Chelm 127 D1
Tindal St. Chelm 127 D1
Tinker St. Rams 56 B4
Tinker's La. Roch 178 C1
Tinker Side. Basil 185 D3
Tinnocks La. St L 135 D1
Tintagel Way. Mald 144 C4
Tintern Ave. South 190 B1
Tippersfield. S Ben 187 F2
Tippett Cl. Colch 68 C3
Tiptree Cl. South 189 F2
Tiptree Gr. Wick 174 B4
Tiptree Hall La. Tipt 100 A1
Tiptree Rd. Gt Brx 99 E1
Tiptree Rd. Lit Brx 115 F3
Titania Cl. Colch 68 C4
Tithe Cl. With 97 F2
Tithe The. Wick 174 A3
Tobruk Rd. Chelm 126 C3
Tobruk Rd. Colch 67 E2
Tofts Chase. Lit Bad 129 F3
Tog La. Gt Hor 31 D2
Toledo Cl. South 200 A4
Toledo Rd. South 200 A4
Tollesbury Cl. Wick 174 C3
Tollesbury Rd. Toll D 118 C1
Tollesbury Rd. Tolle 118 C1
Tolleshunt D'arcy Rd. Toll M 117 F2
Tollgate Dr. Stanw 66 B4
Tollgate East. Stanw 66 B3
Tollgate W. Stanw 66 B3
Tollgate Rd. Thund 188 B3
Tolliday Cl. Wiv 69 D1
Tom Tit La. Woo Mor 143 F4
Tonbridge Rd. Hock 177 F4
Tongres Rd. Canv 197 D2
Tony Webb Cl. Colch 50 B2
Took Dr. S Woo F 165 E3
Top Rd. Toll K 101 D1
Top Rd. Woo Wa 130 B1
Toppesfield Ave. Wick 174 B3
Toppesfield Rd. Gt Y 4 C4
Toppesfield Rd. Gt Y 15 D4
Torquay Cl. Rayl 176 B3
Torquay Dr. South 189 F1
Torquay Rd. Sprin 127 E3
Torrington Cl. Sprin 127 F3
Torrington. South 201 E4
Torsi Rd. Canv 197 E2
Tortoise Cl. Colch 68 A2
Torver Cl. Bl Not 77 E3
Totham Hill Green. Gt Tot .. 116 C3
Totlands Dr. Clact 110 A4
Totman Cl. Rayl 188 B4
Totman Cres. Rayl 188 B4
Totnes Wlk. Sprin 127 F3
Totteridge Cl. Clact 109 E3
Toucan Way. Basil 185 D2
Toucan Way. Clact 109 F3
Toulmin Rd. Hat Pev 114 A2
Tower Ave. Chelm 127 D2
Tower Court Mews. South .. 199 F4
Tower Cut. Brigh 106 C3
Tower Rd. Clact 109 F1
Tower Rd. Wiv 69 D1
Tower St. Brigh 106 C3

Towerfield Cl. South 201 F4
Towerfield Rd. South 201 F4
Towers Rd. Mald 132 B3
Town Croft. Chelm 127 D3
Town End Field. With 114 C4
Town Sq. Basil 185 D3
Townfield Rd. Roch 178 C1
Townfield St. Chelm 127 D2
Townfield Wlk. Gt Wak 192 C2
Towngate. Basil 185 D3
Townsend Rd. Tipt 100 B4
Towse Cl. Clact 109 E3
Traddles Ct. Chelm 126 C3
Trafalgar Rd. Clact 109 F2
Trafalgar Rd. Colch 66 C3
Trafalgar Rd. South 201 E4
Trafalgar Way. Brain 60 A2
Travers Way. Basil 186 A3
Tree Cl. Clact 109 F4
Treecot Dr. South 190 C2
Treelawn Dr. South 189 F2
Treelawn Gdns. South 189 F2
Trenchard Cres. Sprin 127 E4
Trenders Ave. Rayl 176 A4
Trenham Ave. Basil 186 B4
Trent Cl. Burn 170 A3
Trent Cl. Wick 174 B3
Trent Rd. Chelm 126 B3
Trent Rd. With 97 F1
Trews Gdns. Kelv 81 E2
Trimley Cl. Basil 185 E4
Trimley Cl. Clact 109 C2
Trinder Way. Wick 174 A3
Trinity Ave. South 199 F4
Trinity Cl. Chelm 127 E2
Trinity Cl. Elmst M 69 E1
Trinity Cl. Mann 35 E2
Trinity Cl. Rayl 176 C1
Trinity Cl. W Mers 121 E4
Trinity Ct. Chelm 127 E2
Trinity Rd. Hals 25 E1
Trinity Rd. Mann 35 E2
Trinity Rd. Rayl 176 C1
Trinity Row. S Woo F 165 F4
Trinity Sq. South 200 A4
Trinity Sq. S Woo F 165 F4
Trinity St. Hals 67 F4
Trinity St. Hals 25 F1
Trinity Wood Rd. Hock 178 A4
Triton Way. Thund 188 A3
Triumph Ave. Clact 124 C4
Trotters Field. Bran 60 A2
Trotwood Cl. Chelm 126 C4
Troubridge Cl. S Woo F 165 F4
Trunette Rd. Clact 109 E2
Trunnions The. Roch 178 C1
Trusses Cres. Rayl 176 B3
Trusses Rd. Brad O S 136 C2
Tryon Ct. Hals 25 E1
Tudor Cl. Brigh 106 C4
Tudor Cl. Clact 109 D1
Tudor Cl. Rayl 176 C1
Tudor Cl. Rayl 189 E4
Tudor Cl. Sud 7 F1
Tudor Cl. Thund 187 F3
Tudor Cl. With 76 B1
Tudor Cl. With 97 F1
Tudor Gdns. South 189 E2
Tudor Gdns. South 201 E3
Tudor Green. Clact 124 C4
Tudor Green. Sud 7 F1
Tudor Rd. Canv 196 B2
Tudor Rd. Rayl 189 E4
Tudor Rd. South 190 C1
Tudor Rd. Sud 7 F1
Tudor Way. Hawk 177 F2
Tudor Way. Wick 174 B4
Tudwick Rd. Tolt 100 C1
Tudwick Rd. Toll D 117 F3
Tudwick Rd. Toll M 117 F3
Tufnell Way. Colch 49 E1
Tugby Pl. Chelm 126 C3
Tulip Cl. Sprin 127 F4
Tulip Way. Clact 109 D2
Tulip Wlk. Colch 68 B4
Tumbler's Green. Stis 61 E4
Tunbridge Rd. South 190 C1
Tunstall Cl. Basil 186 B3
Tunstall Cl. St O 108 A3
Turkentine. Sud 13 E3
Turkey Cock La. E A Gr 65 F4
Turkey Oaks. Chelm 127 E2
Turner Ave. Lawf 35 D3
Turner Cl. South 201 F4
Turner Ct. Wiv 69 E1
Turner Rd. Colch 67 F4
Turnstone End. Colch 68 C4
Turpins Ave. Clact 110 B3
Turpins Cl. Clact 110 B3
Turpins La. Walt 93 F4
Turpins The. Basil 185 E4
Turstan Rd. With 114 C4
Tusser Cl. With 64 A4
Tusser Ct. Gt Bad 140 B4
Tusset Mews. Colch 67 F4
Tutors Way. S Woo F 165 F4
Twain Terr. Wick 174 B3

Tweed Cl. Hals 43 E4
Twining Rd. Colch 66 C2
Twitten La. Chelm 140 A1
Twitty Fee. Dan 143 D4
Twyford Ave.Gt Wak 193 D2
Twyzel Rd. Canv 197 E3
Tyburn Hill. Wic Bis 46 A3
Tydeman Cl. Stanw 66 B2
Tye Green. Glems 2 A3
Tye Hill. Lawf 34 C2
Tye La. Elmst M 69 F2
Tye Rd The. Gt Ben 90 A4
Tye Rd. Elmst M 69 F4
Tye The. E Han 153 E4
Tyefields. Basil 186 B4
Tyehurst Cres. Colch 50 B1
Tyler Ave. Clact 109 D2
Tyler St. Rams 39 F3
Tylers Ave. South 200 A4
Tylers Cl. Chelm 140 A4
Tylers Ride. S Woo F 165 F4
Tylewood. S Ben 188 B1
Tylney Ave. Roch 178 C2
Tylneys Rd. Hals 26 A2
Tyms Way. Rayl 176 C1
Tyndale Cl. Hull 165 E2
Tyndale Dr. Clact 109 D1
Tyndales La. Dan 143 D3
Tyne Way. Chelm 126 B3
Tynedale Ct. Colch 50 A2
Tynedale Sq. Colch 50 A2
Tyrell Dr. South 200 A4
Tyrells Cl. Sprin 127 F2
Tyrells Way. Gt Bad 140 C4
Tyrells. Hawk 177 E3
Tyrone Rd. South 201 D4
Tyrrel Ct. Basil 186 B3
Tyrrell Rd. S Ben 187 F1
Tyrrell Rd. Thund 187 F3
Tythe Cl. Sprin 127 F4
Tythings The. Hals 43 E4

Ullswater Cl. Bl Not 77 E3
Ullswater Rd. Thund 187 F4
Ulster Ave. South 201 E3
Ulting Hall Rd. Ult 130 C4
Ulting La. Langf 130 C3
Ulting La. Langf 130 C3
Ulting Rd. Hat Pev 114 B1
Ulting Way. Wick 175 D4
Ulverston Rd. Ashi 167 E1
Una Rd. Basil 186 A4
Una Rd. Rams 39 F3
Undercliffe Gdns. South 198 C4
Underhill Rd. S Ben 187 F2
Underwood Squ. Hadl 189 E1
Union La. Roch 178 C1
Union Rd. Clact 125 D4
Unity Cl. Colch 68 B2
Upland Cres. W Mers 121 E4
Upland Dr. Colch 50 B1
Upland Rd. South 199 D4
Upland Rd. W Mers 121 E4
Uplands Cl. Hawk 177 F3
Uplands Cl. S Ben 187 D2
Uplands Cres. Sud 7 F1
Uplands Dr. Clact 109 D1
Uplands Dr. Sprin 127 E4
Uplands Park Rd. Rayl 176 B2
Uplands Rd. Clact 109 E1
Uplands Rd. Hawk 177 F3
Uplands Rd. S Ben 187 D2
Uplands Rd. Sud 7 F1
Upp Hall La. Gt T 64 B3
Upper Ave. South 186 C4
Upper Branston Rd. Clact .. 109 E2
Upper Bridge Rd. Chelm ... 127 D1
Upper Chapel St. Hals 25 F1
Upper Chase. With 140 A4
Upper Chase. Chelm 140 A4
Upper East St. Sud 12 C4
Upper Farm Rd. Ashe 8 B4
Upper Fenn Rd. Hals 26 A1
Upper Fourth Ave. Frin 93 F3
Upper Holt St. Ea Col 45 E3
Upper Lambricks. Rayl 176 C2
Upper Market Rd. Runw 174 B4
Upper Park Rd. Brigh 106 C4
Upper Park Rd. Clact 109 E2
Upper Park Rd. Wick 174 B4
Upper Roman Rd. Chelm ... 127 D1
Upper Second Ave. Frin 93 F3
Upper St. Glems 2 C4
Upper St. Str S M 22 B1
Upper Third Ave. Frin 93 F3
Upper Trinity Rd. Hals 25 F1
Upton Cl. W Berg 48 B2
Upway The. Basil 185 E4
Upway. Rayl 176 B3
Urmond Rd. Canv 197 D2
Uttons Ave. South 199 E4
Uxbridge Cl. Wick 174 C3

Vaagen Rd. Canv 197 D2
Vale Ave. South 191 D1
Vale Cl. Colch 50 C1
Vale End. Chelm 140 B2
Vale The. Basil 185 E4

Victoria Rd. Mald

Valentine Way. Silv E 79 E2
Valentines Dr. Colch 50 B1
Valentines. Wick 174 B3
Valfreda Way. Wiv 69 D1
Valkyrie Cl. Tolle 119 E1
Valkyrie Rd. South 199 E4
Vallance Cl. South 191 F2
Valletta Cl. Chelm 66 B2
Valley Bridge. Chelm 127 D3
Valley Cl. Stanw 66 C2
Valley Cres. W Berg 48 C2
Valley Rd. Brain 60 A2
Valley Rd. Clact 110 A3
Valley Rd. Colch 68 C2
Valley Rd. Harw 39 E3
Valley Rd. Sud 13 F4
Valley Rd. Wiv 87 E4
Valley View Cl. South 50 A2
Valley View. Glems 2 C4
Valleybridge Rd. Clact 110 A3
Van Dieman's La. Chelm ... 140 B4
Van Dieman's Rd. Chelm ... 140 A4
Van Diemens Pass. Canv ... 197 F2
Van Dyck Rd. Colch 67 D3
Vanderbilt Ave. Rayl 176 B4
Vanderbilt Ave. Canv 197 E2
Vane La. Cogg 63 D1
Vanessa Dr. Wiv 69 D1
Vange Corner Dr. Corr 185 D1
Vange Hill Dr. Basil 185 F2
Vange Park Rd. Basil 185 D2
Vanguard Way. Brain 60 A2
Vanguard Way. South 201 F4
Vansittart St. Harw 40 B3
Varden Cl. Chelm 126 C3
Vardon Dr. Hadl 189 D2
Vaughan Ave. South 191 F1
Vaughan Cl. Roch 178 C3
Vaulx Rd. Canv 197 D2
Vauxhall Ave. Clact 124 C3
Vauxhall Dr. Brain 59 F3
Vellacotts. Chelm 127 D4
Venables Cl. Canv 197 E2
Venlo Rd. Canv 197 D3
Ventnor Dr. Clact 110 A4
Vera Rd. S Han 163 E2
Verlander Dr. Rayl 176 A4
Vermeer Cres. South 202 A4
Vermeer Ride. Sprin 127 F4
Vermont Cl. Basil 186 B4
Vermont Cl. Clact 110 A2
Vernon Rd. Canv 197 E3
Vernon Rd. Hadl 189 E3
Vernon Rd. N Fam 156 A1
Vernon Way. Brain 60 B3
Vernons Dr. Wa Col 46 C3
Vernons Wlk. Basil 174 A1
Veronica Wlk. Colch 68 C4
Vesta Cl. Cogg 62 C1
Veytses End. Str S M 22 B1
Viaduct Rd. Chelm 127 D1
Viborg Gdns. Mald 144 C4
Vicarage Ave. Wh Not 78 C1
Vicarage Cl. Canv 197 D1
Vicarage Cl. Toll D 118 B2
Vicarage Cres. Hat Pev 114 A2
Vicarage Gdns. Clact 109 F1
Vicarage Hill. S Ben 187 F1
Vicarage La. Gt Bad 140 C4
Vicarage La. Mund 145 F1
Vicarage La. Th L S 73 F1
Vicarage La. Till 149 F2
Vicarage La. Walt 94 B4
Vicarage Meadow. Hals 25 F1
Vicarage Meadow. Soum ... 159 E2
Vicarage Mews. Gt Bad 140 C4
Vicarage Rd. Bel S P 5 D1
Vicarage Rd. Chelm 140 A4
Vicars Orchard. Bul 11 F3
Viceroy Cl. Colch 68 A2
Vickers Rd. South 190 B3
Victor Ave. Basil 186 B3
Victor Dri. South 198 C4
Victor Gdns. Hawk 177 F3
Victor Rd. Colch 68 A3
Victoria Ave. Rayl 93 E4
Victoria Ave. South 190 C1
Victoria Ave. Wick 174 B4
Victoria Chase. Colch 67 F4
Victoria Circus. South 200 A4
Victoria Cl. Wiv 69 D1
Victoria Cres. Chelm 2 C4
Victoria Cres. Lawf 35 E2
Victoria Cres. Wick 174 B4
Victoria Dr. Gt Wak 193 E1
Victoria Espl. Wen 183 E3
Victoria Gdns. Colch 50 A2
Victoria Pl. Brigh 106 C3
Victoria Rd. Brigh 106 C3
Victoria Rd. Chelm 127 D2
Victoria Rd. Clact 110 A2
Victoria Rd. Col N 155 F3
Victoria Rd. Colch 67 E3
Victoria Rd. Mald 132 A1

Victoria Rd. Rayl 176 C2
Victoria Rd. S Woo F 165 E3
Victoria Rd. South 198 C4
Victoria Rd. South 200 B4
Victoria Rd. Walt 94 B4
Victoria Rd. Weel 91 D3
Victoria St. Brain 60 A1
Victoria St. Harw 40 B2
Victory Rd. Clact 109 E2
Victory Rd. W Mers 121 D3
Viking Rd. Mald 131 F1
Viking Way. Clact 110 C3
Viking Way. Runw 163 E1
Vikings Way. Canv 196 B2
Villa Rd. S Ben 187 E2
Villa Rd. Stanw 66 B3
Village Cl. Walt 93 E4
Village Dr. Canv 196 C2
Village Gate. Sprin 128 A2
Village Hall Cl. Canv 196 B2
Village Way. Walt 93 E3
Villiers Pl. Bore 112 C1
Villiers Way. Thund 187 F3
Vince Cl. W Mers 121 E3
Vincent Cres. South 201 F4
Vincent Rd. Ashi 167 D1
Vine Dr. Wiv 69 E2
Vine Farm Rd. Wiv 69 E2
Vine Rd. Tipt 100 B3
Vinesse Rd. Lit Hor 30 B2
Vineway The. Harw 40 A2
Vineyard Gate. Colch 67 F3
Vineyard St. Colch 67 F3
Vineyards The. Gt Bad 140 C4
Vint Cres. Colch 67 E3
Vintners The. South 190 C3
Viola Wlk. Colch 68 C4
Violet Cl. Sprin 127 F4
Virgil Rd. With 97 F3
Virginia Cl. Clact 109 D1
Virginia Cl. Thund 187 D4
Virley Cl. Mald 132 B2
Vista Ave. Walt 75 E1
Vista Rd. Clact 110 A2
Vista Rd. Walt 174 C4
Vivian Ct. Walt 94 B4
Volwycke Ave. Walt 144 C4
Voorburg Ave. Canv 197 E2
Voorne Ave. Canv 197 E1
Voysey Gdns. Basil 174 A1

Waalwyk Dr. Canv 197 E2
Waarden Rd. Canv 197 D2
Waarem Ave. Canv 197 D2
Waddesdon Rd. Harw 40 B2
Wade Rd. Clact 110 A4
Wade Reach. Walt 94 A4
Wadham Park Ave. Hock ... 177 D4
Wagtail Dr. Mald 132 B3
Wagtail Pl. Kelv 81 E1
Wakefield Cl. Colch 68 A4
Wakelin Way. With 98 A1
Wakering Ave. South 202 A4
Wakering Rd. Gt Wak 193 D1
Wakering Rd. South 192 A1
Wakes St. Wa Col 46 B3
Wakescolne. Wick 175 D3
Wakeshall La. Bel S P 9 E4
Waldegrave Cl. Lawf 35 D2
Waldegrave Way. Lawf 35 E2
Waldegrave. Basil 185 D2
Waldegraves La. W Mers .. 122 A4
Walden Cl. Gt Tot 116 A2
Walden House Rd. Gt Tot .. 116 A2
Walden Way. Walt 94 A3
Waldingfield Rd. Sud 12 C4
Waldringfield. Basil 185 D4
Walford Cl. Sprin 127 F1
Walford Pl. Sprin 127 F1
Walford Way. Cogg 63 D2
Walk The. E A Gr 66 A4
Walk The. Hull 165 E2
Walker Dr. Hadl 189 D1
Walkers Cl. Sprin 127 E4
Walkey Way. South 202 A4
Walkways. Canv 196 C3
Wall La. Wrab 37 F3
Wall Rd. Canv 197 F2
Wall St. St O 123 E3
Wallace Cl. Colch 50 A1
Wallace Cres. Chelm 140 B4
Wallace St. South 201 F4
Wallace's La. Burn 112 C2
Wallasea Gdns. Sprin 127 F3
Wallflower Ct. Sprin 127 F3
Wallis Ave. South 190 C1
Walls Cl. Colch 68 C4
Walls The. Mist 35 F3
Walnut Cl. Hock 177 F4
Walnut Dr. With 98 A2
Walnut Gr. Brain 59 F1
Walnut Tree La. Sud 12 C4
Walnut Tree Way. Colch ... 67 D2
Walnut Tree Way. Tipt 100 B4
Walnut Way. Brigh 106 C4
Walnut Way. Clact 109 E1
Walpole Wlk. Rayl 177 D1
Walsingham Cl. Sud 13 E3
Walsingham Rd. Colch 67 F3

Walsingham Rd. South 191 D1
Walter Way. Silv E 79 E2
Walters Cl. Chelm 140 B2
Walters Cl. South 189 F3
Walters Yd. Colch 67 F4
Waltham Cres. South 191 D2
Waltham Glen. Chelm 140 B4
Waltham Rd. Bore 112 C3
Waltham Rd. Rayl 176 A2
Waltham Rd. Terl 95 F1
Waltham Way. Frin 94 A3
Walthams Pl. Basil 186 A4
Walthams. Basil 186 A4
Walton Rd. Clact 110 A2
Walton Rd. South 200 C3
Walton Rd. Th L S 74 B1
Walton Rd. Walt 93 E4
Walton Rd. Walt 94 B4
Wambrook. South 192 B1
Wamburg Rd. Canv 197 F2
Wansfell Gdns. South 200 C4
Wantz Chase. Mald 132 A1
Wantz Haven. Mald 132 A1
Wantz Rd. Mald 132 A1
Warburton Ave. Si Hed ... 24 B4
Warde Chase. Walt 94 A4
Wargrave Rd. Clact 109 E2
Warham Rd. Harw 39 F1
Warley Way. Frin 94 A3
Warner Dr. Brain 59 E2
Warners Gdns. South 190 C3
Warnham Cl. Clact 109 D3
Warren Chase. Thund ... 188 A2
Warren Cl. Rayl 188 B4
Warren Dr. Wick 175 D4
Warren La. Stanw 66 B2
Warren La. Writ 126 B2
Warren Rd. Brain 60 B1
Warren Rd. Hadl 189 D2
Warren Rd. Hals 25 E1
Warren Rd. S Han 163 E4
Warrens The. Walt 93 F3
Warrens The. Wic Bis ... 115 F3
Warrenside. Brain 78 A4
Warrior Sq E. South 200 A4
Warrior Sq N. South 200 A4
Warrior Square Rd. South 201 F3
Warwick Cl. Canv 197 D3
Warwick Cl. Mald 132 A1
Warwick Cl. Rayl 176 C1
Warwick Cres. Clact 109 F2
Warwick Cres. Mald 132 A1
Warwick Dr. Mald 132 A1
Warwick Dr. Roch 190 C4
Warwick Gdns. Rayl 176 C1
Warwick Green. Rayl ... 177 D1
Warwick Rd. Clact 109 F2
Warwick Rd. Rayl 176 C1
Warwick Rd. Rayl 189 D4
Warwick Rd. South 200 C3
Warwick Sq. Chelm 126 C2
Wash La. Clact 109 E1
Wash La. Gold 133 D4
Wash La. Lit Tot 133 D4
Washford Gdns. Clact .. 109 E1
Washington Cl. Mald 131 F1
Washington Rd. Harw ... 40 A1
Washington Rd. Mald ... 131 F1
Wat Tyler Way. Basil ... 185 D4
Wat Tyler Wlk. Colch ... 67 F4
Watchfield La. Rayl 176 B1
Watchouse Rd. Chelm .. 140 B2
Water La. Bures 19 F1
Water La. Cav 1 B1
Water La. Colch 67 E4
Water La. Lit Hor 30 C4
Water La. Nay 20 C3
Water La. Peb 27 D4
Water La. Stis 61 E3
Waterdene. Canv 196 C3
Waterford Rd. South ... 201 E3
Waterhall Ave. South .. 192 A1
Waterhouse La. Ard 52 B3
Waterhouse La. Chelm . 126 C1
Waterhouse St. Chelm . 126 C1
Waterloo La. Chelm 127 E1
Waterloo Rd. South 201 E4
Watermill Rd. Fee 81 F2
Waterside Rd. Brad O S . 136 C2
Waterside Rd. Pal Co ... 181 D3
Waterside. Brigh 106 C3
Waterville Rd. Basil 186 A2
Waterworks Dr. Clact .. 109 D3
Waterworks Rd. Tolle .. 119 E1
Watery La. Bradw 62 A1
Watery La. Rayl 165 E1
Watkins Way. South ... 192 C1
Watlington Rd. S Ben .. 187 D1
Watson Cl. South 201 E4
Watson Rd. Clact 109 F2
Watt's La. Roch 178 C1
Watts Rd. Colch 67 D1
Wavell Ave. Colch 67 E2
Waveney Dr. Sprin 127 E4
Waverley Cres. Runw .. 163 E2
Waverley Rd. Thund ... 187 E3
Wavertree Rd. S Ben .. 187 D2

Wavring Ave. Walt 93 F4
Waxwell Rd. Hull 165 F1
Wayfarer Gdns. Burn ... 170 A3
Wayletts. Hadl 189 D3
Wayside. Dan 142 C4
Weald The. Canv 196 C2
Wear Dr. Sprin 127 E3
Weare Gifford. South .. 201 E4
Weaver's Ct. Sud 12 C4
Weaverdale. South 192 C1
Weavers Cl. Colch 66 C3
Weavers Dr. Glems 2 A2
Weavers La. Sud 12 C4
Weavers Row. Hals 25 F1
Weavers. Basil 185 F2
Weaversfield. Silv E ... 79 E3
Webster Cl. Si Hed 24 B4
Websters Way. Rayl ... 176 B1
Wedgewood Way. Hawk . 178 B3
Weel Rd. Canv 197 E1
Weeley By-Ps Rd. Weel . 72 C1
Weeley Rd. Gt Ben 89 F4
Weeley Rd. Lit Cla 91 E2
Weggs Willow. Colch .. 68 B4
Weight Rd. Chelm 127 F1
Weir Farm Rd. Rayl ... 188 B4
Weir Gdns. Rayl 176 B1
Weir La. Rowh 86 B4
Weir Pond Rd. Roch ... 178 C1
Welbeck Ave. Rayl 176 A2
Welbeck Cl. Hawk 177 F3
Welbeck Rd. Canv 197 D2
Welch Cl. South 191 F1
Well Field. Writ 126 A1
Well La. Birch 83 D3
Well La. Chelm 140 A1
Well La. Cla 4 A4
Well La. Dan 143 D3
Well La. Dan 142 B4
Well Side. Mks T 64 C2
Well Terr. Mald 132 A3
Well's St. Chelm 127 D2
Welland Ave. Chelm ... 126 B3
Welland Rd. Burn 170 A3
Wellands Cl. Wic Bis .. 115 E3
Wellands. Wic Bis 115 F3
Weller Gr. Chelm 126 C4
Wellesley Rd. Clact ... 109 F2
Wellesley Rd. Colch ... 67 F3
Wellfield Way. Walt ... 93 F3
Wellington Ave. Hull .. 176 B4
Wellington Ave. South . 190 A1
Wellington Cl. Brain ... 60 B2
Wellington Cl. Chelm .. 126 B3
Wellington Rd. Ashi ... 166 C1
Wellington Rd. Harw .. 40 C3
Wellington Rd. Mald .. 131 F1
Wellington Rd. Rayl ... 176 C2
Wellington St. Brigh .. 106 C3
Wellington St. South .. 199 E4
Wellmeads. Chelm 140 A4
Wells Ave. South 190 B3
Wells Cl. Sprin 127 E3
Wells Gdns. Basil 185 F4
Wells Hall Rd. Sud 13 E2
Wells Rd. Colch 68 A4
Wellsfield. Rayl 176 C2
Wellstead Gdns. South . 190 A2
Wellstye Green. Basil .. 185 F4
Welshwood Park Rd. Colch .. 50 C1
Wembley Ave. May 158 A4
Wendene. Basil 185 F2
Wendon Cl. Hawk 178 B2
Wenham Dr. South 190 C1
Wenlock Rd. Weel 90 C3
Wensley Rd. Thund 188 A3
Wents Cl. Gt Ben 71 F1
Wentworth Cl. Hat Pev . 114 A2
Wentworth Cres. Brain . 59 F3
Wentworth Meadows. Mald .. 131 F1
Wentworth Rd. South .. 191 D2
West Ave. Chelm 126 C4
West Ave. Clact 109 F1
West Ave. Hull 165 E2
West Ave. May 146 C1
West Beech Ave. Wick . 174 C4
West Beech Cl. Wick .. 174 C4
West Belvedere. Dan .. 142 C4
West Bowers Rd. Woo Wa .. 130 B2
West Chase. Mald 131 F2
West Chase. Mald 145 D4
West Cres. Canv 196 C4
West Dock Rd. Rams .. 39 F3
West End Rd. Tipt 100 A2
West Green. S Ben 187 D3
West Hanningfield Rd. Sand .. 141 D1
West Hanningfield Rd. W Han .. 140 C1
West House Estate. Soum .. 159 E2
West Lawn. Chelm 140 B1
West Ley. Burn 170 B3
West Lodge Rd. Colch .. 67 E3
West Point Pl. Canv ... 196 B2
West Rd. Clact 109 F1
West Rd. Hals 25 F1
West Rd. South 190 C1

West Rd. South 201 E3
West Sq. Chelm 127 D1
West Sq. Mald 131 F2
West St. Cogg 62 C1
West St. Colch 67 F4
West St. Harw 40 C3
West St. Roch 178 C1
West St. Rowh 86 C4
West St. South 190 C1
West St. South 198 C4
West St. Tolle 119 E1
West St. Walt 94 B4
West St. Wiv 87 D4
West Station Yd. Mald .. 131 F1
West Stockwell St. Colch . 67 F4
West Thorpe. Basil 185 E3
West View Cl. Colch ... 50 A2
West View Dr. Rayl 176 A1
West Wood Cl. Thund .. 188 B2
Westborough Rd. South . 190 B1
Westbourne Cl. Hadl ... 188 B3
Westbourne Cl. Hock ... 178 A4
Westbourne Gr. Gt Bad . 140 B4
Westbourne Gr. South .. 190 A2
Westbourne Gr. South .. 190 A2
Westbury Cl. Copf 65 E3
Westbury Rd. Frin 93 D3
Westbury Rd. South ... 191 E1
Westbury. Hawk 178 B2
Westcliff Ave. South .. 199 F3
Westcliff Dr. South 189 E1
Westcliff Par. South ... 199 F4
Westcliff Park Dr. South .. 190 B1
Westcliffe Gdns. Canv . 197 F1
Westcott Cl. Clact 109 F3
Westerdale. Sprin 127 F4
Westergreen Meadow. Brain .. 59 F1
Westerings The. Gt Bad . 140 C3
Westerings The. Hawk .. 177 F3
Westerings. Purl 144 B1
Westerings. S Woo F .. 142 C1
Westerland Ave. Canv . 197 E2
Westerlings The. T Gr .. 78 C3
Western Ave. South ... 190 A4
Western Cl. Silv E 79 F2
Western Espl. Canv ... 197 D1
Western Espl. South .. 199 F4
Western La. Silv E 79 F2
Western Prom. Brigh .. 106 B3
Western Prom. St O ... 106 C2
Western Rd. Brigh 106 C3
Western Rd. Burn 170 B2
Western Rd. Hadl 188 C3
Western Rd. Hadl 189 D1
Western Rd. Rayl 176 A1
Western Rd. Silv E 79 F2
Western's End. Catt ... 35 E4
Westfield Ave. Chelm .. 126 C4
Westfield Cl. Wick 174 C4
Westfield Dri. Cogg ... 63 D2
Westfield. Cla 4 A3
Westgate. South 201 F3
Westlake Ave. Basil ... 186 C3
Westlake Cres. Wic 69 D1
Westleigh Ave. South . 189 E1
Westman Rd. Canv 197 F2
Westmarch. S Woo F .. 165 E3
Westminster Dr. Hock . 177 E3
Westminster Dr. South . 190 A1
Westminster Gdns. Brain . 60 A2
Westmorland Cl. Mist .. 36 A2
Weston Rd. Colch 68 A3
Weston Rd. South 200 A4
Westridge Rd. Clact ... 110 A3
Westropps. L Mel 7 E3
Westway. S Ben 187 D2
Westway. Colch 67 F4
Westway. Colch 67 F4
Westway. S Woo F 165 E3
Westwood Dr. W Mers . 121 F3
Westwood Gdns. Hadl . 188 B3
Westwood Hill. Colch .. 49 D2
Westwood Rd. Canv ... 197 D2
Wet La. Box 31 F3
Wetherfield Cl. Rayl ... 176 A2
Wetherfield Rd. Colch . 86 A4
Wetherfield Rd. Si Hed . 15 E1
Wetherfield Way. Wick . 175 D3
Wetzlar Cl. Colch 68 A2
Weybourne Cl. South .. 190 C4
Weybourne Gdns. South . 190 C4
Weybridge Wlk. South . 192 C1
Weymouth Cl. Clact ... 125 E4
Weymouth Rd. Sprin .. 127 F3
Whaley Rd. Colch 68 A4
Wharf La. Bures 28 C4
Wharf Rd. Chelm 127 E1
Wharf Rd. Mald 132 C2
Wharfe Cl. With 97 F1
Wheatfield Rd. Stanw . 66 B3
Wheatfield Way. Chelm . 140 A3
Wheatlands. Elmst M .. 69 F3
Wheatley Ave. Basil ... 186 B2
Wheatley Cl. Hawk 178 B2
Wheaton Rd. With 98 A1
Wheatsheaf Cl. Wrab .. 37 D3
Wheatsheaf La. Wrab .. 37 E2
Wheeler Cl. Colch 68 C3
Wheelwrights The. South . 191 D3

Whernside Ave. Canv ... 197 E3
Whist Ave. Runw 163 F1
Whistler Rise. South ... 202 A4
Whitby Rd. Soum 159 D2
White Cotts. Fair 95 E2
White Elm Rd. S Woo F . 143 D1
White Hart La. Gt Wak . 193 D2
White Hart La. Hock 177 F3
White Hart La. Sprin ... 127 F4
White Hart La. W Berg . 48 C3
White Horse Ave. Hals .. 43 E4
White Horse La. Mald .. 131 F1
White Horse La. With .. 97 F2
White House Chase. Rayl . 176 C1
White House Rd. South . 199 E4
White Lodge Cres. Th L S . 74 B1
White Rd. Canv 196 B2
White Trees Cl. S Woo F . 165 E3
Whitefriars Cres. South . 199 E4
Whitefriars Way. Colch . 67 D3
Whitegate Rd. Brigh ... 107 D3
Whitegate Rd. South .. 200 A4
Whitehall Cl. Colch 68 B2
Whitehall Ct. With 98 A1
Whitehall La. Th L S ... 73 E1
Whitehall Rd. Colch ... 68 B2
Whitehouse Cres. Gt Bad . 140 B4
Whitehouse Hill. Virl .. 119 D4
Whitehouse La. Bel S P . 5 D1
Whitehouse La. W Berg . 48 B2
Whitehouse Meadows. South . 190 A3
Whitehouse Rd. S Woo F . 165 E4
Whitelands Cl. Runw ... 163 F1
Whiteshott. Basil 185 D2
Whitethorn Gdns. Chelm . 140 B4
Whiteways Cl. With 97 F2
Whiteways. Canv 197 E1
Whiteways. South 189 F3
Whitewell Rd. Colch ... 67 F3
Whitlands. Glems 2 A3
Whitmore Cl. Basil 185 F4
Whitmore Way. Basil .. 185 E4
Whittier Way. W Mers . 121 D4
Whittingham Ave. South . 191 F1
Whytewaters. Basil 185 F2
Whyverne Cl. Sprin 127 F3
Wick Beech Ave. Wick . 174 C4
Wick Chase. South 191 F1
Wick Cres. Wick 174 C4
Wick Dr. Wick 174 B4
Wick Farm Rd. St L ... 148 B4
Wick La. Ard 51 D4
Wick La. Fing 87 E2
Wick La. Harw 40 A1
Wick La. St O 90 B2
Wick La. Wick 174 C4
Wick Rd. Burn 170 C3
Wick Rd. Colch 68 B1
Wick Rd. Gt Ben 90 A3
Wick Rd. High 21 E1
Wick Rd. Langh 32 C2
Wickfield Ash. Chelm .. 126 B3
Wickford Ave. Basil ... 186 A3
Wickford Rd. S Woo F . 165 E3
Wickford Rd. South ... 199 F4
Wickham Hall La. Wic Bis . 115 E2
Wickham Pl. Basil 185 E3
Wickham Rd. Colch ... 67 D3
Wickham Rd. With 114 C4
Wickham's Chase. S Woo F . 143 E1
Wicklow Ave. Chelm ... 126 B3
Wickmead Cl. South ... 191 F1
Wicks Cl. Brain 59 E2
Widford Chase. Chelm . 139 F4
Widford Cl. Chelm 139 F4
Widford Gr. Chelm 139 F4
Widford Park Pl. Chelm . 139 F4
Widford Rd. Chelm 139 F4
Widgeon Pl. Kelv 81 E1
Widgeons. Basil 185 D3
Wigboro Wick La. St O . 107 F1
Wigborough Rd. Lay H .. 84 C1
Wigborough Rd. Peld .. 103 E2
Wignall St. Lawf 34 C2
Wilbye Cl. Colch 67 D2
Wilkin Ct. Colch 67 D2
Wilkinsons Mead. Sprin . 128 A2
Willett Rd. Colch 67 D2
William Boys Cl. Colch . 68 B4
William Cl. Wiv 69 E2
William Dr. Clact 109 E1
William Groom Ave. Harw . 40 A1
William Rd. Basil 186 C3
William St. Brigh 67 F4
Willingale Ave. Rayl ... 176 C2
Willingale Way. South . 192 A1
Willingham Way. Colch . 68 C4
Willmott Rd. South ... 190 B3
Willoughby Ave. W Mers . 121 E3
Willoughby's La. Brain . 60 B4
Willow Ave. Walt 93 F4
Willow Cl. Brigh 106 B3
Willow Cl. Burn 170 B3
Willow Cl. Canv 196 C2
Willow Cl. Hock 177 E3
Willow Cl. Rayl 176 B2
Willow Cl. South 189 F3

Willow Cres. Hat Pev

Willow Cres. Hat Pev 114 A2
Willow Dene. Si Hed 15 E1
Willow Dr. Rayl 176 B2
Willow Gr. S Woo F 154 A1
Willow Hall La. Wix 55 E4
Willow Hall La. Wix 13 D4
Willow Meadows. Si Hed 24 C4
Willow Rise. With 98 A3
Willow Tree Way. Ea Col 45 D3
Willow Way. Clact 125 D4
Willow Way. Harw 39 F1
Willow Wlk. Cane 168 B1
Willow Wlk. Hadl 188 B2
Willow Wlk. Hock 177 F3
Willow Wlk. Tipt 100 B4
Willow Wlk. Weel 90 C4
Willowbank. Chelm 140 A2
Willowdale Centre. Runw 174 B4
Willows The. Basil 186 B3
Willows The. Bore 128 C4
Willows The. Colch 68 A2
Willows The. S Ben 187 D2
Willows The. South 192 A1
Wilmington Rd. Colch 50 B1
Wilmslowe. Canv 197 F3
Wilrich Ave. Canv 197 E2
Wilshire Ave. Sprin 127 F2
Wilsner. Basil 186 B4
Wilson Cl. Wiv 69 D1
Wilson Marriage Rd. Colch 50 B1
Wilson Rd. South 199 F4
Wilson's La. Mks T 64 C2
Wimarc Cres. Rayl 176 A2
Wimborne Rd. South 191 D1
Wimbourne Gdns. Walt 93 F4
Wimbush Ct. Basil 186 A4
Wimbush End. Basil 186 A4
Wimbush Mews. Basil 186 A4
Wimhurst Cl. Hock 177 F4
Wimpole Rd. Colch 68 A3
Winbrook Cl. Rayl 188 C4
Winbrook Rd. Rayl 188 C4
Winchcombe Cl. South 189 F2
Winchelsea Dr. Gt Bad 140 C4
Winchelsea Pl. Brigh 106 C4
Winchester Cl. South 189 F4
Winchester Dr. Rayl 176 A3
Winchester Rd. Colch 68 A3
Winchester Rd. Frin 94 B3
Wincoat Cl. S Ben 187 E2
Wincoat Dr. S Ben 187 E2
Windermere Ave. Hull 165 E1
Windermere Dr. Bl Not 77 E3
Windermere Rd. Clact 110 B3
Windermere Rd. South 200 B4
Windermere Rd. Sud 13 D4
Windermere Rd. Thund 187 F4
Windham Rd. Sud 13 D4
Windmill Fields. Cogg 62 C2
Windmill Gdns. Brain 60 A4
Windmill Park. Clact 109 F3
Windmill Rd. Brad 36 B1
Windmill Rd. Hals 25 E1
Windmill Row. Glems 2 B3
Windmill View. Tipt 100 B3
Windrush Dr. Sprin 127 E3
Windsor Ave. Clact 109 E2
Windsor Cl. Canv 197 D2
Windsor Cl. Colch 68 A1
Windsor Ct. Brigh 106 C3

Windsor Gdns. Brain 60 A2
Windsor Gdns. Hawk 178 A2
Windsor Gdns. Runw 163 E1
Windsor Gdns. Thund .... 188 B2'
Windsor Pl. Sud 13 D4
Windsor Rd. Basil 186 C4
Windsor Rd. South 190 C1
Windsor Rd. W Mers 121 E4
Windsor Way. Chelm 126 C1
Windsor Way. Rayl 176 C1
Windward Way. S Woo F 165 F3
Winfields. Basil 186 B4
Wingate Cl. Brain 59 F2
Winifred Rd. Basil 186 A3
Winnock Rd. Colch 68 A3
Winsford Gdns. South 190 A2
Winsley Rd. Colch 68 A3
Winsley Sq. Colch 68 A2
Winston Ave. Colch 67 D2
Winston Ave. Tipt 100 C3
Winston Way. Hals 26 A2
Winstree Cl. Lay H 84 C3
Winstree Rd. Burn 170 A3
Winstree Rd. Stanw 66 B3
Winstree. Basil 186 A4
Winter's Hill. Lay B 83 F1
Winter's Rd. Lay B 83 F1
Winterbournes. Walt 94 A4
Winterswyk Ave. Canv 197 F2
Winton Ave. South 199 F4
Winton Ave. Wick 174 A4
Wisdoms Green. Cogg 63 D2
Wistaria Pl. Clact 109 E3
Wiston Rd. Bures 30 B4
Witch Elm. Harw 39 F1
Witch La. Cogg 63 D4
Witchards. Basil 185 D3
Witham Lodge. With 114 C4
Witham Rd. Bl Not 78 A3
Witham Rd. Langf 131 E4
Witham Rd. Lit Brx 115 F3
Witham Rd. T Gr 79 D2
Witham Rd. Terl 96 C1
Witham Rd. Toll M 117 E3
Witham Rd. Wh Not .... 78 A3'
Withrick Wlk. St O 108 A3
Withypool. South 192 B1
Withywindle The. S Woo F 165 E3
Witney Rd. Burn 170 B2
Wittem Rd. Canv 197 D3
Witterings The. Canv 197 D2
Witting Cl. Clact 109 E3
Witton Wood Rd. Frin 93 F3
Wivenhoe Cross. Wiv 69 E1
Wivenhoe Park Cnr. Colch 69 D3
Wivenhoe Rd. Alres 88 A4
Wivenhoe Rd. Ard 51 E1
Wix By-Ps. Lit Ben 7 E4
Wix Rd. Brad 36 C1
Wix Rd. Gt Oak 55 E2
Wix Rd. Gt Oak 56 A2
Wix Rd. Rams 38 C1
Woburn Ave. Walt 93 E4
Wolfe Ave. Colch 68 A3
Wollards Gdns. L Mel 7 E4
Wollaston Cres. Basil 174 B1
Wollaston Way. Basil 174 B1
Wolseley Ave. Clact 124 C3
Wolseley Rd. Chelm 127 D1

Wolton Rd. Colch 67 D1
Wolves Hall La. Tend 54 C1
Wonston Rd. Soum 159 E2
Wood Ave. Hock 177 F4
Wood Dale. Gt Bad 140 C3
Wood End. Hawk 177 E3
Wood Farm Cl. South 189 E2
Wood Field End. Lay H 85 D3
Wood Green. Basil 174 A1
Wood La. E A Gr 47 F1
Wood La. Mald 132 A3
Wood Rd. Mald 132 A3
Wood St. Chelm 140 A4
Woodberry Cl. Canv 197 D3
Woodberry Cl. Hadl 189 E3
Woodberry Rd. Wick 175 D3
Woodberry Way. Walt 94 A4
Woodbridge Gr. Clact 109 D2
Woodburn Cl. Thund 188 A2
Woodbury Cres. South 190 C3
Woodcock Cl. Colch 68 C3
Woodcote Cres. Basil 186 B3
Woodcote Rd. South 190 A1
Woodcote Way. Thund 187 D4
Woodcotes. South 192 C1
Woodcroft Cl. Thund 188 B2
Woodcutters Ave. South 189 E3
Woodend Cl. Thund 188 B2
Woodfield Cl. Walt 94 A4
Woodfield Cotts. Mald 132 B3
Woodfield Dr. W Mers 121 D4
Woodfield Gdns. South 198 C4
Woodfield Park Dr. South 190 A1
Woodfield Rd. Brain 60 A2
Woodfield Rd. Hadl 189 D2
Woodfield Rd. South 199 D4
Woodfield Way. Hat Pev 114 A2
Woodfield. Wick 174 B3
Woodford Cl. Clact 109 F4
Woodgrange Cl. South 200 C4
Woodhall Cl. Sud 7 F1
Woodhall Rd. Chelm 127 D4
Woodhall Rd. Sud 7 F1
Woodham Dr. Hat Pev 114 A2
Woodham Halt. S Woo F 165 E4
Woodham Mortimer Rd.
Woo Ma 143 F4
Woodham Park Dr. S Ben 187 E1
Woodham Rd. Rett 164 C3
Woodham Rd. S Ben 187 D1
Woodham Rd. S Woo F 155 D2
Woodham Rd. Stow M 155 D2
Woodhays. Basil 186 B4
Woodhill Rd. Dan 142 A3
Woodhill Rd. Sand 142 A3
Woodhurst Rd. Canv 196 C2
Woodland Cl. Hadl 188 C2
Woodland Cl. Hat Pev 114 A3
Woodland Rd. Chelm 127 D2
Woodland Rise. Weel 72 C1
Woodland Way. Gos 42 C4
Woodland Way. Wiv 69 D1
Woodlands Ave. Rayl 188 C2
Woodlands Cl. Basil 185 F2
Woodlands Cl. Clact 110 A4
Woodlands Cl. Hock 177 D3
Woodlands Cl. Rayl 188 B4
Woodlands Dr. Basil 185 E1
Woodlands Park. Hadl 189 D2

Woodlands Rd. Hock 177 E3
Woodlands Rd. Wick 174 B4
Woodlands The. Brigh 106 C4
Woodlands The. South 201 F4
Woodlands. Ath 158 A2
Woodlands. Brain 60 B2
Woodlands. Colch 50 C1
Woodlands. Gt Oak 56 A1
Woodleigh Ave. South 189 E2
Woodlow. Thund 188 A3
Woodpecker Cl. Colch 68 C4
Woodpond Ave. Hock 177 F3
Woodroffe Cl. Sprin 128 A2
Woodrolfe Farm La. Tolle 119 F1
Woodrolfe Park. Tolle 119 F1
Woodrolfe Rd. Tolle 119 F1
Woodrow Way. Colch 68 C4
Woodrows La. Clact 109 D3
Woodrush End. Colch 66 A3
Woods The. Hadl 188 C2
Woodside Ave. Thund 187 E4
Woodside Chase. Hawk 177 F2
Woodside Cl. Colch 50 C1
Woodside Cl. South 189 D3
Woodside Rd. Ashi 198 C3
Woodside Rd. Hock 177 D3
Woodside View. Thund 187 E4
Woodside. Hadl 189 D3
Woodside. Lit Bad 129 F1
Woodside. Mund 145 E1
Woodside. Walt 94 A3
Woodstock Cres. Hock 177 E3
Woodstock. W Mers 121 E4
Woodview Cl. Colch 50 B2
Woodview Dr. Gt Le 95 D4
Woodville Cl. Hawk 178 B2
Woodville Rd. Canv 197 E2
Woodyards. Brad O S 136 C2
Woolards Way. S Woo F 165 E4
Woolner Rd. Clact 109 E3
Woolpack La. Brain 59 F3
Woolpack. South 201 E4
Woolwich Rd. Clact 109 E3
Worcester Cl. Brain 60 A1
Worcester Cl. South 191 D1
Worcester Cl. Steep 147 D1
Worcester Cres. Alres 88 A4
Worcester Ct. Gt Bad 141 D3
Worcester Dr. Rayl 176 C1
Worcester Rd. Burn 170 B3
Wordsworth Ave. Mald 145 D4
Wordsworth Cl. South 191 D1
Wordsworth Ct. Chelm 127 D3
Wordsworth Rd. Brain 59 F4
Wordsworth Rd. Colch 66 C3
Workhouse Hill. Box 31 F2
Workhouse La. S Woo F 154 A1
Workhouse Rd. Lit Hor 30 B1
Worlds End La. Fee 81 E2
Worthington Way. Colch 66 A2
Wrabness Rd. Rams 38 B2
Wrabness Rd. Rams 39 D1
Wren Ave. Rayl 189 E4
Wren Ave. South 189 E4
Wren Cl. Gt Ben 71 E1
Wren Cl. South 189 E4
Wren Cl. Thund 187 D3
Wrendale. Clact 109 F3
Wright's Ave. T Gr 78 C3

Writtle Cl. Clact 109 D2
Writtle Rd. Chelm 139 F4
Writtle Wlk. Basil 185 F4
Wroxham Cl. Colch 67 D3
Wroxham Cl. South 189 D3
Wryneck Cl. Colch 49 F2
Wulvesford. With 114 B4
Wyatts Dr. South 200 C4
Wyatts La. Sud 19 E4
Wyburn Rd. Hadl 188 C3
Wyburns Ave E. Rayl 188 C4
Wyburns Ave. Rayl 188 C4
Wych Elm. Colch 68 A2
Wycke Hill. Mald 144 B4
Wycke La. Tolle 119 F1
Wycliffe Cl. Colch 49 F1
Wycombe Ave. Thund 187 D3
Wyedale Dr. Colch 66 C3
Wykeham Rd. Writ 126 A1
Wykes Green. Basil 185 E4
Wyncolls Rd. Colch 50 B3
Wyndham Cl. Colch 86 A4
Wyndham Cres. Clact 110 A3
Wynters. Basil 185 D2
Wyharns. Basil 186 B4
Wythefield. Basil 186 A3

Yale Mews. Colch 50 A2
Yarmburg Rd. Canv 197 E2
Yare Ave. With 97 E1
Yarnacott. South 201 E4
Yarwood Rd. Chelm 127 F1
Yeldham Lock. Sprin 128 A1
Yeldham Rd. Ca Hed 15 E2
Yeldham Rd. Si Hed 15 E2
Yeovil Chase. South 190 A2
Yew Cl. With 98 A3
Yew Tree Cl. Colch 68 C4
Yew Tree Cl. Hat Pev 114 A3
Yew Tree Gdns. Chelm 140 B3
Yew Way. Clact 124 C3
Yorick Ave. W Mers 121 E3
Yorick Rd. W Mers 121 E3
York Cl. Rayl 189 D4
York Cl. Sud 12 C4
York Gdns. Brain 60 A2
York Pl. Colch 68 A4
York Rd. Ashi 178 B4
York Rd. Brigh 106 C3
York Rd. Burn 170 B2
York Rd. Chelm 140 A4
York Rd. Clact 110 C3
York Rd. Ea Col 45 D3
York Rd. Rayl 189 D4
York Rd. South 200 A4
York Rd. Sud 12 C4
York Rise. Rayl 189 D4
York St. Mann 35 E2
Young Cl. Clact 109 E3
Young Cl. South 190 A4
Ypres Rd. Colch 67 F2

Zandi Rd. Canv 197 E1
Zealand Dr. Canv 197 F2
Zelham Dr. Canv 197 F2
Zider Pass. Canv 197 F2

Zider Pass. Canv

O|S ORDNANCE SURVEY
STREET ATLASES

The Ordnance Survey / Philip's County Street Atlases provide unique and definitive mapping of entire counties

Counties available

- Berkshire
- Buckinghamshire
- East Essex
- West Essex
- North Hampshire
- South Hampshire
- Hertfordshire
- East Kent
- West Kent
- Nottinghamshire
- Oxfordshire
- Surrey
- East Sussex
- West Sussex
- Warwickshire

The County Street Atlases are revised and updated on a regular basis and new titles are added to the series. Many counties are now available in full-size hardback and softback editions as well as handy pocket-size versions.

The series is available from all good bookshops or by mail order direct from the publisher. However, the order form opposite may not reflect the complete range of titles available so it is advisable to check by telephone before placing your order. Payment can be made by credit card or cheque/postal order in the following ways:

By phone *Phone your order through on our special Credit Card Hotline on 0933 410511. Speak to our customer service team during office hours (9am to 5pm) or leave a message on the answering machine, quoting CSA94, your full credit card number plus expiry date and your full name and address*

By post *Simply fill out the order form opposite (you may photocopy it) and send it to:*
Cash Sales Department, Reed Book Services, PO Box 5, Rushden, Northants, NN10 6YX

CSA94	Hardback QUANTITY/TOTAL	Softback QUANTITY/TOTAL	Pocket QUANTITY/TOTAL	
	▼ £12.99	▼ £8.99	▼ £4.99	
East Essex	£ ISBN 0-540-05848-3	£ ISBN 0-540-05866-1	£ ISBN 0-540-05850-5	➤ £
West Essex	£ ISBN 0-540-05849-1	£ ISBN 0-540-05867-X	£ ISBN 0-540-05851-3	➤ £
North Hampshire	£ ISBN 0-540-05852-1	£ ISBN 0-540-05853-X	£ ISBN 0-540-05854-8	➤ £
South Hampshire	£ ISBN 0-540-05855-6	£ ISBN 0-540-05856-4	£ ISBN 0-540-05857-2	➤ £
Nottinghamshire	£ ISBN 0-540-05858-0	£ ISBN 0-540-05859-9	£ ISBN 0-540-05860-2	➤ £
East Sussex	£ ISBN 0-540-05875-0	£ ISBN 0-540-05874-2	£ ISBN 0-540-05873-4	➤ £
West Sussex	£ ISBN 0-540-05876-9	£ ISBN 0-540-05877-7	£ ISBN 0-540-05878-5	➤ £
	▼ £10.99		▼ £4.99	
Berkshire	£ ISBN 0-540-05738-X		£ ISBN 0-540-05835-1	➤ £
Buckinghamshire	£ ISBN 0-540-05660-X		£ ISBN 0-540-05711-8	➤ £
Hertfordshire	£ ISBN 0-540-05720-7		£ ISBN 0-540-05840-8	➤ £
East Kent	£ ISBN 0-540-05661-8			➤ £
West Kent	£ ISBN 0-540-05662-6			➤ £
Oxfordshire	£ ISBN 0-540-05665-0			➤ £
Warwickshire	£ ISBN 0-540-05642-1			➤ £
	▼ £10.99		▼ £3.99	
Surrey	£ ISBN 0-540-05694-4		£ ISBN 0-540-05708-8	➤ £

I enclose a cheque/postal order, made payable to *Reed Book Services*, for **£**_____

or please debit my ☐Access ☐American Express ☐Visa account by **£**_____

Account number ☐☐☐☐ ☐☐☐☐ ☐☐☐☐ ☐☐☐☐

Expiry date ☐☐ ☐☐ Signature

☐ Please tick this box if you do not wish your name to be used by other carefully selected organisations that may wish to send you information about other products and services

Name

Address

Postcode

◆ Free postage and packing ◆ All available titles will normally be dispatched within 5 working days of receipt of order but please allow up to 28 days for delivery

Registered office: Michelin House, 81 Fulham Road, London SW3 6RB. Registered in England, number 1974080